# THE SAME, ONLY DIFFERENT

OTHER BOOKS IN THE COLLECTION

Political Law in Canada

Canada's Parliament: A Primer

The Senate of Canada

The Recognition of Two Official Languages in Canada

Drafting, Interpreting, and Applying Legislation

Federalism in Canada: Evolving Constitutional, Political, and Social Realities

The House of Commons of Canada

Canadian Immigration Law and Policy: Then and Now

A Treatise on Treaties: Crown-Indigenous Treaties in Canadian Law

UNDERSTANDING CANADA

# THE SAME, ONLY DIFFERENT

UNDERSTANDING CANADA AND
THE UNITED STATES

Gregory J. Inwood and Robert W. Speel

UNIVERSITY OF TORONTO PRESS
Toronto  Buffalo  London

INSTITUTE OF PARLIAMENTARY AND POLITICAL LAW
INSTITUT DE DROIT PARLEMENTAIRE ET POLITIQUE

© University of Toronto Press 2025
Irwin Law
An imprint of University of Toronto Press
Toronto Buffalo London
utorontopress.com
Printed in the USA

ISBN 978-1-4875-6630-2 (paper)   ISBN 978-1-4875-6632-6 (EPUB)
                                 ISBN 978-1-4875-6631-9 (PDF)

All rights reserved. No part of this publication may be reproduced, stored in or introduced into a retrieval system, or transmitted in any form or by any means (electronic, mechanical, photocopying, recording, or otherwise) without the prior written permission of both the copyright owner and the above publisher of this book.

**Cataloguing in Publication available from Library and Archives Canada**

Cover image: Adobe Stock

We wish to acknowledge the land on which the University of Toronto Press operates. This land is the traditional territory of the Wendat, the Anishnaabeg, the Haudenosaunee, the Métis, and the Mississaugas of the Credit First Nation.

University of Toronto Press acknowledges the financial support of the Government of Canada, the Canada Council for the Arts, and the Ontario Arts Council, an agency of the Government of Ontario, for its publishing activities.

# Contents

**Foreword** *vii*

**Introduction** *1*

*chapter one* **Canadians and Americans — The Same, Only Different: Comparative History and Political Culture** *11*

*chapter two* **Comparative Political Institutions: Where Does Power Lie in Each Country?** *67*

*chapter three* **Comparative Elections and Voting: Do Canadians Have Too Few Electoral Choices, or Do Americans Have Too Many?** *109*

*chapter four* **Federalism and Regionalism** *137*

*chapter five* **Comparative Public Policy: Similar Countries, Dissimilar Policies** *179*

*chapter six* **Trade and Economic Policy: The Long and Winding Road** *217*

*chapter seven* **Foreign Policy: Friends and Allies (Mostly)** *263*

*chapter eight* **Looking Ahead: Comparing Canada and the United States and Canadian-American Relations** *295*

**Notes**  *307*
**Bibliography**  *333*
**Index**  *369*
**About the Authors**  *387*
**About the Editor**  *389*

# Foreword

Seen from distant or partial perspectives, Canada and the United States may appear to be similar in several respects. Following Indigenous rule, both countries were at times composed of colonies of various European powers, most significantly of the British Crown. This endowed them with inescapable similarities. Today, they enjoy democratic political systems and they espouse capitalism as their respective economic models. They share numerous socio-political and even cultural features. They are not only each others' allies, but also cooperants in many global initiatives. Glances from overseas can, however, be incomplete or even misleading. There is no intellectual link between the perspectives of Sir John A Macdonald and Sir Georges-Étienne Cartier on one hand and George Washington, Thomas Jefferson, and Benjamin Franklin on the other. While Canada has endeavoured to find a political *modus vivendi* to accommodate its anglophone and francophone components, the United States has emphasized its unicultural English character, despite recent Hispanic inroads. In the era when the United States has been either a world power or the sole superpower, the Canadian imprint on world politics has been far less profound. Each country has earned respect for its legal system and its version of democracy, though the Canadian and American versions of each are distinct from each other.

The foregoing imagery sets the scene for this volume in the Understanding Canada collection. As much as it is possible to analyze a country by focusing individually on various of its political, legal, historical, social, or economic features, it is also useful to get to know a jurisdiction by comparing and contrasting it with its closest neighbour. This is the methodology professors Inwood and Speel have adopted. They have devised a comprehensive grid for looking at Canada and the United States from a variety of necessary perspectives: democracy; political institutions; elections and voting; federalism and regionalism; public policies; trade and economic policy; and foreign policy. They cap the analysis with a look ahead. Using this methodology, they reduce the distance between the two countries and sharpen the perspective of readers on the similarities and differences between these two North American countries. Among Understanding Canada authors, this methodology is new and uniquely helpful.

Two factors militate in favour of the comparative approach. First, mutual knowledge and awareness are irreplaceable. No one can be a good citizen without understanding both their own country and familiarizing themselves with its closest comparator. This is true, first, in an environment of absence of genuine information compounded by a pervasive lack of over-the-horizon curiosity. Moreover, genuine information is also a vital necessity in a world seriously damaged by the superficial, the unimportant, the fake, and the deliberately misleading. Thus, in an environment crying out for analysis and comparison based on facts, this book will provide both.

In addition, there is the issue of timing. One can think of the short-term, looking at the electoral calendar in the neighbouring countries. In a more long-term perspective, the internal characteristics of Canada and the United States are evolving in response to domestic political, social, and economic tensions. If, as some once perceived, history ended in the late 1980s, it is now resuming its march. In a global environment of increasing, indeed renewed, competition for power, the role of each country on the world stage is evolving in as-yet-unknown directions.

## Foreword

In sum, there is no better reason to engage with this book than the comparative perspectives it offers and there is no better time to absorb the realities it investigates than now. Professors Inwood and Speel have drafted a text that will serve academics, students, and indeed interested citizens well on both sides of the forty-ninth parallel. United States, meet Canada! Canada, meet the United States! Get to know each other!

Gregory Tardi, DJur.
Editor, *Understanding Canada* collection
May 2024

# Introduction

*Geography has made us neighbours. History has made us friends. Economics has made us partners, and necessity has made us allies.*
— President John F Kennedy[1]

*Living next door to the United States is like an elephant sharing a bed with a mouse. No matter how friendly and even-tempered the beast... one is affected by every twitch and grunt.*
— Prime Minister Pierre Trudeau[2]

*A Canadian is "an American who rejects the Revolution."*
— Professor Northrop Frye[3]

*Americans are benevolently ignorant about Canada, while Canadians are malevolently informed about the United States.*
— Historian James Brebner[4]

This book provides a brief comparative analysis of the Canada-United States relationship, including its political, economic, cultural, and international-relations dimensions. To this end, it explores the comparative history and political cultures of the two countries; the institutions of their respective political systems; elections, political parties, and voting; regionalism; public policies; and issues in Canadian-American relations. Across these many dimensions of comparison, it is clear that Canada and the United States are the same, only different.

## A Complicated Relationship

If you sat in a university classroom with both Canadian and American students, as we have done many times, you would be hard pressed to tell them apart. Their manner of dress and comportment would be largely the same. The diversity within each of the two groups would be roughly similar. The technology in their hands or on their desks would be practically identical. And if you could access their browsing histories, you would likely find comparable news, educational, cultural, sports, and entertainment sites. Many of the political themes they articulate would be alike, such as a belief in democracy, security, and freedom. Perhaps their accents would differ once they started talking. But their turns of phrase and colloquialisms would probably be alike (although many Canadians might be identifiable by their resort to "eh?" at the end of some sentences and the Americans mystified by mention of Toonie coins).

And yet, these students belong to two distinct and varied political communities. Their dominant political cultures, values, forms of democracy, political institutions, and place in the world resemble each other in interesting ways, but also differ in substantive ways. One might say that the paradox of Canadians and Americans is that they are the same, only different.

Recent polls have confirmed that paradox, finding many similarities between Canadian and American political and cultural attitudes, but also significant differences. An Innovative Research Group survey in 2020 found similar beliefs in the two countries about government involvement in the economy and free trade, with Canadians being slightly more favourable on both issues. Poll respondents in both countries also had similar attitudes toward immigration and remedying racial discrimination, which might surprise consumers of American news. The main differences found in the polls were in cultural issues such as abortion, where Americans were far more likely to favour restrictions, and on support for strong dominant political leaders, which were more popular in the United States than in Canada during the last year of Donald Trump's first term as president and which likely played a role in Trump's victory in the 2024 presidential election.[5]

Survey researchers Michael Adams and Andrew Parkin also found similarities and differences in the two countries in a 2022 survey. While attitudes toward economic opportunities and access to social services as well as opposition to the criminalization of drugs were similar in the United States and Canada, a majority of Canadian Conservatives supported women's right to abortion, and 61 percent of Canadians wanted possession of handguns to be illegal, compared to 29 percent of Americans.[6]

Television shows in both countries have satirized some of the differences between Canada and the United States, focusing on stereotypes that are a source of humour to residents in both countries. In a 2002 episode of *The Simpsons* television show, young Bart Simpson develops an interest in a girl whose father moves from Springfield to Toronto to film a movie. When Bart tells his father Homer that they need to travel to Toronto, Homer whines "Why should we leave America to visit America Junior?" Upon arrival in Canada on a bus with a Canadian Mountie and a hockey player as other passengers, Marge exclaims, "It's so clean and bland, I'm home." When a security officer at the CN Tower lets Bart and Homer know the attraction will be closing in five minutes, Homer offers a $1 bribe to stay open, and the officer accepts the "American currency" with excitement. Later, Bart and his friend Milhouse fight over the girl they both like and end up interrupting a live episode of *Curling for Loonies*.

Another long-time animated show, *South Park,* also frequently lampoons American stereotypes about Canada, and the 1999 movie version of the show was nominated for an Academy Award for the song "Blame Canada," in which the parents of a South Park character blame a Canadian children's television show filled with profanity and crude humour for the crude behaviour of their own children.

In Canada, comedian Rick Mercer had a popular segment titled "Talking to Americans" on the comedy satire show *This Hour Has 22 Minutes*. During the segments, Mercer would travel to the United States and get oblivious Americans, including prominent political leaders, on camera, to congratulate Canada on its national igloo and on adopting a twenty-four-hour day, and to discuss Canadian Prime Minister Jean Poutine and the Saskatchewan seal hunt. These are all made up, of course, to show how little many Americans seem to know about Canada.

However popular culture portrays the (mis)perceptions of citizens between the two countries, at the political level, relations are more serious. When Joe Biden became the president of the United States in 2020 after four years of Donald Trump's "Make America Great Again" belligerence, tariffs, and protectionism, politicians and public servants in Ottawa — and a lot of other Canadians — breathed a sigh of relief, anticipating a return to some form of normalcy in the Canadian-American relationship.

Biden and Prime Minister Justin Trudeau knew each other, having dined together in Ottawa when Biden was vice president. Biden talked up his family connections to Canada, noted his vice president Kamala Harris grew up in Montreal, and claimed that Canada's friendship — its "family connection" — was vital to the United States. "This is one of the easiest relationships you can have as an American president, and one of the best,"[7] Biden said when Trudeau was sitting beside him at the White House on 18 November 2021. But that family analogy may have glossed over the extent to which dysfunction can be part of a family dynamic, including, for example, a bullying older sibling or perhaps a neglectful parent. Did Biden treat Canada as "family"? Has any American president?

One of the first things Biden did after his inauguration was cancel the planned cross-border Keystone XL pipeline as part of the climate change agenda he had campaigned on. But Trudeau's government, and the province of Alberta, had considered the pipeline vital to Canada's economic health and a key part of its energy policy. In the past, when American policy choices had adversely affected Canadian interests, Ottawa was often able to quietly negotiate some other concessions or compensation, or even exemptions. There might have been a quid pro quo to follow, perhaps a softening of "buy American" positions as they affected Canada, for instance. However, in this case, quite the opposite occurred.

Instead, Biden ramped up the "buy American" rhetoric on government procurement. He doubled tariffs on Canadian lumber. As the COVID-19 pandemic eased, he took his time on reopening the land border after Canada had already started welcoming Americans back. He did not intervene on Canada's behalf as Michigan's governor attempted to shut down a critical oil and gas pipeline that serviced central Canada. He signed a new nuclear submarine pact with Australia and the United Kingdom for Pacific defence and left Canada out (although Trudeau claimed not to want in). He proposed the *Inflation Reduction Act* in 2022, which was a massive subsidy program for electric vehicles built in the United States, leading Canada (and Mexico) to charge that it violated trade agreements and would destroy the Canadian (and Mexican) auto industry. As if to pour salt on the wound, Biden visited a Michigan electric auto plant on the very day before Trudeau was scheduled to visit the White House.

Despite all of this, Trudeau insisted Biden was his "friend" and made apologies for the president's behaviour toward Canada: "Biden has huge, huge domestic responsibilities that he's trying to navigate. He's one of the good guys on climate change, on inclusion, on gender, on the things that we know are building blocks to safe, successful societies and democracies. He's on the right side of things, so he needs to be successful."[8] It is true, after all, that the president of the United States is always a busy person with countless distractions and responsibilities to attend to, besides the concerns of its small neighbour to the north. Biden faced numerous profound threats to his country, from climate change to attacks by his predecessor's anti-democratic supporters, while desperately trying to pass major economic and justice reforms that would reshape his country. He did so while facing a divided electorate that seemed at times to be on the brink of civil war.

It was not until March 2023 that Biden visited Canada as president. That was more than halfway through his first term in office — later than any American president since the 1970s. Admittedly, the pandemic and civil disruption in the United States stemming from the deep polarization there forced the president to be more inward-looking and domestically focused. But those facts did not lessen the importance of the Canada-United States relationship for Canada.

With friends like these, Canada must have been wondering, who needs... Trump? Anxiety about cross-border relations and politics among Canadian government officials and many other Canadians returned after Trump won the 2024 presidential election. One journalist put the issues facing Canada in dramatic terms:

> Now that the people of the United States have elected a fascist to lead them — a felon to "take care that the laws are faithfully executed," an insurrectionist to "preserve, protect and defend the Constitution," a rapist, a racist, and a narcissistic psychopath to hold the country's highest position of honour — the question on everyone's lips, naturally, is: what does it mean for Canada?[9]

So great was the concern that Deputy Prime Minister Chrystia Freeland felt compelled to tell everyone to calm down, saying "I want to say with utter sincerity and conviction to Canadians that Canada will be absolutely fine." Still, two days after the American election, the prime minister announced he was resurrecting the defunct cabinet committee on Canada-US relations, originally created in 2016 when Trump was first elected president.

The Trudeau-Trump relationship had been fraught during Trump's first presidency, and during his campaign for re-election Trump was openly contemptuous of Trudeau. At one point, Trump called Trudeau "a far-left lunatic."[10] Trump also repeatedly proclaimed his plan to impose a 10 percent across-the-board import tariff, the impact of which would result in about $30 billion per year in economic costs to Canada, according to the Canadian Chamber of Commerce.[11] On foreign policy, Trump took a view diametrically opposite to the view of Canada, NATO, and the European Union on the question of supporting Ukraine in its war against Russia. Trump also attacked the United Nations, an institution Canada strongly supports. During the months between the 2024 election and the start of his second term, Trump threatened a 25 percent tariff on Canadian products. He also repeatedly made "jokes" about Canada becoming the fifty-first state and insulted Trudeau by referring to him as the "governor" of the "great state of Canada."

Before he began his second term, Trump announced his plan to include in his administration a number of key players who had been outspoken critics of Canada. These included Congressman Mike Waltz as national security adviser. Waltz, from Florida, had repeatedly criticized Trudeau on social media, particularly regarding his handling of issues related to China. Waltz also predicted on X that Conservative Leader Pierre Poilievre was going to "send Trudeau packing in 2025" and "start digging Canada out of the progressive mess it's in."[12] Trump and Waltz also criticized NATO members that had not met their defence spending targets, including Canada, although Trudeau had committed to reaching the target of spending the equivalent of 2 percent of the country's GDP on defence by 2032. Florida Senator Marco Rubio, Trump's choice for secretary of state, expressed concerns about the Canada-United States border, and he had attacked Canada's move to accept Palestinian refugees, claiming without evidence that "terrorists and known criminals continue to stream across US land borders, including from Canada."[13] Trump's choice for ambassador to the United Nations, New York Congresswoman Elise Stefanik, had been a member of the Northern Border Security Caucus, which had called for Homeland Security to secure the northern border, claiming there had been an increase in human and drug trafficking. "We must protect our children from these dangerous illegal immigrants who are pouring across our northern border in record numbers," she claimed, again without evidence.[14] Tom Homan, Trump's choice to be a "border czar," said that "the problem with the northern border is a huge national security issue," and suggested he was prepared to have some tough conversations with Ottawa.[15] In addition, Robert Lighthizer, Trump's former trade representative, was an informal adviser for the president-elect's transition. Lighthizer had been in charge of the American team that renegotiated the North American Free Trade Agreement, and that took a particularly tough stance against both Canada and Mexico in the process.

Whether an outwardly pro-Canada but inwardly protectionist Democrat is president or an outwardly anti-Canada and inwardly protectionist Republican is president, what is the challenge for Canada's leadership under these circumstances? To not be overlooked. A former clerk of the Privy Council and secretary to Cabinet (the highest position in the Canadian federal public service) offered the following advice to prime ministers on how to manage relations with the United States: "At a minimum . . . you may have to work hard to vaccinate against the risk that the Americans will take Canada for granted, forget about the impact on Canada of actions aimed at other countries, and side-swipe us unintentionally."[16] This is essentially a historically rooted condition that changes very little from administration to administration. Canada had to continuously find ways of reminding Biden that he was the one who said the friendship between Canada and the United States "is absolutely critical to the United States, our well-being, our security, our sense of ourselves."[17] He needed to be convinced that Canada's success is not a distraction from America's success, but a central element of it. After Biden was replaced by Harris as the Democratic presidential nominee in July 2024, and after Trump won the 2024 election, this challenge remained, as it does at all times in the Canadian-American relationship.

But how . . . ?

## The Plan of the Book

This is the never-ending Canadian dilemma in Canadian-American relations that this book will address. To do so, it applies a lens that reveals the extent to which Canada and the United States are the same, only different. The book begins, in Chapter 1, with an exploration of the political cultures of the two countries. Chapter 2 examines comparative political institutions. Chapter 3 looks at comparative elections and voting. Federalism and regionalism in both countries are the subjects of Chapter 4. Chapter 5 compares public policies in the two countries. Chapter 6 examines trade and economic policies. Chapter 7 assesses other aspects of the foreign policies of both countries. Finally, Chapter 8 looks ahead and engages in some informed speculation on the future trajectory of the Canadian-American relationship. Focusing on the differences and similarities of domestic politics, government institutions, and policy choices in the two countries will help to inform the analysis of the Canadian-American relationship. Ultimately, it is hoped that this text will contribute to understanding Canada.

CHAPTER ONE

# Canadians and Americans — The Same, Only Different: Comparative History and Political Culture

## Introduction

Why do Canada and the United States have different governing systems? How did those systems originate? How do they function to provide for "Peace, Order and Good Government" for Canadians and "Life, Liberty and the Pursuit of Happiness" for Americans? What factors in the two countries' history and political cultures lead to the conclusion that Canada and the United States are "the same, only different"? This chapter addresses these factors. It sets out the predominant historical factors that have contributed to this paradox by examining the development of each country's political culture, values, and democracy. This will set the table for a comparative examination of the political institutions in both countries in Chapter 2.

### A. Political Culture, Values, and Democracy

#### 1) The Indigenous Antecedents in North America[1]

Canadian-American relations have antecedents that pre-date the arrival of the Europeans in the sixteenth century. Thus, there are two broad periods to consider in the history of North America that gave rise to the nation-states of Canada and the United States. The first period is the history of Indigenous peoples from their earliest arrival up to the sixteenth century. The specific date marking the arrival of Indigenous peoples in North America is a matter of some contention and is difficult to definitively assign. The second period is from the arrival of the Europeans to the present. While it is the latter period we are mainly concerned with, this can only be understood by reference to what preceded it.

It is generally thought that the Indigenous peoples of North America began arriving about 10,000–30,000 years ago by crossing the ice bridge across the Bering Strait, the eighty-two kilometres (51 miles) wide straight at its narrowest point joining the Arctic and Pacific oceans between modern-day Russia and Alaska. The Neolithic age beginning 6,000–8,000 years ago saw the domestication of plants and growth in basic tools leading to higher populations, permanent settlements, and increasing complexity of life, which in turn gave rise to specialization. Agricultural surpluses in Mesoamerica (present-day southern North America and most of Central America) led to developments in agriculture, architecture, science, mathematics, art, cultural, political, economic development, etc. This period lasted until about 900 AD and was followed by the rise of the Toltecs and Aztecs. Cahokia was the site of a pre-Columbian Native American city directly across the Mississippi River from modern St. Louis, Missouri. The largest such settlement north of Mexico City, it was a major trade hub for Indigenous peoples 1,000 years before the Vikings landed in present-day Newfoundland around 1000 AD.[2]

Estimates of the populations of Indigenous peoples in North America before the arrival of the Europeans vary. There were thought to be 3.8–7 million Indigenous people in North America overall, of which roughly 1.8[3]–5 million[4] were in present-day United States, and 500,000–2 million were in what is now Canada. By the time of the achievement of independence by the Thirteen Colonies in 1776, there were 500,000–700,000.[5] By Confederation in Canada in 1867, about 140,000.

In Canada, relations between Indigenous peoples and the French in New France (present-day Quebec) and later, the British in British North America were at first straightforward. The Indigenous peoples and French regarded each other as vital trading partners who each brought valuable new goods to the other. They also evolved into military allies who assisted in consolidating power and protecting against the British and hostile neighbouring Indigenous peoples. The French regarded the Indigenous peoples as vital economic partners who helped extend the fur trade to the Pacific and as military allies in their contest with the British for control of North America. In addition, Indigenous peoples helped establish the eventual boundary between Canada and the United States. Later, different tribes served as allies to the Americans against British designs on a newly independent United States, while others assisted the British in protecting against American incursions into British North America. A fluid and shifting series of alliances, treaties, deceptions, and double-crossing by both the Europeans and the Indigenous peoples characterized much of the 200-year history of contact up until the nineteenth century. By that point, the Indigenous peoples were largely marginalized, isolated, alienated, and oppressed by both civil society and governments, which saw little remaining utility in an economic or military partnership with them.

In British North America, the relationship with the Indigenous peoples was constitutionalized in the Royal Proclamation of 1763, which recognized Native land rights and described a rough Proclamation Line that divided hunting grounds from land that could be settled by Europeans. The Crown retained title to the land mass of Canada, but recognized the rights of Indigenous peoples to use and occupy the land, although the exact eastern and western boundary of the reserved lands was not specified. The relevant part of the Royal Proclamation reads as follows:

> And whereas it is just and reasonable, and essential to our interest and the security of our colonies, that the several nations or tribes

of Indians with whom we are connected, and who live under our protection, would not be molested or disturbed in the possession of such parts of our Dominion and territories as not having been ceded to, or purchased by us, are reserved to them, or any of them, as their hunting grounds.[6]

The Royal Proclamation provided the constitutional basis of the idea that the Indigenous peoples constituted nations whose sovereignty had never been surrendered or taken away, and it sustains arguments for Indigenous self-government to the present day. Notwithstanding the theoretical constitutional relationship between the British Crown and Indigenous peoples, war, disease, discriminatory policies, religious imperialism, attempts at assimilation, and other similar practices resulted in the marginalization of the Indigenous population in Canada, a condition from which it still struggles to recover today.

The earliest years of British colonization of what became the United States also included examples of economic and social cooperation between the Europeans and Indigenous residents. Generations of American school children have learned about Native American assistance to early English settlers through stories like the first American Thanksgiving in Massachusetts and Pocahontas in Virginia.

Many of the British colonies were created with the recognition that the land first belonged to the Indigenous peoples and should be purchased to avoid wars. Roger Williams, who created a colony at modern Providence, Rhode Island, after his banishment from Massachusetts, spoke Algonquin languages and criticized policies in other New England colonies that did not recognize Indigeous title over local land.[7] But early episodes of violence between European settlers and the Indigenous population led to growing distrust between the groups and a series of wars, conflicts, and massacres that became more common on the lands that became the United States than those that became Canada.

Skirmishes and wars broke out between Native American groups and English, Dutch, French, and Spanish settlers, and colonial militaries in New England, New York, Virginia, North and South Carolina, the Great Lakes region, the Louisiana Territory, and New Spain (in what is now the southwestern United States). Even Roger Williams later in his life supported the sale into slavery of members of defeated Indian tribes after King Philip's War ended in the 1670s.[8]

By 1763, European settlers had begun to head westward, away from the Atlantic coast, to new territories inhabited by Native Americans, creating more conflicts. Attempts to forestall such conflicts were a key reason for the Royal Proclamation of 1763 to limit European settlers from moving west of the Appalachian Mountains. Daniel Boone is famous in American history for flouting the Proclamation and settling in Kentucky, thereby provoking conflicts with local Native Americans. Even George Washington, due to his military service in the French and Indian War, claimed ownership of western lands and wrote that he planned to ignore the Proclamation's prohibitions of such settlements.[9] Many American historians have attributed American anger at this limit on western settlements as a key cause of the American Revolution.[10]

The different relationships between Indigenous peoples and the Europeans who settled the northern half of the continent and those who settled the southern half suggest reasons why Canada and the United States developed along different lines. Both groups of Europeans had to determine the nature of their connections and interactions with Indigenous peoples. In New France and British North America, the emphasis was initially on trade and economic relations, particularly to foster and develop the fur trade. In the British colonies which became the United States, a different set of conditions contributed to a different set of relations. A more temperate climate, longer growing season, and access to ice-free ports year-round meant that the colonists were less concerned with cooperative economic relations with the Indigenous peoples, and more concerned with westward expansion for the purposes of settlement. This led to ongoing clashes with Indigenous peoples and eventually a state of ongoing warfare to forcibly destroy the Indigenous people, and confiscate the land needed for the growing populations of settlers.

## B. Colonialism

Patterns of colonial settlement in Canada and the United States differed markedly. North America became a location for the great military-political struggles of European powers as Europe tried to remake North America in its own image. Consequently, waves of Spanish, French, English, and Dutch settlers contributed to the gradual emergence of distinct societies. At first under the control of the imperial powers, each emerged seeking more and more political, economic, and cultural self-control over time.

### 1) American Settlement

The Spanish arrived in New Spain in 1492 in the West Indies; military conquest, economic exploitation, and settlement quickly followed. The French arrived in New France in 1534 at Quebec; growth was slow and incremental, and focused on the expansion of the fur trade. The English arrived in Virginia in 1607 with a settlement at Jamestown and in New England in 1620 when a religious community known as Puritans founded Plymouth (present-day Massachusetts). The Dutch followed and founded New Amsterdam (New York) in 1624.

By the 1750s, New Spain had developed as a tightly controlled, deeply religious society dominated by the Catholic church. It had the largest Indigenous population, and largest overall population of about 6 million by the 1750s. The thirteen English colonies on the Atlantic seaboard had a population of about 1.5 million by the 1750s, with political, economic, and cultural institutions of great complexity and variety. New France was characterized by more isolated and remote communities; it was a conservative and church-dominated (Catholic) society, which included a huge land mass from the Gulf of St. Lawrence to the Gulf of Mexico but with a smaller, scattered population of only 65,000 by the 1750s. The Dutch had an early influence on colonial New York, but the colony was captured by the British in 1664 and renamed.

## 2) The French and Indian War (aka Seven Years' War), 1756–1763

The drive toward separate American and Canadian independence began, to a large extent, in western Pennsylvania with disputes between the British and French in the French and Indian War (also known as the Seven Years' War in Canada). The outnumbered French were particularly dependent on alliances with the Indigenous tribes of the Great Lakes and Ohio Valley regions. Western Pennsylvania was very important to the fur trade of the mid-1700s, and the French established four forts in the region: Fort Duquesne (present-day Pittsburgh), Fort Presque Isle (present-day Erie), Fort Le Boeuf (present-day Waterford), and Fort Machault (present-day Franklin). In 1752, the governor of Virginia sent a twenty-one-year-old major named George Washington to Fort Le Boeuf to tell the French to leave the area, but after a cordial meal together, the French refused, and Washington returned to Virginia to give his report. Thus began the French and Indian War.

## 3) The Treaty of Paris and the Royal Proclamation, 1763

The British eventually defeated the French in 1759 at the Battle of the Plains of Abraham in Quebec City, the capital of New France. In the Treaty of Paris signed in 1763, the French gave up New France to the British. King George III of England signed the Royal Proclamation of 1763, which forbade American colonists from settling west of the Appalachian Mountains without approval of the British government to avoid conflicts with Indigenous tribes. In Canada, the Royal Proclamation is seen as part of the Constitution and provides the legal basis for some modern Indigenous land claims (discussed in Section D below), as well as the basis of English-French accommodation as opposed to assimilation of the French population (also discussed in Section D below).

## C. The American Story of Revolution

One of the most significant differences between Canada and the United States results from their unique formative experiences. As we have seen, the American colonists had a different relationship to the Indigenous peoples than the Canadian colonists did. Moreover, the formative ideas shaping American democracy and the origins and development of the American constitutional order differ from the Canadian experience. We can sum up the differences as revolution versus evolution.

### 1) Taxation Without Representation

With the Seven Years' War over, the British Parliament needed to raise revenue to pay for war debts and for future defences of the American colonies against Indigenous tribes and the Spanish. The British Parliament did not want to tax people in Great Britain to defend colonies on the other side of Atlantic, which would have been very unpopular with voters in Britain. Therefore, the British Parliament instead imposed taxes on American colonists, who immediately began trying to avoid paying them. Given that the American colonists were not directly represented in the British Parliament, this led to the complaint of "taxation without representation," which became a rallying cry for the revolution.

The British passed the *Stamp Act* of 1765, which taxed legal documents, permits, newspapers, wills, pamphlets, and playing cards. The American colonists protested, and mobs attacked British government officials in the colonies. Secret societies formed, such as the Sons of Liberty. The British repealed the *Stamp Act* and replaced it with the Townshend Acts of 1767, which were new taxes imposed on American colonies for lead, paper, paint, glass, and tea imports. Boycotts of British products ensued, as did large-scale smuggling by American merchants who did not want to pay import taxes. One key centre of smuggling was Narragansett Bay in the colony of Rhode Island. In 1772, the British ship the *Gaspee*, a customs schooner that enforced the Navigation Acts in and around Newport, Rhode Island, was chasing a smuggling ship in Narragansett Bay to enforce import taxes, but ran aground. In an act of civil defiance, John Brown, a leading merchant of Rhode Island, organized a group who secretly boarded the ship at night, shot and wounded the captain, and set fire to and burned down the *Gaspee*. The episode was emblematic of the colonists' growing disposition to use violence against British authorities. In modern Rhode Island, every summer, the city of Warwick celebrates Gaspee Days where people stage a parade, dress in Revolutionary War uniforms, and burn an effigy of the *Gaspee*.

In 1773, the British Parliament passed the *Tea Act,* making tea imported by the British East India Company to the colonies less expensive than tea smuggled by American merchants. When British ships filled with tea docked in Boston Harbor later that year, the Sons of Liberty dressed up as Indians, boarded the ships at night, and dumped the tea overboard in what became known as the Boston Tea Party. This became an iconic event, emblematic of the strong current of political protest in the United States. For example, a group called the Tea Party movement emerged in 2009 as a fiscally conservative political movement within the Republican Party, calling for lower taxes, among other reforms, and often referring to themselves as historical successors to the Boston protest of 1773.

The British Parliament in 1774 reacted harshly, determined to punish the colonists, but ultimately feeding the grievances that resulted in the American Revolution. The Intolerable Acts (known as the Coercive Acts in Britain), which shut down the port of

Boston until the British were repaid for the lost tea, were passed. It also forced Boston residents to allow British soldiers to billet in their homes. More generally, the Acts took away self-governance and rights that Massachusetts had long enjoyed. Many Americans across the Thirteen Colonies reacted with outrage.

The *Quebec Act, 1774* (one of the Intolerable Acts) restored the rights of the Catholic church over much of Quebec society to ensure the loyalty of the French-Canadian *habitants*. But more importantly for the Americans, it made most of the area around the Great Lakes part of the province of Quebec, including Southern Ontario; the disputed territory of Ohio, Michigan, Indiana; and even parts of modern-day Wisconsin, Illinois, and Minnesota. This territory also included what was then called the "Land of the Indians" that the Royal Proclamation had recognized as Indigenous land where the Royal Proclamation had restricted European settlement.

In response, in 1774 and 1775, the American colonies set up their first Continental Congress, and established local militias. The first shots of the American Revolution were fired in 1775, when the British sent a regiment to Massachusetts to confiscate the arms of local militias. In another formative event in the American creation story, Paul Revere famously rode west to warn the militias "the British are coming, the British are coming" (although Revere probably never said those exact words), whereupon the militias mustered and fired on the British at Lexington and Concord, Massachusetts. This event later became one basis for the Second Amendment to the United States Constitution about well-regulated militias and the right to bear arms (discussed in Chapter 5). The United States declared independence in 1776, and with some help from France, defeated the British. The British then signed a peace treaty with the Americans in 1783, and the disputed Great Lakes area was made a part of the United States.

While some Native American communities supported the American side during the revolution, and even more supported the British side, neither side had consulted with the Native Americans about the western territorial borders set in the peace treaty for their opinion on these issues.

## 2) A Revolution or a Civil War?

The American colonists were very divided over going to war against the Crown, even if they opposed the oppressive taxation policies of the British. As historian Stephen Azzi says:

> The sympathies of most residents of British North America were difficult to pin down, both before and during the uprising. The conflict was a revolution, but it was also a civil war, one that pitted neighbour against neighbour, rebellious Americans against those who fought for the British Crown. The majority of Americans opposed the taxes Britain had forced upon the colonies, but most were also wary about resorting to violence.[11]

The colonists who supported the British and opposed the revolution were known as United Empire Loyalists. After the American Revolution, many of these Loyalists fled to Quebec and Nova Scotia and pushed for the creation of the new colonies of Upper Canada and New Brunswick. They become the first large English-speaking population of modern Canada, more than doubling the existing English population. However, they possessed a "contradictory identity"— at once American and anti-American, and in many ways laid the basis for Canada's ambivalent relationship with the United States.

The American Revolution also contributed to the development of distinct political cultures in the two countries. The American sociologist and political scientist Seymour Martin Lipset characterized the Revolution this way:

> Americans do not know but Canadians cannot forget that two nations, not one, came out of the American Revolution. One was Whig and classically liberal or libertarian — doctrines that emphasize distrust of the state, egalitarianism, and populism. . . .

The other was Tory and conservative in the British and European sense — accepting of the need for a strong state, for respect for authority, for deference.[12]

The differences between the two countries, rooted in these long-ago events, help explain many policy differences between them, right down to the present day, as we will see throughout this book.

### 3) A New Constitution

The first governing document of the newly independent United States was the Articles of Confederation, drafted during the American Revolutionary War. The Articles assumed a system of government dominated by states with the same colonial geographical boundaries that had been set by the British. Most government powers were granted to states and very few were granted to the national government that initially met in Philadelphia. The powers to declare war, negotiate treaties and alliances, regulate Indian affairs, establish a post office, raise a national treasury funded by state contributions (voluntary state donations), and coin money (which states could also do) were given to the new United States national government. That was it. The national government could declare war but had no national military to fight it, and lacked the means to raise money to finance an army unless the state governments were willing to provide donations for funding, which many were reluctant to do.

Article XI said that nine current states would need to approve admission of a new state into the country, but made an exception for Canada, which had the automatic right to join the United States whenever Canada wanted. Since Canada never had an interest in becoming a part of its southern neighbour, Americans periodically invaded over the next hundred years to try to move the process along.

The Articles of Confederation provided a long list of governance problems for the United States in the 1780s. Because the national government had no power of taxation and lacked any national military or even a federal executive branch, it was dependent on state governments to enforce federal policies. There were also no federal courts, only state courts. Each state got exactly one vote in the national Congress, no matter the state population, and a unanimous vote of all states was required to amend the Articles. States imposed tariffs on products from other states and were printing and coining their own money, making commercial trade and travel difficult in the new country. There was no effective way to settle boundary disputes between states, leading to skirmishes like the Pennamite-Yankee wars between settlers from Pennsylvania and settlers from Connecticut in what is now northeast Pennsylvania. King Charles II of England in the seventeenth century had granted the area to both states in separate documents.

In 1787, political leaders from around the United States called for a convention in Philadelphia to amend the Articles of Confederation. Twelve of the thirteen states sent delegates to the convention. The government of Rhode Island, which had been printing up inflationary state paper money, refused to send any delegates to the convention; consequently, it was impossible to amend the Articles. So the delegates in effect threw out the Articles, created a new Constitution, and said only nine states would need to approve the new Constitution to go into effect, actions which in the twenty-first century might be labelled as a form of a coup, though without violence. Rhode Island would later become the last of the original thirteen states to ratify the Constitution after the state was threatened with an economic blockade by the other twelve states in 1790. The Federalist Papers, written by James Madison, Alexander Hamilton, and John Jay to convince the New York state legislature to ratify the new United States Constitution, contained frequent critical comments of Rhode Island.

Most of the delegates from the twelve states at the Constitutional Convention of 1787 were elite members of society, including wealthy Northern merchants, Southern plantation owners, lawyers, doctors, and clergy. No urban workers, women, Westerners, African Americans, or Native Americans served as delegates. Seventy-four delegates were approved to attend the convention; fifty-five actually did, and twenty-five of those delegates were slave owners. Many historians and political scientists have argued that the delegates at the Constitutional Convention focused on their own economic interests when writing the United States Constitution, but others have pointed out that the delegates were well-educated and held certain broad principles, and the resulting Constitution represents a mix of self-interest and principles from the late eighteenth century.[13]

There were conflicts about ideas of governance among the delegates at the Convention and compromises made to resolve those conflicts, many of which affect the operations and effectiveness of American government in the twenty-first century. Delegates from larger states argued for representation based on population, while those from smaller states argued for equal representation for each state in the Congress. In addition, advocates of democracy argued for a directly elected Congress, while delegates who were suspicious of the "passions of the people" argued for indirect selection of Congress. The two-chamber Congress was intended to address both of those sets of arguments. The House of Representatives was to be directly elected by voters every two years, and states with larger populations would get more members, while the Senate would have two members from each state and its members would be chosen for six-year terms by state legislatures (that would change with the Seventeenth Amendment to the United States Constitution in 1913, which provides for direct voter election of senators).

The most notorious compromise made at the Constitutional Convention involved an effort by Southern states to count enslaved people as part of their populations in order to increase representation in the House, even though the economic elites of those states treated slaves as property and had no intention of allowing them to vote (as the slaves would then vote to abolish slavery). Several Northern states had begun to abolish slavery by the time of the Convention and objected to Southern states obtaining more political power through retention of the practice. So a compromise was written into the United States Constitution, in which enslaved people would count as three-fifths of a free person when determining numbers of representatives in the House, a practice that remained in effect until the Thirteenth Amendment abolished slavery in 1865.

## 4) Manifest Destiny

The White population of the new United States of America consisted largely of the descendants of people escaping religious or political persecution in Europe. They proved to be a restless people and soon wanted to move inland across the continent. Thus began the American policy known as manifest destiny, understood as the need to move westward and spread the revolutionary spirit and ideas of democracy and liberty across the American continent. This need to spread American ideals remains a key component of the foreign policy of the United States to this day.

## 5) Nineteenth-Century Growth

Far-reaching political changes were accompanied by economic and social change not just in the United States, but in British North America and Mexico as well. The early transition from rural to urban and from agricultural to industrial societies began in the nineteenth century, but was most pronounced in the United States. While the Mexican and American populations were roughly even in 1800 (5.3 million versus 5.8 million) and Canada was a mere 400,000, by the 1850s the American population was more than 31 million, Mexico's was 8 million, and Canada's was 2.4 million.

## 6) The War of 1812

Resistance by the British to the idea of manifest destiny eventually contributed to the War of 1812, in large part because the British kept forts along the border between Canada and the United States, including in cities like Detroit, making it difficult for the Americans to move westward. Moreover, the Americans accused the British of trading weapons with Indigenous tribes, who used them against American settlers. The United States declared war on Britain in 1812, claiming its key goal was to conquer Canada and expel the British. So sure of success were the Americans that former President Thomas Jefferson called the conquest of Canada merely "a matter of marching."[14]

Many of the key battles in the war took place in the Niagara region of southwestern Upper Canada (Ontario). Some Indigenous tribes played key roles, particularly for the British. The Shawnee Chief Tecumseh tried to unite various Indigenous tribes, having been promised their traditional lands would be secured with a British victory. But in the end, they were generally abandoned and subsequently marginalized.

The war has sometimes been characterized as more like a civil war, since many families were divided in their allegiances, with some members on one side of the border, others on the other side. Americans won some lake battles in the War of 1812. In 1813, American forces crossed Lake Ontario and attacked York, the capital of Upper Canada, today known as Toronto. Sensing defeat, the British retreated. As they departed, though, the British set a magazine storehouse on fire and the resulting explosion killed thirty-seven American soldiers, including their general, Zebulon Pike, and resulted in more than 220 casualties. Partly in retaliation, the Americans burned down the Parliament buildings and several other government offices, looted the town, and took the parliamentary mace of Upper Canada back to Washington; it was only returned in 1934 as a goodwill gesture by President Franklin Roosevelt. (Fort York has been rebuilt in Toronto and today is a major tourist destination.)

In 1814, British forces sailed up Chesapeake Bay and burned down Washington, including the White House, Capitol, Treasury, and Library of Congress, specifically in retaliation for the burning of York. The British then sailed on to Baltimore, Maryland, on the Chesapeake Bay and bombarded Fort McHenry, which protected Baltimore Harbor. A young lawyer named Francis Scott Key was on a British naval ship negotiating the release of American prisoners and observed the British bombardment of Fort McHenry at night. When

Key woke up the next morning, he saw the American flag still flying over Fort McHenry. Key wrote a poem about this — "The Star-Spangled Banner" — which later became the American national anthem.

In 1814, with neither side able to exploit an advantage, the United States and Britain signed the Treaty of Ghent to end the war. To this day, the Canadians claim they won, while history classes in the United States focus on American battle victories and usually teach that the war ended in a draw. Most everyone agrees, though, that the Indigenous peoples lost.

## 7) The Southern Border

After the War of 1812, the Americans returned to their policy of manifest destiny. In 1803, President Thomas Jefferson purchased the Louisiana territory from France, but it was felt there was still not enough space for some American settlers who continued to move further west. In the 1820s, Mexico allowed some American settlers with slaves to move to the northern Mexican province of Tejas (Texas). More and more Americans with slaves moved there in the 1830s, even though a new Mexican government no longer wanted such settlers. Still, American settlers continued to move into Tejas illegally. Meanwhile, Spain's domestic European relations and preoccupations with Napoleon opened an opportunity for Mexicans agitating for independence. The 1821 revolution was successful in overthrowing Spanish rule, but implanted a conservative Mexican regime rather than representative democracy. Powerful ideological and political tensions resulted in instability and insecurity.

## 8) The Mexican-American War

Eventually in the 1830s, Mexico removed rights to local government previously granted to settlers in Tejas. The American settlers rebelled, war started, and Texas declared independence from Mexico in 1836. The Mexican government never fully accepted this state of affairs, though, and American settlers appealed for annexation to the

United States, which came about in 1845. In 1846, the United States government sent troops to the border of Mexico and Texas along the Rio Grande River and shots were fired. Sixteen Americans ended up dead, and the Mexican-American War began. It ended in 1848 with a treaty in which the United States took over all of modern California, Arizona, New Mexico, Nevada, Utah, and most of Colorado.

Of course, no one asked the opinions of the Native Americans who lived there about these territorial changes.

## 9) 54-40 or Fight!

Meanwhile, a dispute also occurred over the territory of what is now Washington, Oregon, Idaho, and British Columbia — areas claimed by both the United States and by Britain on behalf of Canada. Both countries had forts near the mouth of the Columbia River. The Hudson's Bay Company (which exists to this day as a department store) ran the British fort and its purpose was to conduct the fur trade with Indigenous groups. In the American elections of 1844, a key campaign slogan was "54-40 or fight," suggesting the latitude (fifty-four degrees) at which the Americans believed the boundary should be set. But President James Polk was concerned at the same time about the Mexican-American War, and decided to negotiate with the British and settled on the forty-ninth parallel as the border between the United States and Canada in 1846.

## 10) Slavery and the Civil War

A key distinguishing feature between Canada and the United States is the latter's history of slavery. Whereas Canada outlawed the importation of slaves in 1793, and abolished slavery itself on 1 August 1834, it persisted in the southern United States plantation economy up to the Civil War of the 1860s. The divisions over slavery were stark. The northern states were abolitionist and wanted to prevent the extension of slavery to new states as they entered the Union. The Southern states were pro-slavery and wanted new states to permit slavery. Republican Abraham Lincoln was elected as president in 1860 when the Democratic Party split into factions over the slavery issue. The southern states seceded and formed an independent confederacy, leading to the Civil War (1861–1865), in which about a half million Americans died. The North won, and slavery was abolished with the Thirteenth Amendment, ratified in December 1865; Lincoln was assassinated in April 1865.

Among the lessons of the Civil War for Canada was that giving the state governments too much power at the expense of the national government was disastrous. Thus, when Confederation occurred in 1867, the Fathers of Confederation made sure the central government in Ottawa enjoyed the preponderance of powers compared to the provinces, points we will take up below and in Chapter 4 when we discuss federalism in the two countries.

Meanwhile, American political leaders had growing security concerns about their Northern neighbours. Most Canadians were anti-slavery and supported the Union cause. But some British and Canadians favoured trade and recognition of the Confederacy, and Confederate agents operated in British Canada, engaging in spying and obtaining military supplies. This caused some Union leaders in the United States to see British North America as a potential military threat. The American secretary of state, William Seward, among others, called for the annexation of Canada.[15] While the United States never annexed Canada, it "purchased" Alaska from Russia in 1867, causing Canada to be more geographically surrounded by United States territory. At the time, Alaska contained 700 Russian settlers and 40,000 Alaska Natives, who were never consulted about the "purchase."

## 11) American Imperialism

In the latter half of the nineteenth century, with the Civil War behind it, the United States began a period of rapid economic expansion, industrialization, and railroad building. The concept of manifest destiny spread to interests outside the continental United

States. In 1898, the United States declared war on Spain over colonial control of Cuba, defeated Spain, and took over Cuba until 1902, the Philippines for almost fifty years, and the territories of Guam and Puerto Rico, which it controls to the present day. Also in 1898, the United States annexed Hawaii after American settlers overthrew the local Hawaiian queen. In short, the United States engaged in a period of hemispheric imperialism, extending its influence and power as it gradually expanded and grew into one of the world's great economic, cultural, and military powers.

## 12) The First World War, the Great Depression, and the Second World War

Despite all this, the United States was very reluctant to get involved in world affairs outside the western hemisphere and Pacific Ocean. When the First World War broke out in Europe, Canada immediately joined the war effort as part of the British Empire, but the United States stayed out of it for several years. In 1916, President Woodrow Wilson won re-election with the slogan "he kept us out of war."

However, in 1917, soon after his second term started, Wilson persuaded Congress to declare war on Germany and the Central Powers of Europe. Why the change of policy? One reason is that Wilson told Congress that Germany was negotiating with Mexico to form an alliance so Mexico could get territory back from United States. The United States formally entered the war in 1917, and the "war to end all wars" was brought to a conclusion with Germany's surrender in November 1918. Wilson played a key role in the postwar settlement with the Treaty of Versailles and the creation of the League of Nations, but the United States generally returned to its earlier isolationist policy; it largely stayed out of world affairs and ironically, given Wilson's role, did not join the newly formed League of Nations.[16]

In 1929, the stock market crashed, ushering in the greatest period of economic disruption in modern capitalism to that date. The

American response included President Franklin Roosevelt's New Deal with a vastly expanded role for the state in the economy (not unlike President Barack Obama after the 2008 economic crash, or the response to the COVID-19 pandemic). Drawing on the economic theories of British economist John Maynard Keynes, policies were devised to stimulate economic growth through government spending, creating jobs, managing production, subsidizing agriculture, improving rural life, regulating banks and the stock market, and providing social security pensions. These initiatives marked a sharp departure for the United States from its traditional faith in rugged liberal individualism with its suspicion of the state and insistence on a limited role for government.

However, the United States never went as far as most Western European democracies eventually did in support for economic and social welfare policies advocated for by socialists or social democrats. Many theories relating to political culture have offered explanations as to why. Political scientist Louis Hartz argued in 1955 that America's liberal individualist tradition, lack of a feudal tradition, and large amount of land for settlement led to a widespread consensus among most that socialist solutions were unwise.[17]

Such beliefs are often labelled as American exceptionalism, the idea that the United States is different (or perhaps better) than other countries around the world. These ideas can be connected to the nineteenth-century ideology of manifest destiny. Political scientist Seymour Martin Lipset is among those who agreed with Hartz's central arguments and also cite the exceptional nature of American history and political culture in the diversity of its immigrant populations and the enduring strength of its two-party system as factors in the lack of strength of socialism in the United States.[18]

Others have emphasized the prominent role that race has played in United States politics, especially in the American South. Canadian political scientist Gerard Boychuk has argued that opposition to racial equality played a key role in why the United States never developed universal health care insurance, while regional forces in

Canada led to an opposite result (more about regionalism in both countries is covered in Chapter 4).[19]

When war broke out again in Europe in September 1939, Canada again came to the defence of Britain, although to signal a more independent stance in world affairs, it waited a few days before Parliament actually declared war on Germany and its allies. The United States, however, stayed out of direct action in the war until December 1941, when Japan bombed the American naval base at Pearl Harbor, Hawaii. Prior to that, continuing isolationist attitudes among many Americans, combined with some antisemitism, led to a strong anti-involvement America First campaign, in part led by famous aviator Charles Lindbergh. After the attack in Hawaii, both Canada and the United States played key roles in bringing about victory for the Allies; but as significant was the process of integration of the military-industrial complex on a continental scale, with coordinated efforts to manufacture weapon systems and their supporting industrial and raw material inputs.

### 13) The Cold War

After the Second World War, the United States switched to a more involved foreign policy, helped create the United Nations, and declared a policy of containment to prevent the spread of Communism in Korea in the 1950s, in Vietnam in the 1960s, and in the western hemisphere generally. In Korea, the war was officially a United Nations exercise, but the United States took the lead and for all intents and purposes was the key protagonist against the North Korean communist regime.

In Vietnam, the United States supported a corrupt anti-communist South Vietnam regime against a communist nationalist North Vietnam military force. The American policy in Vietnam was strongly criticized by much of the rest of the world, including Canadian prime ministers Lester Pearson and Pierre Trudeau. The United States had a military draft wherein young males were required by law to serve in the military. Many young people in the United States opposed the war, however, and between 30,000 and 50,000 American draft dodgers fled to Canada. This had a big impact on Canadian politics and society, especially in cities like Toronto, Montreal, and Vancouver. Canadian Prime Minister Pierre Trudeau welcomed the American draft dodgers to Canada, famously calling Canada "a refuge from militarism" in 1970, and in the process angering the administration of President Richard Nixon.

By the beginning of the twentieth century, America had emerged as an imperial power with overseas territories and global commercial and military interests. By the end of the twentieth century, America was essentially the world's only superpower. Support and opposition to American military intervention overseas have existed in both of the two major political parties over the past fifty years, with Democrats sometimes favouring intervention to prevent predicted genocides, in cases like Bosnia, Kosovo, or Libya, and Republicans sometimes favouring intervention to fight claimed enemies of the United States in Panama, Afghanistan, Iraq, and throughout the Middle East.

## 14) Indigenous Relations: Assimilation or Territorial Autonomy?

After the United States' colonies won independence, the new national government returned to policies of expulsions, fighting wars, and making treaties with Native American tribes. Treaties were often broken by White leaders, with negotiations forced on Native Americans. Some treaties were signed by tribal members who were not tribal leaders.

A key United States Supreme Court case that defines the modern relationship between Native American reservations and government officials is *Cherokee Nation v Georgia* (1831).[20] The state of Georgia was annexing land promised to the Cherokee in treaties for use by White people in cotton farming or gold exploration. The Cherokee filed a lawsuit in the Supreme Court. The Supreme Court under the United States Constitution has original jurisdiction (hears the case first) in cases involving foreign officials. The Cherokee filed their lawsuit in the United States Supreme Court because they said Cherokee leaders were foreign officials from a foreign nation. The Supreme Court ruled that the Cherokee are not a foreign nation, so their case must start in a lower court. The Supreme Court said that instead, Indian tribes like the Cherokee are "domestic dependent nations" living on their original territory with rights to self-government. The Court ruling compared the relationship as similar to that of a ward with a guardian. While many later laws also define the relationships between Native American tribes and United States government entities, that domestic dependent nation status with rights to self-government still underlies many policies on Indian reservations, including land use, taxation, and access for federal or state police authorities.

In 1830, President Andrew Jackson signed the *Indian Removal Act* into law, which forced Native American tribes of the American South to leave their homelands and move to what is now Oklahoma, violating promises in earlier treaties. Federal soldiers marched tribes westward, finishing in 1838. Between 4,000-8,000 Native Americans died during the forced march — a journey today known as the Trail of Tears.

In 1871, Congress abandoned all treaty making with Indian tribes, ending any recognition of tribes as foreign nations, and made all Native Americans on reservations wards of the United States government. Previously signed treaties had promised tribes cash assistance, food and clothing, technical and agricultural advice, and educational services in perpetuity, due to relocation and "willingness" to allow White settlers on traditional lands. Those treaties are mostly still in effect today. Since then, United States government policies toward relations with Native Americans have vacillated between attempts at forced or encouraged assimilation into a dominant European culture or emphasis on tribal sovereignty on reservations.

In 1887, the American government tried to end the territorial autonomy of reservations through the passage of the *Dawes Act*. The *Dawes Act* was considered progressive at the time for "helping" Native Americans to assimilate to European ways. The *Dawes Act* broke up reservations and tribally owned land and awarded 160 acres each of tribal land to reservation heads of household, making them private property owners. All surplus tribal land was put up for sale to White settlers. The law had the biggest impact in Oklahoma, which was majority Indian territory at the time. In 1889, some White settlers entered Indian territory sooner than the legal date on which they were allowed to do so to stake land claims before others did, leading to the modern Oklahoma Sooners nickname. The *Dawes Act* of 1887 failed to improve the economic status of Native Americans. Tribal identities were lost, and many children were forced into residential boarding schools away from home. Native Americans were allowed to sell the 160 acres after twenty-five years, with much land bought or swindled away by White settlers.

In 1934, Congress decided that the *Dawes Act* was largely a failure and passed the *Indian Reorganization Act*. That law allowed tribes to get back official tribal status under American law and regrouped and recreated reservations. The Bureau of Indian Affairs (BIA) was organized as part of the Department of the Interior to oversee tribal courts, schools, social services, and use of resources on reservations.

In the 1950s, the federal government tried assimilation again. Operation Relocation began in 1952 and gave Native Americans financial assistance if they left reservations to find jobs in urban areas. Forty thousand Native Americans took assistance, usually found low-wage jobs, and lived in low-income areas in cities. Some assimilated, but most moved back to reservations, and the program officially ended in the 1960s. The head of the BIA who designed this program was Dillon Myer, who was the same man who ran Japanese internment camp programs in the United States during the Second World War.

In 1953, Congress passed the *Termination Act*, which offered money to tribes to end official tribal government status and all treaty promises in return for one-time government funding. The largest tribe to use the law was the Menominee of Wisconsin. Tribal members were given $1,500 each (about $17,000 each in 2024 US dollars) to terminate tribal status. Following the termination decision, most tribal members had to sell their land, and could not afford doctors or schools in their rural area. Most Menominee depended on government financial assistance programs, which meant the United States government saved no money. In 1973, Congress approved, and President Nixon signed a repeal of the *Termination Act* and restoration of Menominee tribal status.

In recent decades, the territorial autonomy status of Native American reservations has allowed the opening of several hundred casinos on tribal land across the United States. Some tribal members have derived great economic benefits from casinos located near large population centres, but in recent United States census statistics, the five counties with the highest poverty rates in the country were all on rural Sioux reservations in South Dakota.[21]

## 15) The Modern Political Culture of the United States

In the twenty-first century, American political culture continues to evolve, with many historical factors continuing to play a role and combining with modern technology and the use of social media to spread political ideas and often misinformation. The ideas of manifest destiny and American exceptionalism continue to play a role with widespread use of concepts like "shining city upon a hill" and similar rhetoric. Derived from a lecture by Massachusetts Puritan leader John Winthrop in 1630 and based on the biblical Sermon on the Mount, the perception of the United States as representing a "shining city upon a hill" has been used in speeches by a wide variety of American political leaders, including presidents Kennedy, Reagan, and Obama.[22]

In 1964, historian Richard Hofstadter suggested a recurring strand of politics in the twenty-first century United States. Originally written to describe Cold War fears of Communism, "The Paranoid

Style in American Politics" traces political conspiracy theories from the anti-Masonic movement of the 1820s and 1830s, through the Know-Nothings of the 1850s, the Populists of the 1890s, and among the anti-Communists, White racist groups, and some Black Muslim groups of the 1950s.[23] Social media and online sources help to continue that conspiracy tradition today, which includes fears about vaccines; beliefs in space alien visits to Earth (but that Americans never landed on the moon); the claim that Barack Obama was not born in the United States; the claim that the 2020 presidential election was "stolen" from Donald Trump; the all-encompassing QAnon set of beliefs involving celebrities and political leaders running a child sex slave ring that includes a Washington, DC, pizza restaurant, and Donald Trump's secret plan to save the country; and even continued disputes about who assassinated President John F Kennedy. Such belief in mostly nonsensical conspiracies now plays a major role in American voting behaviour and the actions of some political leaders.

Trust in American government institutions plummeted in the 1970s after the Vietnam War and Watergate scandal and never recovered. Trust levels have remained below 25 percent since the final years of the George W Bush administration.[24] Yet while Americans distrust their government in the abstract and are prone to believe in conspiracy theories, the same Americans profess to have favourable views toward many government agencies, such as the US Postal Service, NASA, and even the CIA, and Americans continue to expect their government to provide key services, such as national defence, protecting consumers and the environment, maintaining infrastructure, and preventing discrimination.[25]

Meanwhile, modern American and Canadian political culture has also been greatly influenced by increased diversity in both societies. The United States was only 58 percent non-Latino White (a category that includes those who responded that they were White, but not Hispanic or Latino) in the 2020 Census, compared to 83 percent non-Latino White fifty years earlier. Unlike the nineteenth and early twentieth centuries, when most immigration to the United States came from Europe, the ten countries with the highest immigration numbers to the United States in the twenty-first century are all in Latin America or Asia. In 2023, 32 percent (about one-third) of members of the United States House of Representatives indicated that their racial background is non-White.

## D. The Canadian Story of Evolution

The American story of revolution reveals the many factors that contributed to the United States' character and its political, economic, and cultural makeup. Many of the formative events that shaped the United States overlap with those that shaped Canada. Yet there are also clearly many uniquely Canadian formative events as well. Many contributed to a distinctive Canadian-style democracy, constitutional order, and political culture.

### 1) The Road to Confederation

Unlike the American colonists, the Canadian colonists did not seek to overthrow the established order; however, they did seek to reconstitute it peacefully. The outlines of the Canadian story are clear: conservative, loyal Canada turned its back on and rejected the American revolutionary experience, and decided instead to take the slow, evolutionary path to nationhood. Thus, the move from colony to nation was qualitatively different. However, in the context of Canadian-American relations, some regarded the movement to nationhood compromised by the mid- to late twentieth century and suggested that Canada had moved from colony to nation to colony — this time of the newly emergent American Empire. Canada also faced the very real possibility of dissolution due to internal tensions and conflict between French and English Canada and, by the twenty-first century, increasing tensions regarding Indigenous relations. We will trace these developments below, beginning with the colonial period and how it compares to the American experience.

## 2) Jacques Cartier and Samuel de Champlain

Jacques Cartier was a French explorer who led three expeditions to Canada — in 1534, 1535, and 1541 — while looking for a route to the Pacific through North America (a Northwest Passage). While he did not find one, Cartier paved the way for French exploration of North America, travelling some thousand miles up the St. Lawrence River. He also tried to start a settlement in Quebec in 1541, but it was abandoned after a terribly cold winter. Cartier named Canada; "Kanata" means village or settlement in the Huron-Iroquois language. Cartier was given directions by Huron-Iroquois Indians for the route to "kanata," a village near what is now Quebec, but Cartier later named the entire region Canada. He was, however, unable to establish the conditions for an ongoing settlement after having made his three journeys to Canada.

On 3 July 1608, French explorer Samuel de Champlain landed at the "point of Quebec" and set about fortifying the area against attack by building three main two-storey buildings and a moat fifteen feet wide. This was to become the city of Quebec. Of the twenty-five people who stayed the first winter, only eight survived, most having died of scurvy and some of smallpox. But Champlain laid the basis for the expansion of settlement and the fur trade, and was gradually followed by a modest influx of French settlers.

## 3) The French-English Battle for Supremacy

The relatively slow growth of the French colony stood in contrast to the relatively rapid expansion of the thirteen British colonies. Clashes were inevitable, though, as the French colony stretching from the Gulf of St. Lawrence to the Gulf of Mexico blocked the westward expansion of the British. Alliances with Indigenous peoples by both powers led to numerous bloody conflicts. As we noted above, these conflicts culminated in the French and Indian War (aka Seven Years' War), 1756–1763, the conclusion of which saw the conquest of the French by the British on the Plains of

Abraham at Quebec City in 1759. In 1763, the Treaty of Paris ended the war and ceded all lands in northeast North America to the British. In addition, the Royal Proclamation of 1763 created the colony of Quebec.

Subsequently, with unrest in the thirteen American colonies growing, and realizing they were greatly outnumbered by the French in British North America, the British passed the *Quebec Act* in 1774 to ensure French, Catholic loyalty to English, Protestant Britain. This initiative allowed for the continuation of key elements of the French society and culture, including the French civil law and the Catholic religion. It is important to note that these long-ago initiatives established the precedents for accommodation of the minority French in Canada, as opposed to the possibility of assimilating them. The latter option was rightly seen as impossible given the huge numerical advantage of the French population over the British at the time. These developments continue to resonate in French-English relations in Canada to this day.

As the American Revolution unfolded and the Declaration of Independence of 1776 was proclaimed, the impact in British North America was essentially to reinforce the "Britishness" of Canada. This was one of the main impacts of the arrival of the United Empire Loyalists, who, as noted above, represented a powerful ideological, political, and cultural force that remained faithful to the British Crown in the northern colony.

### 4) Tensions and Conflicts

Pressure from the thousands of United Empire Loyalists for a representative model of government based more closely on British parliamentary institutions led to the *Constitutional Act, 1791*. The Act divided the colony of Quebec into Upper Canada (Ontario) and Lower Canada (Quebec). It also introduced a form of representative government, extending the franchise to all, including women, who owned property in Lower Canada. But it mainly entrenched the power of the governor and the non-elected legislative assemblies while constraining the powers of the elected assemblies. This gave rise to rule by the elite groups known as the Family Compact in Upper Canada and the Château Clique in Lower Canada, with consequences that would violently play themselves out some forty years later.

Population growth in Canada was greatly stimulated by the arrival of the United Empire Loyalists. Compared to the Spanish and American regions of North America, however, it was quite a bit slower. By 1800, the Mexican and American populations were roughly even at about 5.3 million versus 5.8 million, respectively. The American population then accelerated at a rate greater than that of Mexico and Canada. By the 1850s, the American population was more than 31 million, Mexico's was 8 million, and Canada's was under 3 million. Canada's much slower growth can be attributed to its harsher climate, difficult geography, and the political economy being caught in a "staples trap," as political economist Harold Adams Innis put it, which set the stage for Canada as "hewers of wood and drawers of water" — that is, producers of natural resources (staples) for export while importing finished goods rather than manufacturing them domestically.[26]

## 5) The War of 1812

By the early 1800s, the colonies of Upper and Lower Canada were confronted with a belligerent America that sought to drive the British out of North America and assume dominion over the entire northern half of the continent. An unforeseen impact of the War of 1812, though, was to inculcate a new Canadian nationalism. Episodes such as the burning of York (Toronto) and triumphs like the burning of Washington helped foster this newly emergent attitude. So too did the emergence of heroic figures such as General Isaac Brock and Tecumseh who together led the military resistance to the American invasion, and the settler Laura Secord who hiked through dense woods over many kilometres to warn the British of American military plans she had overheard. These events all contributed to a sense of "Canadianness" with which colonists could distinguish themselves from the Americans to the south. It may be possible to overstate this point, though. In 2012, the Conservative government of Stephen Harper tried to stir up Canadian nationalism with events commemorating the 200th anniversary of the war. Few Canadians participated. It may be more accurate to note that, like the American Revolution, the War of 1812 was more like a civil war, with opinions and loyalties divided on both sides.

## 6) Growing Pains

By the 1830s, demands for responsible government were growing, leading to rebellions in Upper and Lower Canada in 1837 and 1838 against the ruling elites known as the Family Compact in Upper Canada and the Château Clique in Lower Canada; both rebellions were easily put down. But they signalled a growing dissatisfaction with the elitist style of governing that had entrenched itself wherein the governor rewarded a small, interconnected group of loyal supporters with land and important positions, and largely ignored the democratic wishes of the elected assemblies. A ruling oligarchy had emerged composed of prominent business owners, religious leaders, and the governor's appointed members of government. Political institutions reflected the dominance of the elite; the executive council was appointed by and gave advice to the Governor General, who was free to accept or reject it. Additionally, an upper house called the Legislative Council, also appointed by the Governor General, could veto legislation coming from the elected assembly. The trappings of responsible government appeared to be in place, but it was largely a charade. As Lord Durham characterized it, "It is difficult to understand how any English statesman could have imagined that representative and irresponsible government could be successfully combined."[27]

The result over time was constant tension and friction in the colonies. Had the governor been required to choose the executive council members from the elected assembly and retain the support of a majority of the members of that assembly, there would have been a system that resembled real responsible government. But it is worth recalling that one of the formative events of British North America was its rejection of the democratic experiment coming out of the American Revolution. Democracy was not an attractive proposition among those who had monopolized power in Upper and Lower Canada, and indeed was regarded as contrary to the natural order of a governing class whose sense of *noblesse oblige* would presumably produce the best outcomes for the masses of the people. One Governor General of Upper Canada, Sir Francis Bond Head, an ardent opponent of democracy, defended the Family Compact in this way:

> The family compact of Upper Canada is composed of those members of its society who, either by their abilities and character have been honoured by the confidence of the executive government, or who, by their industry and intelligence, have amassed wealth. The party, I own, is a comparatively small one; but to put the multitude at the top and the few at the bottom is a radical reversion of the pyramid of society which every reflecting man must forever see end only in its downfall.[28]

In Lower Canada, a dissident group called *les Patriotes* under the leadership of Joseph Papineau emerged to contest the Château Clique and champion responsible government. They argued for a system of government in which the Governor General would have to choose advisers from those who supported the will of the elected assembly in order to protect French Canadian society. Some brief violent episodes resulted in 1837 that were put down, but they signalled the depth of dissatisfaction with the status quo.

As in Lower Canada, dissatisfaction in Upper Canada revolved around the religious, economic, and political power relations between the ruling oligarchy and the people as represented in the elected assembly. William Lyon Mackenzie was a rabble-rousing newspaper publisher and member of the Legislative Assembly who agitated for the overthrow of the Family Compact. He railed against its corruption and monopolization of all the best public offices. He claimed, "they fill every office with their relatives, dependents and partisans ... they are paymasters, receivers, Auditors, Kings, Lords and Commons!"[29] Moreover, Mackenzie claimed there was no effective check on their power since the Governor General and executive council were not accountable to the elected assembly. Frustrated that his pleas for reform went unanswered, Mackenzie led a brief armed insurrection in 1837 that was easily put down; he subsequently fled to the United States.

## 7) Lord Durham's Report, 1839

Despite their failures, the rebellions in Upper and Lower Canada concerned the British colonial authorities, who dispatched Lord Durham to investigate the root causes and propose remedies. Lord Durham was a British aristocrat who embodied the imperialist attitudes of the British ruling class of the nineteenth century. This included an attitude of superiority over the French, whom he claimed had neither a history, literature, nor culture, and were clearly an inferior race compared to the British. Durham wrote that "there can hardly be conceived a nationality more destitute of all that can invigorate and elevate a people, than that which is exhibited by the French in Lower Canada, owing to their retaining their peculiar language and manners. They are a people with no history and no literature."[30] It was on the basis of this ignorance that he made the following recommendation:

> I entertain no doubts as to the national character which must be given to Lower Canada; it must be that of the British Empire; that of the majority of the population of British America; that of the great race which must, in the lapse of no long period of time, be predominant over the whole of the North America Continent. Without effecting the change so rapidly or so roughly as to shock the feelings and trample on the welfare of the existing generation,

it must hence forth be the first and steady purpose of the British Government to establish an English population, with English laws and language, in this Province, and to trust its government to none but a decidedly English legislature.[31]

Durham did support the aspirations of the French Canadians for self-government. But he asserted that their motivations were less about representativeness or responsible government and more about maintaining "an old and stationary society, in a new and progressive world."[32] Durham spent five months in Canada, all but two weeks of which were in Lower Canada. He issued what has become a landmark document in Canadian political history, *Lord Durham's Report*, in 1839.

Durham famously stated that he found "two nations warring in the bosom of a single state." He recommended both responsible government and the unification of the two colonies of Upper and Lower Canada as remedies. Responsible government would still be twenty years away, but the second goal was achieved by the *Act of Union* in 1840.

Durham argued that the dominant British liberal institutions were key to preventing any future rebellion by the colonists. To ensure their success, he advocated a legislative union of the two provinces with representation in the new assembly to be based on population. Of course, this would guarantee an English majority; by 1840, there were about 400,000 English in Upper Canada, and 150,000 English and 450,000 French in Lower Canada. Future immigration would favour the growth of the English. In other words, this was transparently a recommendation to hasten the assimilation of the French. It would be another twenty-five years before a federal model of government would be proposed and accepted in Canada, wherein minority groups would be protected from this type of the tyranny of the majority.

Durham made a second recommendation derived from his observations of the abuses of power by the oligarchies in the two colonies. The favouritism evident in the granting of land, positions, and favours to the governor's circle of family, friends, and supporters led Durham to decry this concentration of power. The solution he prescribed was responsible government through which the governor and executive council would have to be accountable to the elected assembly. Thus, a more democratic model of government was proposed, which would resolve the power struggle between the Family Compact and Château Clique, and the elected assemblies in favour of the latter.

The principle of responsible government differs in important ways from the "checks and balances" instituted in the American governing system. Rather than create a *separation of powers* between the executive, legislative, and judicial branches of government, as in the United States, responsible government creates a *fusion of powers*. This is because the executive branch of government (the prime minister and Cabinet) must also be members of the legislative branch (the Parliament) and answer directly to it. Thus, the divergent paths taken by the United States and Canada were institutionalized politically in two quite different systems of government. We will return to the details of the political institutions in both countries in more detail in Chapter 2.

## 8) The *Act of Union, 1840*

The unification of Upper and Lower Canada, as recommended by Durham, proceeded in 1840. But the unforeseen result was virtual deadlock and stalemate for the next twenty-five years. This was the result of a design flaw — the Act created an elected assembly with an equal number of members from each of the two colonies, and the members acted and voted according to their own separate interests in the newly named Canada East and Canada West. The positive consequence of this design, though, was that it pushed the colonies toward the set of reforms that resulted in Confederation and the creation of a federal system of government in 1867.

The *Act of Union* created a kind of political dualism.[33] It reflected both the interdependence and separateness of the English and French. This was seen in a number of ways — the capital and Parliament were alternated between Toronto, Kingston, Montreal, and Quebec City, for instance. An English public service was established, as was a French one. For each portfolio in Cabinet, two ministers — one English and one French — headed government ministries. There were even two prime ministers! Legislation was passed by a "double majority"; issues of concern to one part of the Union had to be supported by a majority from that part as well as by a majority of the entire Parliament.

The emergence and importance of cultural dualism in Canada contrasts strikingly with the melting pot experience derived from the American Revolution in the United States. In the Canadian case:

> The Quebec Act laid the basis for this cultural dualism by allowing for the protection of French civil law and the continuance of the Catholic religion. The Constitution Act helped solidify that dualism geographically by extending the boundaries of the colony. Lord Durham's Report recognized French-English dualism as the key problem confronting the colony, and the Act of Union helped institutionalize political dualism.[34]

There were built-in problems with the *Act of Union*, however, which portended its demise. Even though the population of Canada East still outnumbered that of Canada West, both had the same number of Members of Parliament. In any event, there were divisions among the English merchants of Toronto and Montreal. There was disagreement among some English politicians over the advisability of moving to responsible government. When, by 1851 according to the census of that year, the English of Canada West outnumbered the French of Canada East, calls emerged for representation by population from some English politicians. Politicians in Canada East were opposed, not surprisingly. Moreover, the situation was aggravated by deadlock over a number of pieces of legislation throughout the 1850s.

George Brown, publisher of *The Globe* newspaper and a prominent English politician, took the position that overcoming the political problems of the colony required a form of federal government. He said, "We have two races, two languages, two systems of religious belief, two systems of everything, so that it has become almost impossible that, without sacrificing their principles, the public men of both sections could come together in the same government."³⁵ Brown later played a key role along with Sir John A Macdonald and others in the Confederation debates, which resulted in the creation of a new government, based on a type of federalism roughly modelled on the American federal system, as we will see below.

But Union government remained desirable to the French because the dualist institutional features of the Union government gave them the mechanisms to resist assimilation and protected them from domination by the English. French leaders had occupied important posts, including prime minister; had helped create a French language public service; and had gained a sort of equality with English Canada. They feared being overtaken by the now more-populous Canada West. Nonetheless, by the late 1850s and early 1860s, it was clear that significant reforms were needed.³⁶

## 9) Confederation, 1867

Following a series of conferences in Charlottetown in 1864, Quebec City in 1866 and London in 1867, the *British North America Act, 1867* (BNA Act, 1867) was passed by the British Parliament and brought about the Confederation of the colonies Upper and Lower Canada, New Brunswick, and Nova Scotia. There was no revolution, unlike in the United States — only a lot of talking. And the talking was limited to a small group of political, economic, and social elites; there was no consultation with the masses or participation by them in the discussions or the ratification of Confederation. It was not a "declaration of independence." Alexander Hamilton wrote in the Federalist Papers that the American system of government was based on the "consent of the people." Indeed, the American Constitution states, "We, the people of the United States, in order to form a more perfect union. . . ." There were no such pronouncements in the Confederation of Canada; in other words, there was no acknowledgement of popular democracy. The elites who concocted the deal made no pretense of seeking popular legitimacy through elections or referenda, for instance. The Confederation agreement was not even submitted to the legislatures of New Brunswick or Nova Scotia for approval. In the Province of Canada the agreement was debated, but without the opportunity to move amendments. The BNA Act, 1867 was simply a British statute that united the four colonies into a single "Dominion" under the name of Canada.

There were several interrelated motivations that drove the political and economic elites of the time toward Confederation. These included the desire to overcome the stalemate between French and English in Upper and Lower Canada caused by the *Act of Union*. In addition, there was the desire among French delegates to the conferences to ensure that they were provided with ongoing linguistic and cultural protections. Guarantees for the ongoing prosperity of the business class was a key driver too. Lord Durham had pointed out in his Report of 1839 that the facilitation of economic development by colonial administrations was vital. This included building canals, ports, roads, bridges, and other infrastructure to facilitate the extraction of staples products and delivery to markets. It also included government loans and grants, the awarding of tracts of land and positions, and the fostering of trade. Economic concerns were heightened when the United States abrogated the Reciprocity Treaty with Canada in 1866. This essentially ended a period of free trade of a number of goods, and led to the logical conclusion that east-west economic markets within Canada needed to be developed and exploited. Indeed, the economic arguments for Confederation were among the most persuasive. Historian Frank Underhill noted the need to secure the interests of the colonial capitalist class. He wrote:

> The essential work of the Fathers of Confederation was to weld the scattered British possessions in North America into a unity within which Canadian capitalism could expand and consolidate its power, to provide for the capitalist entrepreneurs of Montreal and Toronto a half-continent in which they could realize their dreams and ambitions.[37]

On the military front, the American Civil War ended in 1865, leaving the United States with a large, well-trained mechanized army with nothing to do; some American politicians looked north and contemplated the takeover of Canada as punishment for Britain's tacit support of the South in the Civil War. In addition, a group of Irish nationalists called the Fenian Brotherhood, many of whom had served in the Union army during the war, executed raids on Canada as a means to attract British military resources to North America and away from Ireland, thus aiding the Irish in their fight for independence. A popular song of the day went, "Many battles have been won/Along with the boys in blue/And we'll go and capture Canada/For we've nothing else to do."[38] The Fenian raids and the prospect of American invasion meant the Canada-United States relationship was fraught with tension.

Was there Canadian support for the option of annexation by the United States? The spread of democratic institutions was slower in Canada than in the United States, and this aggravated some in the Canadian colonies. But Canadians had generally rejected the option of American republicanism several times when offered the opportunity to rebel against the British Crown, for instance during the American Revolution in 1776, the War of 1812, and the Rebellions in Upper and Lower Canada in 1837 and 1838. It would seem that the presence of thousands of United Empire Loyalists whose fealty to the Crown remained strong meant that adopting American style democracy was not realistic. Moreover, the powerful Catholic church in Lower Canada preferred the political arrangements it had worked out with the British rather than absorption into the "godless republic" to the south.[39]

## 10) The *British North America Act, 1867*

The *British North America Act, 1867* (BNA Act, 1867) was the legislation passed by the British Parliament that brought the Dominion of Canada into being. Why "Dominion," which is a term unique in the annals of naming countries? Originally, the Fathers of Confederation expected the new country to be called the Kingdom of

Canada, since the British monarch remained as head of state. However, the British felt the prospect of a "kingdom" on the border of the American republic would further strain relations with the Americans. Dominion was chosen as a less provocative term; it was part of the Canadian coat of arms, whose motto is "*A mari usque ad mare*," which in turn comes from the Latin translation of Psalm 72:8 in the Bible: "*Et dominabitur a mari usque ad mare, et a flumine usque ad terminos terrae*" ("He shall have dominion also from sea to sea, and from the river unto the ends of the earth").

The BNA Act, 1867 established a bicameral national Parliament with representation by population in the elected lower house — the House of Commons — and representation by region in the appointed upper house — the Senate. It also created a federal system and divided powers between the federal and provincial governments. Nova Scotia and New Brunswick retained their existing legislatures and other institutions of government, while the province of Canada was divided into two new provinces, Ontario (the old Canada West, formerly Upper Canada) and Quebec (the old Canada East, formerly Lower Canada). The Act also established a legislature and other institutions of government for each of Ontario and Quebec.

By 1867, Canada West had surpassed Canada East in population, so Confederation's offer of representation by population in the new national Parliament, as well as a separate provincial legislature, was an attractive proposition. For Canada East, fear of being swamped by the majority of English-speaking Canadians was offset by the creation of a separate provincial legislature controlled by the French-speaking majority, whose authority related mainly to matters like language, education, and civil law directly touching on the survival of their distinct linguistic and cultural society.

## 11) Confederation, Not Independence

The BNA Act, 1867 did not follow the American model of codifying all of the new nation's constitutional rules, and it was definitely not a "Declaration of Independence." Indeed, the Act stated the new Dominion was to have "a constitution similar in principle to that of the United Kingdom." Unlike the American revolutionaries, the Fathers of Confederation wanted the old rules to continue in both form and substance exactly as before. The major difference, though, was the adoption of federalism — much like the American system and contrary to the unitary model in Britain. (Federalism is discussed in more detail in Chapter 4.)

The independence of the United States could be characterized as incorporating a visionary political philosophy articulated in the Federalist Papers written by Alexander Hamilton, James Madison, and John Jay; no such vision accompanied Canadian Confederation. Instead, it was a pragmatic set of compromises concerned less with political theory and more with how to create profitable conditions for the expansion of capitalism across the colonies. A document of "monumental dullness,"[40] the BNA Act, 1867 was a rather dry and legalistic expression of the new country's founding laws. This outcome of the Confederation debates, and the debates themselves, lacked the stirring rhetoric and discourse emanating from the American experience, or indeed that of many other countries.

Nonetheless, Confederation was a nation-building exercise of impressive achievements. The differences among the colonies were deeply entrenched and difficult to overcome. While lacking a charter or expression of newly articulated and innovated first principles of governing, philosophy, or politics, it did represent a pragmatic compromise that ensured the continuation of British political practices and institutions wedded to American-style federalism in the context of a newly created society. This type of marriage was unique in the world and had never before been attempted.

## 12) Still a Colony?

There were many features of the new political system that retained the features of a British colony. For instance, Canada remained subordinate to Great Britain in international relations. It also remained subject to important imperial limitations in local affairs, including the power of the British Parliament to enact statutes extending to Canada. Moreover, the British monarch continued to appoint Canada's Governor General. The new Dominion was prevented from enacting any statute repugnant to an imperial statute extending to Canada. Canada did not establish a Supreme Court, but instead continued sending appeals from Canadian courts to the British Judicial Committee of the Privy Council.

## 13) From Confederation to Independence — Sort Of[41]

Canada's predominantly staples-based economy required a strong central government to promote economic development, and that is what Confederation appeared to create. The 1867 agreement was followed in 1868 by the purchase of Rupert's Land (including all of present-day Manitoba, most of Saskatchewan, southern Alberta, southern Nunavut, and northern parts of Ontario and Quebec) from the Hudson's Bay Company. This allowed for the expansion of Canada to include Manitoba in 1870 and British Columbia in 1871. Prince Edward Island joined in 1873.

As prime minister, Sir John A Macdonald sought to construct an economic and political union across the geographically massive but sparsely populated northern half of North America. He instituted an aggressive approach encapsulated in his National Policy of 1879. This political-economic blueprint guided the development of the Canadian political economy for more than 100 years and was a broad-based platform whose central planks included the construction of a transcontinental railway, an aggressive policy of promoting immigration to Canada to develop the West, and a system of tariffs on the importation of foreign goods. This ambitious plan for the further evolution of the "Empire of the St. Lawrence," as the early Canadian political economy was termed, was a type of "defensive expansionism"[42] against the emerging American empire in favour of an east-west political economy rather than a north-south one.

The Canadian government was endowed by the constitutional division of powers to intervene in the economy and enact laws to foster accumulation and growth. This it did through promoting, financing, and supporting a variety of infrastructure initiatives such as roads, canals, waterways, and the distribution of land. In addition, it provided grants and subsidies to businesses. The key element of this state-led effort, however, was the construction of the transcontinental railway. This massive undertaking was used to entice British Columbia to join Confederation and ultimately to unite the new Canadian nation on an east–west basis while offsetting the increasing north–south economic and cultural pull of the United States. A main result of the National Policy was to make central Canada the financial, industrial, and manufacturing centre of Canada. It became the metropole to the hinterlands of western, eastern, and northern Canada, shipping its finished goods to these more remote regions in return for a supply of staples products.

As a nation-building exercise, the National Policy succeeded tremendously — if you lived in central Canada. If you lived in the outer regions, it became a symbol of domination and exploitation. For instance, the excessive costs of construction of the railway combined with excess rail capacity meant that the line was never as profitable as intended. This resulted in high freight rates borne by those shipping staples to central Canada. This was compounded by the high cost of importing American goods due to the high tariff of the National Policy. Consequently, Western Canada in particular came to see itself as an exploited hinterland to central Canada, which contributed to strains on national unity that continue to manifest themselves to this very day in Canada.

There is another striking contrast between Canada and the United States that can be traced to the interventionist state that the National Policy helped to foster in Canada. While American capitalist development was largely driven by the private sector, the Canadian federal state assumed the major responsibility for the development of the Canadian nation, even as it was working mainly at the behest of private economic interests. The Canadian political economy was primarily driven by the state heavily involving itself in finance, credit, tariffs, transportation, infrastructure, land disposition, and other areas.

However, the Constitution gave other powers to the provinces, namely control over natural resources, which laid the groundwork for the ongoing regionalization of the political economy. Because Canada was predominantly a staples-based economy, divisive competition between the regions of Canada, as well as between many provincial governments and the federal government, was fostered. Innis argued that staples economies contain paradoxical tendencies of freedom and domination *within* societies as well as across societies. By this he meant that, for example, in constructing a railroad to foster a national economic union, a new political dynamic of Western versus central Canada and the phenomenon of "Western alienation" arose.[43]

Gradually and incrementally, Canada developed as a nation and a nascent sense of nationalism emerged, but not without some severe growing pains. Apart from the strains associated with the National Policy, French-English tensions predominated in the evolution of Canada. For example, westward expansion into present-day Manitoba by English settlers ran up against the already-established communities of French and Metis, many of whom had originally been involved in the fur trade. Seeking access to farmland, the English settlers engaged in confrontations with the French and Metis, who were led by the firebrand Louis Riel. These tensions erupted into the rebellions of 1870 and 1885. The French and Metis were defeated, and Riel was hung as a traitor.

Later, English-French tensions were heightened by the *Manitoba Schools Act, 1890*. In this episode, English Protestant Manitobans, who constituted a majority of the population, persuaded the Manitoba provincial government to end funding and support for French-language schools, which were Catholic. The French Catholic minority implored the federal government to act to protect their constitutionally guaranteed rights. The federal government had the power to overturn provincial legislation, but the governing Liberal Party under Prime Minister Wilfrid Laurier were champions of provincial rights and were reluctant to step into provincial affairs. With significant support from Quebec, where the majority of French Catholics opposed federal intervention in provincial affairs, Laurier opposed disallowing the *Manitoba Schools Act*. Similarly, Ontario's Regulation 17/1913 also sought to end constitutional guarantees for the provision of French language education to the French-speaking minorities in that province. No federal action was taken to protect minority interests in that case either.

As the twentieth century began, Prime Minister Wilfrid Laurier made a bold prediction. In 1904 he said, "As the nineteenth century was that of the United States, so I think the twentieth century shall be filled by Canada."[44] Laurier's optimism was commendable, but he apparently got the two countries futures' reversed! Several events and episodes in the twentieth century would test the new nation; in some ways Canada lived up to Laurier's advance billing, but in many ways it did not.

## 14) Marginalization of Indigenous Peoples

By 1900, the marginalization of the Indigenous population of Canada had accelerated and taken on dark and sinister characteristics. As noted earlier, the Royal Proclamation of 1763 was the first constitutional document to define and set the basis for the relationship between the colonial government and Indigenous peoples. It guaranteed certain rights over traditional hunting and fishing lands, and established the process by which the government could acquire Indigenous lands. In 1850, the *Act for the Better Protection of the Lands and Property of the Indians in Lower Canada* was passed. It was one of the first pieces of legislation to define a person legally as Indian, a concept that evolved into the notion of Indian "status." The definition essentially said that people shall be considered as Indians if they were of "Indian blood" and were members of a "Body or Tribe of Indians," and further that all their descendants were considered to be Indian. Non-Indians who "intermarried with such Indians," people whose parents (one or both) would have been considered

Indians, and "all persons adopted in infancy by any such Indians" were also eligible to be given status.

Ultimately, assimilation of Indigenous people became the official policy of Canadian colonial governments. The *Gradual Civilization Act* of 1857 and *the Gradual Enfranchisement Act* of 1869 were examples of this effort. They were both aimed at removing any special rights Indigenous peoples might have enjoyed in order to assimilate then into the broader mainstream culture and society. An Indigenous person could be voluntarily enfranchised if they gave up their status in return for the vote and some land. Indigenous peoples rejected this deal, and subsequently the federal government began unilaterally enfranchising Indigenous peoples.

The BNA Act, 1867 contained but one short line about Indigenous Canadians: Section 91(24) said the federal government shall be responsible for "Indians and lands reserved for Indians." As with the masses of other Canadians who were excluded from the Confederation debates and the adoption of the BNA Act, 1867, the Indigenous peoples were also not consulted. The federal government assumed a paternalistic and domineering role through the *Indian Act, 1876* in sublimating and controlling the Indigenous peoples. It set up elected band councils whose limited powers were delegated by the federal minister, and could be revoked at will. A category of "status Indian" was created for the purposes of administering the *Indian Act* and determining who was eligible for federal benefits flowing from treaties signed by the Indigenous peoples and the Crown.

## 15) The First World War, the Great Depression, and the Second World War

Meanwhile, the First World War served as a test of the degree to which Canada retained its "Britishness," or whether it was due to set sail as a sovereign and independent nation. When Great Britain declared war on Germany and its allies in September 1914, Canada was automatically at war as well. This was a direct consequence of the fact, noted above, that the BNA Act, 1867 did not confer on

Canada any independent power over its foreign affairs. But the sacrifices of Canada's fighting forces were immense, and contributed in no small way to a new sense of patriotism and national pride.

However, there was a cleavage in Canadian society over participation in the war. French Canadians, long since cut off from any ties to France, had little sympathy for entangling Canada in European affairs. When voluntary enrollment in the armed services failed to provide sufficient numbers of recruits, the federal government began considering conscription, an option that fostered deep and profound opposition among French Canadians. A furious debate ensued. Eventually, the government of Prime Minister Robert Borden enacted the *Military Service Act* in 1917, which made all male citizens between the ages of twenty and forty-five years subject to military service. The Borden government also introduced the *Wartime Elections Act*, which gave the vote to the wives, mothers, and sisters of soldiers, the first women permitted to vote in Canadian federal elections. Notably, they tended to favour conscription because it supported their men who were already soldiers.

While divisions over conscription were not solely between French and English, it served as a key flashpoint in straining the existing cultural accommodations between the two groups. Tens of thousands of French Canadians joined others from across Canada in refusing to register for the selection process. Applications for exemptions among those that did register approached 93 percent of conscripts. Attempts to arrest suspected draft dodgers resulted in several days of rioting and street battles in Quebec City at Easter in 1918, leaving four dead and dozens injured. The war ended in 1918, but the tensions between French and English persisted.

The Great Depression affected Canada in much the same way it affected the United States. Many businesses failed and thousands of Canadian lost their jobs. Unemployment approached 20 percent in 1933; Canada was particularly adversely affected because of its reliance on the export of staples products, whose prices fell by more than 50 percent. At the time, about 25 percent of the Canadian gross national product was derived from exports. Canada's international trade levels dropped precipitously, and the cost of many imported goods increased. Drought conditions, especially in the West, persisted for about a decade, undermining agricultural production. Plagues of grasshoppers and fierce hailstorms periodically added to the misery. Poverty rates skyrocketed. Unemployment "relief camps" were created to house unemployed men. Social unrest, strikes and protests grew in number and intensity. Protest movements emerged, some of which morphed into political parties that challenged the traditional Conservative and Liberal two-party system.

The Conservative government of Prime Minister RB Bennett initially rejected the idea of a Roosevelt-style "New Deal" to ameliorate the effects of the Great Depression. But by 1935, conditions were so bad he had a change of mind and introduced a package of Keynesian-style reforms. In January 1935, he broadcast a series of live radio speeches outlining a "New Deal" for Canada. It included a more progressive taxation system, a maximum workweek, a minimum wage, closer regulation of working conditions, unemployment insurance, health and accident insurance, a revised old-age pension, and agricultural support programs.

But it was too little, too late. The Canadian electorate replaced Bennett with Liberal William Lyon Mackenzie King in the election of 1935. King had also been reluctant at first to admit that the national government had a role to play in providing relief for the unemployed, believing as Bennett did that this was a matter best left to the family, religious or charitable organizations, or local or provincial governments. This was a commonly held view, even as those groups were clearly incapable of dealing with a problem of the magnitude of the Great Depression. Indeed, by the early 1930s, some provincial governments were technically bankrupt and hundreds of municipalities collapsed; they could offer no substantive help.

King enacted a number of reforms based on Keynesian theory. Keynes argued that if private investment in the free market failed to produce full employment, the state must initiate public investment through deficit spending to create jobs. The Great Depression had changed the way King and indeed many Canadians thought about the economy and the role of the state. There ensued a dramatic expansion of state responsibility for the economy, and the first bricks in the foundation of the modern social welfare state were laid. But it took the outbreak of the Second World War to pull Canada out of the Great Depression. Unemployed men enlisted in the military and by 1939, with demand for goods and materials rising in Europe, both the Canadian and American economies began to recover.

The issue of Canada's participation in the Second World War was treated slightly differently than it had been in the First World War. This time, while Canada remained resolutely loyal to the British Empire, it waited several days after Britain declared war to do so itself. And Canada made sure its own declaration of war was made by its own Parliament. This reflected the growth of Canadian nationalism in the early twentieth century. Two important constitutional documents contributed to this newfound notion that Canada was evolving to become a fully self-governing nation. The first was the Balfour Declaration of 1926, which declared that Britain and its Dominions were constitutionally equal. The second was the Statute of Westminster in 1931. The Act proclaimed that the countries that were formerly colonies of Great Britain would remain in allegiance with the Crown, but each would be granted full legal autonomy. The countries agreeing to this new state of affairs became known as the British Commonwealth of Nations. The one exception to full legal autonomy for Canada, though, related to the power to amend the Canadian Constitution. Because Canadian federal and provincial governments had never been able to agree on a mutually acceptable amending formula, it was decided to leave the power to amend the Canadian Constitution in the hands of the British Parliament. This situation persisted until 1982, when Canada finally created a domestic amending formula and patriated its Constitution (discussed in Chapter 2). But the fact that Canada waited a few days and had its own Parliament declare war in 1939 essentially enshrined the principle that the Statute of Westminster conferred this sovereign power to Canada.

Canada's contribution to the Second World War was immense relative to its population. It created the fourth-largest air force and third-largest navy in the world, contributed to nearly every theatre of the war, and sent some 1.1 million soldiers to fight. But as with the First World War, tensions existed within Canada between the English and French. Conscription once again became an issue, and the old fault lines reopened. King was deeply averse to enacting conscription during the Second World War, having seen how it tore the country apart during the First World War. In 1939, King had promised there would be no conscription. But as the war dragged on and the need for more soldiers grew, he recognized the possibility that conscription would be needed.

King decided to hold a referendum on the issue in the hope that it would help release him from his no-conscription pledge. On 27 April 1942, Canadians were asked, "Are you in favour of releasing the Government from any obligations arising out of any past commitments restricting the methods of raising men for military service?" During the debate over conscription, King sought to reassure French Canadians that even a yes vote would not automatically ensure the introduction of conscription, explaining his new policy to Parliament as "not necessarily conscription, but conscription if necessary." Across Canada, 64.5 percent voted in favour of conscription, including 83 percent of English Canadians. But in Quebec, 72.9 percent of voters opposed. In the end, only a relatively small number of Canadians were conscripted before the war ended. But clearly the old French-English divisions had resurfaced.

## 16) Post-War Canada

The post-war years in Canada were initially a period of prosperity and growth, with a newly confident and outward-looking Canada playing an important role in the construction of the post-war world (discussed in more detail in Chapter 7). On the home front, Canada developed a more diversified economy with a growing manufacturing sector that had been stimulated by wartime production and that exported goods to European countries rebuilding after the devastation of the war. As a staples-based economy, the country's primary resources were also in demand, as evidenced by the dramatic symbol of the post-war boom represented by the discovery of oil in Alberta in 1947 (see Chapter 7).

In order to manage the huge numbers of returning soldiers and to ensure they had opportunities to make a good living, the federal government launched an early "affirmative action" program for veterans, taking many into the public service as the government rapidly expanded the provision of social services during the construction of the social welfare state. Educational opportunities were also given to veterans in the form of reduced or free tuition and expansion of both technical training and academic education in the burgeoning post-secondary education system. Jobs were plentiful in the private sector as well. A housing boom and growing consumerism fed the growth of the middle class as returning veterans married and had families. A growing array of modern conveniences accompanied this growth, including the latest technological innovation known as television. On 6 September 1952, the Canadian Broadcasting Corporation (CBC) began television broadcasting for the first time.

## 17) The Quebec Question

Perhaps the most dramatic transformation heralding the arrival of modern Canada took place in Quebec where far-ranging political, economic, and social/cultural change accompanied the emergence of a new Quebec. The period known as the "Quiet Revolution" began in 1960. On the political front, the Union Nationale, a conservative and corrupt party that had ruled almost continuously since the 1940s, was defeated by the Quebec Liberal Party in 1960 under Jean Lesage, ushering in an era of progressive reform. The emergence of new parties and movements advocating greater powers for the provincial government appeared; some went further, arguing for the idea of separating from Canada and creating an independent and sovereign Quebec. These included a radical and violent faction known as the Front de libération du Québec (FLQ) who engaged in bombings and, during the so-called October Crisis of 1970, the kidnapping of a British diplomat and the murder of a Quebec Cabinet minister. These events precipitated the invoking of the *War Measures Act*, the precursor to the *Emergencies Act*, calling in the army and suspending all civil liberties. The sentiment in favour of separatism eventually resulted in the victory of the separatist Parti Québécois in the provincial election of 1976 under René Lévesque, sending shockwaves throughout the nation.

On the economic front, the Lesage government adopted the slogan *Maitre Chez Nous* (masters in our own house) and embarked on exercises in economic nationalism to enhance opportunities for the French in Quebec who had historically been denied control of the economy by a powerful English elite minority. Symbols of this shift included the creation of Hydro Quebec, and government-run pension and investment funds. New economic opportunities for French-speaking Quebecers in the executive and managerial offices of these corporations emerged. A process of industrialization and urbanization, already a reality in English Canada, was accelerated.

On the social/cultural front, the Catholic church, which for decades had dominated Quebec life as part of an unholy trinity with the English economic elite and French political elite, began to lose its status and power. For example, the Catholic church's control over education was diminished by the creation of a provincial education ministry. As well, there was a flowering of secular French-Canadian literature, music, and the arts fuelled by the emergence of a distinctive Québécois nationalism within the province.

All of these changes occurred rapidly and with far-reaching consequences. The question "what does Quebec want?" became the central preoccupation in Canada. The separatist Parti Québécois held a referendum in 1980 on "sovereignty association," which was defeated by a vote of 60 percent *non* to 40 percent vote *oui*. The federal government responded by promising to "renew federalism" and proceeded to engage Quebec and the other provinces over intense constitutional negotiations. Ultimately, an agreement was struck, but without the approval of Quebec. The Constitution was patriated in 1982. It included a domestic amending formula, the termination of authority over Canada of the United Kingdom Parliament, and a *Charter of Rights and Freedoms*. But Quebec's isolation led some Quebecers to claim they had been betrayed, and they referred to the patriation deal as the "night of the long knives." This led to a second referendum in 1995 wherein 51 percent voted *non*, while 49 percent voted *oui* in a traumatic "near-death" experience for the Canadian nation.

### 18) Meanwhile, in English Canada . . .

The "Quebec question" dominated politics in Canada for much of the second half of the twentieth century. It has not disappeared, but it has been accompanied by issues arising out of English Canada. Politically, the party system, long dominated by the Liberal and Progressive Conservative parties at the national level, fractured, with left and right wing and regional parties forming and dissolving, although only the Liberal and Conservative parties continued to win power at the national level (the party and electoral system are discussed in more detail in Chapter 3 and regionalism in Chapter 4).

Economically, manufacturing and industrial production grew, especially in central Canada. The integration of the Canadian economy into the American economy rapidly increased, with massive levels of foreign direct investment mainly into central Canadian manufacturing, while the hinterlands continued primarily as staples-producing and exporting economies. Eventually, growing continental integration culminated in free trade agreements with the United States and, later Mexico, in the 1980s, 1990s, and early 2000s (see Chapter 6).

Culturally, English Canada emerged in the post-war years as an urban multicultural society searching for an identity in the shadow of the American cultural hegemon. Concerns over the expression of Canadian culture resulted in a growing nationalism often thinly disguised as anti-Americanism. The national government initiated an important royal commission entitled the Royal Commission on National Development in the Arts, Letters and Sciences (known as the Massey Commission) in 1951, which resulted in wide ranging recommendations for state funding and support for Canadian television and radio broadcasting, literature, music, and the arts. Meanwhile, changes to Canada's immigration policies resulted in a massive influx of new immigrants who were neither English nor French. The multicultural face of Canada emerged, leading the federal government to eventually modify its traditional dualist conception of the country, appending to it an official policy of multiculturalism.

Overall, Canada transformed itself through the twentieth century from colony to nation. But modern Canada suffered growing pains in the process, including the stresses and strains associated with divisions between the French and English, which led perilously close to the breakup of Canada. Nonetheless, a newfound Canadian identity and nationalism was forged by the experiences of two World Wars and the Great Depression, and symbolized by the adoption of a distinct Canadian flag in 1965 and the patriation of the Constitution in 1982. But in addition, the old east-west ties that once bound the nation as encapsulated in Macdonald's National Policy gradually frayed and were replaced with a much more pronounced north-south orientation. Driven by continental economic integration and reinforced by American cultural imperialism, many Canadians were both drawn into the American orbit and repulsed by it.

Like the United States, Canadian population diversity has rapidly increased due to immigration in the past fifty years, adding to the already diverse populations of English and French speakers, Indigenous residents, and descendants of previous European and Asian immigrants. In Canada, "visible minorities" or "racialized" people (neither of those terms is commonly used in the United

States) have increased from 5 percent of the population in 1981 to 27 percent in 2021, with another 5 percent indicating an Indigenous identity. In recent years, a majority of immigrants to Canada have come from Asian countries. While immigrants to Canada come from countries everywhere, Canada continues to get a higher percentage of immigrants from Europe than the United States and a lower percentage from Latin America. In 2023, 21 percent (about one-fifth) of members of the Canada House of Commons indicated that they are either visible minorities or Indigenous.

## Conclusion

We asked at the outset of this chapter: Why do Canada and the United States have different governing systems? How did those systems originate? How do they function to provide for the "Peace, Order and Good Government" or "Life, Liberty and the Pursuit of Happiness" of the citizens in each country? Given the distinct yet overlapping historical trajectories that Canada and the United States followed, what are the important factors that make them "the same, only different"? The next chapter explores this phenomenon in the context of comparing the main political institutions of each country.

CHAPTER TWO

# Comparative Political Institutions: Where Does Power Lie in Each Country?

## Introduction

Did you ever wonder — who has more power, a prime minister or a president? What is the difference between Parliament and Congress? How much influence does each country's Supreme Court have, and how does the judiciary influence democratic decision-making? Returning to the theme of similarities and differences, we note how the core political institutions of both countries — the executive, legislative, and judicial branches — are strikingly similar, yet equally strikingly different. Power may in fact be vested in the people in both countries, but distinctive institutions bring that abstract concept to life in different ways. This chapter outlines and explains those differences by comparing political institutions while keeping in sight the core similarity that defines the political systems of Canada and the United States — democracy.

### A. Comparing Democracies: Executive and Legislative Institutions

Canada and the United States are both representative democracies and share certain characteristics as such. They both observe the rule of law (no one is above the law, not even the makers of the law); they constitutionally guarantee certain rights and freedoms (in a Charter of Rights of Freedoms in Canada and a Bill of Rights in the United States); and power is vested in the people in both countries and exercised by their freely chosen representatives.

## 1) Checks and Balances Versus Fusion of Powers

In the United States, a system of checks and balances ensures that power is divided between the legislative branch (Congress, made up of the Senate and House of Representatives), the executive branch (the President and Cabinet), and the judicial branch (the Supreme Court and all the courts below it). The founders felt that "ambition must be made to counteract ambition," as James Madison wrote in the Federalist Papers, in order to avoid hasty decision making or abuses of power. The United States Constitution even forbids members of Congress from holding office in the executive branch of the federal government.

In Canada, power is much more centralized, with the executive branch (the prime minister and Cabinet) being the key decision-makers in the system, giving orders and directives to the legislative branch (the Parliament, made up of the appointed Senate and elected House of Commons). But note that the system of checks and balances does not apply in Canada. Instead of an American-style *separation of power*, there is a *fusion of power*, as the executive and legislature sit together in Canada in Parliament. Indeed, the executive branch has to be chosen from among the members of the legislative branch. That is why the Canadian prime minister and Cabinet must be Members of Parliament (MPs), and is the central feature of responsible government, the history of which we briefly traced in Chapter 1.

In Canada, we could say that the executive and legislative branches work together more efficiently than in the American system. However, the price for efficiency is a concentration of power in the hands of the executive, as the prime minister appears to have almost unchecked power to direct the government. This is largely a function of something called party discipline in which all the members of a given party take direction from their leader and vote together as a bloc. This is necessary because the prime minister needs the support of a majority of the MPs to pass legislation. In return, the executive branch must be accountable to the legislative branch, and explain its actions. Thus the prime minister and Cabinet stand up in the House of Commons during Question Period and answer for their policies. This is the core of the system of responsible government. The executive is responsible to the legislative branch, and ultimately through it, to the citizens.

In contrast, in the United States, the president is constitutionally prohibited from being a member of Congress. There is no system of responsible government in the Canadian sense of the term. The president does not appear in Congress as the leader of the party with the most seats and command Congress to do his bidding. There is no system of party discipline — although there is deep partisanship that differentiates Democrats and Republicans. But there is no prohibition in Congress from members "crossing the floor" to vote with the other party, as there is in the Canadian Parliament. There is a need to negotiate and bargain about policy decisions in the American system between the executive and legislative branches. In the United States, when apportioning blame for policies that are not working, a president will often blame Congress, leaders of Congress will blame the president, and the voting public, which is to blame for electing those people, gets frustrated.

It can be said that in the United States Congress, more than 90 percent of proposed bills never get passed, but members of Congress can and do have the opportunity to represent their constituents' interests very closely because they have much more freedom of action and independence than MPs in Canada. In Canada, 98 percent of government bills do get passed, but constituent interests are often sacrificed due to party discipline.

## 2) Power in the Executive Branch: Constitutional Monarchy Versus Republic

In the United States (and most of Latin America), the president combines the powers of head of state and head of government, but those powers are separate in Canada (and most of Europe). In Canada, the head of state is the queen or king of England, and when she or he is not in Canada (which is most of the time), the appointed Governor General. The Governor General represents the country to the outside world, signifies continuity and legitimacy for the regime, and presides over major ceremonial occasions. The head of government is the prime minister, who runs the day-to-day operations of policy making for the government.

In Canada, the executive branch is marked by a combination of real political power and symbolic power, each of which is located in a different place in the political system. Symbolic power is found in the head of state. The queen or king and Governor General's powers are mainly symbolic, but constitutionally they are impressive. They include:

- Giving royal assent to all legislation before it can become law
- Officially choosing the prime minister
- Officially determining when national elections occur
- Acting as Commander-in-Chief of the Canadian Armed Forces
- Officially choosing the Supreme Court justices
- Hosting foreign government dignitaries who visit Canada

Despite this impressive roster of powers, the head of state does not exercise them independently, but only acts at the behest of the prime minster. For instance, no Governor General would refuse to give royal assent to legislation duly passed by Parliament. Nor would they refuse a prime minister's request to dissolve Parliament in order to call an election. The one incident in Canadian history where this did occur created a constitutional crisis in 1926 known as the King-Byng affair; Governor General Lord Byng refused Prime Minister William Lyon McKenzie King's request to call an election

**TABLE 2.1. RECENT USAGE OF THE PRESIDENTIAL VETO AND NUMBER OF TIMES CONGRESS OVERRODE IT AS OF DECEMBER 2024**

| President | Vetoes | Times Overridden |
| --- | --- | --- |
| George W Bush | 12 | 4 |
| Barack Obama | 12 | 1 |
| Donald Trump | 10 | 1 |
| Joe Biden | 13 | 0 |

and instead invited the leader of the Opposition to try to govern. Similarly, it is in reality the prime minister who chooses senators, Supreme Court justices (see below), ambassadors, and hundreds of other high-level government appointments, while the Governor General's approval is symbolic.

In the United States, the president has all the powers of head of government plus head of state. The president signs into law legislation passed by Congress. The president is the Commander-in-Chief of the Armed Forces, and receives foreign dignitaries as head of state. Presidents can veto legislation passed by Congress instead of signing it, although two-thirds of both Houses of Congress can override the president and pass something into law without the president's signature. As of 2023, there had been 2,590 presidential vetoes in American history, of which only 112 were overridden by Congress.[1] Recent usage of the presidential veto is shown in Table 2.1. While the president chooses Supreme Court justices, the Senate must approve those choices. The president has no influence over the timing of elections, which are on a fixed schedule, as we note in Chapter 3.

### 3) Selection of Executive Branch Leadership

In Canada, the head of state inherits his or her position. The Governor General is appointed formally by the queen or king but in reality is selected by the prime minister, usually for a five-year term, which can be extended. The Governor General formally appoints the prime minister, but in reality, the role is determined to be the leader of the party with the largest number of members elected to the House of Commons. In the United States, the Congress has played no role whatsoever in choosing the president since 1824.

## 4) Terms of Office and Removal Before Term or Mandate Is Complete

In Canada, according to the Constitution, elections must occur for the House of Commons within a five-year period after the previous election. Historically, the prime minister has enjoyed a tremendous amount of discretion as to the timing of an election within that five-year window. More recently, fixed election dates have been legislated for national elections as well as for many provincial elections. However, under certain circumstances, the prime minster can still call an election before the fixed election date — for instance, if there is a minority government. This is a situation where no one party has a majority of seats in the House of Commons, but the prime minister's party has the most seats and relies on the support of one or more opposition parties to pass legislation. If that support is withdrawn, and there is a vote of non-confidence in government, the prime minister must call an election.

Fixed election dates came to Canada in 2006 when Parliament passed a law to hold elections in October every four years. However, then-prime minister Stephen Harper, heading up a minority government, called an early election in 2008. Harper won another minority government and then lost a vote of non-confidence in the House of Commons in 2011. He finally won a majority in the 2011 election, and subsequently waited four years, as the new law prescribed, until October 2015 to have the next election, which the Liberals won under Justin Trudeau. The next election, 2019, returned Trudeau to power, but with a minority government. Trudeau, like Harper before him, called another election before the fixed election date, and won yet another minority in 2021.

Parties can also remove their own leader as prime minister any time they want and replace the prime minster with their preferred choice. Each party has its own mechanisms to conduct regular leadership reviews, along with rules for voting a leader out of office. No sitting prime minister has ever been removed officially in this way as parties generally recognize that deposing a prime minister would shake the voters' confidence in the party and likely produce discord and division within the party and among its supporters. Moreover, prime ministers have tremendous powers to dole out rewards and penalties to party members in order to keep them in line. Sitting leaders of opposition parties have been removed occasionally, however. For instance, in 2022, Conservative Party leader Erin O'Toole was ousted by a margin of seventy-three to forty-five in a secret ballot vote by Conservative Party MPs according to the terms of the Party's *Reform Act*.

Canadian party leaders and activists, however, have sometimes pressured prime ministers to step down between elections with claims that party popularity is dropping and implied threats of forced removal. For example, in 2003, partly due a scandal about promotion of the Canadian government in Quebec, Liberal Prime Minister Jean Chrétien was convinced to resign by supporters of former Liberal Finance Minister Paul Martin, who was then chosen as Liberal Party leader and became prime minister without any intervening elections. In 2024, a significant number of disgruntled Liberal MPs tried to pressure Trudeau to step down given their party's dismal standing in the polls and the apparent popularity of their Conservative Party opponents. Trudeau eventually gave in and announced he would resign in early 2025.

In the United States, there are fixed dates for all elections for all offices. The presidential election occurs every four years, the House of Representatives every two years, and the Senate every six years (one-third of senators face re-election every two years to get additional six-year terms). General elections have been held on the first Tuesday after the first Monday in November since 1845. The fact that presidents cannot choose election dates reveals the vagaries of politics. For instance, in February 1991, 89 percent of Americans said President George HW Bush was doing a great job and deserved re-election. But by the time of the presidential election in November 1992, Bush won only 37 percent of votes, losing to Bill Clinton.

There is a complicated procedure to attempt the removal of an American president during their four-year term, which we witnessed in 2019 and again in 2021. It requires a majority vote by the House of Representatives to impeach a president (the modern word "impeachment" derives from an Old French term "empêcher," meaning to hinder, trap, or entangle). Impeachment is followed by a trial in the Senate, which needs a two-thirds vote to convict and remove a president for treason, bribery, or "high crimes and misdemeanors."

In 2019, Donald Trump was impeached by the Democrat-dominated House on charges of abuse of power and obstruction of Congress, but acquitted by the Republican-dominated Senate. The charges related to Trump's phone call with the president of Ukraine about military assistance to Ukraine. During the phone call, Trump asked the Ukrainian president for a favour to investigate political opponent Joe Biden. Trump became just the third president in American history to be impeached after Bill Clinton (1998) and Andrew Johnson (1868). The Senate voted 52:48 to acquit Trump on abuse of power and 53:47 to acquit him on obstruction of Congress. Senator Mitt Romney (R–Utah) was the only senator of either party to break ranks, voting to convict Trump on the abuse of power charge.

Then, in 2021, Trump became the only president in American history to be impeached a second time. This impeachment originated with Trump's attempts to overturn the 2020 presidential election results with false claims of election fraud and efforts to pressure election officials in Georgia to overturn the results there. The impeachment resolution stated that Trump incited the violent attack on the Capitol in Washington, DC, on 6 January 2021, while Congress was convened to count the electoral votes and certify the victory of President Joe Biden and Vice President Kamala Harris.

The Senate voted 57:43 to convict Trump of inciting insurrection, falling ten votes short of the two-thirds majority required by the Constitution, and Trump was therefore acquitted. Seven Republican senators joined all Democratic and Independent senators in voting to convict Trump, the largest bipartisan vote ever for an impeachment conviction of an American president or former president. While Trump was no longer president during the Senate trial, a conviction would have allowed the Senate to bar Trump from ever being president again. Remarkably, the fact of Trump's two impeachments did not seem to play a role in dissuading Americans from electing him to another term as president in 2024.

## 5) Legislative-Executive Communications: The Speech from the Throne and the State of the Union

In both countries, the general agenda and goals of the government are presented annually to the people through similar, but different, means. The Canadian counterpart to the American State of the Union Address is the Speech from the Throne, or the Throne Speech. It is read by the monarch (when they are in Canada) or Governor General in the Senate (the Crown never enters the House of Commons) and marks the official opening of every new session of Parliament. The Throne Speech also acts as a declaration of the goals of the government for the upcoming parliamentary session. But the far more important means of communication is that the prime minister and their Cabinet, as members of Parliament, are present in the House of Commons most days in session and participate in Question Period, the forty-five minutes each day during which MPs can ask any question they want to of the prime minister or the Cabinet.

In contrast, the State of the Union address stems from Article II, Section 3 of the United States Constitution, which states, "The President shall from time to time give to Congress information of the State of the Union and recommend to their Consideration such measures as he shall judge necessary and expedient." Since George

Washington, presidents have generally given either a speech or written message to the nation annually. Much like the Canadian Throne Speech, the State of the Union Address is used by the president to outline the goals and agenda for the coming year. The president addresses Congress formally only once a year in the State of the Union Speech; otherwise the president is almost never seen in the Capitol Building.

The presidential address to Congress was given in person by the first two presidents, George Washington and John Adams. But the third president, Thomas Jefferson, felt that a presidential address to Congress was too similar to the British Speech from the Throne tradition and that the United States needed to avoid monarchical traditions. Jefferson instead sent a message in writing, as did all nineteenth-century presidents. The tradition of a direct address to Congress in person restarted with President Woodrow Wilson in 1913, who saw the public relations advantages of the media reporting on the spectacle of a president addressing Congress. It has continued ever since.[2]

## 6) Formation and Role of Cabinets

In Canada, the prime minister chooses all the Cabinet members who run the various government departments and determines the size and composition of the Cabinet. Over time, different prime ministers have created Cabinets of different sizes with different portfolios. Justin Trudeau initially had twenty-nine members of Cabinet, which he later increased to thirty-nine. Stephen Harper had twenty-six, and Paul Martin had thirty-seven. The discretion of the prime minister in this role is virtually absolute; Parliament has no role in either selecting or approving the prime minister's Cabinet choices. The number and type of Canadian government departments have changed dramatically since 1867 as new issues and government responsibilities have arisen. In Canada, the Cabinet is the key decision-making body and a very powerful political actor.

## Comparative Political Institutions

In the United States, the size of the Cabinet is fixed by Congress, not the president. Moreover, the Senate must approve all presidential appointments to lead those departments. It does so by a simple majority vote after public hearings into the suitability of the president's nominees. The House of Representatives and Senate must vote to create new Cabinet departments. The Department of Homeland Security is the newest, having been created in 2003. In the United States, the Cabinet administers departments but is otherwise powerless.

The last nominated American Cabinet member to be rejected in a full Senate vote was John Tower in 1989, who President George HW Bush had nominated to be Secretary of Defense. Tower had been a Republican Senator from Texas from 1961 to 1984, chair of the Senate Armed Services Committee from 1981 to 1984, and had a reputation for supporting every weapons system requested by the Department of Defense. When Tower retired from the Senate in 1984, he became a lobbyist for American defense contractors. In 1989, Democrats had a 55:45 majority in the Senate, and most Democrats opposed the Tower nomination due to his ties to the defense industry. But in 1989, the Senate still had many conservative Democrats from the South who agreed with Tower's views on military spending. So Democrats who opposed Tower raised allegations about "drinking and womanizing" against him. As a Senator, Tower had sometimes appeared possibly inebriated in public and was also seen with women who were not his wife when he was still married. Democrats argued that Tower was not the right person to lead the Defense Department. That was enough to convince more conservative Democrats, and the Tower confirmation was rejected 53:47.[3] President Bush then had to choose a different Secretary of Defense. He chose Dick Cheney, a Congressman from Wyoming who would go on to become vice president under President George W Bush.

Since 1989, numerous presidential Cabinet nominees have also been unable to gain Senate confirmation approval in a vote, but their nominations were either withdrawn before the formal vote, or they have been retained as "acting" department leaders, until legal or political requirements forced them out.

## 7) Ministerial Responsibility

Responsibility and accountability of government are handled differently in Canada compared to the United States where Cabinet is concerned. In Canada, one of the most important mechanisms to ensure the accountability of government are the doctrines of individual and collective ministerial responsibility.[4] Under these doctrines, ministers are ultimately responsible for all of the undertakings of their departments. If a mistake is made, they must answer for it. Resignation of a minister is the ultimate penalty if the mistake is significant enough and is the consequence of actions that can be directly attributed to the minister. However, if it is one of the minister's officials who makes a mistake, ministerial responsibility is expressed through the minister answering to the House of Commons for the mistake and implementing remedial action. This is referred to as the doctrine of answerability, a somewhat milder version of ministerial responsibility. No minister in Canada has ever resigned because of a mistake made directly by a subordinate.

The key principle underlying the doctrine of ministerial responsibility is that the ultimate responsibility for government action or inaction belongs to the political head — that is, the minister. As the political master in charge, all the official acts undertaken by public servants beneath them must be held accountable. This is the case even though a department might employ thousands of people, make thousands of decisions, and spend millions of dollars per year.

Reinforcing this doctrine is the concept of collective ministerial responsibility. As members of Cabinet, ministers are required to act in solidarity; once a decision has been taken behind closed doors in a Cabinet meeting, all ministers defend the decision in public, regardless of their personal position or whether they lost the debate in Cabinet. Cabinet keeps its internal disagreements to itself. In this way, the government is seen to be speaking with one voice, thereby reinforcing political stability and unity, and the appearance of consensus, important considerations for the electorate. Cabinet acts collectively in every government decision, and therefore must accept collective ministerial responsibility. Cabinet confidentiality is a corollary of collective ministerial responsibility. What goes on in Cabinet stays in Cabinet. Even when individual ministers disagree with decisions taken at the Cabinet table, they keep their disagreements to themselves. Open debate and a frank assessment of all alternatives occurs in the privacy of the Cabinet meeting. This leaves ministers confident that divisions within government will not be publicly aired.

In the United States, there are no such doctrines, and the Cabinet's political role is to serve as an appendage of the elected president in the executive branch. Presidents meet with their Cabinets periodically in the White House Cabinet Room. Cabinet members sometimes give advice to presidents, but no formal Cabinet votes are taken or needed. In recent decades, Cabinet meetings have mostly been ceremonial in nature, with presidents inviting in television cameras to provide video to the public, and then asking the cameras to leave before discussions begin. At one famous Cabinet meeting in 2017, President Trump's appointed Cabinet members spent the first several minutes of the meeting praising Trump and exclaiming about what a wonderful president Trump was before the cameras; one reporter said it was "the most exquisitely awkward public event I've ever seen."[5]

While there is nothing in the United States directly equivalent to Canadian ministerial responsibility, American presidents do have the power to fire any Cabinet member at any time for any reason, whether due to incompetence or for political reasons. For instance, if a policy in a Cabinet department is perceived poorly by the public, a president can fire a Cabinet member to protect the president's own popularity.

In the nineteenth century, there were questions in the United States about whether the Senate needed to approve the presidential firing of a Cabinet member, since the United States Constitution requires the Senate's approval to hire a Cabinet member. In 1867, Congress passed the *Tenure of Office Act* over President Andrew Johnson's veto, which required Senate approval for any presidential decision to fire a Cabinet member. Andrew Johnson had been the vice president under Abraham Lincoln and became president after Lincoln's assassination. Johnson had previously been a Democrat from Tennessee, but had supported the Union cause during the American Civil War and was chosen by Lincoln to form a Union ticket in the 1864 election. Johnson, however, continued to sympathize with Southern White opposition to civil rights for newly freed slaves and was politically opposed by the Republicans who controlled Congress at the time. Johnson ignored the *Tenure of Office Act* and fired Lincoln's Secretary of War, Edwin Stanton, who opposed Johnson's policies of leniency toward Confederate states and support for White dominance in South. Stanton then barricaded himself in his office to prevent his removal. The House of Representatives then voted to approve eleven impeachment articles, all having to do with Johnson's violations of the *Tenure of Office Act*, with most Republicans voting for impeachment and most Democrats voting against. The Senate held a trial and voted 35:19 to convict and remove Johnson on the first three articles, one vote short of what was needed. At that point, the Senate gave up and ended the trial. There was lots of evidence of bribery of senators on both sides of the issue.[6] The *Tenure of Office Act* was repealed by Congress in 1887.

In 1926, the Supreme Court resolved the issues about presidential firings of agency leaders in the executive branch in the case *Myers v United States*. Frank Myers had been appointed as a postmaster in Portland, Oregon for a four-year term by President Wilson under a law passed by Congress saying the president could remove someone early with the advice and consent of the Senate. Myers did some unpopular things (such as not rehiring First World War veterans right away at the post office) and made political enemies. President Wilson fired him in 1920 without Senate approval. Myers then sued for back pay, calling his firing illegal.

The Supreme Court ruled 6:3 that requiring Senate approval to fire top executive branch officials was unconstitutional and interfered with the Constitutional power of the president "to take care that the laws be faithfully executed."[7]

## 8) The Public Service

The public service in Canada and the United States differ in some significant ways. The Canadian public service was originally derived from the British model, and many of the titles used to this day — such as clerk of the Privy Council and secretary to Cabinet (the head of the public service) — reflect that. However, there has also been a significant American influence on the history and trajectory of the Canadian public service. For example, the transition from a patronage-based public service to a merit-based one beginning in the early twentieth century came about because of the influence of American reformers' struggling against big city corruption. Reformers spread the gospel of putting public service in the hands of trained professionals rather than cronies of corrupt big city boss-mayors and their supporters.

In 1881, President James Garfield was assassinated by Charles Guiteau. Guiteau, who often showed signs of mental illness, was convinced that he had played a key role in Garfield's election victory and made repeated requests to Garfield administration officials to get appointed to a diplomatic position. This political event allowed reformers to claim that a "disappointed office seeker" had killed the president due to the patronage system and led to the passage of the *Pendleton Act* of 1883 that established a civil service system for hiring people based on merit in the federal executive branch.[8]

While American-style corruption was not a central issue in Canadian politics, American-style reforms inspired change in Canada. A group of Canadian businesspeople interested in more efficient government appealed to Conservative Party leader Robert Borden to reform the public service in return for their support in the upcoming election. Borden did win the election and implemented the *Civil Service Act, 1918*, which called for the creation of the

Civil Service Commission (later the Public Service Commission) to oversee appointments to the public service and take them out of the hands of politicians. In addition, competitive exams were instituted as the basis of appointments, public servants were prohibited from engaging in political activities, and the public service organization was rationalized and restructured with a job classification system.[9]

In Canada, as in Great Britain, a change in government does not also mean a change in the public service; most appointed officials retain their jobs even when a new party takes power. Their ministers, in contrast, are often in their positions for a relatively short time, are not usually specialists in their areas of responsibility, and rely heavily on their bureaucratic advisers starting with the deputy minister, the top ranking bureaucrat in each department, for advice and support. The deputy minister is the administrative head of the department and conveys the minister's instructions to the bureaucracy.

In the United States, the public service size, style, and use of patronage versus merit distinguishes it from the Canadian model and experience. For instance, about 4,000 public service jobs are direct appointments of the president, and the top ranking officials of every federal department are replaced after each election. Cabinet ministers are selected from outside the ranks of elected members of Congress. An American Cabinet secretary typically serves for the duration of the administration, unless they are replaced or resign. Each one must be confirmed by the Senate. This means the appointment process can be fraught with political intrigue since the Senate may be controlled by the opposition party. Originally nearly all civil service positions were assigned by patronage. However, since the *Pendleton Civil Service Reform Act* of 1883, the majority of the civil service, especially at the lower levels, is appointed by merit and many belong to the American Federation of Government Employees labour union. The jobs of these employees, like in Canada, are not dependent upon election results. The *Hatch Act* of 1939 further entrenched the non-partisan role of the civil service by restricting political activities among federal civil service employees and even state and local government employees who administer federal programs.

## 9) Power in the Legislative Branch

In both countries, the House and Senate must pass all laws and all budget items. The original intention of the Canadian Senate was two-fold: to represent regional interests, and to protect minority rights. Where regional interests are concerned, the purpose was undermined by the distribution of Senate seats across the country. Ontario and Quebec each received twenty-four seats, but the Western provinces were lumped together and given twenty-four seats, as were the original Atlantic provinces. Therefore "region" in two cases coincided with "province," but not in the other eight cases. The result was to enhance the influence of the two central provinces in Confederation and contribute to the feelings of political alienation and discrimination in the rest of the country. Where protecting minority rights is concerned, it is worth recalling that there is a qualification for Senate membership that requires potential candidates to own at least $4,000 of property. This stipulation, included in the *British North America Act, 1867* (BNA Act, 1867), was to fulfill the Senate's role in protecting minority rights because, as Prime Minister John A Macdonald said, "We must protect the rights of minorities, and the rich are always fewer in number than the poor."[10]

Traditionally, the Canadian Senate passes almost all legislation approved by the House of Commons; as an appointed body, the Canadian Senate lacks the democratic legitimacy to defy the will of the elected House of Commons. This does not mean that approval is automatic, though. For instance, in 2010, the Harper Conservative minority government was unable to prevent the opposition parties from joining together to support a bill to cut greenhouse gas emissions, but the Conservative-dominated Senate blocked the bill. In 1990, the Conservative government of Brian Mulroney passed the Goods and Services Tax (GST) in the House of Commons, but it met resistance in the Liberal-dominated Senate, which threatened to vote against the legislation. Upon consultation with constitutional experts, Mulroney activated a never-before-used section of the Constitution, which allowed him to boost the Senate ranks by eight members, thereby giving him the numbers to pass the bill.

The Canadian Senate often undertakes a process of applying "sober second thought" to legislation, looking for ways to enhance or improve it without distorting the intention articulated by the House. In any event, traditionally the prime minister has controlled appointments to the Senate, and typically stacked it with partisan supporters. More recently, steps have been taken to enhance the non-partisanship of the Senate. Trudeau announced in 2016 that there would no longer be any Liberal senators, and that future appointments would be made on the basis of merit rather than partisanship. There are still senators that identify as Conservatives, however, and the goal of an entirely nonpartisan Senate has yet to be realized. Trudeau also created an Independent Advisory Board for Senate Appointments. It is charged with making recommendations for nominees to fill vacant Senate seats, although its recommendations are non-binding. But now, any Canadian citizen meeting certain criteria can apply to the advisory board to be considered for nomination. The result of the change has been that independent senators now outnumber those with a political affiliation.

In the United States Congress, partisanship has historically not been as dominant as in the Canadian Parliament. In the past, Republicans and Democrats regularly "crossed the floor" to vote. There was no principle of party discipline and for many years, conservative Democrats and liberal Republicans held positions of power in Congress. However, partisanship in the Congress has increased in recent decades as conservative Democrats and liberal Republicans have almost disappeared, and more votes have partisan outcomes than in the past, though still not to the same extent as the party solidarity found in the Canadian House of Commons.

The United States Senate, like the Canadian Senate, was originally intended to represent "minority" interests. In the eighteenth-century views of the American Constitution's creators, the minorities of concern were smaller states, who were guaranteed two seats in the chamber, just like large states, and educated men with better judgment, who would be chosen for six-year terms by state legislatures (this was modified to direct public votes for senators by the Seventeenth Amendment, approved in 1913). The Senate has a few special powers not given to the House, including the confirmation of presidential nominations to be federal judges, Cabinet officials, or ambassadors, and ratification of international treaties.

The House and Senate block each other all the time in the United States, especially when controlled by different parties; but even when the same party controls both bodies, this happens. For example, in 2013, the Democratic Senate passed an immigration reform bill, but the Republican House refused to pass the bill. Between 2010 and 2013, the Republican-dominated House voted fifty-four times to repeal all or part of the *Affordable Care Act* (Obamacare). But the Democratic Senate never agreed. In 2017, the Republican House voted again to repeal Obamacare, but the Republican-majority Senate voted against repeal. During the Congress of 2021–2022, 1,780 bills passed one chamber of Congress and not the other. Most proposed significant legislation never passes both Houses, though more mundane laws to name courthouses or post offices after locally famous people pass frequently.

The Canadian Parliament is dominated by the executive branch to the extent that "governing from the centre" is an accurate description.[11] One of the impressive powers held by the prime minister is the right to terminate a session of Parliament, called prorogation. This differs from a recess or adjournment, which do not end a session, and from a complete dissolution of Parliament, which ends both the session and the entire Parliament, requiring an election for the House of Commons. In Canada, Parliament is typically prorogued upon the completion of the agenda set forth in the Speech from the Throne. Parliament remains in recess until the Governor General summons parliamentarians once the prime minister has signalled a date for the resumption of Parliament.

Proroguing Parliament has proved contentious in several recent cases. On 4 December 2008, Harper recommended Governor General Michaëlle Jean prorogue Parliament after two opposition parties formed a coalition with the support of a third party and threatened to pass a vote of non-confidence. The Governor General granted the prime minister's request after she consulted with constitutional experts followed by a two-hour meeting with the prime minister. Some constitutional experts later called Harper's move an abuse of the power to prorogue. Harper again advised the Governor General to prorogue Parliament on 30 December 2009, to keep Parliament in recess for the duration of the upcoming XXI Olympic Winter Games in Vancouver, British Columbia. Opposition Members of Parliament claimed it was a way for Harper to avoid ongoing investigations into a scandal involving the detention and abuse of Afghan detainees. Trudeau prorogued Parliament in January 2025 to avoid a non-confidence vote and give his party time to select a new leader after he resigned.

## 10) The Democratic Basis of and Representation in Congress Versus Parliament

The United States House of Representatives has 435 members, with the number fixed by Congress since 1913. Each state gets at least one, with the rest apportioned based on population from the most recent census. As of 2023, each House district had about 760,000 people. California, the largest state with 39 million people, gets fifty-two representatives during the decade of the 2020s. Wyoming, the smallest state with 580,000 people, gets one representative. The Senate has 100 members, two per state, and has been elected since 1913.

The American territories get non-voting delegates in the House (including Washington, DC), but no representation in the Senate. This explains the Washington, DC, licence plate slogan, "Taxation Without Representation." The District of Columbia statehood movement is a political movement that advocates making the District of Columbia a state. On 10 January 2023, Congresswoman Eleanor Holmes Norton (D-DC) introduced a District of Columbia statehood bill into Congress, one of the more than 150 constitutional amendments and bills introduced to provide representation to the District of Columbia (but never passed) since 1803. Indeed, Norton's bill passed the House for the first time in history in June 2020 and passed again in April 2021, but neither passed the Senate. All Congressional legislation "dies" at the end of each even-numbered year and must be reintroduced and start the lawmaking process over.

In Canada, the House of Commons chamber is divided into Government and opposition sides. Any member not affiliated with the governing party is part of the opposition. As noted above, unlike in the United States Congress, "party discipline" is a key feature and rigorously enforced. The Canadian House of Commons has 338 members as of 2024. Each province gets a minimum number of ridings (House of Commons districts) based on a formula in the Canadian Constitution. In 2024, there were about 115,000 people per riding. Ontario, the largest province with a population of 15.5 million, has 121 ridings, with about 128,000 voters per riding; Prince Edward Island, the smallest province with a population of 176,000, has four ridings with 44,000 people per riding. Because of a constitutional stipulation that no province can have fewer MPs than senators, and because Prince Edward Island was granted four senators, it can be said that Prince Edward Island is probably among the most overrepresented jurisdictions in the democratic world. The three northern territories of Yukon (44,000), Northwest Territories (45,000), and Nunavut (41,000) each get one riding.

The Canadian Senate has 105 appointed members (see Table 2.2). The distribution of senators produces great inequalities in representation. Apart from the example of Prince Edward Island noted above, New Brunswick has ten senators for 832,000 people, whereas British Columbia has six senators for 5.4 million people. This might shock the many Americans who complain that California's 39 million people get two senators, the same as Wyoming's 580,000 people.

In 2023, the Canadian Senate had fifteen Conservatives, thirty-eight from the Independent Senators Group (mostly appointed by Trudeau), eleven from the Progressive Senate Group, fifteen from the Canadian Senators Group (founded on 4 November 2019, mostly centrist in membership, and intended to focus on regional concerns), twelve Non-Affiliated, and fourteen vacancies. There are

**TABLE 2.2. DISTRIBUTION OF SENATORS IN THE CANADIAN PARLIAMENT**

| Region | Distribution of 105 Senators |
|---|---|
| Maritime Provinces (New Brunswick, Nova Scotia, and Prince Edward Island) | 24 |
| Quebec | 24 |
| Ontario | 24 |
| Western Provinces (Manitoba, Saskatchewan, Alberta, and British Columbia) | 24 |
| Newfoundland and Labrador | 6 |
| The Territories (Yukon, Northwest Territories, and Nunavut) | 3 |

no official New Democratic Party (NDP) members in the Senate, because the party's constitution prohibits New Democrats from accepting an appointment so long as the body is appointed and not elected. Canadian senators serve until death or age seventy-five, whichever happens first.

Because the United States Congress and Canadian House of Commons are all elected, there is no maximum age limit. The oldest MP in Canadian history was William Anderson Black who was first elected to the House of Commons of Canada in 1923 when he was seventy-six years old. He held his seat until his death in 1934 at the age of eighty-six.

In 2023, the United States Senate had sixteen members age seventy-five years or over, including the oldest, Dianne Feinstein (D-CA), age ninety, who died in September 2023 after several incidents caused other members of Congress to question her mental acuity. The oldest member of Congress ever was Senator Strom Thurmond (R-SC). He served in the Senate until age 100 in 2002. Thurmond was openly racist and a supporter of racial segregation during his career. At age sixty-six, he married Miss South Carolina (a beauty pageant winner) who was twenty-two years old, and they had three children together. Six months after Thurmond died at the age of 100 in 2003, his mixed-race, then seventy-eight-year-old daughter Essie Mae Washington-Williams (1925–2013) revealed publicly that he was her father. Her mother Carrie Butler (1909–1948) had been working as his family's maid, and was either fifteen or sixteen years old when twenty-two-year-old Thurmond impregnated her in 1925. His mental fitness was frequently questioned during his last twenty years in office, although this did not stop the voters of South Carolina from re-electing him repeatedly.[12]

A comparison of the Canadian Parliament and United States Congress is summarized in Table 2.3.

## 11) Proposal and Passage of Laws

In Canada, the prime minister and Cabinet introduce almost all laws, and they almost always pass due to the convention of party discipline. However, if a majority opposes the legislation, they can vote non-confidence to remove the prime minister and their government. Motions of non-confidence are restricted to major bills such as the annual budget that involve the raising and spending of money.

There are some limited opportunities for MPs not in Cabinet to introduce legislation, including private members' bills. These cannot include provisions for the spending of funds nor raise taxes, although they can reduce taxes. However, most private members' bills fail to pass, although the chances for success are increased in minority governments. An example of a private member's bill that was successfully passed (in 2021) was an Act authorizing the Canada Revenue Agency to enter into an agreement with a province or a territory regarding the collection and disclosure of information required for an organ and tissue donor registry. Also in 2021, *An Act to amend the Criminal Code regarding sports betting* was passed as a private member's bill. The bills that do get passed most often are those involving relatively minor issues like changing the name of a riding.

In the United States, only members of Congress can introduce laws. Presidents and Cabinet members have no constitutional authority to introduce legislation and must depend on members of

**TABLE 2.3. COMPARING THE CANADIAN PARLIAMENT TO THE UNITED STATES CONGRESS**

| American Congress | | Canadian Parliament | |
|---|---|---|---|
| House of Representatives | Senate | House of Commons | Senate |
| 435 members | 100 members | 338 members | 105 members |
| Two-year term, unlimited | Six-year term, unlimited | Term lengths last up to five years, unlimited terms | Lifetime term up to age seventy-five |
| Members chosen from local districts | Two members chosen from entire state | Members chosen in individual constituencies | Twenty-four members chosen from each of four regions: the Maritimes, Quebec, Ontario, and the Western regions. Newfoundland and Labrador and the Territories are not part of any region. Newfoundand and Labrador gets six senators, while the three territories get one member each |
| Each member represents about 770,000 people | Representation varies by state population | Each member represents about 115,000 people | Representation varies by province and territory |
| Directly elected in each district | Directly elected in each state since 1913 | Directly elected in each constituency | Appointed by the Governor General on the advice of the prime minister |
| Members must be at least twenty-five years of age | Members must be at least thirty years of age | Members must be at least eighteen years of age | Members must be between thirty and seventy-five years of age |

**TABLE 2.3.** (*Continued*)

| American Congress | | Canadian Parliament | |
|---|---|---|---|
| House of Representatives | Senate | House of Commons | Senate |
| Members must live in the state they represent | Members must live in the state they represent | No residency requirements, but members typically live in the constituency they represent | Members must be a resident of the province or territory for which they are appointed and must also own property worth at least $4,000 above their debts and liabilities |
| Members required to have been a US citizen for at least seven years | Members required to have been a US citizen for at least nine years | Members must be Canadian citizens | Members must be Canadian citizens |
| Average cost for election campaign: about $5 million per district in direct spending by candidates 2022 | Average cost for election campaign: about $50 million per state in direct spending by candidates 2022 | Total spending by parties and candidates 2021: About $1.8 million per riding ($1.4 million in US dollars) | N/A |

Source: Data Compiled by Authors.

Congress to initiate proposed laws. But more than ninety percent of proposed laws never pass; rather, they are sent to a committee and "killed" there. A committee chair (always a senior member from the majority party in the chamber) either opposes the proposed legislation or decides it's not that important and will decline to schedule any votes or procedural motions to move the legislation forward. In many cases, bills are simply introduced so members of Congress look good to their constituents back in their home state; they have no realistic possibility of ever passing.

For example, in 2022, Representative Paul Gosar of Arizona introduced the *Granite Mountain Hotshots Commemorative Coin Act* to honour firefighters who had died while fighting an Arizona wildfire. In 2021, Representative Brenda Lawrence of Michigan introduced the *Aretha Franklin Congressional Gold Medal Act* to honour the late singer from Detroit. Senator Amy Klobuchar of Minnesota in 2022 introduced the *Prince Congressional Gold Medal Act* to honour the late singer from her state. After their introduction, these bills were referred to committees, where their legislative processes ended.

## B. Judicial Institutions

### 1) Power in the Judicial Branch

In both Canada and the United States, the judiciary plays an important role in three regards. The judges and courts are called upon to act as arbiters in the event of disputes between:

- the other branches of government (executive and legislative)
- the two levels of government (federal and provincial/state)
- citizens and government

The historical context for the courts in both Canada and the United States is the same; both are rooted in the rule of law tradition that is traceable to *Magna Carta* in 1215, and the Glorious Revolution of 1688 in England, which deposed the Stuart kings and established Parliament's supremacy over the Crown. John Locke's influential defence of the idea of "rule by consent" in his *Second Treatise in Government* of 1690 is also reflected in the political-legal systems that evolved in Canada and the United States. So too is Locke's advocacy of the notion that even the legislature must rule "by declared and received laws ... interpreted by known authorized judges."[13]

Moreover, Locke based his view on the idea that the "law of Nature" also places certain restrictions on the power of the state and restricts it from interfering with the natural rights all citizens possess. The American Declaration of Independence very much justified the revolution and founding of the new republic on these two fundamental principles of Locke's political theory. The American revolutionaries proclaimed that "all men are by Nature equal" and that they possess certain inalienable natural rights. However, majority rule sometimes produces laws that do not respect the rights of minorities. And avoiding the "tyranny of the majority," to use the phrase coined by French philosopher Alexis de Tocqueville, was left in the hands of the founders of both the United States and Canada.

Both countries sought to address these issues, at least implicitly if not explicitly, by producing written constitutions. But while the American Constitution added a Bill of Rights ensuring fundamental freedoms within a few years, the Canadian Constitution initially relied on the unwritten conventions more common in the British parliamentary tradition, where rights are not written down but are the product of parliamentary laws. Consequently, the role of the courts is different in Canada and the United States. The American Supreme Court plays a more explicitly political role, interpreting and enforcing the "constitutional law" alongside all other law. This is the process of judicial review whereby the Supreme Court checks legislative and executive actions and ensures they are consonant with the Constitution. Within these parameters, judicial review combined with a Bill of Rights helps ensure finding the tricky balance between majority versus minority and individual versus collective rights.

In the latter half of the twentieth century, the American Supreme Court became active in striking down legal barriers of racial discrimination. Using the Fourteenth Amendment's guarantee of "equal protection of the laws" by state governments, it also gradually expanded its judicial activism into other areas of public policy. This led to questions about the undemocratic nature of judicial review. While individual rights were often protected and expanded, judicial activism brought into question the issue of "rule by consent."

The British tradition, upon which Canadian jurisprudence is largely based, contained no written constitutional prohibitions to check the power of Parliament. Moreover, the courts do not interpret or enforce the unwritten constitutional conventions. But this opens up the possibility of violations of individual rights, and does not necessarily prevent the tyranny of the majority. However, the protection of rights does not simply depend on their articulation in a constitution. Instead, a society's values, attitudes, beliefs, and the moral quality of civic life may be enough to guarantee those rights. Alexis de Tocquville made this observation when he compared Great Britain to another country that has a written constitution, Switzerland, when he said, "In England there seems to be more liberty in the customs than in the laws of the people."[14]

While the Canadian Constitution was modelled on British practices, there was one major deviation from the start. This was the introduction of federalism (see below), or two levels of government, in contrast to Great Britain's unitary model of government. The BNA Act, 1867 contains a division of powers between the federal and provincial governments. The Supreme Court came to be an arbiter or umpire when the two levels of government could not agree over the jurisdiction of a given law. In this role, it frequently adjudicated questions of rights and civil liberties disguised as disputes over the division of powers. Thus, parliamentary supremacy combined with the rule of law, the division of powers, and the moral quality of civic life to protect Canadians.

Strangely, though, the Fathers of Confederation were blithely disinterested in the issue of judicial review of a federal system of government. This was the case even though the American experience with judicial review had, by 1867, clearly revealed the crucial importance of the Supreme Court in influencing the distribution of powers between the state and national governments. Indeed, the BNA Act, 1867 gave the federal Parliament the power to create a "General Court of Appeal for Canada," but said nothing about its powers or role in adjudicating disputes between the levels of government. In the United States, Chief Justice Marshall had articulated a role as constitutional arbiter for the American Supreme Court in the case *Marbury v Madison* in 1803.[15] This case gave the Supreme Court the power to strike down any act of government that, in the court's view, violated the Constitution. The Canadian Supreme Court and its predecessor, the British Judicial Committee of the Privy Council (JCPC), assumed the same power, "without explicit acknowledgement and despite the incompatibility of judicial review with the traditional British theory of parliamentary supremacy."[16]

Nonetheless, apart from the British legacy, living next door to the heart of modern liberal democracy inevitably influenced the trajectory of Canada's legal and constitutional system. In 1960, the government of Prime Minister John Diefenbaker enacted a Bill of Rights, although it was not entrenched in the Constitution and only applied to federal law. Then, in 1982, the *Canadian Charter of Rights and Freedoms* (*Charter*) was added to the Constitution along with a constitutional amending formula as part of the patriation of the Constitution. This step fundamentally altered the relationship between the executive, legislative, and judicial branches by allowing the courts to place explicit limitations on the law-making power of Parliament. However, out of respect for the doctrine of parliamentary supremacy, a compromise was added to the *Charter* in section 33 that allowed Parliament and provincial legislatures to pass laws "notwithstanding" that they might violate certain rights. Thus, the principle of the consent of the governed was reinforced.

As a result of these developments, it could be said that the Canadian system contains important elements of both the British and American models of liberal democracy. Both the United States and Canada impart an important role for the courts in interpreting and enforcing constitutional rights. They are essentially the same, only different, as with so many other Canadian-American comparisons. The differences include the means by which Supreme Court rulings can be reversed. In the United States, this requires either constitutional amendment or packing the Court with partisan judicial appointments who will endeavour to overturn legal precedents. Such was the case when Republican President Trump selected three conservative judges to fill vacancies on the Court and join three other conservative justices to overturn the *Roe v Wade* abortion ruling in

2022 (see Chapter 5). In Canada, the path to reversing judicial decisions can involve invoking section 33, the notwithstanding clause, which allows governments to pass legislation that violates certain *Charter* rights for a period of up to five years at a time. Traditionally, governments have been reluctant to do so, but several provincial governments and one territorial government have used it (see Box 2.1).

---

**Box 2.1. The Use of the Notwithstanding Clause in Canada**

The notwithstanding clause can be invoked to pass controversial laws that override the rights of citizens. Four provinces and one territory have passed laws invoking the notwithstanding clause, most frequently by Quebec. It invoked a blanket application of the clause to every law from 1982 to 1985, a French-only sign law in 1988, a law prohibiting public sector employees from wearing religious coverings in 2019, and a law strengthening the use of French in 2022. Saskatchewan passed a back-to-work law invoking the clause in 1986, and passed a law in 2018 (never brought into force) invoking the clause to permit the government to pay for non-Catholics to attend publicly funded Catholic schools. Alberta passed a law invoking the clause in 2000 to define marriage as "between a man and a woman"; this law was effectively declared *ultra vires* by the Supreme Court of Canada because only the federal Parliament can define marriage. In 2021, Ontario passed a law invoking the clause to limit third-party group activities in the lead-up to an election. Ontario also threatened to use the clause in 2022 to limit workers' collective bargaining rights, but a public outcry and a court challenge caused the government to back down. Yukon used it once, but the law to which it would have applied never passed. The federal Parliament has never introduced legislation invoking the clause.

Source: Tsvi Kahana, "The Notwithstanding Clause in Canada: The First Forty Years" 60 *Osgoode Hall Law Journal* (Winter 2023), online: https://canlii.ca/t/7n3xs.

## 2) The Role of the Judges and Courts: Federalism and Criminal Justice

As noted above, in a system of federalism, there are two or more levels of government. The Canadian Constitution expressly enumerates powers of both levels of government in a division of powers; federal powers are listed in section 91 of the Constitution, while provincial powers are listed in section 92. The powers listed for the federal government includes the residual power that says the federal government may make laws for the "peace, order and good government of Canada."

The United States Constitution lists all the powers of the national government in article I, section 8, then says in the Tenth Amendment that any powers not listed remain those of the states. So while provincial government powers are listed explicitly in the Canadian Constitution, state government powers are not listed in the American Constitution. The American Constitution contains a supremacy clause that states that whenever a national law and state law are in conflict, the national law is supreme.

In Canada, major criminal offences are violations of the federal *Criminal Code*, and penalties are devised by the national government. The administration of justice is a provincial matter, so trials occur in provincial courts. The major courts are funded by the federal government, which also appoints most judges. In the United States, most crimes such as murder, rape, and theft are violations of state laws, and each state has its own laws regarding what is criminal and what penalties are applied. This explains the variation in laws across states, including with regard to the death penalty, legalization of marijuana, abortion, and other issues. States fund and administer their own court systems, and federal courts have their own system of trial courts for crimes under federal law, like counterfeiting, kidnapping across state lines, postal fraud, murder of a federal employee, etc.

## 3) The Court Systems and the Supreme Courts

In Canada, the law is bijural. This awkward term simply means Canada employs both the English common law and the French civil law traditions in the administration of justice. The basis of common law is the cumulative body of law dating from the thirteenth century in England wherein judges dispense justice on the basis of past custom and on the precedents built up over the years in prior legal findings. The civil law is derived originally from Roman law; the Emperor Justinian ordered the consolidation of all laws in 529. Later, Napoleon ordered the codification of French law on this basis of Roman law, and the *Napoleonic Code* was created in 1804 as an authoritative written record of all laws. The *Civil Code* in Quebec, a key part of the distinctive political culture of the province, is a legacy of the early relationship between French and English after the Conquest in 1759. It was the *Quebec Act* of 1774, which permitted the continuation of civil law, that made Canada a bijural country. The common law is applied outside Quebec in matters of private law, and the *Civil Code* is applied to private law matters inside Quebec. Common law is used, though, for public law both inside and outside Quebec.[17]

Increasingly, these two legal systems have been influenced by the growing jurisprudence found in Indigenous legal traditions as well. According to the federal Department of Justice:

> Aboriginal peoples in Canada have also contributed to our legal system. Aboriginal rights and treaty rights are recognized and protected under the Constitution. Aboriginal rights are those related to the historical occupancy and use of the land by Aboriginal peoples; treaty rights are those set out in treaties entered into by the Crown and a particular group of Aboriginal people. Reserves, for example, are the responsibility of the federal government.
>
> Aboriginal customs and traditions have also contributed to new ways of dealing with people, such as healing and sentencing circles, community justice and restorative justice.[18]

In 1982, Aboriginal rights were recognized and affirmed in the *Canadian Charter of Rights and Freedoms*. This was a first, as was the appearance of the terms "Aboriginal," "Inuit," and "Metis" in the Canadian Constitution. Several contemporary developments contributed to an increasing interest in Indigenous jurisprudence, including the 1996 Royal Commission on Aboriginal Peoples (RCAP), and numerous ongoing civil rights, treaty, and land claims settlement processes. Indigenous law is still evolving; the Supreme Court of Canada has delivered a number of ground-breaking decisions regarding Aboriginal legal issues, but it has not yet authoritatively determined the content of Aboriginal law.[19]

The legal system in Canada reflects the presence of federalism in that there are both federal and provincial courts. There is some horizontal integration between them in that some cases heard in provincial courts can be appealed to the Supreme Court of Canada. The Constitution references the courts in several sections. The creation of courts by the provinces is authorized in section 92; the provinces also appoint the judges to these courts. Section 96 also authorizes the provinces to create courts, but with judges appointed by the federal government. Section 101 authorizes the creation of courts by the federal government, which also appoints the judges.

A rather elaborate federal judicial system was thus brought into existence, at the apex of which sits the Supreme Court of Canada. Established in 1875, it did not actually become "supreme" as the final court of appeal until 1949.[20] The Supreme Court is empowered to hear all kinds of cases, including common, civil, criminal, statutory, administrative, constitutional, federal, and provincial.

Beyond this, a rather complicated and somewhat confusing court system exists in Canada. While England provided the template for the court system, it was a unitary country, not a federal one. So while Canada attempted to fuse the features of two systems into one, it did not take the logical path that the United States took — create two parallel independent sets of courts. For matters falling within state jurisdiction, the United States has state supreme courts and courts of appeal; for matters falling within federal jurisdiction, it has federal district courts and courts of appeal (discussed below). Instead, England's basic structure of inferior and superior trial courts and two appeal courts was appended to a federal structure in Canada. The most significant features of this system include the following.

First, most matters arising under federal or provincial law are dealt with by courts that are administered by the provinces. These courts have remained largely as they had been when the province entered Confederation. Unlike the United States, there is no distinction between the courts that try matters of federal law and those that try matters of provincial law. Second, the judges of these courts may be federally — or provincially — appointed. The seriousness of the matter determines whether a case goes to a superior court for trial before a federally appointed judge. Third, all appeals from provincially appointed courts, including matters of provincial law, are heard by federally appointed judges. However, superior and provincial appeal courts are administered by each province while the Supreme Court of Canada is administered by the federal government.[21]

In the United States, below the federal Supreme Court are the federal courts of appeal, and below them are the district courts, which are the general trial courts for federal law. Separate from, but not entirely independent of, this federal court system are the individual court systems of each state, each dealing with its own laws and having its own judicial rules and procedures. The Supreme Court of each state (which does not always have "Supreme Court" as an official name) is the final authority on the interpretation of that state's laws and constitution. A case may be appealed from a state court to the federal Supreme Court only if there is a federal question (an issue arising under the Constitution, or laws/treaties of the United States). The relationship between federal and state laws is quite complex; together, they form the United States law.

The federal judiciary consists of the Supreme Court, whose justices are appointed for life by the president and confirmed by the Senate, and various "lower" or "inferior courts," among which are the courts of appeals and district courts. The first Congress divided the nation into judicial districts and created federal courts for each district. From that beginning has evolved the present structure: the Supreme Court, thirteen courts of appeals, ninety-four district courts, and several courts of special jurisdiction. Congress retains the power to create and abolish federal courts, as well as to determine the number of judges in the federal judiciary system. It cannot, however, abolish the Supreme Court.

There are three levels of federal courts with general jurisdiction, meaning that these courts handle criminal cases and civil lawsuits between individuals. The other courts, such as the bankruptcy courts and the tax court, are specialized courts handling only certain kinds of cases. The bankruptcy courts are branches of the district courts, but technically are not considered part of the "Article III" judiciary because their judges do not have lifetime tenure. Similarly, the tax court is not an Article III court. The United States district courts are the "trial courts" where cases are filed and decided. The United States courts of appeals are "appellate courts" that hear appeals of cases decided by the district courts, and some direct appeals from administrative agencies. The Supreme Court hears appeals from the decisions of the courts of appeals or state Supreme Courts (on constitutional matters), as well as having original jurisdiction over a very small number of cases.

The federal judicial power extends to cases arising under the Constitution, an Act of Congress, or a United States treaty; cases affecting ambassadors, ministers, and consuls of foreign countries in the United States; controversies in which the United States government is a party; controversies between states (or their citizens) and foreign nations (or their citizens or subjects); and bankruptcy cases. The Eleventh Amendment removed from federal jurisdiction cases in which citizens of one state were the plaintiffs and the government of another state was the defendant. It did not disturb federal jurisdiction in cases in which a state government is a plaintiff and a citizen of another state the defendant.

The power of the federal courts extends both to civil actions for damages and other redress, and to criminal cases arising under federal law. Article III has resulted in a complex set of relationships between state and federal courts. Ordinarily, federal courts do not hear cases arising under the laws of individual states. However, some cases over which federal courts have jurisdiction may also be heard and decided by state courts. Both court systems thus have exclusive jurisdiction in some areas and concurrent jurisdiction in others.

The Constitution safeguards judicial independence by providing that federal judges shall hold office "during good behavior." Usually they serve until they die, retire, or resign. A judge who commits an offence while in office may be impeached in the same way as the president or other officials of the federal government. While no American president has ever been convicted and removed as president after an impeachment trial, eight federal judges have been convicted and removed, often due to allegations of bribery. The most recent such conviction was in 2010. United States judges are appointed by the president and confirmed by the Senate. Another constitutional provision prohibits Congress from reducing the pay of any judge. Congress could enact a new lower salary applying to future judges, but not to those already serving.

## 4) The Supreme Courts

In both countries, the Supreme Court is the highest court in the federal court system. The American Supreme Court deals with matters pertaining to the federal government, disputes between states, and interpretation of the Constitution, and can declare legislation or executive action made at any level of the government as unconstitutional nullifying the law and creating precedent for future law and decisions.

In Canada, both the federal and provincial governments can ask the Supreme Court to give an opinion on a constitutional issue. This is called a "reference case." In the United States, the Supreme

Court will not give advice and generally does not rule on hypothetical situations, hence there are no reference cases. In the American legal system, someone must have standing to bring a case to court; they must prove that a law has individually and directly affected them before a court will hear the case. For instance, if the Congress wanted to declare an official religion, this clearly violates the Constitution's First Amendment, which forbids the establishment of an official religion. But Congress could pass the law anyhow. If Congress asked the court first if they could do it, the court would not answer. After the law passed, someone could sue and say the law was in violation of the Constitution, and it would be that person who brought the case to the courts and eventually to the Supreme Court if it got appealed through the system.

We noted above that in Canada, the BNA Act, 1867 allowed for the creation of a Supreme Court, but it was not actually created until 1879 and not made "supreme" until 1949. Prior to 1949, the Judicial Committee of the Privy Council (JCPC), a panel of British law lords who advised the monarch, heard appeals from Canadian courts. The Governor General on the advice of the prime minister appoints the nine judges of the Supreme Court. A powerful constitutional convention dictates that three of the judges must come from Quebec and be versed in the civil law; three judges come from Ontario, two from Western Canada, and one from Atlantic Canada.

The appointment process has recently undergone reforms intended to ensure it is more transparent and not tainted by overt political considerations. While partisanship among the Canadian judges has not been an issue in the past, the perception that the appointments made by the prime minister alone lacked legitimacy occasionally surfaced. An eight-member independent, non-partisan Advisory Board first identifies suitable candidates for appointment, and then receives and seeks out applications. The Advisory Board then develops a shortlist of three to five names using specific criteria that have been made public and that reflect that the nominees are eminently qualified jurists, bilingual, and representative of the wider Canadian society. Then, a broad-based set of consultations is undertaken by the minister of justice. It includes feedback from the Chief Justice of Canada, relevant provincial and territorial attorneys general, relevant Cabinet ministers, and opposition justice critics, as well as members of both the House of Commons Standing Committee on Justice and Human Rights and the Standing Senate Committee on Legal and Constitutional Affairs. A recommendation is then made by the minister of justice to the prime minister who chooses and announces the nominee. The minister of justice and the chairperson of the Advisory Board will then appear before the House of Commons Standing Committee on Justice and Human Rights to explain why the nominee was selected. Finally, members of the House of Commons Standing Committee on Justice and Human Rights and the Standing Senate Committee on Legal and Constitutional Affairs, along with a representative from each party with seats in the House, are invited to take part in a question-and-answer period with the nominee, which is moderated by a law professor. This process is described by the government of Canada as an opportunity "to get acquainted with" the future justice.[22]

This vetting process has proven to be far less political and controversial than the Senate ratification of American Supreme Court judges often is (discussed below). In any event, political scandal and controversy over Canadian Supreme Court appointments are rare. One recent exception was the so-called Nadon affair in 2014. Prime Minister Stephen Harper attempted to fill a vacancy on the Court that by convention goes to a Quebec judge versed in civil law. Marc Nadon was a Federal Court of Appeal judge from Quebec, but he had been retired for two years, had practised maritime law when a judge, and had not practised at the Quebec bar for twenty years. His appointment was challenged by a Toronto constitutional lawyer who said that it was a violation of the constitutional convention that stated that three judges must come from Quebec and be trained in civil law. The Supreme Court heard the case and ruled 6:1 that Nadon was not eligible to be appointed. This was a major slap in the face for Harper, but demonstrated the importance of the constitutional convention that three judges must come from

Quebec and that certain legal and constitutional principles were judged inviolable even over the wishes of a prime minister.

Political partisanship is also less pronounced in the Canadian legal system, including on the Supreme Court, where judicial philosophy outweighs partisan considerations in the judges' deliberations. For instance, the Harper government lost several high-profile cases before the Supreme Court, including the striking down of prostitution laws, two of the government's tough-on-crime provisions, and Senate reform provisions, even though the majority of judges on the highest Court were his appointments. The Trudeau government has sometimes experienced the same fate:

> Take *R. v. Ndhlovu*, which dealt with the *Criminal Code* provisions requiring lifetime mandatory registration on the national sex offender registry. A majority of five — all but one appointed by Liberal prime ministers — found that law infringed the *Canadian Charter of Rights and Freedoms* and could not be saved under the "reasonable limits" clause. A partial dissent was written by Justice Russell Brown, who was appointed by former prime minister Stephen Harper, and it was joined by three other judges who were also appointed by Harper. One could reasonably wonder what role partisanship plays in a case such as this.[23]

The American Supreme Court was established pursuant to Article III of the United States Constitution in 1789 as the highest federal court in the United States. The nine judges of the Supreme Court are appointed by the president and confirmed by the Senate. The judges often divide along partisan lines on important issues. The 2022 overturning of the abortion case *Roe v Wade* is an example.

Political scandal and controversy over American Supreme Court appointments is more common compared to the Canadian experience. Appointment of United States Supreme Court judges attracts considerable attention from the press and advocacy groups, which lobby senators to confirm or to reject a nominee depending on whether their track record aligns with the group's views. The Senate Judiciary Committee conducts hearings and votes on whether the nomination should go to the full Senate with a positive, negative, or neutral report. In 2016, the Republican-dominated Senate refused to hold any vote on whether to confirm President Obama's Supreme Court nominee, Merrick Garland.

Among the many high-profile scandals attached to American Supreme Court appointments was the Kavanaugh case. President Trump nominated Brett Kavanaugh to the Supreme Court on 9 July 2018 to fill the position vacated by retiring justice Anthony Kennedy. Palo Alto University Professor of Psychology Christine Blasey Ford contacted a *Washington Post* reporter with allegations that Kavanaugh had sexually assaulted her in the early 1980s while the two of them were in high school. Two other women also accused Kavanaugh of sexual misconduct. Kavanaugh denied all three allegations. Media attention on the appointment process was extensive. Following a supplemental Republican-controlled Senate Judiciary Committee hearing, a majority of the Committee voted to send the nomination to the full Senate floor. After an additional FBI investigation, which Democrats criticized, the Senate confirmed Kavanaugh's nomination by a vote of 50:48 on 6 October, and he was sworn in later that day.

Kavanaugh was but one of several Trump appointments that affected the partisan balance of the Supreme Court. Any president whose party controls the Senate, as Trump did from 2017 to 2020, has the opportunity to pack the Court with partisan judges. This has made the Court a far more political body than is the case for the Canadian Supreme Court. Comparing the two countries in this regard invites assessment of the merits of partisan appointments of judges.

## Conclusion

In the United States, the "checks and balances" system divides power between the legislative branch (Congress), the executive branch (the president), and the judicial branch (the Supreme Court and courts below it) on the understanding that, as noted above, "ambition must be made to counteract ambition," and to avoid hasty decision making or abuses of power. In Canada, the legislative branch (Parliament) and the executive branch (prime minister and Cabinet) are fused. Power is more centralized with the executive and legislative branches working together, but with the former clearly dominating the latter. The system is more efficient than the American model, but arguably suffers from a greater democratic deficit. The judicial system in Canada is, however, separate from the other two branches.

In the United States, there is a single accountable executive democratically chosen by the people who acts as both the head of state and head of government. There is no role for a leader like the queen or king of England who serves because their ancestors were the most successful at killing their opponents. In Canada, the separation of head of state and head of government makes the prime minister less a symbol of the nation than the president, but since the prime minister has by convention taken on many of the Governor General's constitutional roles, this has not acted as a limit on the prime minister's power.

In the United States, there is more of a role for local interests in policymaking (choosing candidates, weaker parties). In Canada, there is more emphasis on national interests in federal policymaking, since national political institutions have largely failed to be as representative of regional interests as was originally intended. In the United States, the government is more stable overall, with fixed terms of office and no such thing as a minority government that can lose a vote of no confidence. It is hard to remove a president, and House incumbents who run again almost always win re-election (about 98 percent of the time in recent years). There have been only five changes of party control in the House in the last seventy years. In Canada, if the people are unhappy with the current prime minister, a vote of no confidence can be initiated, a process arguably much easier than the impeachment and conviction of a president. Alternately, in Canada, the prime minister's party can overthrow them. In the past seventy years, the largest party in the House of Commons has changed eight times.

The judicial branches are similar in many ways, but differ in the relationship between federal courts and state or provincial courts, in the appointment process for judges, and in the special role for the Quebec *Civil Code*, which has no equivalent in the United States. Canada's Notwithstanding Clause in the *Canadian Charter of Rights and Freedoms* also has no equivalent in the United States Bill of Rights, nor do Canadian reference questions to seek Supreme Court advice exist in the United States. In Canada, criminal law is mostly determined at the federal level, and in the United States, it is mostly determined at the state government level.

Comparing political institutions reveals the similarities and differences in the political systems of both countries. The powers of prime ministers and presidents have been assessed, the distinctions between Parliament and Congress have been described, and the influence and role of the Supreme Courts in each country have been outlined. How the executive, legislative, and judicial branches influence and are influenced by democracy has been described as well. Returning to the theme of similarities and differences, we note how the core political institutions of both countries — the executive, legislative, and judicial branches — are strikingly similar, yet equally strikingly different. A pattern of similarities and differences is also found in the two nations' electoral systems and voting, subjects of the next chapter.

CHAPTER THREE

# Comparative Elections and Voting: Do Canadians Have Too Few Electoral Choices, or Do Americans Have Too Many?

## Introduction

Do Canadians have too few electoral choices, or do Americans have too many? Why are there so many more viable political parties in Canada than in the United States? Why are there more elected positions in the United States, where voters vote with much more frequency than Canadians? What role does money play in elections in the two countries? This chapter looks at the similarities and differences between the two countries in terms of how they conduct elections and voting, and the party systems in Canada and the United States.

## A. Elections in Canada and the United States

### 1) Frequency of Voting

Both Canada and the United States are democracies, but they run their electoral systems and practise party politics in strikingly different ways. Consider the frequency with which a citizen votes, for instance. Most Americans can vote at least twice a year every year — Canadians do not vote anywhere near as often. In the United States, primary elections, in which official candidates for Democratic and Republican parties for various offices are chosen, occur every year. Primary election dates vary by state; in Pennsylvania, for instance, they are always in April or May. Texas usually holds them in March. California and several other states hold them in June, while Florida holds theirs in August and Massachusetts in September. The United States general election is always in November, where voters choose between Democrat, Republican, or (sometimes) Independent candidates for office. That is a lot of voting!

If you live in the city of Toronto, you would normally vote for five offices over a four-year period. In September 2021, you would have had the opportunity to vote in a federal election for one candidate for Member of Parliament (MP) in Ottawa; in June 2022, you could have voted in a provincial election for one candidate for Member of the Provincial Parliament (MPP). In October 2022, you could have voted in a municipal election for a city councilor, school board trustee, and mayor. Due to the resignation of the mayor, Torontonians voted for that office again in June 2023, but normally, most Toronto voters would have had no government elections in 2023 or 2024.

If you live in Erie, Pennsylvania, over that same four-year period, you could have voted for up to eighty offices in elections that occur twice per year. Over half of these elections are for judges, whereas in Canada, no judges are elected. In 2022, Pennsylvania elected a governor; a lieutenant governor; a United States senator in Washington, DC; a United States Representative in Washington, DC; and a state representative in Harrisburg, the state capital. In 2023, Erie residents even voted for county coroner. A local funeral director has always won the job. While it might not be clear what a funeral director would know about criminal forensic investigations, the good people of Erie made that choice nonetheless. And who could argue with *vox populi*? According to one 2022 study, there were 519,682 elected officials in the United States, 96 percent of whom were local, 3.6 percent were state, and 0.1 percent were federal.[1]

Comparative Elections and Voting

## 2) Candidate Selection

Another difference between the two countries is in how candidates for office are chosen. In the United States, national or state party leaders have no input into who local voters choose in primaries to run as candidates under the party label. This can result in some odd and controversial choices. For example, in 2010 a United States Senate election was held in Delaware to replace Joe Biden, who had become vice president. National Republicans wanted United States Representative Mike Castle to be their party nominee; he was a moderate and polls showed he would easily beat the Democratic candidate in the November general election. But Republican rank-and-file voters in the primary instead chose Christine O'Donnell to be their nominee. O'Donnell had never held political office; she was best known for speaking out against evolution and for being an anti-masturbation activist. After she won the primary, comedian Bill Maher revealed that O'Donnell once said she dabbled in witchcraft, which became something of a national joke and which prompted O'Donnell to release a rather unusual campaign ad with the opening line "I'm not a witch. I'm nothing you've heard. I'm you."[2] In the end, O'Donnell still got 40 percent of the vote in the general election against the winning Democrat.

In 1990, Republican voters in Louisiana chose David Duke to be the official candidate for the United States Senate in a primary election over the objections of many national party leaders. Duke was a former grand dragon of the racist Ku Klux Klan (KKK) and student leader of the American Nazi Party. Duke lost the general election to a Democrat. Local Republican voters chose Duke again as their candidate in the 1991 election for Louisiana governor, and he lost to a Democrat again.

In 2017, a special election (the United States equivalent of a by-election in Canada) was held in Alabama for the United States Senate to replace Jeff Sessions, who resigned to become United States Attorney General. National and state Republican leaders favoured Alabama State Attorney General Luther Strange to be the Republican nominee, but Republican voters instead chose Roy Moore in a primary election to be their candidate. Moore had twice been elected as Chief Justice of the Alabama Supreme Court, and had been removed both times by panels of Alabama judges. The first time, in 2003, it was for installing a Ten Commandments monument in the Alabama Supreme Court building and refusing to remove it after federal judges said the monument violates the United States Constitution regarding the separation of church and state. Moore was elected Alabama Chief Justice again in 2012 and removed a second time in 2017 after he ordered all Alabama judges to ignore a United States Supreme Court ruling about same-sex marriage and ordered Alabama judges not to allow same-sex marriages. Moore was also a leader in the birther movement between 2008 and 2016 — the racist movement that falsely claimed that President Barack Obama was not born in the United States. (Donald Trump was also a leader in that movement.) Moore also called for a ban on Muslims serving in the American Congress. After he won the nomination, news stories came out that when he was in his thirties, Moore liked to date high school girls. Allegations about sexual contact with a fourteen-year-old girl, the alleged rape of a sixteen-year-old girl, and many others that Moore dated or tried to date, along with his being banned from Gadsden Shopping Mall where he would troll for young girls, all emerged. Moore denied it all, but lost to a Democrat in the general election, 50 percent to 48 percent. Alabama is a state that almost always voted Republican, so this was seen as a major repudiation of Moore and of Trump who had publicly endorsed Moore.

In Canada, candidates for MP or MPP are chosen at local riding association meetings by local party activists. If you join a political party, you can have direct input into who you want your candidate to be, as in the United States. But in Canada, all candidates must be approved by national party leaders for federal elections or by provincial party leaders for provincial elections, so there is far less chance that an O'Donnell, Duke, or Moore would be selected to run for a party in Canada. Occasionally it is discovered after the election campaign is under way that a candidate has an unsavoury past, and the party will remove them as their official candidate. Such was the case in 2021, when Conservative Party candidate Lisa Robinson was revealed to have authored Islamophobic tweets when she had been a city councilor, a charge that she denied. Because the campaign was under way, her name was already on the ballot for the election despite having been disowned by the Conservative Party. She lost to the Liberal candidate. In that same election, Liberal candidate Kevin Vuong won his riding in a close-fought race after the Liberals cut ties with him just days before the election over a sexual assault charge that was later dropped. Vuong subsequently took his seat as an Independent. The New Democratic Party removed two candidates — Dan Osborne in a Nova Scotia riding and Sidney Coles, the candidate for a downtown Toronto riding — after both made antisemitic comments.

There is also the opportunity for party leaders to override the choices made by local riding associations and "parachute" their preferred candidate into a riding. This is often done if a high profile or famous person wants to run, and the party leadership thinks that person will almost certainly help win the riding. This can be a very controversial process, though, as rank-and-file members often resent this usurpation of their local control over the candidate selection process.

Both systems represent democratic models of candidate selection, but they are clearly different. In the United States, candidate selection is entirely in the hands of the rank-and-file party members. National and state party leaders have no say in who the local people select. In Canada, party leaders have the opportunity to veto choices made by rank-and-file party members if they think the candidate is too controversial, or if they want to install their own preferred candidate.

## 3) The Party Systems in Canada and the United States

The two largest political parties in both the United States and Canada contained supporters from a broad ideological spectrum during the late 1800s and for most of the 1900s. These "big tent" or "catch all" parties included strong conservatives and strong liberals in both the United States Republican and Democratic parties and frequent moderate dominance of the Canadian Liberal and Conservative parties (the latter known as the Progressive Conservative party during the second half of the twentieth century).

The modern Canadian multi-party system consists of parties that range from socialist to neoconservative. Liberal ideological positions typically predominate nationally. At the provincial level there is a great deal of variation across the country. The national Liberal Party can be said to be ideologically to the right on the economy, and to the left on social policy. The national Conservative Party, which has undergone several name changes in the past three decades and is an amalgamation of the Progressive Conservative, Reform, and Alliance parties, is ideologically to the right on the economy and on social policy. The New Democratic Party (NDP), whose original name until 1960 was the Cooperative Commonwealth Federation, is ideologically to the left on the economy and on social policy. The Bloc Québécois is a federal party that runs candidates only within the province of Quebec and its main *raison d'être* is to promote the independence of Quebec. Ideologically, it is generally to the left. There is also a minor party focused on environmental issues, the Green Party, with both right and left ideological elements. Over Canada's history, various minor protest parties of the right and left have appeared and disappeared. They have provided the important function of introducing innovation in policy as well as acting as an outlet for protest.

The American party system consists of two main parties. The Republican Party is ideologically to the right on the economy and on social policy. Some elements have embraced radical populism as well. The Democratic Party is ideologically to the left on the economy and on social policy. It contains some socialist elements as well. There are, in addition, Independents. They come from across the political spectrum. For example, in 1991, Bernie Sanders began to represent Vermont in Congress as an Independent, although he sat with, worked with, and became a candidate for the leadership of the Democratic Party. He is the longest-serving Independent in congressional history.

One major difference in the party systems in the two countries occurs at the state and provincial levels. In the United States, the Democratic and Republican parties are by far the two largest parties in all fifty states. In 2024, all fifty governors were either Democrats or Republicans, and all fifty state legislatures were controlled by one of those two parties. In Canada, provincial party systems differ greatly from those at the national level. A majority of right-leaning provincial parties retain the Progressive Conservative name that the national party abandoned two decades ago. In Alberta, the governing party in 2024 was called the United Conservatives. In Quebec, the governing party was called Coalition Avenir Québec and had no national equivalent. In Saskatchewan, the governing party was the Saskatchewan Party. The Liberal Party had no presence in provincial government in the Western provinces, and the NDP barely had any prominence in provincial politics in some of the Eastern provinces.

## 4) Electoral Systems in Canada and the United States

As we noted above, Canadians usually vote no more than five times over four years, and Canada does not have primary elections. Canadian elections must occur within a five-year time period after the last election, but the date can vary. Fixed election dates were introduced in 2007 by the government of Stephen Harper, although it is still possible for a prime minister to call an early election (see Chapter 2).

The Canadian electoral system is a "single-member plurality" or "first-past-the-post" system. In every electoral district, the candidate with the most votes wins a seat in the House of Commons and represents that riding as its MP. This means that candidates need not receive more than 50 percent of the vote (an absolute majority) to be elected. This has proven to be very controversial, since parties that

**TABLE 3.1. COMPARISON OF THE PERCENTAGE OF POPULAR VOTE VERSUS SEATS, 2019 AND 2021 CANADIAN FEDERAL GENERAL ELECTIONS**

|  | 2019 % Popular Vote | 2019 % Seats | 2021 % Popular Vote | 2021 % Seats |
|---|---|---|---|---|
| Liberals | 33.1 | 46.4 | 32.62 | 47.34 |
| Conservatives | 34.4 | 35.8 | 33.74 | 35.21 |
| Bloc Québécois | 7.7 | 9.5 | 7.64 | 9.47 |
| NDP | 15.9 | 7.1 | 17.82 | 7.40 |
| Green | 6.5 | 0.9 | 2.33 | 0.59 |
| Independent | 0.4 | 0.3 | 0.19 | 0.00 |
| People's Party | 1.6 | 0.0 | 4.94 | 0.00 |

capture less than half the popular vote are frequently rewarded with more than half the seats in the House of Commons or provincial legislatures (see Table 3.1).[3] The provinces of Prince Edward Island, British Columbia, and Ontario have all held referenda on electoral reform, but all failed to pass. Justin Trudeau campaigned in 2015 on a promise to reform the electoral system, but abandoned that promise once elected.

All American states also have single-member district systems for the United States House of Representatives, in which states are carved into districts of equal populations, each district electing one member to the House. For the United States Senate, states operate statewide as dual-member districts. Most states also elect members of Congress by plurality or first-past-the-post.

However, six states have modified their electoral systems to require majority votes (more than 50 percent) to get elected to Congress and some other offices. In Georgia and Louisiana, if no candidate wins more than half of the vote in a first election, a runoff election will occur between the top two candidates. In California and Washington State, all candidates for an office from all parties run on the same ballot in a primary election, and the top two automatically go on to the general election in November. Maine and Alaska have systems of ranked choice voting, where voters can rank all the candidates for an office instead of just choosing one. In usually Republican Alaska, this led to a surprise victory for a Democratic Congressional candidate in 2022 against two less popular Republicans.

## 5) Creating Legislative Districts

Creating legislative districts differs substantially in Canada compared to the United States. In the former, setting electoral boundaries has been a non-partisan affair since 1964, handled by an arm's-length agency; in the latter, it is usually a partisan affair run by the political parties that control state governments at any given in time.

"Gerrymander" is a term derived from the early 1800s in the United States. It is a portmanteau of "Gerry" and "salamander." Elbridge Gerry was governor of Massachusetts in 1812, and he signed a law to create state Senate districts that favoured his party, including one district that a local cartoonist said looked like a salamander. The American Constitution says that states determine how elections occur, so most states have partisan state legislatures that create districts for the House of Representatives. Most modern gerrymandering is done by majority parties in state legislatures to create partisan advantages through two main methods: "packing," in which voters of the opposing party are packed into as few districts as possible; and "cracking," in which voters of the opposing party are divided up so they cannot form a majority anywhere.

Partisan gerrymandering has been criticized as the politicians selecting the voters instead of the voters selecting the politicians. It has become more extreme in the United States in the past thirty years due to sophisticated computer and mathematical modelling. For example, Pennsylvania's seventh congressional district between 2013 and 2018 is often cited as an example of partisan gerrymandering and made CNN's list of most obscenely gerrymandered congressional districts in America. Its shape has been

**FIGURE 3.1. PENNSYLVANIA'S 7TH CONGRESSIONAL DISTRICT, 2013-2018**

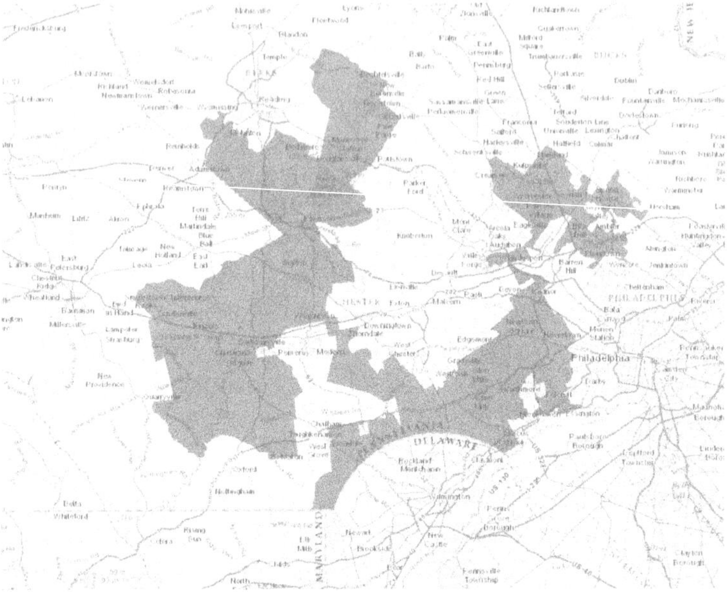

Source: United States Department of the Interior.

mockingly said to resemble Goofy kicking Donald Duck (see Figure 3.1).[4]

The United States Supreme Court has typically ruled in previous cases that partisan gerrymanders are allowed by the United States Constitution, but challenges continue. In January 2018, the Pennsylvania State Supreme Court ruled that gerrymandered congressional districts violated the Pennsylvania state constitution, which requires that elections "shall be free and equal." The court enlisted the aid of Stanford law and politics professor Nathaniel Persily to create new districts.[5] In 2022, four other State Supreme Courts ruled that partisan gerrymanders violated their state constitutions. Not all states resort to gerrymandering; ten states use bipartisan or non-partisan commissions to create congressional districts, including California.

In 1964, the *Electoral Boundaries Readjustment Act* ended "gerrymandering" in Canada. A non-partisan commission was created for each province chaired by a judge with two other members appointed by the Speaker of the House of Commons.[6] According to Elections Canada, the commissioners work to propose a new electoral map for their province by considering such criteria as average population numbers, communities of identity and interest, historical patterns of an electoral district, and geographic size of electoral districts. The districts can deviate from the average population figures by up to 25 percent to ensure representation in geographically under-populated and remote areas. As a result, some electoral districts are huge and sparsely populated, while others are small and densely populated. For example, the geographically largest district, Nunavut, sprawls over some 1,800,000 square kilometres and serves about 40,000 people, while the geographically smallest electoral district, Laurier–Sainte-Marie in Quebec, occupies only ten square kilometres, but serves a population of almost 117,000 residents.

The commissions consult with Canadians through public hearings, and submit a report on their considerations and proposed electoral map to the House of Commons. Objections from members of the House of Commons are considered as well, and a final report is prepared outlining the electoral boundaries for each province. However, as independent bodies, the commissions make all final decisions as to where these boundaries will lie.

## 6) (S)electing Party Leaders and Presidential Candidates

In Canada, there is no nation-wide election for prime minister, unlike for president in the United States. The prime minister is simply the leader of the party that wins the largest number of seats in the House of Commons in a general election. Leaders of parties are chosen in leadership conventions attended by party members selected as delegates from each riding across the country, and/or by all members of a party through an internet- or phone-based vote. For example, on 14 April 2013, 130,744 Liberal Party members chose

Justin Trudeau over five other candidates. On 10 April 2016, 65,782 New Democratic Party members chose Jagmeet Singh over three other candidates. On 10 September 2022, nearly 418,000 members cast ballots, choosing Pierre Poilievre as leader of the Conservative Party over four other candidates on the first ballot.

The American presidential primary election process is quite unlike anything in the Canadian system. Candidates from within a party declare that they want to seek the nomination to run for their party as the presidential candidate against the other party's presidential candidate. Party members in state primary elections vote for delegates to a national convention, not directly for a candidate. These delegates are pledged to a presidential candidate. A few states choose pledged delegates though a presidential caucus system rather than a primary. In a caucus, people show up to vote at one specific day and time, listen to speeches about each candidate, and then vote. Voter turnout tends to be dismal at these caucuses. For example, in 2024, the 110,000 voters who participated in the Iowa caucuses accounted for just less than 15 percent of the state's 752,000 registered Republicans. Nonetheless, some states continue to use caucuses to give more power to party activists.

Each party awards each state a certain number of delegates to the national convention, mostly based on its population but with other factors included, such as past support for the party. Party leaders like governors and members of Congress also attend conventions as unpledged delegates. Each party also awards the various territories small numbers of delegates. Candidates require more than half of the delegate votes to win. The process is often forgone, however, since one candidate has usually won a majority of pledged delegates before the convention is even held.

In 2024, unprecedented events occurred for the first time since the modern presidential primary process began in the 1970s. After a disastrous performance in an initial presidential candidate debate with Donald Trump, Joe Biden, who was 81 years old and showing strong signs of impaired mental acuity, was convinced to drop out of the race after all the primaries were over. Under Democratic Party rules, his pledged delegates were then free to cast their votes at the party convention for another candidate, Vice President Kamala Harris, who Biden endorsed to replace him after he had won almost all pledged delegates in primaries.

The selection of national party leaders in Canada has begun to take on some characteristics of American primary elections during the twenty-first century, with party members nationwide all voting for the national leaders rather than those national leaders being chosen at a national convention filled with local party leaders. But a major difference remains in that the selection of national party leaders in Canada is a national process that occurs across the country at the same time. In the United States, each state decides separately when to hold a presidential primary or caucus, and they can occur any time between January and June of a presidential election year. By tradition, Iowa and New Hampshire have gone first for many decades. They even have state laws saying they get to go first. But the early results in those two states tend to skew perceptions of candidate viability, because both states are very small and not at all representative of the broader American population. By the time states with later primaries in May or June get to vote, usually all but the winning candidates have dropped out of the campaign.

## 7) Presidential Elections and the Electoral College

As mentioned previously, there is no national election for prime minister in Canada. That position goes to the leader of the largest party in the House of Commons. But in the United States, voters elect the president through the Electoral College system. The Electoral College is used only for presidential elections. Each state gets a number of Electoral College votes exactly equal to the number of members it has in Congress (House + Senate = 535). For example, Pennsylvania got nineteen electoral votes in 2024, California got fifty-four, Texas got forty, New York got twenty-eight, and Delaware got three. Washington, DC, which is not part of any state, has no voting representation in Congress, but the Twenty-third Amendment to the Constitution (1961) gives DC voters three electoral votes for president, which adds up to a total of 538 electoral votes nationwide

A candidate must receive 270 or more Electoral College votes (more than half of 538) to win the presidency. Each party chooses electors to represent their state. These are usually long-time party loyalists who have served the party or occupied important positions within the party. Electors are supposed to vote for the presidential candidate who gains the largest popular vote in their state, but they are not legally bound to do so in every state. The winner of the most popular votes for a state gets all the Electoral College votes for that state in the forty-eight states that use "winner-take-all" systems for their electoral votes; if a candidate finishes first in one of those forty-eight states, they win all the electoral votes for that state. Two states — Maine and Nebraska — do not have winner-take-all systems for electoral votes; they award one electoral vote in each House of Representatives district and two more for the statewide winner. This allowed Donald Trump to win exactly one electoral vote in Maine in 2024 (with Harris winning Maine's other three electoral votes) and allowed Harris to win one electoral vote in Nebraska (with Trump winning Nebraska's other four electoral votes). Maine and Alaska now also use ranked choice systems to determine the winners of their electoral votes.

The 2016 presidential election is indicative of the quirks of the Electoral College system. In Pennsylvania, Republican presidential candidate Donald Trump won 48.6 percent of the vote, while Democratic presidential candidate Hillary Clinton won 47.9 percent of the vote; Trump won by only 44,292 votes, but won all twenty Electoral College votes. In Michigan, Trump won 47.5 percent of the vote, Clinton won 47.3 percent of the vote; Trump won by only a 10,704 vote margin, but won all sixteen Electoral College votes. In Wisconsin, Trump won 47.2 percent of the vote, while Clinton won 46.5 percent of the vote; Trump won by only a 22,748-vote margin, but won all ten Electoral College votes. In these three states combined, Trump won by only a combined 77,744-vote margin, but that gave him all forty-six electoral votes. In contrast, in Hawaii, Clinton won 61 percent of the vote, Trump won 29 percent of the vote; Clinton won Hawaii by a 138,044-vote margin, and won all four electoral votes. In Massachusetts, Clinton won 60 percent of the vote, and Trump won 33 percent of the vote; Clinton won by a 904,303-vote margin to win all eleven electoral votes. Overall, Clinton won the popular vote nationwide by about 3 million votes, but lost the Electoral College vote, thus allowing Trump to assume the presidency.

Occasionally, an elector does not keep their pledge in a presidential election. These are called "faithless electors." But there has never been a circumstance where there were enough faithless electors to change the outcome of a presidential election.

In the 2016 presidential election, there were seven faithless electors for president, the most in United States electoral history and the first time there was more than one since 1832, when there were two. In 2016, four faithless electors were Democrats from Washington state; three voted for Colin Powell, secretary of state under President George W Bush, and one voted for Faith Spotted Eagle, a leader of a North Dakota pipeline protest, who became the first Native American in United States history to win an electoral vote. One Democratic faithless elector was from Hawaii, and voted for Bernie Sanders, a member of Congress who had lost the Democratic primaries to Clinton. Two faithless electors were Republicans from Texas, one of whom voted for Ron Paul, former Congressman and Libertarian activist, and one for John Kasich, governor of Ohio. In 2020, the Supreme Court heard a case where plaintiffs argued that punishments meted out to the faithless electors from Washington state (a $1,000 fine) were unconstitutional, but the Court unanimously upheld the fines in its ruling.

Reform of the Electoral College is often called for — mainly by those who lose as a result of its vagaries. Reform would require a constitutional amendment. According to previous polling, most Republicans and most Democrats thought that the Electoral College should be replaced with a direct popular vote. For example, in 2013, 61 percent of Republicans supported abolishing the Electoral College, as did 66 percent of Democrats. But in December 2016, only 19 percent of Republicans supported disbanding the Electoral College, while 81 percent of Democrats agreed. Trump famously proclaimed his utter disdain for the Electoral College in 2012, saying "The Electoral College is a disaster for democracy. . . . Let's fight like hell and stop this great and disgusting disaster. . . . The phony Electoral College made a laughing-stock of our nation. The loser one!" But after winning the 2016 Electoral College (while losing the popular vote) Trump said, "The Electoral College is actually genius in that it brings all states, including the smaller ones, into play."[7] There are many common and easily disproven myths about the benefits of the Electoral College, myths usually cited by those who feel that the Electoral College provides a partisan advantage to their side.[8]

## 8) The Timing, Frequency, and Style of Elections

As we have seen, Americans hold elections for president every four years, for senators every six years, and for the entire House of Representatives every two years. General elections in the United States have always been the first Tuesday after the first Monday in November since 1845. All states have constitutions that also set fixed terms of office and election dates. The length of terms of office for governors and state legislatures and other officials vary by state, usually four years for governors, and two or four years for legislators. Local governments in most states have charters similar to constitutions that set terms of office for local officials. Local elections in many states occur in odd-numbered years.

Because of fixed election dates in the Unites States, the entire House of Representatives is up for election in November of every even-numbered year and has led to the "Midterm Effect" in the United States. Because a presidential term is four years, that means the entire House is up for election the same time as the president and again halfway through the presidential term (midterm). Since political parties formed in the United States 200 years ago, the party of the president has lost seats in the House of Representatives in all but a few of those midterm elections, as voters tend to blame the president's party for any political or economic situation they do not like. In 2022 with Democratic President Biden, Republicans gained nine seats in the House and took it over. In 2018 with Republican President Trump, Democrats gained forty-one seats in the House and took it over. The Midterm Effect has led frequently to one party controlling the federal executive branch and another party controlling the federal legislative branch, something that never happens in Canada.

When is a general election held in Canada? The Governor in Council sets the date of a general election. According to section 4(1) of the *Canadian Charter of Rights and Freedoms*, "no House of Commons and no legislative assembly shall continue for longer than five years from the date fixed for the return of the writs of a general election of its members." Any date within that five-year period may be chosen to hold the election.

However, some jurisdictions have moved to fixed election dates — Canada, British Columbia, and Ontario. On 6 November 2006, Parliament passed Bill C-16, *An Act to Amend the Canada Elections Act*. Each general election is to take place on the third Monday in October in the fourth calendar year after the previous poll, starting with 19 October 2009. With the minority government falling twice and elections being held in October 2008 and May 2011, no Parliament had yet reached its maximum life. The majority government produced in the 2 May 2011 election made it possible for the subsequent election to be determined by the fixed-date section of the *Canada Elections Act* on 19 October 2015. But a minority government was returned in the 2019 election, and the subsequent election was held in 2021, which produced yet another minority government. In these circumstances, the prime minister has tremendous discretion in setting the timing of the election, as long as they conform to the five-year period as set out in the *Canadian Charter of Rights and Freedoms*. Despite the fixed-date election legislation, under the *Parliament of Canada Act*, the prime minister is still free to request an election at any time. An amendment to the *Canada Elections Act* clearly states that "Nothing in this section affects the powers of the Governor General, including the power to dissolve Parliament at the Governor General's discretion." To be clear, it is the prime minister who requests the Governor General dissolve the House, a supplication that has only been refused once in Canadian political history in 1926 and which sparked a constitutional crisis as a result (discussed below and in Chapter 2).

Occasionally, by-elections are necessary when a Member of Parliament resigns before their term is up or dies in office. When a seat in the House of Commons becomes officially vacant, the prime minister has about 170 days within which to call a by-election. The Speaker of the House must inform the chief electoral officer immediately, and between the eleventh and the 180th day after receiving notification, the chief electoral officer issues a writ to the returning officer of the electoral district concerned, directing them to hold a by-election. In the United States, when vacancies in Congress occur in between scheduled election dates due to the deaths or resignations of members, state governors call "special elections" to fill those vacancies.

As noted above, the prime minister by convention has tremendous discretion as to the timing of elections within a five-year period. What are the implications of this power? For one thing, it reflects the strength or weakness of the sitting government; a prime minister can use the timing to capitalize on political popularity, or avoid calling an election in periods of unpopularity. This permits considerable political strategizing by the prime minister. In turn, this reinforces the power of the prime minister and helps them keep a grip on the party caucus. Nothing inspires team loyalty like the prospect of a well-timed election that bolsters the chances for re-election! In this context, there is the issue of symbolic versus real power to be considered. The Governor General must approve the prime minister's request to dissolve Parliament to call an election, and normally does so automatically. Only once has a Governor General refused such a request — in 1926.[9]

The prime minister's power is not absolute, however. In the British Cabinet-parliamentary system, the executive (prime minister and Cabinet) must answer to the legislative branch (the House of Commons). This is the principle of responsible government raised in Chapter 1. Thus, the executive must have the support or *confidence* of a majority of the Members of Parliament to govern and pass legalization. Defeat of a government through the mechanism known as a non-confidence motion in the House can precipitate an election. This is where a majority of the members of the House vote against a piece of legislation introduced by the executive. The matter of the legislation must be of a significant nature to trigger a vote of non-confidence, and that means it must relate to a major financial issue, such as the government's annual budget. If a motion of non-confidence passes, the prime minister, having been denied the support of the majority of the Members of Parliament, must call an election as their government has lost the legitimate right to govern This is a mechanism that is completely absent in the American political system.

## 9) Election Administration

As for the administration of elections, we see another major difference between the Canadian and American systems. Elections Canada is the non-partisan agency responsible for conducting federal elections, by-elections, and referendums. Election officers must be politically neutral: they may not favour one political party or candidate over any other. Special precautions ensure that no political leanings can affect the administration of electoral events. All election workers must take an oath to uphold voters' rights and the secrecy of the vote, and to perform their duties without favouritism. Each candidate can have representatives present on election day during both the voting and the counting of the votes to verify that everything is carried out fairly and properly.

In the United States, however, partisan officials administer elections in most of the country, a framework that helped inspire various conspiracy theories about the 2020 presidential election as well as many past elections. The United States Constitution says that states administer elections. The person who runs elections at the state level, called a secretary of state in most states (not to be confused with the national secretary of state, who runs American foreign affairs), is either a partisan elected position (in a majority of states) or appointed by other partisan elected officials. At the county level, the people who run local elections are also elected or appointed by elected officials.

In the Georgia election for governor in 2018, the Democratic candidate was Stacey Abrams, a former leader of Democrats in the Georgia State House of Representatives. Abrams was aiming to be first African American woman ever elected governor anywhere in the United States. The Republican candidate was Brian Kemp, the Georgia secretary of state in 2018, who was in charge of running the election where he was on the ballot. Polls were very close, and Kemp was accused frequently by Abrams prior to the election, including with lawsuits that did not succeed, of fixing election rules and policies to favour himself. He won the election with 50.2 percent of the vote to her 48.8 percent. In 2022, Abrams ran against him again, and he won again, 53 percent to 46 percent.

In 2022, the Republican candidate for governor of Arizona was Kari Lake, a former TV news anchor and big supporter of Trump, and the Democratic candidate was the secretary of state Katie Hobbs, in charge of running the election in which she was on the ballot. Hobbs won the election 50.3 percent to 49.7 percent. Lake, who claimed that the 2020 presidential election was stolen from Trump, also claimed that the election for governor was stolen from her and filed several lawsuits, all of which she lost. As these examples and others show, partisanship plays an important role in the administration of elections in the United States.

## 10) Money and Elections

The *Canada Elections Act* and the *Income Tax Act* include a series of financial provisions designed to entrench openness, fairness, and accessibility within the Canadian electoral system. In contrast to the United States, there are strict regulations as to who may contribute and how contributions must be received and reported. As well, how much a candidate, political party, or third party may spend during the election period is regulated.

Contribution limits have been set for individuals, corporations, trade unions, and unincorporated associations. As of 2024, at the federal level a citizen or permanent resident of Canada can contribute up to $1,725 in total each year to each registered political party, together with the party's candidates, nomination contestants, and registered electoral district associations; up to $1,725 in total per contest to the leadership contestants of a registered party; and up to $1,725 to a candidate in an election who is not endorsed by a registered party. The first $5,000 an individual contributes to their own campaign as a candidate, nomination contestant, or leadership contestant will be exempt from the individual contribution limits listed above. The net result is that a candidate, nomination contestant, or leadership contestant can contribute a maximum of $10,000 in total to their own campaign.[10] As of 1 January 2007, corporations or trade unions that operate in Canada are forbidden from making contributions to federal leadership contestants, candidates for election, or registered parties.

There are also election expenses limits for candidates. A candidate's election expenses limit is the maximum amount of money that they are allowed to spend in an election campaign based on a formula in the *Canada Elections Act*. Spending limits are initially based on the number of names appearing on the preliminary lists of electors or on the revised lists of electors for the electoral district, whichever is greater. The limit is then calculated at the following rates: $2.17 for each of the first 15,000 electors; $1.09 for each of the next 10,000 electors; and $0.54 for each elector over 25,000.

Election expenses limits for political and third parties also condition the financing of elections. The maximum amount allowed for the election expenses of a registered party for an election is calculated by multiplying $0.70 by the number of names on the preliminary lists of electors for electoral districts in which the registered party has endorsed a candidate. As for third party spending, in 1983, Parliament banned this form of advertising during elections; however, a right-wing interest group called the National Citizens Coalition successfully challenged the law as a violation of the *Canadian Charter of Rights and Freedoms* the following year. In 2000, Parliament passed the current limits on spending by third parties, which the Supreme Court upheld in 2004.

There are almost no limits to spending on elections, campaigns, and candidates in the United States; it is the "Wild West" of electoral politics. As some observers have suggested, "The legal and regulatory framework in the US for spending is one that makes little sense from either a practical or a principled perspective."[11] In 1976, the United States Supreme Court in *Buckley v Valeo* ruled that most limits on campaign spending were unconstitutional for abridging freedom of speech.[12] The one limit the Supreme Court allowed was on contributions to candidate campaigns "to avoid the appearance of corruption." In 2024, that limit was set at $3,300 per individual per campaign per candidate (the amount goes up with inflation). Political Action Committees (PACs) set up by interest groups to donate money to campaigns can donate $5,000 per campaign per candidate. That amount has been fixed since 1974.

Because the Supreme Court said that limits on campaign spending are unconstitutional and abridge freedom of speech:

1. Governments cannot limit overall spending by candidate campaigns, so in 2020, the Biden campaign spent more than $1 billion, and the Trump campaign spent $774 million raised through individual contributions.
2. Governments cannot limit candidates from spending their own money, so Trump spent $66 million of his own money on the 2016 campaign. Billionaire Michael Bloomberg, former mayor of New York City, spent more than $900 million of his own money in his failed quest for the Democratic nomination for president in 2020.

3. Governments cannot limit money raised and spent by "independent" groups not officially connected to a candidate's campaign. You cannot limit fundraising or spending by a group called "People Who Love Donald Trump" if it is not connected to the official Trump campaign. You cannot limit a group called "People Who Hate Donald Trump" if it is not connected to an official candidate campaign. Outside groups sent more than $1 billion to help the Biden and Trump campaigns in 2020.

In 2010, the United States Supreme Court ruled 5:4 in *Citizens United v Federal Election Commission* that corporations have freedom of speech under the Constitution and that corporations and unions can contribute unlimited amounts to independent groups not connected to candidate campaigns.[13] A 1907 federal law still in effect bans all corporation and union donations directly to candidate campaigns. The *Citizens United* decision led to the creation of Super PACs under United States tax law, which can collect unlimited donations for "independent" political groups from corporations, unions, or individuals. But few corporations donate to Super PACs, whose donations are mostly public, because that could lead to consumer boycotts or shareholder and investor anger. Almost all modern Super PAC money comes from wealthy individuals, the same as with independent groups before the *Citizens United* decision. For example, Sheldon Adelson, a casino billionaire, donated $215 million to pro-Republican Super PACs in 2020. Michael Bloomberg donated $151 million to pro-Democratic Super PACs in 2020. In 2022, George Soros, a Hungarian-American investment banker and target of several antisemitic conspiracy theories in Europe and the United States, donated $177 million to pro-Democratic Super PACs, and Richard Uihlein, heir to the Schlitz Beer fortune and owner of the Uline shipping company, donated $86 million to pro-Republican Super PACs. All the top donors to Super PACs are wealthy individuals, not corporations.[14]

It is estimated that in the United States, 1 percent of donors contribute 90 percent of the money candidates receive.[15] In the decade after their creation, Super PACs spent almost US$3 billion on

**Box 3.1. The Influence of Lobbyists in American Elections**

According to Canadian businessperson Frank Guistra, one of the problems with the role of money in the American political system is the super-sized influence of lobbyists:

*Adding to the problem of money in politics, consider that there are approximately 12,000 lobbyists in DC representing primarily corporate and foreign interests. In 2021, the total lobbying spending in the United States amounted to $3.73 billion. Lobbyists ensure that legislation works in their favour and there is plenty of evidence the results are not always in the best interests of the general public.*

*In 2020, the pharmaceuticals and health products industry in the United States spent the most on lobbying efforts, totaling to about $357.85 million. It's no wonder the American health-care system is one of the worst in the developed world. The US spends more on health care as a share of the economy — nearly twice as much as the average OECD (Organisation for Economic Cooperation and Development) country — yet has the lowest life expectancy among the eleven nations.*

*The United States spent $754 billion on national defence during fiscal year 2021, which amounted to eleven per cent of federal spending, more than the next nine countries combined. And guess what? The defence industry spends approximately $120 million per year on lobbying in Washington. It's no wonder the US is mired in forever wars.*

*The same can be said of many other industry groups, including the fossil fuel industry. The five largest oil and gas companies alone spend about $200 million a year on lobbying to control, delay, or block binding climate policy. Severely curtailing the lobbying industry and reversing Citizens United would help direct funding to where it is truly needed, as both of these phenomena are exacerbating the gap between rich and poor.*

Source: Frank Giustra, "America Is a Broken Nation. Here's How to Fix It in Four Easy Steps (and Why It Will Never Happen)" *Toronto Star* (7 September 2022), online: www.thestar.com/business/opinion/2022/09/07/how-to-fix-a-broken-america-in-four-easy-steps-which-will-never-happen.html.

federal elections. This unfettered approach to campaign revenues and expenses has made it prohibitively expensive to run for many public offices in the United States. Political spending in the 2020 election totalled $14.4 billion, more than doubling the total cost of the record-breaking 2016 presidential election. In contrast, Canadian political parties raised a mere $30 million during the 2021 federal election. In just the month of March 2020, Joe Biden raised $46,741,037 in his run for the presidency; in the same month, Trump raised $13,635,668.[16] During the 2024 presidential campaign, Biden held a glitzy fundraising gala at Radio City Music Hall in New York City accompanied by former presidents Obama and Clinton; in a single night Biden raised more than $25 million.[17] When Vice President Kamala Harris became the Democratic presidential nominee after Biden withdrew in July, 2024, her campaign had raised $1 billion by October.[18] The Federal Election Commission reports also indicated that Super PACs who supported the Trump and Harris campaigns had raised over $1 billion. Overall, the Harris campaign outspent the Trump campaign on advertising by an estimated $460 million, although that did not win her the election.[19]

## 11) Ballot Initiatives

General referendums are ballot questions created by a government, allowed in all fifty states. For example, in forty-nine states (all except Delaware), when state legislatures pass amendments to a state constitution, voters must approve the amendment in a referendum. The United States Constitution has no provisions for a national referendum, and there has never been one. Canada, in contrast, has had three national referendums:

1898: A non-binding referendum to prohibit alcohol was accepted by 51 percent nationwide, but 81 percent of Quebecers voted no, and Prime Minister Laurier decided not to enact national prohibition.

1942: Conscription was supported by 65 percent nationwide, but 72 percent of Quebecers voted no, and Prime Minister King avoided imposing the draft until nearly the end of the Second World War.

1992: The Charlottetown Accord to broadly reform and amend the Canadian Constitution was rejected by 55 percent of Canadian voters.

Quebec has held two failed provincial referendums on sovereignty association (a form of independence), in 1980 and 1995. Most Canadian provinces have held referendums on a variety of subjects.

In the United States, twenty-three state constitutions also allow voter initiatives, in which voters sign petitions to put a proposed law or state constitutional amendment directly on the ballot and bypass the state legislatures. The number of signatures needed varies by state, usually between 5 percent to 10 percent of voters in a recent election. If a majority of voters approves the proposal on election day, it becomes law even if the elected officials oppose the idea. Initiatives differ from referendums, which are put on the ballot by the elected government of a state or province. Only one province in Canada allows voter initiatives — British Columbia, which has held only one so far (in 2011), to repeal the harmonized sales tax (HST).

Use in the United States is far more frequent and widespread. Most western states allow voter initiatives, and a few eastern states do as well. For instance, in 1996, 56 percent of California voters approved a medical marijuana initiative over the objections of the governor and most elected officials in the state. The initiative allowed Californians to grow and possess personal amounts of marijuana if they had a medical condition and got a doctor's note. Since then, thirty-seven more states have also made medical marijuana legal; the first five states through voter initiative, and then some state legislatures also approved it. Medical cannabis remained illegal in eleven states as of early 2025.

In November 2012, voters in Colorado and Washington state approved initiatives to make possession and cultivation of personal amounts of recreational marijuana legal, and to have the state regulate, tax, and license legal marijuana dealers, similar to the way states regulate alcohol sales. In 2014, the first legal recreational marijuana stores in North America opened in Colorado and Washington. Since then, eleven other states have also approved voter initiatives to make recreational marijuana legal, including California. Eleven state legislatures made recreational marijuana legal; recreational marijuana was legal in twenty-four states as of 2024. However, all types of marijuana remain completely illegal under United States federal law as of 2024, adding to the legal complications of marijuana use and sales in the United States. So far, the federal government in the past decade has generally declined to enforce federal marijuana laws in states that have made it legal.

Other voter initiatives have covered various public policies of concern to Americans. In November 2022, Colorado voters made psilocybin (magic mushrooms), thought to help with depression and post-traumatic stress disorder (PTSD), legal for medical purposes. Oregon made psilocybin legal for medical purposes in a voter initiative approved in 2020, and its use in medical settings began in 2023. Californians in 2022 approved a voter initiative to require that at least 1 percent of all public education spending by state and local governments go toward arts and music education due to frequent budget cuts in those programs. Michigan voters in 2022 approved an initiative over the objections of the Republican state legislature that provides the right to reproductive freedom under the state constitution. In the 2024 election, seven states passed similar initiatives protecting or expanding abortion rights. Overall, almost seventy voter initiatives on a wide variety of policy issues — including how to handle marijuana regulations, voting procedures, economic issues, and immigration laws — were on ballots in various states.

## Conclusion

There are many distinguishing features between Canada and the United States insofar as how each country manages elections and voting. For instance, Americans vote at least twice a year every year. Canadians usually will not vote as often. The United States employs a primary system wherein dates are set separately by each state to choose official candidates for Republican and Democratic parties for all offices. The American general election, in which voters nationwide choose between Republican, Democrat, Independent, or other party candidates for each office, is always held in November. If you live in Toronto, Ontario, you would vote for a total of five government offices; if you live in Erie, Pennsylvania, you would vote for a total of eighty offices, over one-half of them judges. Erie even elects a county coroner. In short, Americans vote for a lot more offices in a lot more elections than do Canadians.

With presidential elections every four years and congressional elections every two years, American politicians are in campaign mode 365 days a year. The twenty-four-hour cable news cycle ensures non-stop political reporting, often focusing on the horse-race rather than the substance of policy. The public gets inundated with every moment of the campaign process. The United States does not have an officially demarcated campaign period. For example, Republican Ted Cruz announced his 2016 presidential candidacy 596 days before election day. Meanwhile, in Canada, an election period must be a minimum of thirty-six days and a maximum of fifty days.

As this chapter has revealed, Canada and the United States are similar in that they are both democracies, but different in that, in comparison, each have strikingly unique electoral systems and party politics. The question of whether Canadians have too few electoral choices, or Americans have too many is difficult to answer. While ideology, formative events, and differing historical experiences explain why there are so many more viable political parties in Canada than in the United States, this tells us little about the quality of democracy in each country. Neither does the mere fact of voting for more public offices in the United States than in Canada. The role of money, likewise, plays a role in elections in the two countries in quite different ways. But the extent to which one system is more or less democratic than the other is a matter of ongoing debate.

CHAPTER FOUR

# Federalism and Regionalism

## Introduction

The similarities and differences between Canada and the United States extend to the manner in which they both adopted federal systems of government, which are now two of the oldest such systems in the world. The Americans innovated modern federalism; the Canadians copied it — sort of. Federalism is a system of two or more levels of government. It exists to square the circle of diversity and unity in societies that are divided regionally, linguistically, culturally, economically, or in other ways. In federal systems there is one national government for the entire country plus any number of sub-national governments. In Canada, there is a national government, ten provinces, and three territories. In the United States, there is a national government, fifty states, five territories, and the District of Columbia. In this chapter, we will look first at the impact of regionalism on Canada and the United States, and then link that factor to the quite similar but also different systems of federalism in both countries.

## A. The Origins of American Federalism and the Canadian Adaptation

Both Canada and the United States exhibit a propensity to base voting and policy-making on the factor of regionalism. Regional political differences within Canada and within the United States explain a lot about the development of different political values, policy solutions, and election outcomes in both countries.

### 1) American Regionalism

Building on the work of Daniel Elazar on the United States, some political historians have looked at the development of regional political cultures based on original European colonial settlement patterns.[1] They have identified four broad political cultures based on the region of colonial European settlement, the original European settlers, how each community organized itself, and the view of government held by the settlers. Beginning in the seventeenth and eighteenth centuries, these groups arguably laid the basis for modern American society. These four political cultures are the moralists, the individualists, the traditionalists, and the populists.

*Moralists* landed mainly in New England. They originally represented Puritan small-town culture, holding a view that governments should play a role improving the local community as well as society as a whole. They believed in the good of the commonwealth as represented by the power of government to advance the public interest. Citizens run for public office with the belief that government and bureaucracy is a force for good and that issues matter. A strong ethos of public service coupled with an aversion to corruption in politics are significant aspects of this way of thinking. These views were later reinforced by large numbers of Scandinavian immigrants and spread across the upper Great Lakes into the Midwest and the Northwest.

*Individualists* landed mainly in the mid-Atlantic states and included Dutch and Quakers engaged in commercial merchant activities. They were in some ways the opposite of the moralists.

They represent big city culture, and see government as a tool to promote individual interests. Many Catholic immigrants who saw politics as a way to improve their status in society joined them. Individualists expressed faith in the free market and saw government's role as ensuring the functioning of the market. Bureaucracy is regarded negatively to the extent that it interferes with patronage, which is in turn reflected in the politicians' aspirations for material gain that is at the base of their motivations for running for office. The individualists and their political culture eventually migrated to the central Midwest and western states.

*Traditionalists* landed in the South, and were typically the second or third sons of British aristocrats who emigrated because they would not inherit the family estate back in Britain (which went to the eldest son). They created a rural, agricultural-based plantation culture. Given their aristocratic background, they saw the role of government as preserving the traditional social order. Politicians sought office with an attitude of *noblesse oblige*; with great wealth comes the responsibility to give back to those who are less fortunate. Politics was regarded as an exclusive competition between rival factions which were often family-based. Bureaucracy is seen with suspicion as it interferes with the personal relationships at the heart of an elitist and closed governing circle. Compared to other areas, the Traditionalist areas got few new immigrants in the 1800s and early 1900s, although their descendants moved westward through the southern and southwestern states.

*Populists* landed in the colonial West region near the Appalachian Mountains, and were typically of Scottish-Irish background. They included the settlers constantly pushing westward across the Ohio Valley into Indian territory during and after the Seven Years' War (1756–1763). They had an extended family culture, and often resisted government authority. They saw it as limiting their opportunities and infringing on their freedoms. The Populists moved westward, often into other hilly or mountainous areas, and were joined by many German political and religious dissidents who also tended to distrust government.[2]

Each of these regional cultures spread westward during the 1800s and were reinforced by later immigrant groups. Political movements in American history can be linked to regions such as these with their distinct political cultures. For example, with the Moralists, we see advocates of prohibition (of alcohol), abolition (of slavery), environmentalism, and support for the social democratic policies like those of Vermont Senator Bernie Sanders. We can associate the Individualists with merchant capitalism, big city corruption (Donald Trump was raised in New York City), and social tolerance (Hillary Clinton was raised in Chicago). The Traditionalists have historically been associated with support for slavery, discrimination, and the most opposition to immigration in American politics. The Populists, with their emphasis on individual rights, are associated with gun rights and various conspiracy theories such as those about the "deep state." The right-wing Tea Party movement, which originated in 2009, grew largest here.

Regionalism as represented by these divisions affects voting and policy demands. The modern Blue States (Democratic states) tend to contain Individualist and Moralist areas and non-White voters. The Red States (Republican states) tend to contain Populist and Traditionalist voters. Support for the Democratic Party and the Republican Party often reflect some of these characterizations of the broad American political culture, although demographic changes are underway in the United States. European Americans now constitute about two-thirds of American voters and are declining as a share of the American electorate. Nationwide, most European-Americans vote Republican, but percentages are much higher in Red States than in Blue States. African Americans vote about 90 percent Democratic. Latino and Asian Americans have voted about 60–65 percent Democratic in recent elections.[3] It is noteworthy, though, that in the 2024 election, a 14-percentage-point swing in Trump's share of Hispanic voters helped propel him to victory. About 46 percent of Hispanic voters picked Trump, up from 32 percent in the 2020 election.[4]

Divisions in the United States Congress reflect these trends: as of 2023 the Blue States of the Northeast had elected twenty-three Democrats (although two of the Democrats were officially

Independents — Bernie Sanders of Vermont and Angus King of Maine — who both caucused with the Democrats) and one Republican to the United States Senate, while the Pacific Coast states had elected eight Democrats and two Republicans (both from Alaska) to the Senate. The Red States of the South were represented by twenty-three Republicans and three Democrats (two of them from Georgia), and the six Midwest states that do not border the Great Lakes had twelve Republicans in the Senate and no Democrats. Democrats constituted the majority of senators in 2023 in the Great Lakes Midwest states and the Rocky Mountain states as well.

The Blue States are concentrated in the Northeast, Great Lakes Midwest, and the Pacific Coast. The Red States are concentrated in the South, Great Plains Midwest, and northern Rocky Mountains. Formerly Red States in the Southwest have been trending Democratic recently due to increased voter populations of Latino Americans. While these voting patterns are not always replicated exactly, they are indicative of broad trends that may be explainable by the patterns of immigration and settlement described above. Figure 4.1 shows the distribution of Blue and Red States in 2022.

## 2) Canadian Regionalism

What about the Canadian case? Regionalism plays no less a role in Canada than in the United States. Again, we can turn to patterns of immigration and settlement in the past to help understand politics of the present. We can also note how the two countries came to be so different, yet similar.

The first factor of significance is the first contact between the European explorers and the Indigenous peoples. Economic partnerships were struck early on to facilitate the fur trade. French and later English fur traders penetrated the continent travelling from east to west in pursuit of pelts for export back to the metropolitan centres in Europe. Indigenous peoples assisted in this activity, and until the fur trade declined in significance, it dictated patterns of

**FIGURE 4.1. DISTRIBUTION OF BLUE AND RED STATES, 2022**

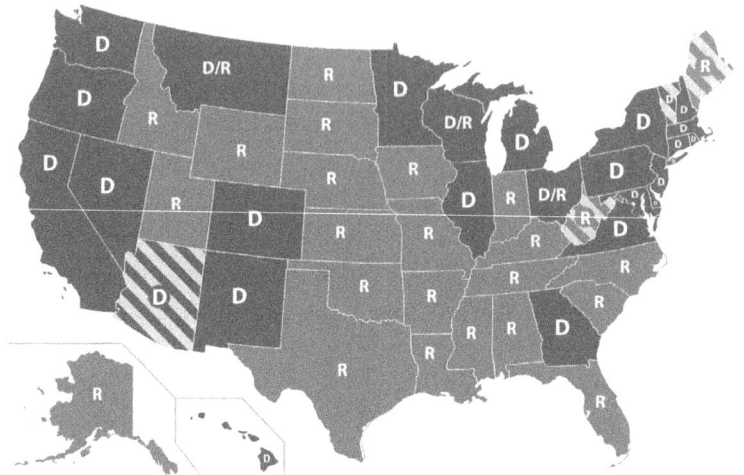

Legend: D denotes two Democratic senators. R denotes two Republican senators. D/R denotes one Republican and one Democrat from the state. Stripes denote one Independent senator (that caucuses with the Democrats).

Source: Adapted from "Composition of the United States Senate at the Beginning of the 118th Congress," by Assorted-Interests — Own work, CC BY-SA 4.0, online: https://commons.wikimedia.org/w/index.php?curid=126415650. Letters have been added to the original map to identify Democratic and Republican states.

development, which were incremental and uneven. It was not until diversification of the economy focused on other forms of staple extraction and small-scale industrial and craft-based production models that the Canadian population began to grow in the latter half of the nineteenth century. But once that process began to unfold, the relationship between Indigenous peoples and the settler societies went into decline, and assimilation of Indigenous peoples rather than partnership became the goal of successive Canadian administrations until the twenty-first century.

The next factor of significance was the division between the English and the French in colonial Canada. As noted in Chapter 1, when the English defeated the French on the Plains of Abraham in Quebec City in 1759, the English were confronted with a stark demographic reality — the French settlers massively outnumbered them. The British were also concerned about unrest in the American Thirteen Colonies and wanted to forestall the possibility of the French joining the American Revolution. Therefore, they embarked on a policy of accommodation rather than assimilation, allowing for the preservation of the French culture, language, religion (Catholicism), and legal system of civil law. Given the geographic concentration of the French in Quebec, they evolved into a powerful political, economic, and cultural force in the politics of Canada. Indeed, much of Canada's history is captured in Lord Durham's evocative phrase describing Canada as "two nations warring in the bosom of a single state." French Catholic versus English Protestant came to define the political culture of early Canada with echoes down to the present day.

Largely Scottish and Irish immigrants who settled into a life of staples extraction populated the Atlantic provinces; fishing, farming, and lumber were key economic activities. Notice that these are all economic activities that are dependent on the availability of natural resource stocks, on foreign markets to export unfinished goods, and on the import of more expensive manufactured products from abroad — usually from the metropolitan master. Consequently, a political culture of dependence emerged in which a spirit of proud cultural individualism confronted a sense of political and economic helplessness. Feelings of alienation from the centre — whether that centre was metropolitan England or, later, a dominant central Canada, came to characterize the Atlantic Canadian political culture.

The central Canadian settlement experience was dominated by the massive influx of United Empire Loyalists after the American Revolution. As we noted in Chapter 1, these were British settlers loyal to the Crown who were expelled from or left the United States. They carried a sense of ideological conservatism in which hierarchy and aristocracy represented the proper social order. They were reflected in the emergence of the Family Compact in Upper Canada and the Château Clique in Lower Canada who were the political, economic, and social elites in each society and who established methods of governing that preserved their interests over those of the "great unwashed." They were suspicious of democracy and "mob rule," as they called the American experiment. But they lived alongside advocates for a more democratic order. Small landowners, merchants, and farmers, who were the backbone of the colony, were positively influenced by the notions of democracy wafting up from their southern cousins. A reformist streak existed in central Canada that also influenced the political culture. Hence, the nineteenth- and twentieth-century political culture of Ontario is often labelled somewhat oxymoronically as "progressive conservative."

Western Canada developed a distinct political culture linked to its immigrant experience too. Vast regions of underpopulated Prairies prompted an aggressive immigration scheme by Sir John A Macdonald as one of the three planks of his "National Policy." The result was an influx of "stalwart peasants in sheepskin coats," as his immigration minister Sir Clifford Sifton described the eastern European farmers who were given incentives to populate the Prairies. In addition, large numbers of Americans flooded into Alberta in the late nineteenth and early twentieth centuries, giving that province its own distinctive ethos within the context of the Western provinces as a whole.

But the other two planks of Macdonald's policy caused no end of grievances from western Canadians. The railway — that great symbol of nation building and national unity — was dominated by central Canadian economic interests who set freight rates and gained ownership of thousands of acres of prime western land. Along with the central Canadian banks and insurance companies, they operated in ways distinctly disadvantageous to the farmers of the west, provoking anger, discord, and ultimately dissent. The other plank in Macdonald's policy, the tariff, had similar impacts. Designed to promote the Canadian national economy, it disproportionately benefited central Canadian manufacturers who were protected from their American competitors. But this meant that western Canadians had to pay more for Canadian manufactured goods than if they had unfettered access to American goods. Hence, the western preference for free trade with the United States, rather than the protectionism of the National Policy. But the smaller population of western Canada meant that it always had fewer representatives in national political institutions like the House of Commons and Senate to speak on its behalf. The sum total of all these slights was the phenomenon of western alienation. No wonder that western Canada is home to most of the populist protest movements and political parties that arose in Canada in the twentieth and early twenty-first centuries, not unlike those in the American west.

We can see the effects of these regional patterns of development and settlement in contemporary Canadian politics. Modern regional voting patterns in Canada began to form in the 1980s. Pierre Trudeau had been prime minister for almost sixteen years, and had been popular in Quebec, but then upset nationalist Québécois voters there by patriating and amending the Constitution in 1982 without the approval of Quebec's separatist government.

In the 1984 election, the Progressive Conservatives (PC) led by Brian Mulroney forged a coalition of disgruntled regions constituting much of Atlantic Canada, soft nationalists in Quebec, and alienated westerners. The PC party won fifty-eight out of seventy-five ridings in Quebec and won a big majority nationwide. Mulroney spent much effort trying to get Quebec to sign on to the Canadian Constitution, with disastrous results. In 1987, Mulroney and the ten provincial premiers negotiated the Meech Lake Accord to amend the Constitution to recognize Quebec as a "distinct society," transfer more powers to the provinces, and give provincial governments a role in choosing senators and Supreme Court justices. Pierre Trudeau opposed the Accord, saying it would weaken a unified Canada. Opposition to the Accord gradually built across Canada. Ironically, many Quebec nationalists said it did not give Quebec enough power while many English Canadians said it gave the province too much. Aboriginal Canadians noted it gave them nothing. There was a three-year timeline for the Accord to be approved by all ten provinces, but Manitoba and Newfoundland and Labrador did not approve it. Aboriginal Elijah Harper, asking why the Accord protected Quebec as a distinct society but not First Nations, blocked Manitoba's approval in the Legislative Assembly.

Mulroney tried again. Stung by the criticism that Meech Lake only addressed Quebec's concerns, he negotiated the Charlottetown Accord of 1992. In contrast to Meech Lake, which had only five clauses, Charlottetown contained more than sixty, and came to be known as the "Canada round" of constitutional negotiations. Among the most important clauses were the following:

1. Recognize Quebec as a distinct society
2. Provide new powers for First Nations
3. Provide more powers for provinces
4. Senators were to be chosen by the provinces
5. Every province would get six senators

Sensitive to the perception that the Meech Lake Accord was negotiated in secret by "eleven men in suits," Mulroney and the premiers agreed to hold a national referendum on the Charlottetown Accord. Nationally, 54.3 percent of Canadians voted against the Accord. The citizens of six provinces voted no, including all the Western provinces, Quebec, and Nova Scotia. Ontario voted yes by the slimmest of margins, 50.1 percent. So the Charlottetown Accord failed.

By 1993, Mulroney was very unpopular, and resigned as leader of the PC party. He was replaced by Kim Campbell, Canada's first female prime minister, just in time for an election that brought a seismic shift in Canadian politics. In the latter years of Mulroney's leadership, two new regional federal parties had formed. In Quebec, the Bloc Québécois was created to contest national elections while supporting independence for Quebec. In the West, the Reform Party was created under the slogan "The West Wants In." It expressed the view that the West was tired of the focus on Quebec and upset that Western interests always seemed underrepresented in Ottawa. Notice that the coalition of disgruntled Canadians that Mulroney had created had fractured, mainly along regional lines.

The 1993 federal election brought an earthquake. In the House of Commons, the Liberals under Jean Chretien won 177/295 seats, including almost all of Ontario and the Atlantic provinces. The Bloc Québécois won an astonishing fifty-four seats, which is more than two-thirds of the Quebec seats. Remarkably, a party dedicated to the breakup of Canada became Her Majesty's Loyal Opposition. The Reform Party captured fifty-two seats, including more than three-quarters of the ridings in Alberta and British Columbia, but no seats east of Manitoba. The NDP won nine seats. But perhaps the most astonishing outcome was the almost total decimation of the PC party, which was left with only two seats! Campbell herself was defeated in what most observers reckon was a repudiation of Mulroney more than a rejection of Campbell. PC support collapsed, and there has never been a major federal party since under the PC banner.

The 1997 federal election had similar results, with the Liberals winning 155 seats; the Reform Party, sixty seats; the Bloc Québécois, forty-four seats; the NDP, twenty-one seats; and the PC party, twenty seats. There was also one Independent. Her Majesty's Loyal Opposition shifted from the hands of the separatists to the alienated west.

Recognizing that splitting the conservative vote by having two parties meant that the Liberals might govern forever, in 2004, the Reform Party and the remnants of the PC party merged to become the Conservative Party. The 2011 federal election showed this strategy was the correct one, as the Conservatives won seventy-two out of ninety-two seats in the Western provinces and, more significantly, seventy-three out of 106 seats in Ontario due largely to the split among left of centre voters between the Liberals and NDP.

One of the key factors derived from Canadian regionalism is that when Quebec acts cohesively, it can have a huge impact on Canadian national elections. Quebec mainly supported the Liberals in 100 years of federal elections, then the PC party from 1984 to 1993, and then the Bloc Québécois from 1993 to 2011. In 2011, Quebec voters discovered "Jack" and voted *en masse* for the NDP. Their leader, Jack Layton, was born and raised in Quebec and the NDP view fit well with Quebec voters at the time, so the NDP won fifty-nine out of seventy-five Quebec seats; coupled with the seats the NDP won in the rest of the country, it became the Official Opposition in Ottawa. The Liberals, saddled with a variety of scandals, finished third. The 2015 election was yet another lesson in the power of regionalism. The Liberals won every riding in Atlantic Canada, two-thirds of the seats in Ontario, and a majority in Quebec, while the Conservatives won almost all the ridings in Alberta and Saskatchewan. In 2019, 81 percent of the seats in Atlantic Canada went to the Liberal Party, while in Ontario the figure was 64 percent. The Liberals just missed winning a majority of the seats in Quebec, at 45 percent, while Alberta and Saskatchewan gave forty-seven out of their forty-eight seats to the Conservative Party. Conservatives finished first in Manitoba and British Columbia, but the Liberals and NDP each won many seats in both of those provinces. The 2021 federal election results were almost identical in each region to the 2019 results.

What this overview suggests is that in virtually every national election in Canada, it is impossible to construct a nationwide winning coalition of voters. This phenomenon is traceable to the impact of regionalism on Canadian political culture — indeed, we should more probably say political *cultures*. The original patterns of immigration and settlement in Canada have left a powerful legacy that affects political outcomes to this day. As with the United States, who settled where and when is important.

## 3) Federalism

This brings us to a consideration of federalism in both countries. The founders in the United States innovated a system of government that accounted for the reality of distinct societies and the need to forge some measure of national unity out of the diversity that existed. Their experiment failed, however, because initially they gave too much power to the regions (the states), with the result that the nation was plunged into a bloody civil war in the 1860s. Subsequently, American federalism evolved to give more power to the national government while ensuring regional concerns were addressed within national political institutions — recall that each state sends two senators to Congress, where state concerns are aired and addressed.

As they gathered in Quebec City and Charlottetown to negotiate the founding of the Dominion of Canada, the Fathers of Confederation were very aware of the consequences of giving the regional governments too much power, as had been the case in the United States. As a result, they sought to negotiate a much more centralized version of federalism that gave more power to the central government so that the mistakes the Americans made could be avoided. There was little question that the regional interests of the new entity had to be accommodated; that was clear in the negotiations, even though Macdonald expressed a preference for a single unitary government rather than the two-level system of federalism. Then again, once he accepted the compromise that was the federal system, Macdonald proclaimed, quite incorrectly, "We have avoided all conflict of jurisdiction and authority."[5] Quebec in particular would not accept a model of government that did not have institutions (provincial governments) that were responsible for regional concerns. Neither Nova Scotia nor New Brunswick would accept such an arrangement either. Hence, the adoption of federalism. And hence the long subsequent history in Canada of conflict over jurisdiction and authority.

The irony is that the original version of federalism created by the American founders was supposed to be highly decentralized with most power in the hands of the state governments; however, it evolved into a highly centralized model. In Canada, on the other hand, the original Confederation bargain suggested a highly centralized version of federalism with most power concentrated in Ottawa's hands, but today, Canada is regarded as perhaps the most decentralized federal system in the world. Such is the impact of regional political cultures in these two very similar, yet very different countries.

In Canada, an awful lot of time and energy has been spent debating the very nature of federalism (think about the separatist movements in Quebec, or the constitutional negotiations described above), whereas the Americans have not. They do argue about the policy role of national and state governments, but spend virtually no time arguing about the first principles of power sharing, or about what the Canadian political scientist Peter Russell called "mega-constitutional politics," the way Canadians do.[6] Baron de Montesquieu, the French jurist and philosopher who conceived the separation of powers in *The Spirit of Laws*, offered the framework upon which western states (including those in North America) should draft their constitution in a federal system of government.[7] Although Canada and the United States have federal governments, both of them have different intellectual discourses on federalism. The intellectual discourse on American federalism focuses on limited government and sharing power between all levels of government.[8] Conversely, the intellectual discourses on Canadian federalism largely focus on identity politics; particularly, it focuses on "language, region, and managing difference."[9]

Federalism is a political system with two or more levels of government in which the constitutional authority to make laws is divided between a national government and some number of regional governments. Neither the national government acting alone, nor the regional governments acting together, have the authority to alter the power of the other level of government. They are considered coordinate and equal in their own constitutional spheres. According to KC Wheare, a British authority on federalism:

> [F]ederal government exists ... when the powers of government for a community are divided substantially according to the principle that there is a single independent authority for the whole area in respect of some matters and that there are independent regional authorities for other matters, each set of authorities being co-ordinate with and not subordinate to the others within its own prescribed sphere.[10]

Citizens in a federal state, therefore, are members of two political communities, one national and one regional.

For practical reasons, all countries distribute power to carry out governmental functions across their territories in some manner.

There are currently approximately twenty-six federal states worldwide (out of about 200 countries recognized as sovereign by the United Nations). Federations tend to have larger populations; about half of the world's population live in federal states. Federal states tend to have large territories, many ethnic or language groups, and/or a historical tradition of local/regional autonomy or government (all characteristic of Canada and the United States). Regional differences based on economic, geographic, historical, religious, linguistic, and ethnic divisions may also be present.

Federal systems are designed to square the circle of unity and diversity. Federalism is seen as a system that will provide national harmony in the face of territorially based or regional loyalties. When social pluralism is low, a unitary model makes sense, but when pluralism is high, a federal model seems to work better.

In federal systems, several particular matters are of great significance. First, because governing is divided, there is the question of jurisdiction. Who can do what? This leads to the design of a constitutionally based division of powers. Thus, the constitution and the law play a very important part in politics in federal countries, which also require the means to arrive at various kinds of agreements through negotiations between governments. This necessitates intergovernmental relations — that is, mechanisms through which the two levels of government can foster relationships that hopefully facilitate policy solutions for societal problems.

Money plays a particularly important role in intergovernmental relations within federal systems. Basic questions about who is allowed to spend and on what policy areas are constant sources of tension. While the constitutional division of powers should provide clear guidance in sorting out fiscal responsibilities, politics often leads to conflict over the interpretation of the words in the constitution, including, importantly, about fiscal responsibilities and relationships.

Regionalism, ethnic and linguistic groups, and party systems are all affected by, and affect, federalism. How different interests are recognized and realized within a federal system is often a source of tension. The way political power is arranged is a constant issue. The basic question is whether to provide a strong national government with subordinate local governments, or the opposite? Thus, we speak of centralized federalism if the national government is given the preponderance of power, versus decentralized federalism if the subnational governments (provinces or states) have the most control. Federal constitutions also provide for "concurrency," which indicates shared areas of jurisdiction.

In practice there is no uniform approach to the division of powers. Listed powers differ by subject, number, specificity, etc. The Canadian Constitution expressly enumerates powers of both levels of government, with the main federal powers listed in section 91 and the main provincial powers in section 92. The Canadian Constitution also contains what is called the "residual power" in section 91. This is a power awarded to one level of government or the other to cover issues that may arise that are not enumerated in the Constitution. In the Canadian case, residual power lies in the clause stating the federal government may make laws for the "peace, order and good government of Canada."

The rationale for federalism in Canada was that it was seen as a pragmatic solution to making union possible. The existence of Quebec as a separate cultural, linguistic, and religious nation loomed large in the minds of the Fathers of Confederation. The existence of distinct political, economic, and cultural societies in Atlantic Canada also played an important role in the outcome of negotiations. In creating a strongly centralized model of federalism, Sir John A Macdonald hoped that the provinces would eventually wither away, to be subordinated ultimately by a dominant national government.

Contrary to the Canadian case, residual power in the United States lies with state governments. The United States Constitution lists all the powers of the national government in Article I, Section 8, and then says in the Tenth Amendment that "The powers not delegated to the United States by the Constitution, nor prohibited by it to the States, are reserved to the States respectively, or to the people." State government powers are not listed. The American Constitution also contains a supremacy clause; whenever a national law and state law are in conflict, the national law is supreme. The original rationale for federalism in the United States was to disperse (rather than concentrate) power, similar to the ideas of the separation of powers and the system of checks and balances between the executive, legislative, and judicial branches of government (see Chapter 2). But the original American Constitution, though it was created to replace the state-centred Articles of Confederation in the 1780s, erred in continuing to confer too much power on the states and too little for the national government. The ultimate consequence was the crisis of the Civil War, 1861–1865.

We could say that the rationale for adopting federalism in the United States was philosophical, premised as it was on notions of balancing power. In Canada, it was pragmatic, premised on notions of securing a deal based on the material interests of the uniting colonies. The subsequent development of federalism in Canada and the United States was a response to circumstances in each country.

The elixir that sustains federal systems is a sense of political nationality. This sense legitimizes federalism by allowing citizens to adhere to a common national bond while expressing their own sub-national identities, whether regional, linguistic, religious, or other. Both moral and legal claims underpin this sense of political nationality based as it is on a feeling of community and the desire to achieve common policy goals. But how strong are commitments to the national community versus the sub-national, whether province, state, or region? This fundamental question is complicated in the North American setting by the existence of two massively unequal countries, the larger of which exerts a constant and overarching influence on the smaller. The phenomenon of continentalism is an ever-present reality in the Canadian-American relationship that at times undermines the sense of political nationality in Canada. For example, all the Canadian provinces trade more north–south across the international border than east–west with each other. American foreign direct investment (FDI) has accounted for as much as 75 percent of all FDI in Canada at times. In 2023, the United States continued to hold 46 percent of FDI in Canada.[11] In addition, in

1981 exports to the rest of the world (ROW) and to the rest of Canada (ROC) were roughly equal, but today trade between provinces within Canada is less than trade between provinces and American states. Some suggest this amounts to a loss of economic control, which undermines the sense of a national political identity.

It is also noteworthy that starting in the late twentieth century, provincial and state governments began a process of institutionalizing their cross-border relationships, notwithstanding that foreign affairs is a federal government responsibility in both countries. Hence the Pacific Northwest Economic Region consists of five American states, two Canadian provinces, and one territory; the Western Governors' Association and Western Premiers' Conference consists of eighteen American states, four Canadian provinces, and three territories; the Conference of New England Governors and Eastern Canadian Premiers consists of six American states and five Canadian provinces; and the Council of Great Lakes Governors includes Quebec and Ontario as associate members. Governors and premiers have struck up relationships on a continental basis that exist alongside the traditional federalism relationships of national-to-sub-national governments in each country. In an unusual set of agreements that have gone beyond geographical proximity, California and Quebec partnered on cap-and-trade regulations of carbon emissions, with the state and province reaching an additional agreement with New Zealand at the 2021 United Nations Climate Change Conference in Scotland.[12] The regionalism that infuses federalism in both countries now more than ever has a continental character.

## B. The Division of Powers in Canadian and American Federalism

### 1) Who Does What?

In a federal system of government, the broad ideological question of "what is the role of government?" is immediately followed by a second question: which level of government is responsible? All governments must determine, for example, who is responsible for the health of the population? If the answer is government, and the system is federal, the subsequent question is posed: which level of government assumes responsibility for the health of the population? Similar approaches must be undertaken with regard to issues like the education or equal opportunity of the population, the alleviation of poverty, unemployment, standards of living, environmental protection, labour standards, economic development, and so on. If government is to be involved in these issues, which level of government — federal or provincial/state — should be responsible? These are consequential questions. Responsibility entails a variety of factors, including funding, policy design, policy implementation, and administration, as well as political credit when things go well and blame when things go badly.

Disagreements about the question of jurisdiction often arise in federal systems, and have featured prominently in both Canada and the United States. The division of powers is supposed to guide policy makers in determining jurisdiction, but the wording of the constitutions in both countries contain numerous ambiguous terms and phrases that are subject to widely different interpretations. As a result, the two levels of government often must bargain and negotiate over the meaning of the words and determine where responsibility lies. This is the realm of intergovernmental relations.

In Canada, the conduct of intergovernmental relations mainly occurs at the executive level of government, hence the term "executive federalism." The phrase was coined by political scientist Donald Smiley, who defined it as "the relations between elected and appointed officials of the two levels of government."[13] This means that the prime minister, the premiers, their cabinets, and senior bureaucratic advisers are the key actors in the negotiating and bargaining that goes on between governments. Executive federalism arose as a consequence of premiers acting as champions of regional political economies and aggressively fighting for enhanced provincial autonomy. The implication is that the true spokespersons for the regions of Canada are the premiers, and further that they have the right and obligation to engage the federal government in ongoing negotiations about both local and national concerns. The process of executive federalism is conducted in a manner that bypasses both the people and the legislatures, and has often been critiqued for its elitist and anti-democratic methods. While nowhere in the Constitution are these powers bestowed on the executive branch, a powerful convention developed in Canadian federalism; the executive level of government engages in "federal-provincial diplomacy," as Richard Simeon called it, to sort out the major constitutional, economic, and political issues confronting Canadians.[14]

To serve the prime minister and premier in their intergovernmental negotiations, an entire administrative machinery has arisen. Quebec was first, with the establishment of a Ministry of Federal-Provincial Affairs in 1961; subsequently, all governments in Canada created ministries or departments dedicated to federal-provincial issues.[15] The peak institution of executive federalism is the First Ministers Conference, held from time-to-time at the request of the prime minister who convenes their provincial counterparts to address the issues of the day. A permanent secretariat in Ottawa facilitates meetings and negotiations between the executives of both levels of government. Thousands of ministerial and officials meetings, conferences, and committees are held each year — mostly behind closed doors — between representatives of the provinces and Ottawa. Some are bilateral, some multilateral, and some only between provinces. A premiers-only organization called the Council of the Federation formed in 2003 allows provincial representatives to meet and strategize together regarding their positions *vis-à-vis* Ottawa; the prime minister is not invited. The system of executive federalism deals with policy making, program development, and service delivery in areas as diverse as social, economic, environmental, and constitutional policy, and virtually everything in between.

Interestingly, there is no real counterpart to the Canadian model of executive federalism in the United States. Relations between Washington and the states are better accommodated in the American system through intragovernmental relations — that is, the representation of state interests in the institutions of the national government. This occurs most importantly in the role played by the Senate, as discussed in Chapter 2. There is a National Governors Association that facilitates meetings between state governors and occasionally between state governors and the president. But there is no regularized or systematic coordination of national-state institutions that compares with the Canadian intergovernmental system.

But in both countries, relations between the levels of government, however constituted, can sour; agreements can prove to be elusive. Thus, an independent arbiter is required in federal systems, and this is where the courts come into play.

## 2) Judicial Interpretation in Canada and the United States

One of the advantages of listing the division of powers in the Constitution is that it clearly delineates what jurisdictional authority each level of government enjoys — or so one might think. This would seem to be truer of American federalism than Canadian, however. In fact, the list of federal and provincial powers in sections 91 and 92 of the Canadian Constitution have actually led to more conflict between the two levels of government than perhaps any other institution of government. This is in large part because the powers listed in the Constitution are subject to a variety of interpretations. Powers like "trade and commerce," "property and civil rights," and "direct taxation" may seem straightforward enough. But when important material interests are at stake and constitutional challenges against federal or provincial law are launched, words and phrases take on whole new meanings unintended by the Fathers of Confederation. Thus, the supposedly clear-cut list of powers becomes a source of endless haggling and interpretation. Court interpretations over the division of powers have produced some quite unexpected results that have effectively recast the face of Canadian federalism, for better or worse, in profound ways.

The role of judicial review in any democratic system is important, but its significance in a federal state can hardly be exaggerated.

An independent arbiter is essential to adjudicate jurisdictional disputes between the two orders of government. Before the *Constitution Act, 1982,* with its *Canadian Charter of Rights and Freedoms,* was proclaimed, the role of the Canadian courts was, due to the principle of parliamentary supremacy, limited basically to the delineation of federal and provincial powers within the existing *British North America Act, 1867.*

Judicial review looks at a particular law or government action in light of the Constitution. The court determines whether all or part of the law or action is *intra vires* (within the constitutional jurisdiction of the government passing the law), or *ultra vires* (outside the constitutional jurisdiction of the government passing the law). Judicial review is initiated by governments that feel their legislative jurisdiction is being invaded by the other level of government. It can also be initiated by citizens and corporations. Judicial rulings are authoritative and can act like constitutional amendments in that they are binding. Rulings tend to be zero-sum; there are clear winners and losers because jurisdiction is hard to divide. In addition, decisions tend to be legalistic rather than political in nature.

As we noted in Chapter 2, both the Supreme Court of Canada and provincial courts of appeal are required by law to hear "references" (as distinct from actual cases) upon the request of the federal and provincial governments respectively, unlike the American Supreme Court. The reference procedure has the advantage of securing judicial opinion before complex and costly administrative machinery is set in motion. As well, the clear determination of jurisdiction is helpful so that citizens can know which level of government is legally accountable for particular issues.

The distribution of legislative powers between the federal and provincial governments (sections 91 and 92) originally comprised one of the centralizing elements of Canadian federalism. The greatest judicial activity in relation to these sections has involved Parliament's broad authority in the opening paragraph of section 91 to legislate for "peace, order and good government" in all matters not explicitly assigned to the provinces, and to legislate in relation to "the regulation of trade and commerce."

On the provincial side, the power to make laws in relation to "property and civil rights in the province" has been the most significant (section 92(13)). The other important provincial power has been regarding "all matters of a merely local or private nature in the province" (section 92(16)), but it has been overshadowed by the "property and civil rights" clause. Judicial decisions relating to these "classic issues" were the most fundamental, and certainly the most spectacular, judge-made laws during the pre-*Charter* years.

Before 1949 when the Supreme Court became Canada's highest appeal body, the final judicial authority for Canada was the Judicial Committee of the Privy Council (JCPC), located in England. This body is technically not a court, but rather a body of law lords that advises the monarch. It was possible for Canadian cases to move to the JCPC from the Canadian Supreme Court or from provincial appeal courts; indeed, half (77 of 159) of all the JCPC's cases involving the distribution of powers went directly from provincial courts. The reason that the task of review devolved ultimately upon the JCPC was historical. It had been the court of appeal for colonial Canada before 1867, and the Fathers of Confederation saw no reason to alter this. Thus, the *Constitution Act, 1867* was silent in this matter.

The most significant impact of the JCPC's rulings was on the residual power. Overall, it tended to place a rather narrow interpretation on the federal government's powers to make laws for the "peace, order and good government" (POGG) of Canada. At first blush, POGG may appear to be a pretty wide power, under which a variety of laws could be justified. Over time, this power has been reduced to a power available to the federal government only in times of emergency. Thus, cannot be used by the federal government to justify federal laws during "normal" times or circumstances. Initially, during the first few years of Confederation, the courts interpreted POGG broadly as a residual power. If the matter under dispute was not found under the enumerated heads of section 92, then it automatically fell within federal jurisdiction.

The restrictions on the use of POGG began with the judicial era dominated by Lords Richard Haldane (1856–1928) and William Watson (1827–1899), who moved the federal system toward what may be called the "classical model," which means that each level of government is considered sovereign within its own sphere of jurisdiction. Concerned about federal intrusions into provincial areas of jurisdiction, they articulated an interpretation of POGG that guarded against this possibility. For the provinces to maintain their constitutional sovereignty, the JCPC consistently reflected a narrow interpretation of POGG and of the federal trade and commerce power (discussed below), and a broad interpretation of the provincial power over property and civil rights.

For instance, several of the important early disputes between Ottawa and the provinces dealt with regulating the consumption and sale of liquor, and the restrictions on POGG began with the ruling by the JCPC in a case called *Local Prohibition* in 1896.[16] The JCPC ruled that the POGG clause could not be used to overrule the enumerated powers of the provinces. In rationalizing this decision, the judges argued that the federal government could overrule provincial jurisdiction if the matter under consideration came to acquire "national dimensions" — that is, if it was important nationally. But they left open the question of how to determine what constitutes "national dimensions."

This question was later dealt with in three other court cases. In the 1922 *Board of Commerce* case, the JCPC struck down two federal laws that were intended to prevent the development of monopolies and hoarding of essential goods after the First World War.[17] The courts said that the laws might have been justifiable under the conditions of a national emergency. In so saying, the courts specified that POGG should only be applied during times of war, famine, or some similar condition. In the *Board of Commerce* case, the courts actually made it harder for the federal government to employ this power than if they simply had to argue that an issue had acquired "national dimensions," as the court ruled in the earlier *Local Prohibition* case. The fact that an issue had acquired "national dimensions" would not be sufficient to justify such exceptional legislation.

Subsequent rulings on POGG also suggested that it was essentially a power to be employed only in wartime or other similar, exceptional circumstances. In *Fort Frances Pulp and Paper Company v Manitoba Free Press and others*,[18] for instance, the JCPC declared that war-related circumstances were sufficient to warrant legislating under POGG, and indicated that the courts would be out of line in questioning Parliament's authority to do so under the conditions of a war or war-related emergency. Subsequent court rulings backed up this view.

In fact, in cases where the courts rejected the federal government's use of POGG as a valid basis for federal legislation, the impugned laws were intended to deal with peacetime circumstances. The first of these was the decision in *Toronto Electric Commissioners v Snider and others (Ontario)*,[19] when the JCPC struck down Canada's major industrial relations legislations. The JCPC also struck down the peacetime use of POGG in a 1937 decision, the *Labour Conventions* case,[20] which rejected the federal government's right to make laws regarding unemployment and social insurance. The federal government had attempted to justify the law on the basis that the Great Depression of the 1930s was a national concern and that it threatened the well-being of the country. This argument was considered inadequate by the JCPC.

In the 1970s, the courts were once again confronted with a federal government that wanted to use POGG to justify legislation that was intended to deal with economic problems outside of wartime. In a ruling on the constitutionality of Ottawa's *Anti-Inflation Act, 1975*,[21] a majority of the Supreme Court of Canada agreed that the federal government's argument that mounting inflationary pressures constituted an emergency justifying legislation that infringed on provincial jurisdiction. This ruling effectively liberated the emergency doctrine from strictly war-related circumstances. The Court decided that it was up to Parliament, not the courts, to determine what constitutes an emergency. The result is that Ottawa now seems to have somewhat easier access to the POGG clause. In 2021, the Supreme Court was asked to rule on a federal government policy designed to tackle climate change. In *Reference re Greenhouse Gas Pollution Pricing Act*, the federal government successfully argued that climate change is a pressing matter of national concern, and in a 6:3 decision the Court found that it was constitutionally permissible for Ottawa to take the lead on a threat that crosses provincial boundaries.[22]

Like POGG, the federal jurisdiction over trade and commerce power appears to be a sweeping power, but has been interpreted very narrowly by courts. It has been limited largely to interprovincial and international trade. Meanwhile, the provincial power of "Property and Civil Rights in the Province" has been interpreted more like what might be expected of the trade and commerce power.

*Citizens Insurance of Canada and Queen Insurance v Parsons (Canada)*[23] was the first major case to limit the trade and commerce power. The JCPC ruled that a broad, literal interpretation of trade and commerce would unnecessarily restrict provincial rights under property and civil rights. It said a broad interpretation would bring any and all aspects of economic life under the authority of Ottawa. Never mind that this was the intention of the Fathers of Confederation! Ottawa's powers over trade and commerce in this case were limited to include "political arrangements in regard to trade requiring the sanction of Parliament, regulation of trade in matters of interprovincial concern, and it may be that they would include general regulation of trade affecting the whole Dominion."

In the view of the court, applying the trade and commerce power more broadly than that would deny the provinces control over property and civil rights in the province. The legacy of the *Parsons* case has been that Ottawa's powers to regulate trade and commerce has been limited to international trade, interprovincial trade, and general trade affecting the whole of Canada. But even this definition causes problems of interpretation. For example, it is possible that some federal laws regulating trade between provinces may also affect trade that occurs strictly within a province as well. Is such a law constitutional? Until the 1950s, the courts said no. Over the years, however, a series of court decisions gradually loosened the restrictions placed on the trade and commerce power in the *Parsons* case. Nonetheless, the overall effect of the *Parsons* case and others like it severely restricted the powers of the federal government.

Indeed, in 2011, the Supreme Court appeared to reassert a provincialist interpretation of trade and commerce. The federal government sought to rationalize the regulation of securities (stocks, bonds, and other financial products); remarkably, there were ten securities regulators in Canada, one for each province, and Canada was the only jurisdiction in the world not to have a single national securities regulator. The Supreme Court was asked to rule on the constitutionality of a federal government proposal to create a unified federal regulatory body for securities that would replace the provincial bodies. The federal government thought financial markets were so important to the Canadian national economy that they should be overseen by a single national regulator. In 2011, it asked the Supreme Court whether Parliament would be allowed to pass a federal law to do that, and the Court said no. In a ruling that caught many constitutional observers off-guard, the Court ruled the move *ultra vires*, suggesting securities regulation fell under provincial purview and that the federal government proposal did not address a matter of genuine national importance that was not substantially different from what the provinces were already doing. The Court read the Constitution as saying that only provinces and territories can make laws about securities trading within their borders. However, the Court indicated that a solution might be found if a cooperative approach could be developed in which the provinces would deal with aspects of securities regulation within their power, and the federal government would deal with aspects within its power. The two levels of government engaged in negotiations to devise such an approach. In *Reference re Pan-Canadian Securities Regulation*, the Court ruled that the federal government's second attempt to create a national securities regulator was constitutional.[24]

The courts are one important avenue for settling conflicts between Ottawa and the provinces, but seldom do their decisions put an end to that conflict. Instead, court cases simply become one element in the complex bargaining that goes on between the two levels of government. For example, in the *Employment and Social Service Act Reference*,[25] the JCPC struck down a federal law establishing a program to deal with national unemployment. This was followed by federal-provincial negotiations leading to a constitutional amendment in 1940 that gave the federal government power over unemployment insurance. In *Public Service Board v Dionne*,[26] the Supreme Court confirmed Ottawa's exclusive jurisdiction to regulate television broadcasting. But right after the decision by the Court, Ottawa indicated its willingness to negotiate with the provinces to share authority over this area. In *Canadian Industrial Gas & Oil Ltd v Government of Saskatchewan*,[27] a provincial tax on natural gas was found to be a direct tax and therefore fell outside of provincial jurisdiction. Later, during the constitutional negotiations of 1981–1982, control over natural resources was negotiated and appeared to broaden the powers of the provinces in this area and permit some form of resource taxation that had been ruled *ultra vires* in the *CIGOL* decision.

Finally, in the *Patriation Reference*,[28] the Supreme Court ruled that Ottawa's unilateral proposal to patriate the *British North America Act, 1867* (BNA Act, 1867) and to change it in ways that affected provincial power was constitutionally legal, but that it violated an unwritten constitutional convention that required Ottawa to have the support of a "substantial number" of provinces in order to change the Constitution. This gave the federal government a legal victory, but at the same time suggested that the political consequences for proceeding were too high. This forced the provinces and the federal government back to the negotiating table and resulted in the deal of November 1981, which led to the patriation of the Constitution.

Patriation of the Constitution included the addition of the *Canadian Charter of Rights and Freedoms* to the *Constitution Act, 1982*. One result is that citizens have become more "judicially conscious." It also added a more politicized role for judges in Canada. As well, its impact on federalism has been to contribute to a pan-Canadian national standard of rights, which critics argue diminishes provincial power *vis-à-vis* the federal government.

The impact of the courts on Canadian federalism can hardly be overstated. It is generally agreed that judicial decisions over the years have tended to decentralize power in Canadian federalism; as a result, the federal system of today is far more decentralized than the Fathers of Confederation envisioned. This was especially true of the body of rulings passed down by the JCPC, although it has not been as true for those rulings passed down by the Supreme Court since it became the court of last appeal in 1949. Some decry these developments as a gross distortion of Canadian federalism. Others see them as reflective of Canadian life and political reality. Debates over the impact of the courts have often centred on the ways in which judges interpret the Constitution. Whether the courts should stick to the "intentions of the Fathers of Confederation" in interpreting the Constitution, or assume the Constitution is a "living tree" susceptible to changing interpretations based on evolving conditions in Canadian life, has animated assessments of the impact of judicial review in Canada.

As we noted above, the United States Constitution has evolved from a highly decentralized system of dual federalism in which each level of government basically looked after its own interests to an integrated "marble-cake" federalism of shared responsibilities. Today it is highly centralized, but also very competitive as fiscal restraint and rivalry between Washington and the states persists. The role of the Supreme Court in adjudicating disputes between Washington and the states has been no less significant than in the Canadian experience.

In particular, modern American federalism differs in two important ways from Canada, leading to United States Supreme Court decisions that define the distinct nature of American federalism. First, unlike in Canada, where the *Criminal Code* is federally defined, most criminal laws in the United States are determined at the state government level. So crimes like murder, assault, theft, and burglary are defined separately by each state, with penalties determined under state laws.

However, the United States federal government also has criminal laws, usually involving the federal power to regulate interstate commerce under Article I, Section 8 of the Constitution, or involving federal agencies or federal officials. In some cases, such as those involving drugs or guns, that means that a person's actions may violate federal law and a state law at the same time. In *US v Lanza* (1922), the United States Supreme Court ruled that it was acceptable to prosecute Vito Lanza for violating the federal Prohibition Act and for violating a Washington state Prohibition Act for the exact same actions involving the manufacture and transport of alcohol, because they were different crimes under different jurisdictions.[29] While there is no longer a federal Prohibition Act, the federal government and state governments in the United States both continue to have sometimes contradictory criminal laws about illegal drugs.

The federal and state governments similarly share jurisdiction over gun laws. In 1992, Texas high school student Antonio Lopez was arrested for bringing a gun to school. While that violated Texas state law, he was prosecuted under the federal Gun-Free School Zones Act of 1990, because federal prosecutors wanted to use this new law that they felt would result in stricter penalties against violators than the loose approach often taken toward guns in states like Texas. In *United States v Alfonso D Lopez, Jr*, the Supreme Court ruled 5:4 that possession of a gun in a school is not interstate commerce, and that Congress had no right to pass such a law, and it overturned the Lopez conviction.[30] The following year, Congress passed a new *Gun-Free School Zones Act*, forbidding gun possession in school areas if the gun had been involved in interstate commerce (manufacture, sales, parts, materials), as almost all guns have been. That law has been upheld in American courts ever since.

But because criminal law in the United States can be set at either the federal or state level, contradictions and conflicts can result that often get settled in courts (for example, Chapter 5 examines the contradictions about the legality of marijuana under United States laws). In 1993, Congress enacted the *Brady Handgun Violence Protection Act*, which required local law enforcement officers to conduct background checks on handgun purchases during a five-day waiting period (the FBI Instant Background check system did not yet exist). County Sheriffs Jay Printz of Montana and Richard Mack of Arizona refused to conduct such background checks, and the Supreme Court in a 5:4 decision in 1997 ruled that due to the Tenth Amendment, the federal government cannot "commandeer" local criminal justice authorities to carry out federal laws, upholding the Printz and Mack decisions not to conduct background checks.[31]

A second set of court rulings that distinguish the United States from Canada are derived from the existence of fifty state constitutions that provide rights and freedoms in addition to those found in the national Constitution's Bill of Rights. Canadian provinces operate under the federal constitution and British parliamentary traditions and have no written constitutions of their own. State constitutions also protect freedom of speech and religion, and rights for accused criminals, protections that get interpreted by state supreme courts in ways that may differ from interpretations of the United States Constitution by federal courts.

In 1972, the Supreme Court ruled that a shopping centre was private property, and that the Constitution's right to free speech does not require a private property shopping centre owner to allow anti-Vietnam war fliers to be distributed on their property. The Supreme Court ruled that the Constitution's First Amendment limits government action, not a private property owner's action.

In 1979, the California state Supreme Court issued a ruling in a case about a Jewish student group that was at the Pruneyard Shopping Center getting petition signatures to protest a United Nations resolution that criticized Israel. The shopping centre kicked out the students, who sued. The California Supreme Court ruled that the right to free speech in the California state constitution allows students to get petition signatures in a public area like a shopping centre, so the shopping centre cannot kick out the students. Pruneyard Shopping Center appealed that decision to the

United States Supreme Court. The Supreme Court ruled 9:0 that state constitutions can provide more individual rights and broader rights and freedoms to state residents than are provided under the United States Constitution, and that state Supreme Courts are final interpreters of state constitutions, so the United States Supreme Court upheld the California Supreme Court decision in the *Pruneyard* case.[32]

The United States Supreme Court pointed out that the United States Constitution is a floor on individual rights, not a ceiling. All Americans have rights from the national Constitution, but most states provide additional rights under state constitutions. These types of rulings are known in the United States as judicial federalism. For example, in 2022, after the United States Supreme Court ruled that abortion is no longer a reproductive right under the United States Constitution, California, Michigan, and Vermont voters approved amendments to their state constitutions to protect abortion rights. In 2024, as noted in Chapter 3, seven more states did so through voter initiatives. As also discussed in Chapter 3, while the United States Supreme Court has ruled that partisan gerrymandering does not violate the United States Constitution, Pennsylvania's Supreme Court ruled that it did violate the state constitution. Four other state supreme courts followed Pennsylvania's lead in 2022.

Pennsylvania is also among a few states whose constitutions include an "environmental rights" amendment stating that "The people have a right to clean air, pure water, and to the preservation of the natural, scenic, historic, and aesthetic values of the environment." In 2013, after the Pennsylvania legislature passed a law to forbid local regulation of oil and gas operations, Robinson Township sued and won a case in the Pennsylvania state Supreme Court that allowed the town to regulate hydraulic fracturing (fracking) in the community due to the Environmental Rights Amendment.[33] In 2023, a Montana court ruled that the state's Environmental Rights Amendment required the state to consider greenhouse gas emissions when considering permits for energy development projects. The case was brought to the court by sixteen youth plaintiffs, ages two through eighteen when they filed.[34] As these examples show, the impact of the American courts on American federalism, like the impact of the Canadian courts on Canadian federalism, is far-reaching.

## 3) Accords and Agreements

A feature of Canadian federalism since its inception has been the use of intergovernmental accords and agreements, some of which may be bilateral involving two governments, while some are multilateral involving three or more governments.[35] They are used by governments to facilitate collaboration in virtually all policy areas. The exact number of intergovernmental agreements is thought to be in excess of 1,500, the vast majority of which are bilateral in nature. While they can be important in intergovernmental relations, they often have a dubious legal base, which is to say that while some are enshrined in law, many are simple "gentlemen's agreements" arrived at informally.

Similar agreements in the United States exist when the federal government partners with state governments to achieve federal goals, sometimes with the carrot of federal grants, and sometimes with the stick of federal mandates. Large numbers of interstate compacts also exist in the United States, often dealing with waters that cross state boundaries. Among the interstate compacts that have gotten prominent attention in the United States in recent years is the Regional Greenhouse Gas Initiative that has set cap and trade regulations on power plant carbon dioxide emissions in almost all northeastern states. The National Popular Vote Interstate Compact is an attempt to address criticisms of the Electoral College system of electing a United States president, by awarding a state's electoral votes to the national popular voter winner instead of a state popular vote winner. As of 2024, seventeen states (all Democrat) and the District of Columbia had approved the compact, which will go into effect once states with 270 electoral votes have approved.[36]

## 4) Centralization of Power Versus Decentralization of Power

As noted in Section 2 above in this chapter, the United States has experienced a trend toward greater centralization of power, while Canada has become perhaps the most decentralized federal system in the world. However, as written, the constitutions of both countries suggest the opposite should be true. Why is this the case?

In the United States, a powerful ideology of one nation derived from its revolutionary founding persists as evidenced by the motto "*E pluribus unum*" (out of many, one). In addition, the phrase "one nation under God" is incorporated into the Pledge of Allegiance. And of course, the searing experience of the Civil War demonstrated that too much power in the hands of the sub-national governments could be disastrous. Beyond these reasons, though, centralization is built into the governing institutions. Specifically, there is a strong influence of intrastate federalism, meaning sub-national representation in national institutions. Effective representation of state interests within the federal government undermines regional or state-level power by providing accommodation of state concerns in Washington. Thus, the Senate with two representatives from each state acts as an effective conduit of state issues that receive attention from the federal government as a result of the active presence of state representatives in this national institution.

In contrast is the extent of decentralization of the federal system in Canada. The fact of "two nations warring in the bosom of a single state" meant that the English-French divide had to be accommodated in order for the new nation of Canada to be born. The history of French Canadian assertiveness in defending its people's survival meant that concessions had to continuously be made by Ottawa. But the lack of representation of provincial interests within the federal government meant that representation of provincial/regional interests evolved primarily through the provincial governments. A powerful "provincial rights" movement took hold in the twentieth century that saw aggressive and assertive premiers step up onto the national stage to contend with Ottawa over power. The existence of Quebec provided a major impetus to this movement, particularly through the Quiet Revolution beginning in the 1960s, which had slogans like "*maître chez nous*" (masters in our own house) and "*egalité ou indépendance*" (equality or independence) that spoke to the requirement that Quebec must be accommodated if Canada was to survive. The slogan "the West wants in," the Alberta bumper sticker that read "Let the eastern bastards freeze in the dark" in the 1980s, and the passage by the Alberta government in 2023 of the *Alberta Sovereignty Within a United Canada Act* claiming the provincial government could essentially ignore federal legislation contrary to Alberta's interests are all manifestations of western alienation that also contribute to the tensions inherent in a federal system that struggles to accommodate regional interests. One consequence of these trends is a decentralized system of asymmetrical federalism in which powerful premiers demand policy solutions that are customized for each province even as Ottawa strives to maintain national standards.

## 5) The Residual Power in Canada and the United States

In 1867, the Fathers of Confederation created a centralized form of federalism in which the balance of power rested with the national government. Some scholars called it "quasi-federalism" because the federal government could even violate the sovereignty of the provincial governments through the constitutional powers of "reservation" (whereby a provincial bill could be stalled before becoming law) and "disallowance" (whereby a provincial bill could be disallowed). Several other clauses in the *British North America Act, 1867* suggested ways in which the federal government could legally intrude in areas of provincial jurisdiction. Section 91 of the Act lists twenty-nine exclusive federal powers including trade, commerce, banking, credit, currency, taxation, navigation, citizenship, and defence. Section 92 lists sixteen exclusive provincial powers including direct taxation, hospitals, prisons, property, and civil rights. The provincial powers were considered in 1867 to be of only limited and local concern; later they became the basis of much more significant provincial responsibilities and powers.

The term "residual power" refers to the authority over jurisdictional fields that do not fall under the enumerated sections of the Constitution. In Canada, the original Constitution was heavily influenced by events in the United States that placed the residual power in the hands of state governments. The Civil War was seen by the Fathers of Confederation as an example of what could happen if the central government did not have strong authority; therefore, they wrote the residual clause in such a way as to allow the federal government to act in any area not specifically assigned to the provinces. Section 91 contains the federal powers and the residual clause, which says:

> It shall be lawful for the Queen, by and with the advice and consent of the Senate and the House of Commons, to make laws for the Peace, Order and good Government of Canada, in relation to all matters not coming within the Clauses of Subjects by this Act assigned exclusively to the Legislatures of the Provinces.[37]

In the United States, the residual powers clause applies at the state level. However, court interpretations have tended to enhance federal power to a greater degree than in Canada, for a variety of reasons. The American Constitution does not set out the powers of the two levels of government as specifically as does Canada's Constitution. Washington only has powers such as coining money, regulating interstate commerce, negotiating treaties, and declaring war. Also, due to the Tenth Amendment to the Constitution, the states have powers over areas such as criminal law and intrastate commerce, and both levels of government have jurisdiction in fields such as taxation, health, and auto safety. In both Canada and the United States, provincial/state governments control education, marriage, and divorce.

A key reason for the increased federal government power in the United States that has been supported by court decisions lies in the Article I, Section 8 power of the federal government to regulate interstate commerce. Under that clause, the United States Supreme Court has upheld almost all attempts by Congress to regulate business or society since 1937. For example, in 1964, after Congress passed the *Civil Rights Act* to forbid restaurants and hotels that served the public from discrimination based on race, the owner of the Heart of Atlanta Motel, a segregated facility, sued and argued that nowhere in the United States Constitution is Congress authorized to tell a private business owner what customers must be served. The Supreme Court ruled that because the motel owner served customers from outside Georgia and advertised outside Georgia, the motel was involved in interstate commerce, and Congress could regulate it.[38]

In *Wickard v Filburn*, the Supreme Court even ruled that the federal government could regulate how much wheat a small Ohio farmer grew on his property that was used only to feed his own animals because that wheat affected the national supply and national prices.[39] Using similar logic, the Supreme Court ruled in 2005 that despite the Tenth Amendment, the federal government could confiscate marijuana plants grown by Californian Angel Raich for her personal medical use, legal under California state law, because her marijuana plants affected the national (and nationally illegal) market for marijuana.[40]

## C. Money Matters: Fiscal Federalism

### 1) Raising and Spending Money Under Canadian Federalism

All federal systems are highly conditioned by the power to raise and spend money. The distribution of powers is greatly influenced by the control of funds as fiscal arrangements determine the degree of dispersion of political authority within a territory.

For example, if a state had a federal system in which jurisdiction was divided but all the power to tax and spend was completely in the hands of the federal government, all significant power would rest with the central government, despite the formal division of powers. If, on the other hand, the sub-national governments (provinces or states) had all the fiscal powers, then the country would be completely decentralized despite any constitutional rules to the contrary.

The complexity of fiscal arrangements in Canada is an area of ongoing debate. The basic conundrum of fiscal federalism in Canada is that the federal government has the power to raise money by any means or mode of taxation, but lacks the jurisdictional authority in the most expensive policy areas. The provinces have jurisdictional authority to create programs and policies in the most expensive areas, but lack the capacity to raise sufficient funds to pay for them. Hence, the two levels of government are entangled and must figure out how to cooperate and collaborate.

An important element of fiscal federalism is federal transfers. This is funding provided by the federal government to help the provinces and territories provide programs and services on an ongoing basis. Most transfers are done through four major programs: the Canada Health Transfer (CHT), Canada Social Transfer (CST), Equalization, and Territorial Formula Financing. Transfers help ensure that all Canadians receive reasonably comparable levels of public services at reasonably comparable rates of taxation, wherever they live. They support important provincial programs: health care, post-secondary education, social assistance, and social services, as well as early childhood development and early learning and childcare. In 2022–2023, support through major transfers to provinces and territories was $87.7 billion.[41] Equalization ensures that less prosperous provinces, called "have-not" provinces, have sufficient revenue to provide public services, and is enshrined in the Constitution:

> Parliament and the government of Canada are committed to the principle of making equalization payments to ensure that provincial governments have sufficient revenues to provide reasonably comparable levels of public services at reasonably comparable levels of taxation.[42]

Equalization payments are determined by a complex formula that measures the revenue-generating capacity of each province, and are unconditional; provinces can spend them according to their respective priorities. For 2022–2023, six provinces received almost $24 billion in equalization payments.[43] Other types of grants from the federal government to the provinces are also part of Canadian fiscal federalism; some are conditional, others unconditional. The federal government also has at its disposal the so-called spending power which, although not written into the Constitution, is the principle that the federal government can spend its money in any way it sees fit, including in areas of provincial jurisdiction (the spending power is discussed below).

## 2) Raising and Spending Money Under American Federalism

The American experience with fiscal federalism begins with the Philadelphia Constitutional Convention in 1787, where the delegates present were adamant that the Constitution should assign precise functions to each level of government. The federal government was given those powers that were national in nature (foreign affairs, defence, currency, and the regulation of commerce between the states and among foreign countries). Residual powers were to remain in the hands of the state governments. Today the distinction between state and federal powers has been blurred and bears little relation to the one described in the 1787 agreement. By the twentieth century, a form of "cooperative federalism" had been grafted onto the framework of the original division of powers.

Over time, Washington has collected an ever-greater share of all government revenues and has handed some of them back to the states in the form of grants. Use of these grants is controlled by standards attached by Washington; critics suggest this has distorted state priorities and interests. Different types of financial arrangements have different effects on the relations between the two levels of government: some grants centralize the system while others decentralize it. Categorical grants provide funds for specific programs and are the most common form of federal grant. They come in two forms: (1) formula grants are allocated to state and local governments according to specific criteria, such as population or the percentage of citizens who are poor or unemployed; (2) project grants allow states to apply for funding following federal rules about guidelines and objectives. Some decentralization is provided by block grants that give states and local governments more discretion about how to spend federal money in broad program areas.

Federal grant money sometimes has a coercive component. Under the United States Constitution, the federal government has no clear authority to set a national drinking age. In 1984, under pressure from Mothers Against Drunk Driving and others concerned about the mix of teenagers, alcohol, and cars and trucks, Congress passed a law to require states to raise their legal drinking ages to twenty-one years, under penalty of losing 10 percent of all federal highway grant money if the state did not comply. South Dakota (among other states) objected to this form of extortion and sued. The Supreme Court ruled that Congress's spending power in the Constitution allows it to withdraw that money when it wants, as long as it is not overly coercive, and upheld the law to indirectly establish a national drinking age.[44]

In the 1970s and 1980s, the United States also allowed for general revenue sharing, which was the most decentralizing fiscal instrument of all since it distributed federal funding to the states with no conditions attached about their expenditure. In other respects, the federal system is decentralized: the states play a major role in the Electoral College system that selects the president; two senators are elected from each state; three-quarters of the states are required to pass constitutional amendments; the party system is highly decentralized. Overall, the fiscal relationship between Washington and the states coupled with court rulings has made the country much more centralized than one would predict from reading the Constitution.

## 3) The Federal Spending Power and the "Necessary and Proper Clause"

One very contentious means to get around the basic conundrum of Canadian fiscal federalism is the federal spending power. This is a convention that says that if the federal government chooses to spend its money, it can do so in virtually any way it sees fit — which includes intruding into areas of provincial jurisdiction. It can be used unilaterally by Ottawa or in consultation with the provinces. It is the subject of frequent debate in Canada, though, since it can promote national programs with national standards, but it also can distort provincial priorities and decision making.

In the United States, the Constitution gives shared power to the two Houses of Congress to make laws, declare war, raise an army and navy, coin money, regulate commerce, establish federal courts, set rules on immigration and naturalization, and "make all laws which shall be necessary and proper for carrying into execution the foregoing powers."[45] The "necessary and proper" clause has been used by the Supreme Court to expand federal authority and allow the federal government to act in what might once have been considered exclusive state jurisdiction. This unique feature of the American Constitution, along with the supremacy clause, adds to the formal division of powers between Washington and the states by placing federal laws in a superior position to state laws. Thus, the states can pass laws in many of the same areas as Congress, but they can be overturned by the courts if they conflict with laws enacted by Washington.

National powers were reinforced by *McCulloch v Maryland* (1819)[46] when the Supreme Court ruled the federal government was not restricted to the enumerated powers of the Constitution, but had "implied powers" because of the "necessary and proper" clause. This decision and others vastly expanded the national government's power to intervene in the economy, regulate interstate trade and commerce, protect civil rights, and set national standards for welfare programs.

## Conclusion

Geographically, Canada and the United States are both vast territories, a factor that contributes to the importance of regionalism in both countries. Distinct regional political cultures and identities in both countries make governing challenging. Federalism can be seen as a system of government that is designed to square the circle of unity and diversity, and was adopted first by the Americans and then the Canadians to do just that. Both Canada and the United States are countries where regionalism has a profound impact on both political culture and policy making. Regional political differences explain a lot about the development of distinct political values, policies, elections, and the decision to construct a federal system in the first place. But as with so many other comparisons between Canada and the United States, the intriguing part is the extent to which federalism in both countries is the same, only different.

CHAPTER FIVE

# Comparative Public Policy: Similar Countries, Dissimilar Policies

## Introduction

Examining policy choices in Canada and the United States presents an array of similarities, while also providing sometimes unexpected and profound differences. Whether the policy issue is climate change, social welfare, health care, guns, the death penalty, gay rights, civil rights, immigration, abortion, doctor-assisted death, marijuana, education, religion, free speech, or language, the landscape of comparison can be fascinating. Unfortunately, time and space do not permit us to examine all these areas. We canvass a selection to get a flavour of the policy worlds in the two countries, beginning with a review of the institutional context of making public policy in Canada and the United States.

## A. Policy Making in Canada and the United States

### 1) Constitutions and Policy Making

As we noted in Chapter 2, the Canadian Constitution is a combination of conventions (British parliamentary traditions), the *British North America Act, 1867* (BNA Act, 1867), and the *Constitution Act,*

1982, which contains the *Canadian Charter of Rights and Freedoms* (*Charter*). Prior to 1982, the Canadian Constitution was amended eighteen times. Until 1982, amendment of the Canadian Constitution required petitioning the British Parliament; after 1982, a domestic amending formula was incorporated into the Constitution. It requires the approval of the federal government plus seven out of ten provinces containing at least 50 percent of the population of Canada for most amendments, although some require the unanimous consent of the federal government and all ten provinces. In Canada, there are no written provincial constitutions. Provincial governments' powers either are listed in the national Constitution (mainly in section 92 of the BNA Act, 1867) or are derived from British parliamentary traditions.

The United States Constitution was fully written in 1787, and it has been amended twenty-seven times since then, including the first ten amendments, known as the Bill of Rights. All fifty states in the United States have written state constitutions that establish each state government, list and limit its powers, and set up local government institutions. Amending state constitutions requires voter approval in forty-nine states (the exception being Delaware). This is in contrast to the national Constitution, for which amendments do not require voter approval. The federal Constitution can be amended through approval of two-thirds of each House of Congress and then approval by three-quarters of states.

As the supreme law of the land in both countries, the constitutions set the parameters of policy making. They determine the relationship between the branches of government (executive, legislative, and judicial), the relationship between the levels of government (national and provincial/state), and the relationship of the governments to their citizens (the *Canadian Charter of Rights and Freedoms* and the Bill of Rights). An examination of select policy areas reveals the similarities and differences flowing from each countries' constitutional law. These similarities and differences in policy making also stem from each nation's historical trajectories, and institutional structures such as electoral constraints on elite decision-making, the courts, and the nature of federalism. To illustrate the similarities and differences in policy choices between the two countries, we consider marijuana legalization, abortion, medically assisted death, government funding for religious schools, health care, guns, climate change, free speech, and language.

## 2) Marijuana

One way to measure a country's democracy is to determine if its constitutional framework permits citizen involvement in proposing and approving policy. The policy case of the legalization of marijuana provides an example of the extent to which each country differs in relation to direct citizen approval of laws.

In 2000, the Ontario Court of Appeal in *R v Parker* ruled Canadians have a constitutional right to use medical cannabis.[1] Initially, under a law passed by the government of Conservative Prime Minister Stephen Harper in 2013, users could get medical marijuana only via mail from licensed producers. Medical marijuana dispensaries popped up in Toronto and other cities, but they were illegal. In November 2017, the Canadian House of Commons approved a bill to make recreational marijuana legal nationwide, but the Senate delayed approval. A Senate committee added a large number of amendments, including one to allow provinces to ban homegrown marijuana (the House of Commons bill allowed four plants per residence). The House of Commons bill also allowed each province to regulate how legal marijuana was sold. The Senate finally passed the bill on 28 June 2018. As is typical of the Canadian policy making process, there was no public involvement or ratification of the relevant legislation.

As discussed in Chapter 3, in the United States, twenty-three state constitutions allow voter initiatives, in which voters sign petitions to put a proposed law directly on the ballot in an election and bypass state legislatures. If a majority of voters approves the proposal on election day, it becomes law even if elected leaders oppose the idea. For example, in 1996, 56 percent of California voters approved a medical marijuana initiative over the objections of the governor and most elected officials in the state. The initiative allowed Californians to grow and possess personal amounts of marijuana if they have a medical condition and get a doctor's note. Since then, thirty-eight other states as of 2024, as well as the District of Columbia, have approved legal medical marijuana, either by voter initiative, or by the state legislatures.

In November 2012, voters in Colorado and Washington state approved initiatives to make possession and cultivation of personal amounts of recreational marijuana legal, and to have the state regulate, tax, and license legal marijuana dealers, similar to the way states regulate alcohol sales. Since then, many other states have used voter initiatives to make recreational marijuana legal. As of 2024, a total of twenty-four states have legalized recreational marijuana, thirteen through voter initiatives and eleven by state legislatures. During the 2024 election, three states — Florida, North Dakota, and South Dakota — rejected legalizing recreational marijuana. A majority of Floridians voted to make recreational marijuana legal, but this was less than the 60 percent approval required by the state.

However, all marijuana remains illegal under United States *federal* law. The administration of Republican President George W Bush (2001–2009) frequently raided medical marijuana dispensaries in California. In 2009, President Barack Obama announced that the federal government would stop raiding medical marijuana dispensaries in states that made those legal. And in 2014, Congress passed a law forbidding use of federal government funds to enforce federal marijuana laws in medical cannabis cases in states where that is legal. This law is still in effect, meaning that marijuana is illegal under federal law, but that it is not enforced in medical cannabis cases in most states.

In 2013, the Obama administration announced that the federal government would not enforce federal marijuana laws in states that made recreational marijuana legal, as long as those states enforced regulations to prevent sales to minors, drugged driving, and sales as part of a criminal enterprise. In 2018, Republican Attorney General

Jeff Sessions rescinded all Obama policies that blocked federal enforcement of federal marijuana laws, and directed that federal prosecutors can raid recreational marijuana stores and arrest sellers and users. That never happened, partly because congressional Republicans from states where recreational marijuana was legal opposed any such raids.

In April 2022, the Democratic majority in the House of Representatives voted 220:204 to make marijuana legal under federal law, but the bill did not pass the Senate and died at the end of 2022. President Joe Biden has publicly supported legal medical marijuana, but has opposed legal recreational marijuana. The Biden administration worked in 2023 to reschedule marijuana to lessen the criminal penalties.[2] As of 2023, there had been no federal raids on legal, state-licensed marijuana stores in the previous decade.

Notice the paths to legalization in both countries reflects how policy can be similar, while the means to achieving it can be quite different. In Canada, the law is nationwide — not provincial — with medical use permitted due to a court decision, and recreational use due to federal legislation. In the United States, legal marijuana was initially approved through voter initiative state by state, with federal law still criminalizing it.

## 3) Abortion

In Canada, before 1988, federal law allowed women to have abortions to save the life or health of the mother upon approval of a three-doctor medical committee. Complaints were commonplace that committee rulings took too long, were inconsistent, and committees were typically staffed only by male doctors. In 1969, Dr. Henry Morgentaler of Montreal opened an abortion clinic, and performed thousands of abortions without medical committee approval. He was prosecuted several times in Quebec and Ontario, but juries kept acquitting him. In 1988, the Canadian Supreme Court in *R v Morgentaler* ruled that Canada's abortion restrictions violated rights to liberty and security of the person in the *Canadian*

*Charter of Rights and Freedoms*.³ This was similar to the landmark American case *Roe v Wade* (1973) (discussed below).

In 1990, Progressive Conservative Prime Minister Brian Mulroney had the House of Commons pass a bill to ban most abortions unless a woman's health or life was in danger. But the bill was blocked by the Senate, and Mulroney dropped the issue. As a result, today, Canada has no criminal laws at all regarding abortion at any time during pregnancy and no American-style regulations of abortion. However, unequal access to abortion services across Canada remains an unresolved public policy issue. As we will see below, the legal framework for abortion in Canada contrasts dramatically with the American case.

In 1973, abortion was illegal in most American states. Norma McCorvey of Texas was unmarried and pregnant and sought an abortion; she said at the time she had been raped, which many years later she said was untrue. Some attorneys in Texas took her legal case. Replacing McCorvey's name with that of Jane Roe, they sued the Dallas County District Attorney Henry Wade, creating the case now famously known as *Roe v Wade*.⁴ While the case was going through the courts, McCorvey had a daughter, and put her up for adoption. (As an aside, later, McCorvey became an activist in the anti-abortion movement. But in a documentary about her life released in May 2020, she revealed she had been paid to say that her involvement in *Roe v Wade* was "the biggest mistake of [her] life." She also said that her anti-abortion activism had been "all an act."⁵)

In its 1973 decision, the United States Supreme Court said that "we need not resolve the difficult question of when life begins." Then in its decision, the Supreme Court resolved the difficult question of when life begins. The Court ruled that before viability (the moment a fetus is able to live outside the mother's womb), a woman's constitutional right to liberty under the Fourteenth Amendment means she has an absolute right to have an abortion. The Court ruled that after viability, states can make abortion illegal to protect the human life of the fetus unless the mother's life or health are in danger. Subsequently, forty-three states made late-term abortions illegal in almost all cases. In 1992, the Supreme Court decided in *Planned Parenthood of Southeast Pennsylvania v Casey* to uphold a Pennsylvania law requiring that women seeking abortions get counselling about alternatives, undergo a twenty-four-hour wait period, and get parental or judicial consent for minors.[6] As of 2022, about half of American states had similar regulations.

On 24 June 2022, a largely conservative American Supreme Court overruled *Roe v Wade* in *Dobbs v Jackson Women's Health Organization*, a decision that sent political shock waves throughout America.[7] A majority on the Court argued that the substantive right to abortion was not "deeply rooted in this Nation's history or tradition." Nor was it considered a right when the Fourteenth Amendment's due process clause was ratified in 1868 and under which abortion was seen as legal; indeed, the Court said, it was unknown in the United States law until *Roe v Wade*. The argument was disputed and criticized by the dissenting opinion, which argued that many other rights, such as contraception, interracial marriage, and same-sex marriage, did not exist when the Fourteenth Amendment was ratified in 1868, and would also be unconstitutional according to the Court majority's logic.

Since that historic overturning of *Roe v Wade*, abortion rights in the United States have become a patchwork of state laws, similar to the pattern found with marijuana laws. As of 2024, about seventeen states had banned almost all legal abortions, including most of the South, another four states had banned most legal abortions at some point before viability, and several other attempted state bans on abortion have been tested in court cases. As was true before the *Dobbs* decision, only a small number of states follow the Canadian model of having no legal restrictions on abortion at any time during the pregnancy, and many states where abortion is legal continued to have Pennsylvania-style restrictions on the procedure. While the Supreme Court overturned abortion rights under the federal Constitution, reproductive freedom remains a constitutional right under more than ten state constitutions.[8] In the 2024 election, voters in seven more states expanded protection for abortion rights.

In Canada, abortion at any stage of a pregnancy remains legal nationwide due to the 1988 *R v Morgentaler* Supreme Court decision and the inability to pass a new law to restrict abortion in 1990. Leadership of the Conservative Party of Canada, has long sought to prevent party members from pushing for new abortion restriction laws with the attitude that such laws would lose large numbers of votes for the party. So for the time being, legal abortion remains a settled national policy in Canada. In the United States, abortion remains one of the most polarizing issues in American society, and is one of the issues having the most impact on voter decisions. After the *Dobbs* decision, about half of the states moved to make almost all abortions illegal, while the other half instituted legal or constitutional protections for abortion rights.

### 4) Assisted Death

In February 2015, the Canadian Supreme Court ruled in *Carter v Canada* that the federal *Criminal Code*'s prohibition on assisted death violated the *Canadian Charter of Rights and Freedoms*.[9] It ruled that section 14 and section 241(b) of the *Criminal Code* were unconstitutional because they prohibited doctors from assisting in the consensual death of another person. The Court gave the Canadian government one year to pass a new law on the issue, but the Conservative Harper government stalled, the Liberals won the federal election of October 2015, and the Court gave them until June 2016 to create a new law.

Prime Minister Justin Trudeau's Liberal government patterned the Canadian law almost exactly on an American law pioneered in Oregon and other state laws (see below in this section). The biggest difference is that Canadian law allows the physician to administer the lethal drugs, whereas the American states only permit the patient to do so. The Trudeau bill was opposed by both those on the right who did not support doctor-assisted death, and many on the left who did not like the narrowness of the law, which would not allow assisted death by those without terminal illnesses, those who wished to give advance directives, mature minors, or the mentally ill. The bill passed the House of Commons 186:137; all but four Liberals voted in favour, all but fourteen Conservatives voted against, and all New Democratic Party (NDP), Bloc Québécois, and Green Party Members of Parliament (MPs) voted against. The Senate then approved the bill soon after by a vote of 48:22. As a result, in Canada, medically assisted death is legal nationwide, and almost always administered by doctors.

A decision by a court in Quebec ruled that limits on medically assisted death by those without terminal illnesses violated the *Canadian Charter of Rights and Freedoms*; so the Canadian Parliament amended the law in 2021. The new law allows those with serious and incurable illnesses or disabilities that are not terminal and who have enduring and intolerable suffering to be eligible for medical assistance in dying (MAID). The amended law temporarily excluded those with exclusively mental illnesses until 2023, a deadline extended until 2027 due to the controversy and difficulty of creating regulations over allowing patients with mental illnesses to get medically assisted death.[10] Also in 2023, a special joint committee of Parliament recommended that the law be amended to include the ability to make advance directives to request medical assistance in dying for those with serious and incurable medical conditions that will lead to incapacity (such as Alzheimer's disease).[11] The joint committee also recommended that further research be conducted to determine if mature minors should be eligible for the law. As of 2024, eleven countries in the world had end-of-life treatment. Canada was the fastest-growing adopter as the number of Canadians using medically assisted death grew at a speed that outpaced every other nation.[12]

Assisted death policy in the United States began with another voter initiative. In 1994, 51 percent of Oregon voters approved the *Death with Dignity Act* to allow doctors to prescribe lethal doses of medicine to mentally competent adult patients with less than six months to live. Patients had to request the drugs, could acquire them fifteen days later, and had to self-administer them. The Oregon state legislature, the Catholic church, and organizations for the disabled all opposed the law and fought it in court, losing all lawsuits by 1997. The Oregon state legislature put a general referendum on the ballot in 1997 to ask voters to repeal the *Death with Dignity Act*. Sixty percent of Oregon voters rejected the repeal, voting to keep the law. In 1998, Oregon became the first jurisdiction in North America to make doctor-assisted death legal, and remained the only such jurisdiction in North America for the next decade.

In 2008, Washington state voters passed the same initiative, and Colorado voters approved death with dignity in 2016. Since 2013, Death with Dignity Acts have also been approved by state legislatures in Vermont, Maine, New Jersey, New Mexico, Hawaii, and California, and in the District of Columbia. All these laws were modelled on, or close to, the Oregon law. Statistics compiled by Oregon show that 2,454 patients had used the law to kill themselves between 1998 and 2022. In 2022, the median age was seventy-five, while 85 percent of patients were senior citizens, 64 percent were cancer patients, 12 percent were patients of heart disease, and 10 percent were patients of neurological diseases. Statistics from other states are similar.[13]

In Oregon, a few more requirements were added to the Death with Dignity regulations before they went fully into effect: a doctor determines if you are mentally competent; two doctors must agree with the diagnosis; and you must be a resident of Oregon. As well, there must be two witnesses who approve of the decision, one of whom cannot be a relative or an heir, or a medical treating professional. In 2022, court cases in Vermont and Oregon that questioned the constitutionality of limiting doctor-assisted death only to state residents led to both states removing that restriction, enabling non-residents to be eligible.

Once again, we have a policy issue that was decided differently in both countries. While court rulings were important in both Canada and the United States, voter initiatives also played an important role in the latter country. But there has been no citizen initiative or approval in Canada. In Canada, medical-assistance-in-dying laws have been approved at the national level, while Death with

Dignity-style laws have been approved by some states but remain illegal in most of the United States. The policies in the two countries differ as well, with most medically assisted deaths in Canada administered directly by doctors and eligibility broadened to those without terminal illnesses. In the United States, drugs prescribed for assisted death must be self-administered under state laws, and only those with less than six months to live are eligible.

## 5) Government Funding for Religious Schools

In Canada, education is a provincial government responsibility, but the provinces have responded in quite different ways to the policy problems posed by religious schools. This is, as two scholars put it, a "peculiar reality."[14] Taxpayer-funded Catholic school systems exist in Ontario, Saskatchewan, Alberta, and two territories, Yukon (to grade 9) and Northwest Territories. Newfoundland and Labrador voted to end the denominational school system after a 1997 referendum. Quebec also eliminated its Catholic and Protestant school boards in 1997.

Children in Ontario have four different taxpayer-funded school systems — public English, public French, Catholic English, and Catholic French. Publicly funded Catholic schools in Ontario are allowed to discriminate in the hiring of teachers and allowed to discriminate in elementary school admissions. The United Nations Human Rights Committee in 1999 and in 2005 ruled that Ontario funding for Catholic schools was religious discrimination against other groups. However, the Canadian Supreme Court ruled in *Adler v Ontario* that taxpayer-funded Catholic schools in Ontario are allowed under the BNA Act, 1867 and they continue to exist to this day.[15] In the 2007 provincial election in Ontario, the Progressive Conservative leader John Tory proposed expanding funding to *all* denominational schools. The ensuing storm of protest over the idea contributed to his defeat. Periodically, issues arise that pit the Catholic school boards against broader public opinion on various issues. In 2023, for example, some boards voted not to display the pride flag, a symbol of LGBTQIA2S+ rights and culture. Consequently, the issue of defunding the Catholic system returned to the headlines. Given that just more than 30 percent of Ontarians are Catholic, governments are loathe to tackle the issue head-on by ending Catholic school funding.

The American Constitution says that governments in the United States cannot establish a state religion. In 1968, Pennsylvania passed a state law to provide state funds for all teacher salaries and instructional materials for non-religious courses taught at religious schools (which were 97 percent Catholic). In *Lemon v Kurtzman*, the Supreme Court ruled that the Pennsylvania law was unconstitutional for "fostering excessive government entanglement with religion."[16] However, in *Zelman-Simmons v Harris*, the United States Supreme Court ruled that it was permissible for Ohio to give low-income parents in Cleveland some tuition money to pay for kids to attend Catholic schools (using school vouchers).[17] The Court drew a distinction between direct government payments to Catholic schools (as in the 1968 Pennsylvania law) and providing tuition money to parents who choose to send their children to Catholic schools.

Since then, several other states have started and expanded school voucher programs for low-income children, including Ohio, Wisconsin, Maryland, Louisiana, North Carolina, and New Hampshire. Lower-income children are also eligible for school vouchers in the District of Columbia. But school voucher programs remain controversial with the public in the United States. In 2000, 68 percent of Michigan voters and 71 percent of California voters rejected ballot measures to start school voucher programs in those states. In 2007, after the Utah state legislature approved school vouchers for the state, 62 percent of Utah voters voted for a ballot measure to repeal the school voucher law, which never took effect. And in 2024, voters in Colorado and Kentucky ballot propositions rejected attempts to start school voucher programs, while Nebraska voters repealed a new law passed by the legislature to start school vouchers.

Despite all that, in 2022, Arizona and West Virginia became the first states to approve laws for universal school vouchers for all children, not just low-income children. And in 2023, eight other state legislatures approved universal school voucher programs — Iowa, Florida, Arkansas, Indiana, Oklahoma, Utah (despite Utah voter rejection of such a program in 2007), North Carolina, and Ohio (who eliminated low-income eligibility requirements).[18] These universal school voucher programs can provide $8,000 or more of state funding for middle-income and wealthy parents to send children to private religious schools, potentially constituting a very large expense for state budgets; they remain controversial with voters.

In this case, both countries have involved the courts and citizens in consideration of the policy issue of government funding for religious schools. In addition, a supranational body, the United Nations, weighed in on the issue in Canada, although its findings were non-binding and of no practical effect. While direct government funding of Catholic schools exists in a few Canadian provinces, many American states have moved in recent years to provide a form of indirect funding for Catholic and other private religious schools through parental use of government-funded school vouchers. In both countries, government funding for religious schools remains controversial.

## 6) Health Care

As a case study, the COVID-19 pandemic of 2019 provides a fascinating snapshot of health policy in both countries. By 2021, Canada's total population was around 85 percent fully vaccinated, and more than 40 percent of Canadians had received boosters. In the United States, by comparison, only 65 percent were fully vaccinated, and less than half of the fully vaccinated had received boosters, according to the Centers for Disease Control (CDC). There were also relatively fewer COVID-19 deaths in Canada. The United States had nearly 343 deaths per 100,000 Americans, among the highest rates among developed countries. Canada, meanwhile, sustained 132 deaths per 100,000 people.[19] There were 52,860 COVID-19–related deaths in Canada compared to more than 1.1 million in the United States by 2022.[20]

In Canada, the United States is frequently cited as a model to avoid and as a warning against increasing private sector involvement in health care. In the United States, meanwhile, Canada's health system is seen by different sides of the ideological spectrum as either a model to be followed or avoided. Canada has one of the world's most fully socialized health care systems (with the exception of some services), while the United States is one of only two Organisation for Economic Co-operation and Development (OECD) countries (with Mexico) not to have some form of guaranteed health insurance for all citizens.

The governments of both nations are closely involved in the delivery of health care. The central structural difference between the two is in health insurance. In Canada, where health policy is a provincial area of jurisdiction, the federal government provides funding support to provincial governments for health care expenditures as long as the provinces abide by the five principles of the *Canada Health Act*. These dictate that provincial health care systems must be based on: (1) public administration; (2) comprehensiveness; (3) universality; (4) portability; and (5) accessibility. Provinces that fail to abide by these five principles can have their federal funding clawed back. Moreover, the *Canada Health Act* explicitly prohibits billing end users for procedures that are covered by Medicare. In 2023, Ottawa charged that some provinces were violating the universality provisions of the *Canada Health Act* by allowing private clinics to provide medically necessary services that should be available to patients at no cost. The federal government withheld transfers to those provinces totalling more than $82 million to induce the provinces to stop the practice.[21]

In the United States, before the passage of the *Patient Protection and Affordable Care Act* in March 2010 (also known as Obamacare), federal and state government funding of the health care needs of its citizens was limited to two broad programs. Medicare provided insurance for eligible seniors and those with long-term disabilities (in Canada, Medicare refers to the universal public health insurance system for all), and Medicaid provided insurance for those with low income and assets. Otherwise, health insurance had to be paid for privately; in most cases, a person's employer provided it. However, that left about 46 million Americans (although not all were citizens) without health insurance.

Both countries had roughly similar health care systems until the 1960s. In 1966, the Canadian government, following the lead of the provincial government in Saskatchewan, created a national universal public health care system. The United States, by comparison, did not create such a system, although it did gradually extend government involvement in the delivery of health care. One of the key reasons for the differences between the two countries has to do with the presence in Canada of a vibrant social democratic and socialist political tradition. The Cooperative Commonwealth Federation (CCF, later called the New Democratic Party or NDP) government of Saskatchewan under Premier Tommy Douglas, where the first socialist government in North America was elected in 1944, championed expanding the social welfare state, including through the creation of universal public health care. The reform was met with intense pushback by doctors and insurance companies. Doctors staged an unsuccessful twenty-three-day strike in 1962 to protest universal health coverage. The popularity of the program made it too politically damaging to remove.

In 1966, federal Liberal Prime Minister Lester Pearson headed a minority government and relied in part on the support of the national NDP in Parliament for support. The NDP was thus able to leverage its position to influence the decision to adopt a national universal pubic health care system. A similar political dynamic emerged in March 2022, when the governing Liberal Party under Trudeau struck a "confidence-and-supply agreement" with the NDP that required the government to table legislation on a pharmacare program that covers most prescription drugs by the end of 2023, later extended to 2024, in exchange for the NDP's support on key votes in the House of Commons. This pharmacare initiative represents the single most expensive expansion of the health care system since Medicare was introduced.

The United States, in contrast, lacks the same kind of social democratic or socialist streak in its politics. This is in part because of the more individualistic, free market ideological views that predominate there. The American political culture is historically more suspicious and resistant to state intervention (see Chapter 1). On a more prosaic level, the Cold War was raging at the time when Canada and many western European countries expanded the size and role of their social welfare systems; the United States instead was pouring huge sums of money into its military. Later, with the demise of the Cold War came the rise of neoconservatism, an ideological movement that regarded state intervention as anathema. Still, by the 1990s, improving the American health care system had become a pressing issue. Democratic President Bill Clinton attempted reform of health care during his first term in office (1993–1997), but failed to get Congressional approval. In 2008, Obama also tackled health care reform and he succeeded in having the *Patient Protection and Affordable Health Care Act* passed in 2010. In 2017, Republican President Donald Trump made repeal of Obamacare central to his presidency, but ultimately failed.

In any event, health care is now one of the most expensive items of both nations' budgets. The United States spends more on health care as a percentage of gross domestic product (GDP) and more per capita on health care than Canada. In 2019, the United States spent 16.8 percent of GDP on health care compared to Canada's spending 10.8 percent of GDP; the United States spent US$10,948 per capita, more than twice as much as Canada spending of US$5,370 per capita.[22] There is also a large difference in how much total health care spending is accounted for by government spending. In the United States, only 45 percent of total health expenses is covered by government spending, whereas in Canada 70 percent is covered. The rest of health care spending in both countries is accounted for out of pocket or through supplemental insurance.[23]

Comparisons of spending lead to consideration of outcomes. As well as costing less, Canada's health care system performs considerably better than the American system. As one report expressed it, "Compared to people in most developed nations, including Canada, Americans have for years paid far more for health care while staying sicker and dying sooner."[24] Indeed, the cost of health care in the United States is by far the highest in the world, yet the United States also has the worst health outcomes overall of any high-income nation.[25] Analysis of eleven high-income countries with regard to five health care areas — access to care, care process, administrative efficiency, equity, and health care outcomes — shows the top-performing countries overall are Norway, the Netherlands, and Australia, while the United States ranks last overall, despite spending far more of its gross domestic product on health care. Before Canadians get too smug about these findings, though, this study also showed that Canada was second last in the rankings.[26] Still, infant mortality rates are lower in Canada, as are obesity rates, while life expectancy is longer than in the United States.[27]

Solving health care problems has often seen the provinces and states act as policy laboratories. Several more radical policy solutions in both countries have come from the sub-national level (states and provinces). As noted above, for instance, Saskatchewan innovated universal public health care in the 1960s. The scheme was later adopted by the federal government. Oil-rich Alberta, under the provincial Conservative Party for forty years, experimented the most with increasing the role of the private sector in health care, including the introduction of private clinics that are allowed to bill patients for some of the cost of a procedure. The United Conservative Party, elected in 2019 in Alberta, has also engaged in reforms seeking to extend privatization of health care. Quebec too has experimented with private health care: Quebec now has the highest number of private clinics that deliver publicly funded care, as well as whole hospitals and emergency wards that have opted out of the public system.

A Canadian court decision in 2005 ruled that the Canadian health care system, which outlaws private health insurance, contravened the Quebec Charter of Human Rights and Freedoms guaranteeing the right to security of the person. In June 2005, the Supreme Court of Canada in *Chaoulli v Quebec* overturned a Quebec law preventing people from buying private health insurance to pay for medical services available through the publicly funded system.[28] While the ruling applies only to the province of Quebec, concerns were raised that it would fundamentally change the way health care is delivered across the country, although its long-term impact seems muted thus far. In Ontario in 2023, the Progressive Conservative government of Premier Doug Ford also expanded the use of private for-profit health care facilities in the delivery of medically necessary publicly funded procedures, although this was one of the provincial measures that triggered the federal government invocation of the *Canada Health Act*, mentioned in this section above.

At the national level in Canada, various right wing parties, including the now defunct Reform Party and its successor, the Conservative Party of Canada, have expressed an interest in further privatizing the public health care system. But to many Canadians, public universal health care is symbolic of what it means to be Canadian, and strong public backlashes have often caused these parties to tone down or even abandon overt declarations of favouring private health care. For example, in the 2004 Canadian election, it was alleged by the Liberal Party that the Conservatives had a secret plan to change Medicare, which caused the collapse of the Conservatives' popularity in the last days of the campaign.[29] The issue partly faded into the background in the 2006 and subsequent elections until the arrival of the COVID-19 pandemic in 2019 (see below).

In 2002 in the United States, Massachusetts Republican Governor Mitt Romney introduced health care reform legislation that provided near-universal health insurance access, mostly through a mandate for state residents to have a minimum level of (usually private) insurance.[30] This model was later used in the federal *Affordable Care Act*, though Governor Romney always claimed his

Massachusetts model was different. Hawaii since 1974 has required private employers in the state to provide health insurance for most full-time employees.[31] Vermont's legislature passed a law in 2011 to provide government funded and managed health insurance to all state residents, but its "Green Mountain Care" plan was abandoned in 2014 due to complaints about the taxes involved.[32]

The goals of Obama's *Affordable Care Act* included increasing the quality and affordability of health insurance, lowering the uninsured rate by expanding public and private insurance coverage, and reducing the costs of health care for individuals and the government. It introduced a number of mechanisms to increase coverage and affordability within new minimum standards and offer the same rates regardless of pre-existing conditions or sex. It survived several legal and countless congressional challenges. Twenty million more Americans were covered by 2018 than had been covered in 2010. Repealing Obamacare became a central plank of the Republican Party and president after 2016; all attempts failed, and the Republicans turned to other issues. Meanwhile, public support for the *Affordable Care Act* has grown through the years, especially when former President Obama is not mentioned in polling questions (some Americans did not realize that the *Affordable Care Act* and "Obamacare" were the same thing).[33]

So why were COVID-19-related policies and outcomes different in Canada and the United States? There are several possible explanations.[34] First, Canada's universal publicly funded health care system meant all Canadians have access to health care. Lack of universal access meant that far more Americans ended up in intensive care than in Canada — about seventy-nine per million in the United States compared to thirty-two per million in Canada. Second, mandates were important. In Canada and the United States, individual provinces, territories, and states can implement and lift local mandates governing behaviour such as going to restaurants, gyms, and other public venues as they see fit. But the Canadian federal government had jurisdiction on issues such as vaccine passports for domestic travel, vaccination requirements for federal employees, or cross-border truckers. (The latter was what initially prompted huge protests that paralyzed Ottawa and blocked the Canada-United States border in February 2022 and caused the invocation of the *Emergencies Act* in Canada for the first time in its history.) In the United States, some cities like New York City introduced vaccine passes to access restaurants and bars, but Canada's mandates were stricter and lasted far longer. The more gradual relaxation of these rules, which were dependent on improvements in public health data, allowed it to avoid the same high levels of infections and deaths that were experienced in the United States, where numbers spiked in several locations that rushed to ease regulations.

A majority of Americans continue to receive health insurance through employer-chosen private plans, while almost all Canadians receive provincial health insurance under the *Canada Health Act*. Both systems have some advantages and disadvantages. The Canadian system costs less, ensures that almost everyone can afford health care, and tends to cause a healthier overall population. The profit-driven American health care system leaves out some people and also makes affordability a problem due to monthly premium payments, co-pays, and deductibles. But those profit incentives also provide far faster access to some types of medical treatments and technology, at least for those who can afford it, than the long waits for non-emergency treatments and diagnostics imposed on many Canadians.

## 7) Guns — A "Wicked Policy Problem"

A "wicked policy problem" is a social or cultural issue or concern that is difficult to explain and inherently impossible to solve. Conflicting values and perspectives, uncertainties about complex causal relationships, and debate about the impacts of policy options characterize wicked policy problems. Why gun policy in the United States appears to fit this characterization whereas it does not in Canada is the focus of this section.

Between 1989 and 2020, there were six mass shootings (defined as four or more people shot in one incident) in Canada, resulting in sixty-four deaths. The École Polytechnique massacre on 6 December 1989 in Montreal, Quebec killed fourteen and wounded another fourteen when a man spewing an anti-feminist, anti-women rant ordered all the men to leave a classroom and opened fire on the remaining women. In the Concordia University massacre on 24 August 1992 in Montreal, four were killed and one wounded in a school shooting. In the Vernon, British Columbia massacre on 6 April 1996, nine were killed and two wounded when an estranged husband murdered a wedding party. In the Shedden, Ontario massacre on 8 April 2006, eight were killed in a biker gang killing of its own gang members. In the Quebec City mosque shooting on 29 January 2017, six were killed and nineteen wounded in an Islamophobic attack on the Islamic Cultural Centre. And on 18–19 April 2020 in Nova Scotia, twenty-two were killed and three wounded at multiple locations when the perpetrator committed multiple shootings using illegal firearms and set fires at sixteen locations while disguised as a Royal Canadian Mounted Police (RCMP) officer.

It is possible to summarize mass shootings in Canada over this thirty-one year period (1989–2020) in a single paragraph. It is not possible to do so regarding mass shootings in the United States for even a single month. It is estimated that there is almost one mass shooting per day in the United States. Repeated massacres there have provoked debate regarding gun control laws and the availability of firearms, although with relatively little effective legislative action.

There were 1.5 million firearms deaths between 1968 and 2017 in the United States. That is higher than the number of American soldiers killed in every conflict since the American War for Independence in 1775. In 2020 alone, more than 45,000 Americans died at the end of a barrel of a gun, whether by homicide or suicide, more than any other year on record to that date. This figure represents a 25 percent increase from five years prior, and a 43 percent increase from 2010. In 2021, 48,830 were killed, and there was a slight decline to 44,000 in 2022.[35]

Gun control in Canada and the United States is a policy area that marks profound differences between the two countries. Gun politics in both countries are controversial, though far less contentious in Canada than in the United States. The degree to which firearms can or should be regulated has long been debated, and disagreements range from the practical to the constitutional to the ethical. Thus, questions arise with regard to whether gun ownership causes or prevents crime; how the Second Amendment in the American Constitution should be interpreted; which weapons, if any, the government has the right to regulate; and whether self-defence is a basic individual right.

The statistical story underlines the stark differences between the two countries. In the United States, there are 14.7 deaths by firearms for every 100,000 people. In Canada, there are 2.5 deaths per 100,000. The homicide rate in the United States committed without guns is only slightly higher (1.5 per 100,000) than the Canadian rate (1.2 per 100,000). But the rate of homicide with handguns in the United States (6.3 per 100,000) is eight times higher than the Canadian rate (0.78 per 100,000).[36]

Rates of gun ownership are strikingly different too.[37] Approximately 40 percent of American households own firearms, including about 17 percent owning handguns. Put another way, there are about 120.5 civilian-owned firearms per 100 people in the United States. That makes the United States the country with the highest rate of civilian gun ownership in the world, and that rate is nearly double that of the next highest country. Of the 326,474,000 Americans (2017), civilians own about 393,347,000 firearms, suggesting that the United States is home to more guns than people. There are 34.7 firearms per 100 people in Canada, where only 16 percent of households own firearms, with 3 percent owning handguns. Moreover, new handgun restrictions were enacted in 2022, so this number will drop even lower (see below).

Handguns have been controlled in Canada by statute since Confederation in 1867. The *Criminal Code* of Canada enacted in 1892, required individuals to have a permit to carry a pistol unless the owner had cause to fear assault or injury, and it was an offence to sell a pistol to anyone under sixteen years of age. Vendors who sold handguns had to keep records, including the purchaser's name, the date of sale, and a description of the gun.

*Criminal Code* of Canada amendments between the 1890s and 1990s steadily increased the restrictions on firearms. In the 1920s, permits became necessary for all firearms newly acquired by foreigners. In 1947, the offence of "constructive murder" was added to the *Criminal Code* for offences resulting in death when the offender carried a firearm. This offence was struck down as unconstitutional by the Supreme Court of Canada in the 1987 case *R v Vaillancourt*.[38] Automatic weapons were added to the category of firearms that had to be registered in 1951. The registry system was centralized under the commissioner of the RCMP.

The categories of "firearm," "restricted weapon," and "prohibited weapon" were created in 1968–1969. Police were given preventative powers of search and seizure by judicial warrant if they had grounds to believe that weapons that belonged to an individual endangered the safety of society. Legislative provisions between 1977 and 1979 required firearms acquisition certificates for all weapons and provided controls on the selling of ammunition. Fully automatic weapons were prohibited. Applicants for firearms acquisition certificates were required to take a safety course. The pressure that led to the current legal regime began with the 1989 École Polytechnique massacre. Between 1991 and 1994, legislation tightened up restrictions and established controls on military, paramilitary, and high-firepower weapons.

In 1995, new, stricter gun control legislation was passed with harsher penalties for crimes involving firearm use, licences to possess and acquire firearms, and registration of all firearms, including shotguns and rifles. The law also required all firearms to be registered. The cost of the firearms registry soared to well over 500 times its original $2-million budget, which proved embarrassing for the Liberal government, and led to increased calls for the registry's cancellation. But due to the École Polytechnique massacre, combined with official policies on gender equality in the *Canadian Charter of Rights and Freedoms*, many Canadians also link gun control issues to gender-related issues like violence by men against women. In March 2012, the Harper government, responding to its constituents (including rural, male, Western Canadian voters), excluded long guns from the gun registry when it passed Bill C-19. Quebec objected, and announced it would maintain a provincial long gun registry of its own. In June 2019, the Trudeau government passed new gun legislation, Bill C-71, *An Act to amend certain Acts and Regulations in relation to firearms*, which reintroduced a form of the long gun registry.

Following the worst gun massacre in Canadian history in Nova Scotia in April 2020, the Trudeau government immediately announced legislation to ban assault weapons.

On 30 May 2022, it introduced legislation to buy back assault-style weapons not already banned and freeze the purchase, sale, importation, and transfer of handguns. Critics have long argued that the main source of handguns in Canada are those smuggled illegally into the country from the United States, but the legislation did little to tackle this problem. Overall, the trajectory of Canadian approaches to gun policy has moved fairly consistently toward tightening the rules for ownership and access going all the way back to the late nineteenth century. No such trajectory is evident in the American case.

The gun politics debate in the United States has centred around the meaning of the Second Amendment of the United States Constitution (1791), and also on the right to bear arms clauses in individual state constitutions. The Second Amendment as passed by the House and Senate and later ratified by the states, reads: "A well-regulated militia being necessary to the security of a free State, the right of the People to keep and bear arms shall not be infringed."

Debates about the meaning of the Second Amendment reveal the importance of the interpretation of words in a constitutional document. For some Americans, the wording of the amendment is about a fundamental individual right, which they see as necessary for things like self-defence, hunting, and target shooting. But for some Americans the Second Amendment goes further than that; it affirms the belief that because of the need of a formal military, the people have a right to "keep and bear arms" as a protection from the government, and that it protects their right to revolution. They sustain this argument by pointing out that the Second Amendment is part of the Bill of Rights, and argue that the Bill of Rights, by its nature, defines individual rights. Thus, there is an inalienable individual right to guns. The meaning of this text remains fiercely debated, with some saying that the amendment refers only to official federal entities, such as the Army or the National Guard. Some gun control advocates argue that the Second Amendment does not cover individual gun ownership. They suggest that the right to own firearms rests on other grounds that render it subject to the full force of the state's police powers, and/or that the amendment is anachronistic and its outright repeal is needed.

Gun control advocates and opponents also disagree on practical questions such as the role guns play in crime. Gun rights groups argue that a well-armed citizenry prevents crime and that making civilian ownership of firearms illegal would increase the crime rate by making law-abiding citizens vulnerable to those who choose to disregard the law. Gun control organizations claim that increased gun ownership leads to higher levels of crime, suicide, and other negative outcomes. One thing both sides generally agree on is that the gun rights lobby is among the most effective and organized single-issue political groups in the United States, with the most prominent example being the National Rifle Association (NRA).

Gun control law in the United States is generally connected to major traumatic events like assassinations and massacres. For instance, the 1968 *Gun Control Act* was passed shortly after the assassinations of presidential candidate Robert Kennedy and civil rights leader Dr. Martin Luther King. Many states implemented criminal background checks or "waiting periods" for handgun purchasers in response to the gun control lobby in the 1980s. Other lobbying efforts have resulted in the passage of laws making it a crime to leave guns in locations accessible to children. In 1998, the National

Instacheck System (NICS) came online managed by the FBI to run database checks on criminal records.

Gun control in the United States is a deeply political issue; the political responses to massacres, often led by strong presidential action, illustrates this point. Within one month of the Sandy Hook massacre on 14 December 2012, in Newtown, Connecticut, when a twenty-year-old man shot and killed twenty children between six and seven years old, and six adult staff members, Obama signed twenty-three executive orders and proposed twelve congressional actions regarding gun control. They included universal background checks on firearms purchases, an assault weapons ban, and limits on magazine capacity to ten cartridges. His government formed a Gun Violence Task Force led by Vice President Joe Biden to address the causes of gun violence. The NRA responded by suggesting armed police officers be placed in all schools and proposed an end to gun-free zones in America.[39] After the Marjory Stoneman Douglas school shooting in Parkland, Florida on 14 February 2018, where a nineteen-year-old man opened fire on students and staff, murdering seventeen people and injuring seventeen others, American high school students organized mass mobilizations across the country to demand gun control. Some of the student leaders of the protests were vilified and demonized on social media by pro-gun advocates. One video surfaced of Republican Representative Marjorie Taylor Greene confronting Parkland shooting survivor David Hogg before she was elected to Congress, claiming his activism was funded by billionaire philanthropist George Soros, who is often the subject of far-right antisemitic conspiracy theories.[40]

Because most criminal laws are defined at the state level in the United States, unlike in Canada where the *Criminal Code* is federal, most gun laws in the United States have been enacted at the state level.

Federal regulations and restrictions in the United States include:

1. Bans on the possession and sale of almost all fully automatic machine guns

2. Requirements that all gun manufacturers, importers, and dealers in the gun business get a federal firearms license (FFL)
3. Bans on certain categories of people from legally owning guns — most convicted felons, those addicted to illegal drugs, committed to psychiatric institutions, subjected to protection from abuse orders, and convicted of domestic violence
4. Requiring gun purchasers to be twenty-one years of age to buy a handgun from a licensed dealer, and eighteen years of age to buy a long gun from a licensed dealer
5. Requiring background checks for any firearm purchase from a licensed dealer, but not for purchases from others (known as the "gun show loophole")
6. Only allowing licensed dealers to sell firearms across state borders
7. A ban on semi-automatic "assault weapons" (1994-2004). The ban expired in 2004.
8. Making it illegal to manufacture, import, sell, or possess any firearms not detectable by metal detectors (metal must be added to any gun made by a 3D printer)

Meanwhile, a large majority of states allow the sale and possession of "assault weapons," require no licence or safety course to own or purchase firearms, do not require firearms to be registered, and allow gunowners to carry firearms in public without permits. Some states are more restrictive. Hawaii, California, and Oregon, for example, do require that all firearms be registered with government authorities. Seven states ban all or almost all sales and possession of "assault weapons" as of 2023. Eleven states impose a waiting period for those seeking to purchase some or all types of guns.[41]

Attempts to reinforce gun control in the United States have often failed because of the ability of the NRA to block or impede legislation in a system of weak party discipline, and the related ability of the NRA to exact punishment on members of Congress if they support gun control. This is possible in part because of a deeply embedded "gun culture" in the United States. As pointed out in Chapter 1, the American story is one of revolution; the Canadian story is one of evolution.

## 8) Climate Change

Climate change is of course one of the key issues of our times. Given the integration of the Canadian and American economies, and the fact that pollution has a habit of not respecting borders, environmental policy has proven particularly challenging. According to political scientist Kathryn Harrison, a three-part typology of factors confound concerted and effective North American climate change action, namely: policy makers' beliefs and ideologies; electoral incentives; and political institutions.[42]

Canada and the United States both have among the highest per capita rate of emissions of greenhouse gases. While there has been a longstanding scientific consensus that climate change is occurring and is mainly caused by human activity, and that transitioning away from fossil fuels is a major element in resolving the issue, the governments of both Canada and the United States have been laggards in confronting and dealing with climate change. Both countries have a significant historical investment in staples production, including oil and gas, and are major consumers of fossil fuels. These similarities extend to their common repeated failure to meet global standards for greenhouse gas emission reductions as well.

Shifting political economies in both countries away from dependence on fossil fuels has proven to be a formidable policy task. Citizens who express support for climate change mitigation also frequently express opposition to the costs associated with it. Historically, the oil and gas industry has effectively exploited its ties with provincial and state governments that contain reserves of fossil fuels, and has been extremely effective in resisting policy innovation that threatened its profitability. Support for the industry in both countries frequently comes from right-of-centre parties and politicians.

Continental economic integration has been a prominent feature of Canadian-American relations, with the United States typically playing the role of the hegemonic power. Such is the case with energy policy where the oil and gas industry is concerned; hence, independent efforts by the smaller partner, Canada, are often fraught. The interdependence of the two countries is unbalanced. The United States is clearly dominant and exerts much more influence internationally in areas such as global environmental treaty negotiations. Moreover, as we point out in Chapter 6, the United States accounts for a much larger share of Canada's trade than Canada does of the United States' trade.

Both countries have taken some steps toward alleviating the climate change crisis at the federal or state or provincial level. In Canada, Quebec introduced a carbon tax on energy producers in 2007. British Columbia created the first broad-based carbon tax in North America in 2008 with taxes on fossil fuels that increase each year to discourage consumption and encourage switching to alternative forms of energy. The tax is supposed to be revenue neutral with tax reductions to compensate consumers for the higher taxes on fossil fuels.[43] A key initiative of the Trudeau government was a carbon tax introduced in 2018, an idea that at the time was politically impossible in the United States. The federal government required each province to create a system of carbon pricing that met federal minimum requirements, and the federal government imposed its own carbon tax on provinces that neglected to do so.[44] The Canadian Supreme Court upheld the federal carbon tax regime in *Reference re Greenhouse Gas Pollution Pricing Act* in 2021, ruling that though natural resources are usually a provincial jurisdiction under the Canadian Constitution, the peace, order and good government clause allows the federal government to address the threat of climate change that affects the whole country and the planet.[45] The Conservative Party campaigned aggressively to end federal carbon pricing, with leader Pierre Poilievre saying he would "axe the tax."[46] Several provincial premiers also spoke out against the federal carbon tax.

In the United States, where any new taxes are often political anathema, the recent approach toward climate change policy in the Democratic party has been targeted tax breaks. The approach of most Republican leaders has been to deny that human-caused climate change exists and to avoid any discussion of any inconveniences to prevent climate change disasters. In 2022, President Biden signed the *Inflation Reduction Act* into law. The bill, which received unanimous Democratic support and unanimous Republican opposition in Congress, had little to do with reducing inflation and everything to do with tax breaks and subsidies intended to encourage use of alternative forms of energy to fossil fuels.[47] At the state level, New York in 2023 became the first state to ban use of natural gas for cooking and heating in most newly constructed buildings to cut back on methane emissions. The Regional Greenhouse Gas Initiative combines almost all northeastern states in a cap-and-trade system for power plant carbon dioxide emissions. And California and Quebec partnered in the unusual cross-border Western Climate Initiative for greenhouse gas emissions trading with a cap.

## 9) Free Speech and Hate Speech

The national constitutions of both Canada and the United States have free speech clauses. In the American case, James Madison introduced twelve amendments to the First Congress in 1789, ten of which became the Bill of Rights. The First Amendment adopted in 1791 declares that Congress shall make no law abridging freedom of speech. The Fourteenth Amendment of 1868 applies First Amendment limits on government action to state and local governments. Over time, American courts, and particularly the Supreme Court, have supported a broad and permissive approach to free speech, placing few limitations on how Americans express themselves. Limits on free speech in the United States are relatively few compared to those in Canada.

In the Canadian Constitution, the *Canadian Charter of Rights and Freedoms* was adopted in 1982, constitutionalizing the rights to freedom of thought, belief, opinion, and expression. However, Canadian courts have ruled that laws that restrict free speech to prevent hate speech are constitutionally permissible. For instance, section

319 of the Canadian *Criminal Code* makes it a criminal offence to publicly incite hatred or wilfully promote hatred in public against an identifiable group. Punishment is a fine or prison for up to two years. Identifiable groups are defined by colour, race, religion, ethnic origin, age, sex, sexual orientation, disability, or gender identity or expression (added in 2017).

The case of *R v Keegstra* before the Canadian Supreme Court is illustrative of the Canadian approach to free speech and civil rights. James Keegstra was the mayor and a high school teacher in Eckville, Alberta. He was charged with wilfully promoting hatred against Jews for teaching extreme antisemitic views to students and telling them that the Holocaust was a fraud. Keegstra required students to repeat these views on exams or be marked down in grades. Keegstra was fired from his teaching position, lost re-election as mayor, and was convicted of wilfully promoting hatred. He appealed his conviction to the Canadian Supreme Court, which upheld Canada's hate speech law 4:3, saying that hate speech is not a victimless crime, and that it can lead to discrimination, prejudice, and violence. Keegstra was fined $5,000, which was lowered on appeal to 200 hours of community service.[48]

Another illustrative Canadian case occurred in response to events in 2010 in Nova Scotia. Two brothers, Nathan and Justin Rehberg, burned a cross in the yard of an interracial couple. Convicted of publicly inciting hatred under the *Criminal Code*, they each served several months in jail.[49]

More recently convicted was Kevin Johnston of Mississauga, Ontario, for repeatedly expressing anti-Muslim views in public, on social media, and on a website he created. In 2019, Johnston was ordered by the Ontario Superior Court of Justice to pay $2.5 million in damages to the owner of a chain of Middle Eastern restaurants after the court determined Johnston had displayed "horrific" behaviour when he made "hateful Islamophobic" comments against the restaurant owner. Johnston was also charged with hate speech in 2017 for offering a $1,000 reward in exchange for videos of Muslim students praying in schools. Johnston referred to Canadian Prime Minister Justin Trudeau as "Jihadi Justin" for allowing Syrian refugees into Canada, and called the existence of the Rohingya a fraud.[50] Johnston ran for mayor of the Toronto suburb of Mississauga in 2018 and placed second with 13.5 percent of the vote. In 2021, he was found guilty of continuing hate speech against the restaurant owner and was sentenced to eighteen months in jail.

In each of these cases, and others like them, the Canadian courts explicitly recognized that limits to free speech exist. This contrasts with the American perspective. In 1978, in the case *Smith v Collin* the United States Supreme Court was confronted with a case involving antisemitism. Albert Smith was the mayor of Skokie, Illinois, a mostly Jewish suburb of Chicago, which included many Holocaust survivors. Frank Collin was the leader of the American Nazi Party, which planned to stage a march wearing uniforms with swastikas and other Nazi symbols through predominantly Jewish neighbourhoods in Skokie. Local officials denied a permit for the march, and the Nazi Party asked the Supreme Court to rule on their right to hold the march on the basis of the right to free speech.[51] The Supreme Court agreed the American Nazi Party's right to free speech had been infringed, and said the march could proceed. After the Court decision, the city of Chicago offered a permit for the Nazi Party to march there instead to spare the residents of Skokie.

In the 1990 case *RAV v City of St Paul*, the United States Supreme Court looked at the case of Robert Viktora, age seventeen years, and some friends who had burned a cross on the lawn of an African American couple in St. Paul, Minnesota. St. Paul had a hate speech ordinance that made it a crime to place on public or private property any symbol or object (including a swastika or burning cross) that aroused anger, alarm, or resentment in others based on race, colour, creed, religion, or gender, with punishment of up to ninety days in jail. Viktora was convicted of violating this ordinance, and appealed his conviction to the Supreme Court. The Court ruled 9:0 that the St. Paul ordinance violated the First Amendment of the Constitution, and overturned Viktora's conviction. The Court said Viktora could be prosecuted for vandalism or trespassing, but not for expressing his views.[52]

In *Snyder v Phelps* in 2011, the United States Supreme Court heard the case brought by Albert Snyder, the father of a Marine killed in Iraq, against Fred Phelps, the leader of the Westboro Baptist Church of Kansas, which was a family-based cult that opposed all non-Protestant religions and gay people. Phelps and his church were notorious for protesting at military funerals with signs that contained slurs for gays, claiming that gay members of the armed forces were being killed as part of God's punishment of the United States for tolerating homosexuality. Snyder's family was Catholic, so the protest at his son's funeral also included anti-Catholic signs. The protest itself was about 1,000 feet away from the funeral, but could be seen and heard at the entrance to the funeral site, and Snyder sued Phelps for disrupting it. A jury awarded Snyder $11 million for emotional distress and punitive damages. But the Supreme Court ruled 8:1 that the Phelps protests were constitutionally protected free speech and threw out the jury award.[53]

Clearly Canada and the United States approach the question of free speech from different perspectives. The guarded and limited application of the principle to behaviour in the former contrasts with the almost wide-open application of the principle in the latter. The difference is perhaps articulated in the *Canadian Charter of Rights and Freedoms* in section 1 which says "The *Canadian Charter of Rights and Freedoms* guarantees the rights and freedoms set out in it subject only to such reasonable limits prescribed by law as can be demonstrably justified in a free and democratic society." The United States Constitution has no such clause, nor does it share this philosophy with regard to free speech.

## 10) Official Languages

The Canadian Constitution recognizes two official national languages — English and French. The United States, unusual in the world, has none, though English is used for almost all government work. About 21 percent of Canadians speak French as a first language, most of whom are geographically concentrated in the province of Quebec. About 82 percent of Quebec's population are francophones, and 94 percent of the population can speak French. In the United States, the most common first language spoken after English is Spanish, which is spoken by about 13 percent of the population. More than 62 million Americans are Hispanic, a number greater than the total population of Canada.

In Canada and in Canadian provinces, the establishment of official languages have substantive impacts on business practices, government services, and education. While the United States has no official national language, a majority of states have declared English as an official language, yet the impact is more symbolic than substantive.

Bilingualism is established in the Canadian Constitution at both the federal level and in New Brunswick, the only officially bilingual province. The federal *Official Languages Act*, first passed in 1969 with a new version passed in 1988 and amended since then, requires that all federal government services be offered in English and in French, that federal courts operate in both languages, and that laws and regulations be published in both languages. Other than government services and education, most Canadians and visitors to Canada frequently get reminded of national bilingualism through the *Consumer Packaging and Labelling Act*, which requires all food and product labels to be provided in both English and French, and the signage on federal highways, which similarly is in both languages.

Provincial governments and government services mostly operate in English everywhere in Canada except Quebec, officially bilingual New Brunswick, and certain francophone areas in other parts of the country. Some provinces such as Manitoba and Ontario provide more government services and educational opportunities in French than others do.

In Quebec, French is the sole official language. The pro-independence Parti Québécois won the provincial elections of 1976, and in 1977 passed Bill 101, *The Charter of the French Language*. Bill 101 requires the following:

1. All public signs in Quebec (like street and road signs) are in French only.

2. All outdoor advertising signs must be in French. The agency that enforces that law, the office québécois de la langue française, is known by some English speakers as the language police. That agency issues citations and fines to stores that violate the law. Stores with trademarked English names like Walmart can use those.
3. Only anglophones who grew up in Canada can send their children to English-language schools. All others, including those who immigrated to Canada, have no choice and must send children to French-language schools.
4. French is the official language of Quebec used in all government and court proceedings.
5. All businesses must allow employees to speak French at work, and employees cannot be fired for not knowing English.
6. All restaurant menus, product labels and instructions, and brochures must be available in French if used in Quebec.

In 1982, Canada patriated its Constitution from the United Kingdom and added the *Canadian Charter of Rights and Freedoms*, which includes a free speech clause. In 1988, in *Ford v Quebec*, the Supreme Court ruled that the Bill 101 requirement that all advertising signs in Quebec be only in French violated the new *Charter of Rights and Freedoms*.[54] The Quebec government then invoked another section of the *Charter of Rights and Freedoms*, the notwithstanding clause in section 33 of the *Charter*, which allows a government in Canada to pass a law notwithstanding that the law might violate certain rights protected in the *Charter*. The new law, however, is only in effect for five years before the government must reinvoke section 33. The Quebec government's use of the notwithstanding clause allowed the province to ignore the judgment of the *Ford v Quebec* decision for five years. In 1993, the Quebec government modified the law to allow English or other languages on outdoor advertising signs, but only if French is in larger print.

In 2022, the Coalition Avenir Québec government passed Bill 96, a major reform of Bill 101. The new legislation made French the Quebec government's exclusive language of communication. There were a few exceptions in health care and the courts, for anglophones with previously acquired language rights, and for Indigenous peoples. New immigrants to Quebec were given six months from their time of arrival to adapt before the Quebec government switched to French only. As well, the number of places in Quebec's English-language colleges (called CEGEPs) were limited to 17.5 percent of Quebec's student population. Moreover, companies with twenty-five to forty-nine employees were required to adopt French as their work language. As with previous pieces of legislation aimed at protecting the French language and culture, the Quebec government invoked the notwithstanding clause to protect it against legal challenges based on the *Canadian Charter of Rights and Freedoms*. In addition to these measures to protect the French language, in 2023 the government increased tuition fees for English-speaking Canadian students from outside Quebec.

Thirty-two American states have made English an official state language. Two states have two official state languages — Hawaii with English and native Hawaiian, and South Dakota with English and Sioux. One state has twenty-one official state languages — Alaska with English and twenty Alaska Native languages. However, unlike in Canada, most state laws that proclaim official languages are vague and symbolic only. For example, in 1987, Governor Bill Clinton of Arkansas signed a state law that says "The English language shall be the official language of the state of Arkansas." That is the entire law.

In 1988, Arizona voters approved a more specific law through a ballot measure to amend the state constitution to say that all levels of state and local government in Arizona must "act in English and no other language." The constitutional amendment allowed exceptions for the following:

1. Schools to help non-English speakers
2. Public health and safety
3. The criminal justice system
4. Compliance with federal laws

The Arizona amendment was challenged in court for a decade until the Arizona state Supreme Court ruled in 1998 that the amendment violated the United States Constitution's protection of free speech.[55] The United States Supreme Court turned down an appeal in 1999. The Arizona Supreme Court ruled that the state English-only provision violated the United States Constitution's free speech protection in three ways:

1. It violated the constitutional rights of non-English speakers seeking government access.
2. It violated the free speech of elected officials to speak any language they want to voters.
3. It violated the free speech of government employees to speak another language to residents not fluent in English.

Many bills have been introduced in Congress to mandate English only by the federal government, with various exceptions. A bill was introduced in 2023 in the House of Representatives and Senate with many Republican sponsors to declare English the official language of the United States and require its use in all national government documents and actions, with some exceptions.[56] But this bill and other similar ones before it have never passed into law.

## Conclusion

So, how do we account for the fact that two countries so similar in so many respects produce quite different public policies? Thinking about the policies discussed above, it is clear that there are striking similarities and differences in both the way policy is made in each country, and the content of the polices each produces. The institutional context of policy making differs in both countries, with the constitutional framework providing contrasting legislative and legal approaches to policy problems. The ideological contrast is important too, with the consequence that the content of policy choices in both countries varies to differing degrees. Citizen involvement in policy making, which level of government is responsible, and the actual content of the policy produced can all be different, even when the essential issues are similar. There may be some compelling reasons, therefore, as to why an American might see Canada as the home of a weirdo pot-smoking beaver, while a Canadian might see the United States as the home of a weirdo gun-toting redneck Uncle Sam.

Source: Courtesy of Theo Moudakis.

CHAPTER SIX

# Trade and Economic Policy: The Long and Winding Road

## Introduction

One of the key factors in questions about how similar and how different Canada and the United States are relates to their deep and long trade and economic relationship. On one level, both countries share a fundamental outlook that a democratic political system wed to a capitalist economy is the best model for advancing the interests of their citizens. Consequently, there are many areas of cooperation that reinforce this reality. On the other hand, the two countries often have differing economic goals in competition with one another, which often lead to political conflict requiring the maintenance of a deep and broad set of relations that stretch all the way up to the prime minister's and the president's offices. These relations, furthermore, are always complicated by the great power and size imbalance between Canada and the United States. Hence the many examples wherein trade and economic policy interests are the same, only different, as are the systems employed in each country to manage their respective budgets, as this chapter shows.

## A. The Evolution of Trade and Economic Relations Between Canada and the United States

### 1) Imbalance in Interests

In 1891, Goldwin Smith posed what became known as "the Canadian question" when he wrote, "Whether the four blocks of territory constituting the Dominion can forever be kept by political agencies united among themselves and separate from their Continent, of which geographically, economically, and with the exception of Quebec ethnologically, they are parts, is the Canadian question."[1] This is a question that continues to be asked to this day, but with the added complication of American administrations who often fail to understand the historical importance of the Canadian-American relationship. So, ironically, the question of whether Canada should integrate further into the American empire remains unanswered despite the ongoing intensification of trade and economic relationships between the two countries.

Canada has been characterized as evolving from colony to nation . . . to colony. After Canada moved from the French and British empires in the seventeenth, eighteenth, and nineteenth centuries, did it then simply become an economic vassal of the American empire in the twentieth and early twenty-first centuries? Patterns of trade and economic development between Canada and the United States reveal a lot about Canada's capacity as a sovereign nation to shape its own destiny, as do patterns of foreign investment. The capacity of the United States as a sovereign nation to shape its own destiny, in contrast, never comes into question.

Given the massive imbalance in economic size and population, we might reasonably ask, how much does Canada mean to the United States? As one State Department official put it, "The United States doesn't have a Canada policy. It has Canada policies."[2] *Invisible and Inaudible in Washington* is the title of a book by Edelgard Mahant and Graham Mount on the historical lack of an articulated American policy toward Canada.[3] Other titles like *Neighbours Taken for Granted* and *Forgotten Partnership* hint at the nature of the Canadian-American relationship, at least as seen in Canadian scholarship.[4] There is no State Department unit dedicated to Canada-United States relations, for instance, despite that same department making the observation: "The relationship between the United States and Canada is among the closest and most extensive in the world."[5] This is reflected in the staggering volume of bilateral trade as well as in interpersonal contact, with about 400,000 people crossing the border every day before the COVID-19 pandemic caused restrictions to be placed on cross-border movement. Since the border reopened in 2022, the number of crossings returned to pre-COVID-19 levels.[6]

Presidents Richard Nixon and Ronald Reagan both once referred to Japan as the United States' largest trading partner. Both were wrong. Former Canadian ambassadors to the United States have documented just how hard it is for Canada to be noticed in Washington.[7] Yet Canadian governments and civil society are practically obsessed with relations with the behemoth to the south. Moreover, this obsession vacillates between love and admiration, and fear and loathing insofar as Canadian attitudes toward greater continental economic integration are concerned. This adds up to considerable challenges in articulating and implementing trade and economic policy, and deciding appropriate approaches to attracting foreign investment.

Free trade with Canada, like other Canadian issues, generally attracts little attention in the United States. A *New York Times* editorial on Canada-United States free trade entitled "Worthwhile Canadian Initiative" won a prize for "most boring headline."[8] Canada, on the other hand, has obsessed about free trade with the United States since the 1800s, with the outcome of several elections having been determined by the issue.

Managing the contemporary Canadian-American trade and economic relationship can be roughly divided into two eras — pre-free trade and free trade. Before the current free trade era, there was an implicit set of norms that evolved over decades. Formal and informal behavioural patterns emerged sanctioned by customs and traditional modes of interactions between the two countries. Conflict was usually resolved on an *ad hoc* basis; disputes over one issue were not linked to disputes over other issues. Officials consulted and negotiated behind closed doors through a system that became known as "quiet diplomacy." Usually, when the Americans took economic actions that might be punitive, Canada quietly negotiated a special exemption or provisions for itself. Hence the idea developed in the twentieth century that a "special relationship" existed between the two countries. This was reinforced by the deepening ties in many different socio-economic and military areas, especially during the Second World War and during the latter half of the century.[9] However, by the twenty-first century, the "special relationship" was severely tested on a number of occasions.

## 2) Background

Starting in 1855, the Reciprocity Treaty created limited free trade between the colonies of British North America and the United States. But in 1866, the United States Congress voted to cancel the treaty, partly in retribution for the British government's tacit economic support of the Confederacy during the American Civil War. It also cut off Canadian businesses from accessing year-round seaports in the United States for their trade with Great Britain. As noted in Chapter 1, Confederation was partly a response to this measure by the American government as the colonies of British North America became increasingly protectionist and looked toward each other for more trade opportunities on an east–west basis. Under Canada's first prime minister, Sir John A Macdonald, the protectionist National Policy of 1879 became the economic cornerstone of the new Canadian nation. As also noted in Chapter 1, it consisted of three planks: the building of a railway from sea to sea; an aggressive immigration policy to attract settlers to the Canadian West; and a policy of tariff protection for Canadian industry.

The tariffs proved most significant in terms of shaping the Canadian-American economic relationship. American enterprises quickly discovered they could jump the tariff wall and establish "branch plants" in Canada to serve the domestic Canadian market. Thus, levels of American investment began an upward trajectory in the early twentieth century that saw American firms come to dominate in various key sectors. American direct investment gradually replaced British portfolio investment that had been previously dominant in Canada. There was a key qualitative difference between British and American investment that came to profoundly contribute to the emergence of a continental North American economic region. This difference was that British portfolio investment involved no ownership shares in Canadian businesses, just dividends from profits. American Foreign Direct Investment (FDI) included outright ownership. Consequently, British economic influence began to decline by the early 1900s and was gradually supplanted by an emergent branch-plant economy with growing dependence on the American economy.

In contrast to Macdonald's Conservative Party, the Liberal Party of Canada under Wilfrid Laurier supported free trade. In the 1911 Canadian federal election, free trade in natural resource products became a central issue. The Conservative Party, now under Robert Borden, campaigned using fiery anti-American rhetoric, claiming free trade would cost Canada its soul; the Liberals lost the election. Further political disputes over free trade were shelved for many decades. In 1935 and 1948 Liberal Prime Minister William Lyon Mackenzie King secretly negotiated with the Americans for free trade, but backed off for fear of domestic controversy.

## 3) Continental Integration by Stealth

Even without free trade, from 1935 to 1980, a number of bilateral trade agreements greatly reduced tariffs in both nations. For example, agricultural machinery crossed the border tariff-free starting in the 1940s. The 1952 Paley Report, "Resources for Freedom," commissioned by President Harry Truman, identified twenty-two resources critical to American security, and targeted Canada as the primary source for twelve of them, thus providing a strong rationale for further American FDI in Canada in those important sectors. It also reinforced the idea that Canada was to be a supplier of staples products (that is, natural resources) rather than a more advanced industrial manufacturing economy, thereby retarding the maturation of the Canadian political economy and contributing to its ongoing dependence on American finished products. In addition, defence production was integrated through the 1959 Defence Production Sharing Agreement (DPSA) made up of branch plants of the American military-industrial complex (renewed and updated by Prime Minister Stephen Harper in 2006).

The most significant bilateral free trade agreement was the Canada-United States Automotive Agreement (also known as the Auto Pact), which continentalized production of automobiles. In January 1965, Prime Minister Lester Pearson and President Lyndon Johnson signed the Auto Pact, enabling growth in Canada's auto sector, which was mainly located in Ontario. The deal guaranteed that for every vehicle sold in Canada, one would be built in Canada. The agreement also allowed North American companies to import cars from anywhere in the world tariff-free. However, the forces of globalization having emerged by the late twentieth century, the World Trade Organization ruled in 2000 against a key section of the agreement, effectively killing it.

As the economic influence and control of American enterprise spread in Canada, it extended into the realm of cultural industries. This history actually dates back to pre-Confederation times. In 1849, a postal subsidy was created to allow Canadian newspapers and journals to be mailed at a reduced rate in order to compete with the much larger American publishing sector. In 1932, the Canadian Radio Broadcasting Corporation (CRBC) was established to provide an alternative to the predominance of American radio broadcasts. A famous aphorism was articulated by Canadian broadcaster Graham Spry who said in 1930, "Our choice is the state or the United States." In 1939, the National Film Board was created to support domestic documentary film production as part of a deal with Hollywood to restrict Canadian competition in the more lucrative popular cinema segment of the movie-making business. The integration of American cultural values in Canada through newly developed technology with the invention of radio and television broadcasting, cinema, and the spread of mass media through print caused considerable consternation in some quarters in Canada. The response included the creation of state enterprises (called Crown corporations in Canada) to protect Canadian culture. The Massey Royal Commission on the Arts and Letters was created in 1955 to look at ways to protect Canadian culture more broadly, including literature, poetry, theatre, dance, music, etc. It recommended that the state create funding bodies to support Canadian artists, which gave rise to the Canada Council for the Arts and other similar agencies.

By the 1960s and 1970s, lines had been drawn between continentalists who advocated greater and deeper economic ties to the United States, and nationalists who feared Canadian sovereignty and identity were gradually being eroded by these deepening economic and cultural ties. The continentalist position was actually rooted in the annexationist movement of the mid-nineteenth century, when a group of Canadian businesspeople began to advocate that Canada join the United States. It later reflected the mainstream economics view in the twentieth century expressed in policy terms through a desire for free trade with the United States, more American FDI, and a continental economy unencumbered by the Canadian state.

A left-nationalist stream developed around issues related to American influence over the labour movement in Canada, the manufacturing sector of the economy, natural resource ownership, and foreign policy, among other things.[10] A more conservative nationalism emerged in the politics of Prime Minister John Diefenbaker who unsuccessfully sought to turn back the hands of time and re-embrace Canada's British imperial connections. The nationalist response was encapsulated in the title of a well-known study called "Silent Surrender" by political economist Kari Levitt.[11] She argued that the growth of the branch-plant economy had resulted in the gradual transfer of control over Canada to American multinational corporations, the headquarters of which made all the key economic decisions regarding employment, investment, and expansion for the Canadian economy. Some observers also argued that a Canadian comprador class of business leaders existed as well, essentially serving the interests of American capital and managing the silent takeover of the Canadian economy on behalf of their American bosses.

Whichever view was correct, there is no doubt that the relationship between Canada and the United States was unique, and perhaps even "special." Canadian philosopher George Grant wrote that "To think of the US is to think of ourselves — almost."[12] Canada seemed to have emerged as a dependent American satellite state, voluntarily surrendering much of its economic, military, diplomatic, and cultural control to the United States. This was the cost; the benefit was a generalized prosperity and economic growth. For those who wanted to counter this trend of Americanization of the Canadian political economy, the method was to argue for an aggressive expansion of state enterprises.

Determining the exact nature of Canada's position in this context sparked considerable debate.[13] Was Canada a dependent nation? A satellite? A rich advanced nation? Whatever interpretation was accepted, the debate often was reduced to nationalism versus continentalism. In one regard, this raised questions about the nationality of capital. Did it matter if capitalists were Canadian or American? Was national control of the Canadian economy the key issue? One view was that the high levels of American FDI made it impossible to embark on a path to state socialism and democratic sovereignty. This focus on ownership of the Canadian economy dominated policy and political debate from the 1960s to the 1990s. Some argued for the Canadianization of key sectors of the economy and of legislation limiting FDI. The argument emerged that Canadian capital had matured, that Canadian savings were now adequate to fund domestic development and break the cycle of branch plant foreign ownership, and the economic stagnation that came when American corporations served their own self-interest. The choice was put starkly by philosopher Charles Taylor who in 1966 said, "We must choose: either we do something as an independent power or become annexationists."[14]

While all this economic navel-gazing was going on and angst was bubbling up in Canada, the United States was simply going about its economic business and creating the largest, most powerful economy in the world. To the extent to which it gave much consideration to its position *vis-à-vis* Canada, it was largely limited to consideration of how American protectionist policies could further American interests which, if they could accommodate Canadian concerns, would do so. But accommodating Canadian concerns was rarely top of mind for successive American administrations. In any event, there was certainly never any economic threat from the Canadian mouse to the American elephant.

## 4) The Liberation of Canada

The global economic crisis of the 1970s illustrated the inherent limitations of any "special relationship" that could be said to exist between Canada and the United States. The crisis prompted the American government to act unilaterally. On 15 August 1971, President Richard Nixon instituted a program of devaluation of the American dollar and increased protectionism. However, Canada failed to obtain any of the usual exemptions it expected under the terms of the "special relationship." In a speech to the Canadian House of Commons, Nixon said, "the fact of our mutual interdependence and our mutual desire for independence need not be inconsistent traits. No self-respecting nation can or should accept the proposition that it should always be economically dependent upon any other nation."[15]

Nixon's actions shocked Canada, and led to a rethinking of its vulnerability. The government of Liberal Prime Minister Pierre Trudeau responded with a number of overtly nationalist policies. It created several state agencies to assert greater Canadian control over the economy, most prominently, the Foreign Investment Review

Agency to screen FDI to determine if it was in Canada's best interests, the Canada Development Corporation to pool Canadian capital and assist Canadian capitalists in expanding their businesses, and Petro-Canada to give the Canadian state a window on the foreign-dominated energy sector. The American government and business class responded negatively, fearing Canada was becoming too socialist and anti-free market.

## 5) Countering Integration: The Third Option

In addition to expanding state control of the economy, the Trudeau government undertook a review of Canada's trade policy. It argued that Canada had three choices going forward. First, retain the status quo, wherein the United States was Canada's largest trade partner and little or nothing needed to be done to alter that reality. Second, deepen trade relations with the United States. Or third, diversify trade relations with Europe, Latin America, and Asia. The "Third Option" was chosen, but ultimately failed due to lack of interest by other countries, failure of Canadian business to seek opportunities abroad, and failure of the government to push it hard enough. Nonetheless, it indicated a willingness on the part of nationalists to try to use the Canadian state to redefine Canada's primary economic and trade relationship.

## 6) The Free Trade Agreement (FTA)

By the 1980s, Canada and the United States were each other's largest trading partners, and their bilateral trading relationship was the largest in the world. Brian Mulroney's Progressive Conservative Party was elected to office in the 1984 election where, interestingly, free trade was not an important issue; indeed, Mulroney and his Progressive Conservative Party both announced their opposition to such a move. When Mulroney ran for the leadership of the Progressive Conservative Party, he denounced the prospects for Canada of a free trade deal with the United States. In 1983, when leadership candidate John Crosbie announced that he was in favour of free trade with the United States, Mulroney's response was unequivocally opposed:

> The country could not survive with a policy of unfettered free trade. . . . I'm all in favour of eliminating unfair protectionism, where it exists. [But] this is a separate country. We'd be swamped. We have in many ways a branch plant economy, in many ways in certain important sectors. All that would happen with that kind of concept would be the boys cranking up their plants throughout the United States in bad times and shutting their entire branch plants in Canada. It's bad enough as it is.[16]

Mulroney also said, "Don't talk to me about free trade, that issue was decided in 1911. Free trade is a danger to Canadian sovereignty, and you'll hear none of it from me now during this leadership campaign or at any other time in the future."[17] Astonishingly, Mulroney later admitted in an interview that his opposition to free trade during the leadership race was purely tactical, and merely intended to garner the support of a sufficient number of Progressive Conservative Party delegates to secure victory for himself.[18] A less charitable interpretation might be that he simply lied to win.

But while Mulroney may have once spoken like an ardent opponent of free trade, he soon became its biggest advocate, prompted by mounting American protectionism, pressure from the Canadian business community, and the recommendations of a 1985 Royal Commission on the economy which issued a report to the government of Canada recommending free trade with the United States.[19] Mulroney, once the president of an American-owned Canadian branch plant company, struck up a close relationship with American President Ronald Reagan, and together they agreed to initiate formal free trade talks. Indeed, Mulroney embraced free trade with an almost indecent enthusiasm:

> In October 1985, when he wrote to Reagan formally requesting negotiations between the two countries, he started a process that would start to reconstitute the Canadian state. Replacing Trudeau's Third

Option with the previously unthinkable second option of increased continental integration, he reversed thirteen years of his predecessors' efforts to increase Canada's parlous autonomy vis-à-vis the United States. At the same time, he renounced the protectionism that had been his party's core belief since John A. Macdonald had announced the National Policy in 1879. Rejecting Canadian governments' long-standing instinct to resist formalizing their relationship with the United States, Mulroney embraced trade liberalization with a determination bordering on zealotry. Free trade had become in his mind a panacea for Canada's ills, and nothing could stop him achieving it.[20]

Mulroney met with Reagan three times in 1984–1985, once during his campaign to become prime minister in June 1984, once eight days after being elected in September 1984, and once again in March 1985 at the so-called Shamrock Summit in Quebec City. At these meetings, Mulroney made clear that he was interested in pursuing closer relations with the Americans in both security issues and economic relations. Mulroney agreed to two requests by the Americans at the Shamrock Summit; first that Canada step up its efforts to support American efforts to contain the Soviet threat, and second to examine ways to reduce and eliminate barriers to trade.[21]

In May 1986, Canadian and American negotiators began to work out a trade deal. The agreement arrived at after protracted and contentious negotiations greatly liberalized trade between the two countries, removing most remaining tariffs. The FTA was not fundamentally about tariffs, however. Average tariffs on goods crossing the border were well below 1 percent by the 1980s. Instead, Canada desired unhindered access to the American economy. Americans, in turn, wished to compete in Canada's energy and cultural industries. In the negotiations, Canada retained the right to protect its cultural industries and such sectors as education and health care. As well, some resources such as water were left out of the agreement. However, the Canadians did not succeed in winning free competition for American government procurement contracts. Indeed, Canadian negotiators later admitted they were badly out-negotiated by the

Americans.[22] As political economist Stephen Clarkson noted, "An inherently unequal match made more asymmetrical by the urgency with which the PMO [Prime Minister's Office] defined the need for an agreement and the inflated claims that the government made about the gains expected from 'free' trade meant that it was negotiating on its knees with the world's most powerful nation. Ottawa made major concessions on the big questions — some of them even before the negotiations started."[23]

Once the treaty was announced, it became a source of great controversy in Canada. A wide-ranging group of Canadians, mostly on the centre and left of the ideological spectrum, came out in opposition to the deal. The Liberal Party led by former Prime Minister John Turner, the New Democratic Party (NDP) led by Ed Broadbent, many labour unions, cultural organizations and artists, and popular sector groups strongly opposed the deal. Another wide-ranging group of Canadians, mostly on the right, came out in support of the deal. Mulroney's Progressive Conservatives and most business groups supported it, including the once-nationalist Canadian Manufacturers Association and the Business Council on National Issues (BCNI) made up of the 150 chief executive officers of the largest Canadian multinational corporations (many of them branch plants of American corporations).

The 1988 Canadian election was almost wholly dominated by the issue of free trade. Mulroney's Progressive Conservatives were re-elected with a comfortable majority. Critics argued that the two parties opposed to free trade actually won a majority of the vote, but because of vote splitting between the NDP and Liberals, the Progressive Conservatives managed to win a majority of seats in the House of Commons. On 1 January 1989, the FTA came into effect.

Meanwhile, the issue barely garnered any attention in the United States.

The exact ramifications of the agreement are hard to measure. After the agreement came into effect, trade between Canada and the United States began to increase rapidly. Throughout the twentieth century, exports fairly consistently made up about 25 percent of

Canada's gross domestic product (GDP); after 1990, exports rose to about 40 percent of GDP. After 2000, they reached nearly 50 percent. Some of this growth can be attributed to the FTA, but some must also be attributed to the sharp decrease in the value of the Canadian dollar during this period, and a general global pattern of increasing international trade. The agreement failed to liberalize trade in some areas, most notably softwood lumber, where Canadians have complained that the Americans repeatedly violated the agreement to impose protectionist policies. The fears that the agreement would undermine Canada's sovereignty continue to be debated. But Canada's cultural industries remained healthy for the most part.

## 7) On to Mexico: The North America Free Trade Agreement (NAFTA)

Once enacted, the FTA remained controversial in Canada. The NDP remained opposed to free trade, while the Liberals under Prime Minister Jean Chrétien, who were elected to office in 1993, promised to renegotiate key parts of the agreement. But they continued the deal with only minor modifications, and signed the North American Free Trade Agreement (NAFTA) in January 1994, forming the world's largest free trade area. NAFTA essentially broadened the bilateral FTA relationship to a trilateral relationship by adding a poor, authoritarian, developing economy into the continental system. It removed barriers to the flow of goods and labour between Canada, the United States, and Mexico, under the oversight of an independent dispute-settlement process.

NAFTA was initially pursued by pro-free trade conservative governments in the United States and Mexico. Canada, afraid of the Americans constructing a "hub-and-spoke" trade regime in the Americas with the United States at the centre, asked to be at the table. There was considerable opposition to the accord on both sides of the Canadian-American border as well as within Mexico, but in the United States it was able to secure passage after President Bill

Clinton made it a major legislative initiative in 1993. H Ross Perot, a Texas billionaire running for president as an Independent, was an outspoken critic of NAFTA during his 1992 presidential campaign, claiming that passage would cause a "giant sucking sound" of jobs leaving the United States for Mexico.

After intense political debate and the negotiation of several side agreements, the United States House of Representatives passed NAFTA by 234:200 (132 Republicans and 102 Democrats voting in favour) and the Senate passed it by 61:38. The Canadian House of Commons passed it by a vote of 140:124, and the Mexican Senate passed it by a vote of 52:2.[24] Subsequently, the total value of trade between Canada, the United States, and Mexico more than doubled in ten years, growing from $306 billion a year to $621 billion a year. United States exports to Mexico and Canada increased under NAFTA from $142 billion to $263 billion a year. By 2016, the total value of trade among the three countries had reached more than $1 trillion.[25]

Transnational corporations tended to support NAFTA in the belief that lower tariffs would increase their profits. Labour unions in Canada and the United States opposed NAFTA for fear that jobs would move out of the country due to lower labour costs in Mexico. Environmental, social justice, and other advocacy organizations believed NAFTA would have detrimental non-economic impacts on public health, the environment, and other social policy areas. In the United States, labour unions and other longtime NAFTA critics decried the loss of well-paying manufacturing jobs. Data from the United States Bureau of Labor Statistics reveal that as of 2018 nearly 4.5 million manufacturing jobs had been lost in the United states overall since NAFTA took effect.[26] This amounted to one out of every four manufacturing jobs. Not all these losses were directly due to NAFTA; the United States trade deficit with China soared at this time as well, contributing to lost manufacturing jobs. Still, more than 950,000 workers were certified as having lost their jobs due to imports from Canada and Mexico or the relocation of factories to those countries.[27]

## 8) From NAFTA to CUSMA/USMCA/T-MEC

During a debate with Democratic presidential candidate Hillary Clinton during the 2016 presidential campaign, Donald Trump announced that "NAFTA is the worst trade deal maybe ever signed anywhere, but certainly ever signed in this country."[28] This view resonated with a significant portion of Trump's supporters, "For communities that have undergone significant de-industrialization, it is easy to understand their agreement with Trump's assessment that NAFTA has been a disaster," according to some observers.[29] As president, Trump insisted that Mexico and Canada renegotiate a new trade agreement. NAFTA's successor — called the Canada-United States-Mexico Agreement (CUSMA) in Canada, the United States-Mexico-Canada Agreement (USMCA) in the United States, and Tratado entre México, Estados Unidos y Canadá (T-MEC) in Mexico — was created in 2020 (described below).

All these free trade agreements raised issues about labour, social, and environmental policies coming under pressure in a "race to the bottom." Along with the creation of the World Trade Organization (WTO) in 1995, new forms of global governance that set new limits on the policy making capacity of governments emerged. New continental rules in line with neo-conservative ideology comprised an "economic constitution" of sorts. The "special relationship" and "quiet diplomacy" between Canada and the United States were largely replaced by a new rules-based regime — although the capacity of one country, the United States, to bypass the rules outweighed the capacity of the other to enforce them.

Notwithstanding the creation of a robust free trade regime, several developments in the first quarter of the twenty-first century aggravated the Canada-United States trade relationship. American protectionism reared its head under several presidents. In 2016, for example, protectionism turned into a defining theme of the American election. Both presidential candidates Clinton and Trump opposed the Trans-Pacific Partnership, a trade deal even bigger than NAFTA. But Trump also singled out NAFTA and promised to erect a wall along the United States-Mexico border. In his inauguration speech, Trump promised an "America first" approach to trade, immigration, and foreign affairs.

Even the efforts to modernize and update NAFTA became entangled in the threat of American protectionism. In 2017–2018, Canada, the United States, and Mexico engaged in a highly contentious round of negotiations to reform NAFTA. In July 2017, the United States produced an initial list of 100 broad, sometimes vaguely worded demands, including:

1. Reducing the American trade deficit within NAFTA, which could mean increasing American exports or reducing Canadian and Mexican imports
2. Scrapping NAFTA's dispute-resolution panels, which had sometimes ruled in Canada's favour on softwood lumber and other trade issues
3. Using "Buy American" provisions to bar Canadian or Mexican firms from seeking United States government contracts
4. Making Canadian and Mexican intellectual property rules similar to those found in United States law

The Trump administration's most contentious NAFTA demands began to take shape at the fourth round of talks in Arlington, Virginia from 11–17 October 2017. In the area of agriculture, the United States wanted an end to Canada's supply-management regime for dairy and poultry products, ignoring the massive subsidies paid to American dairy farmers by the United States government. The American negotiators further declared their desire for a "sunset clause," under which the new NAFTA was to expire in five years unless the member countries agreed to renew it.

The Americans were bellicose and aggressive in their negotiating stance, perhaps reflecting the personality of the president at the time.[30] The personal role of presidents and prime ministers is of course always a key part of the Canadian-American relationship. Political historian Stephen Azzi notes that the close personal relationship between Brian Mulroney and Ronald Reagan was the grease in the wheels that made the Canadian-American relationship so smooth and ultimately allowed for the successful attainment of the FTA.[31] But while personal relationships between prime ministers and presidents can be tremendously helpful, it is clear that no such relationship existed between, for example, John Diefenbaker and John F Kennedy, Pierre Trudeau and Richard Nixon, or Justin Trudeau and Donald Trump. Trump insulted Canada on numerous occasions.[32] And of course, Trudeau was literally left speechless in response to Trump's handling of the race riots in the United States, with Trudeau's twenty-one second silence before the cameras in response to a question about Trump going viral.[33]

The negotiations were fraught with tensions, described as "thirteen months of bitter trade talks, complete with shouting outbursts and blunt exchanges" between the trade negotiators.[34] On 8 March 2018, Trump introduced tariffs of 25 percent and 10 percent, respectively, on steel and aluminum, citing the need to protect domestic supply of the metals for United States military needs — a preposterous argument given Canada's integration into the American military-industrial complex as an important supplier of those metals. Although Canada and Mexico were exempted, Trump explicitly linked that exemption to NAFTA, saying, "If we're making a deal on NAFTA, this will figure into the deal and we won't have the tariffs on Canada or on Mexico. . . . I have a feeling we're going to make a deal on NAFTA."[35] The exemptions for Canada and Mexico expired and the tariffs came into effect 31 May 2018. In the end, despite all the histrionics, a new deal was struck. NAFTA quietly died, and the tri-titled and awkwardly named CUSMA/USMCA/T-MEC was born. However, when Trump returned to power after the 2024 election, the threat to the trade relationship returned. Trump campaigned aggressively on instating across-the-board tariffs on imports, including from Canada.

## 9) Meanwhile... American Protectionism Persists: Softwood Lumber

The United States and Canada had been arguing for years over the United States' decision to impose duties on Canadian softwood lumber imports. The two countries manage their softwood lumber industries in different ways. In the United States, prices are established through the competitive marketplace, and lumber companies are private enterprises. In Canada, provincial governments own most timber, and prices are managed through an administrative process called stumpage, which is a fee that businesses or individuals pay when they harvest timber from Crown land and for which export fees may apply when this timber is exported.[36] The powerful and well organized lumber lobby in the United States has long claimed that stumpage constitutes an unfair subsidy to Canadian lumber producers. As a result, according to the government of Canada:

> [T]he United States lumber industry has frequently sought US government restrictions on Canadian softwood lumber imports through the application of US countervailing duty and antidumping laws — laws that allow the imposition of import duties when a US industry is allegedly harmed by subsidies in the exporting country (countervailing duties), or by dumping, which is when a US industry is allegedly harmed by imported products sold at prices that are lower than the cost of production or lower than prices in the domestic market (anti-dumping duties).[37]

Prime Minister Harper compromised with the United States in 2006, signing the Softwood Lumber Agreement (SLA). Some of the penalties paid by Canadian softwood producers were returned to them. But the issue persisted as an ongoing irritant in the relationship. Canada had filed numerous motions to have the duties eliminated and the collected duties returned to Canada, and won every case brought before the NAFTA tribunal. The United States responded in 2005 by suggesting the NAFTA panel's decision would have no impact on the anti-dumping and countervailing duty orders.[38] In 2015, the SLA expired, and the United States again began to impose tariffs on softwood lumber imported from Canada, leading to higher lumber prices in the United States and contributing to construction inflation.[39] In November 2023, following a regular five-year review of the tariffs, the United States International Trade Commission (USITC) voted to maintain the anti-dumping and countervailing duties on softwood lumber from Canada. The USITC argued that it was concerned about potential financial injury to the United States lumber industry.[40] Canada continued to win trade panel rulings on the dispute, but with little effect on American government policies.[41]

## 10) Alternatives? Canadian Free Trade Agreements with Countries Not Named the United States of America

The protectionist mood in America intensified with the Great Recession of 2008–2009 and the passage of a new *Buy America Act*. Weary of the continuing resort to protectionism by successive American governments, the Canadian government pursued enhanced trade relationships with several countries not named the United States of America, reflective of the spirit of the failed Third Option policy of several decades earlier. In the 1990s, Chrétien's government innovated a "Team Canada" approach to trade diversification. The prime minister and the provincial premiers travelled together along with prominent Canadian business leaders to a variety of destinations to drum up business for Canadian companies. One study shows, though, that trade actually dropped off in the countries they visited.[42] Table 6.1 shows the countries with which Canada has concluded free trade deals. In addition, deals with several more countries and associations have been attempted and/or are undergoing negotiation, including the Association of South-East Asian Nations, India, Indonesia, Mercosur (Argentina, Brazil, Paraguay, Uruguay, and Bolivia), and the Pacific Alliance (Chile, Colombia, Mexico, and Peru).

**TABLE 6.1. FREE TRADE AGREEMENTS WITH CANADA**

| Completed Treaties | Year |
|---|---|
| Chile | 1997 |
| Israel | 1997 |
| Costa Rica | 2002 |
| Colombia | 2008 |
| European Free Trade Association | 2009 |
| Jordan | 2009 |
| Peru | 2009 |
| Panama | 2013 |
| Honduras | 2014 |
| South Korea | 2014 |
| Ukraine | 2017 |
| European Union | 2017 |
| Trans-Pacific Partnership | 2018 |
| United States and Mexico | 2020 |
| United Kingdom | 2021 |

## 11) Meanwhile, Continental Integration Proceeds... The Birth and Death of the Security and Prosperity Partnership

At the same time, Canada, the United States, and Mexico sought to broaden and deepen their continental relationship. They announced the Security and Prosperity Partnership (SPP) for North America on 23 March 2005 in Waco, Texas. The agreement provided a framework for collaboration in areas such as security, transportation, energy, the environment, and public health. But opposition pressure from the anti-globalization movement caused the deal to be quietly cancelled in 2008.[43] In 2011–2012, Harper and Obama negotiated a new "shared vision for perimeter security and economic competitiveness," including the creation of a new "Regulatory Cooperation Council" to reduce red tape for business.[44] On 4 February 2011, they issued Beyond the

Border: A Shared Vision for Perimeter Security and Economic Competitiveness:

> The Declaration established a new long-term partnership built upon a perimeter approach to security and economic competitiveness. This means working together, not just at the border, but beyond the border to enhance our security and accelerate the legitimate flow of people, goods and services.[45]

It appeared that the three North American governments were moving toward greater degrees of cooperation and integration.

## 12) And Then Along Came Trump . . .

The movement toward deeper continentalization was rudely interrupted, however, by the arrival of an American president who threw out the playbook on trade, foreign relations, and diplomacy. Typical of the president's approach was the out-and-out lie he admitted to telling Justin Trudeau: "Trudeau came to see me. . . . He said 'No no no we have no trade deficit with you, we have none. Donald please. . . .' I said 'Wrong Justin, you do.' I didn't even know. I had no idea. I just said, 'You're wrong.'"[46] The process of continental integration received a kick in the shins. As noted above, the CUSMA/USMCA/T-MEC was eventually signed. But ongoing trade irritants, belligerent threats, insults, and rampant protectionism came to characterize the American approach to Canada.

The expectation that some normalcy would be restored to the relationship when Joe Biden became president was compromised by the Democratic president's own protectionist proclivities. As noted in the Introduction to this book, Biden undertook a number of protectionist measures that could be seen as detrimental to Canadian interests. In 2023, Biden visited Ottawa and spoke glowingly of the Canadian-American relationship. The president highlighted Canada's role as a Pacific nation as it seeks to create closer ties through the Indo-Pacific strategy, supported Canada's position toward China, and praised Canada's leadership against arbitrary detention.⁴⁷ But the protectionist sentiment of the American government persisted. Biden preserved most of the Trump tariff regime. The *Inflation Reduction Act*, Biden's signature climate bill, favoured American industry in a way that provoked deep concerns from the Canadian government. It contained $375 billion in new and extended tax credits in areas such as renewable electricity generation, hydrogen production, and sustainable jet fuel usage to help the American clean energy industry get off the ground. The magnitude of these tax credits was far beyond anything the Canadian government could match, and represented a real threat to the development of green industries in Canada.

In any event, Trump was re-elected in 2024, sounding even more bellicose and aggressive than in his first go-round as president. Canadian businesses and governments anticipated even more chaos and discord. Clearly, the similarities of both countries derived from their democratic political systems and capitalist economies are not always enough to counter the differences in self-interest, which often appeared to be the driving force behind trade policy.

## B. Foreign Investment

### 1) Foreign Investment and Nation Building

Along with their deep trade relationship, Canada and the United States have one of the world's largest foreign investment relationships. The United States is Canada's largest foreign investor. American FDI in Canada was more than $581 billion or about 46 percent of total foreign direct investment in Canada in 2022.⁴⁸ Much of that investment is primarily in Canada's mining and smelting industries, petroleum, chemicals, the manufacture of machinery and transportation equipment, and finance. Canada is the fifth-largest foreign investor in the United States. Canadian investment stock in the United States was $1,041 billion in 2022. Canadian investment in the United States is concentrated in finance and insurance, manufacturing, banking, information and retail trade, and other services.

As a staples-based economy, reliance on foreign capital has existed since the first Europeans arrived in Canada. As "hewers of wood and drawers of water," Canada has always required the constant inflow of foreign capital to finance infrastructure (canals, railways, ports, roads, etc.) for its resource-dependent development. The transition from British portfolio investment (as noted in Section 1 above), which dominated in the nineteenth century, to American FDI in the twentieth century marked a qualitative shift that was accelerated by the National Policy. In addition, provincial and municipal governments in Canada encouraged investment through tax breaks, cash incentives, free land, and utilities (water and electricity). Why was the transition significant?

Macdonald skillfully positioned the tariff as a symbol of nationhood — a tool to build up Canada economically and help prevent annexation by the United States. Ironically, the policy fostered widespread discontent, rather than feelings of national unity, outside central Canada. It contributed to the rapid industrial expansion of central Canada, where American branch plants tended to locate, while leaving the hinterlands lacking the investment and employment opportunities created by the branch plant economy. Laurier's electoral loss in 1911 (see Section 1 above) ensured that tariffs would remain in place, and consequently, Canada would continue to need high levels of FDI to sustain growth in branch plants throughout most of the twentieth century.

## 2) Foreign Investment in the Twentieth Century

By 1922, American FDI surpassed British investment, and this was initially generally seen as a positive development. During the Great Depression of the 1930s, the Canadian government increased tariffs, thereby boosting the impetus for more FDI too. At about this time, left-leaning intellectuals in Canada began to question the impact of American FDI. The League for Social Reconstruction argued that high levels of FDI might make it difficult for Canadian governments to nationalize (that is, take ownership over) key sectors of the economy if so desired, although they were more focused on the failures of capitalism than on the specific question of foreign ownership of the economy.[49]

As tariffs were gradually reduced in the post-war years, Canadian governments promoted foreign investment. Canada was increasingly in competition with other countries for American capital, but had a good head start. By 1950, 86 percent of foreign investment came from the United States. Minister of Trade and Commerce (and "Minister of Everything") CD Howe, an arch continentalist, aggressively pursued FDI and was even willing to sell Canadian Crown corporations to foreign buyers.

### 3) Backlash: The Nationalist Critique in Canada

Eventually, American FDI came to dominate certain key sectors of the economy. By 1955, Americans owned 63 percent of the petroleum and natural gas industry and 58 percent of mining and smelting. Gradually, unease with American domination of the Canadian economy began to surface by the mid-1950s and 1960s. There was already a growing anti-Americanism generally. Combined with growing Canadian prosperity, this led to the belief that American FDI was no longer as necessary as it once had been.

Toronto businessperson Walter Gordon (later a Liberal finance minister under Pearson) was appointed in 1955 to head the Royal Commission on Canada's Economic Prospects. There was a clash of ideas before the Commission on whether or not FDI was a good thing for Canada. A redefinition of Canadian economic nationalism emerged as part of the intellectual debate, both within the Royal Commission and in the broader society. The Gordon Commission found that there was a tendency of foreign-owned firms to purchase their supplies abroad and/or not to employ Canadians. It suggested some shares should be sold to Canadians to increase domestic ownership. It also hinted that there might be a link between economic and political dependence. This led to a broader political debate in Canada about FDI.[50]

One of the signs that concern about American domination of the Canadian economy was problematic came in the 1956 Pipeline Debate. This debate galvanized around the proposed construction of a natural gas pipeline from Alberta to Ontario by an American company. John Diefenbaker's Conservative Party took up the nationalist arguments, suggesting this was a sell-out to American interests in an area of vital importance to Canada. Diefenbaker successfully used these arguments during the election campaign in 1957, and his Progressive Conservative Party defeated the Liberals for the first time in twenty-two years. However, there was little follow-through once the Conservatives took power.

In 1965, the Liberals returned to power under Pearson, and Gordon became finance minister. However, Gordon was largely unable to convince his Cabinet colleagues, Canadian businesses, or even the public of his nationalist policy ideas. The 1965 budget contained some provision to promote Canadian ownership of businesses in Canada and lessen FDI, but it was widely denounced by the business community, and Gordon resigned as finance minister. He nonetheless helped broaden the discussion about traditional Canadian-American economic relations.

Gordon returned to Cabinet in 1967 and commissioned the Watkins Report, which was charged with further investigating the impact of FDI on the Canadian economy.[51] Chaired by University of Toronto political economist Mel Watkins, it recommended maximizing the benefits of FDI while slightly strengthening controls over it. It suggested creating provisions against "extra-territoriality," whereby the United States attempted to apply American law to corporations within Canada. Specifically, the United States had tried to invoke the *Trading with the Enemy Act* in response to the Ford Motor Company of Canada doing business with communist Cuba. The Watkins Report also recommended laws to strengthen anti-combines legislation to prevent the creation of monopolies and to increase competition. Pearson largely ignored the Watkins Report recommendations, and Gordon resigned once again. But the nationalist arguments were becoming louder and more prominent nonetheless.

Despite Gordon's defeat, a new nationalism was rising up in Canada in the 1960s and 1970s, partly focused on the issue of FDI. Radicalized by baby boomers, Canadian politics sought to distance Canada from the increasingly troubled American empire, which at the time was engaged in the Vietnam War, domestic riots, civil rights abuses, and scandal-ravaged domestic politics that reached all the way up to the president. There was also growing suspicion about American multinational corporations and their outsized influence in Canada.

As a result of the new mood, nationalist organizations formed, critical books and articles were published, and increasing numbers of Canadian academics and journalists began to express critical views about the Canadian-American relationship. Among other things, they argued that overreliance on foreign capital would lead to total American domination of the Canadian economy, result in underperforming branch plants, and contribute ultimately to a sacrifice of Canadian sovereignty.

Different groups of nationalists had different interpretations of the issue. For left-wing nationalists in the NDP — called the "Waffle" — the problem was capitalism as a whole that needed to be replaced. They argued there was little difference between American and Canadian capitalists; both had to go by nationalizing all industries. Followers of Gordon advocated a more moderate approach focusing on simply lowering levels of American FDI. They sought the creation of a government agency to screen applications for foreign takeovers of Canadian interests, for instance.

Most variants of the new nationalism found their home mainly in central Canada. This region was the wealthiest and could arguably most afford to accept the potentially lower standards of living for increased Canadian control of the economy. Other regions objected to controls on FDI as potentially job-killing measures. Moreover, not all Canadians saw things the way the nationalist critiques did. Many were enjoying high levels of prosperity, wealth, and a high standard of living. The middle class was expanding, and it did not want to give up the benefits of being part of the American empire — including access to consumer goods and American cultural products — for some abstract notion of the "Canadian identity."

The Liberal government of Pierre Trudeau was mildly sympathetic to some of the nationalist critique. Trudeau created the Canada Development Corporation (CDC) in 1971 to pool Canadian capital to purchase firms that might otherwise end up in foreign hands. He also created Petro-Canada and the National Energy Program to assert greater control of the vitally important energy sector. And he commissioned yet another study of FDI, this time under Cabinet minister Herb Gray.

Gray argued that FDI resulted in the "truncation" of the Canadian economy, meaning that there was less decision-making by Canadians, fewer export opportunities, less training of Canadian personnel, and less specialized product development. He also suggested there was less spillover in economic activity from sector to sector within Canada. And the Gray Report resurrected the idea of a screening agency for FDI. Consequently, the Foreign Investment Review Agency (FIRA) was created by the Trudeau government in 1973. Foreigners intending to set up a business in Canada or purchase a Canadian business had to first submit a proposal to FIRA to show the business would be a "significant benefit" to Canada. FIRA could also regulate activities of firms to ensure greater benefits to Canada. But FIRA proved to be a paper tiger, approving the vast majority of applications it received.

## 4) Canada Is Open for Business

The global economic decline in the mid-1970s led to the undermining of confidence in the nationalist critique as economic growth slowed, and unemployment and inflation rose. Keynesian-style state intervention as a general policy prescription began to fall out of favour. Public attitudes began to shift, with increased support for further FDI to help Canada get out of the recessionary cycle. As a clear signal of the importance of the American economy to Canada, Conservative Brian Mulroney came to power in 1984 declaring to a Wall Street audience in New York that "Canada is open for business."

Mulroney dismantled Trudeau's nationalist projects while ironically calling himself a Canadian nationalist. He privatized the CDC and Petro-Canada, and replaced FIRA with Investment Canada, an agency dedicated to facilitating foreign investment instead of screening it. Furthermore, he cultivated closer relations with the United States and, as noted in Section 3 above in this chapter, reversed more than 100 years of the National Policy protectionism by negotiating free trade with the United States. Mulroney represented the neo-conservative strain of continentalist thinking in which the marketplace is the arbiter of social values, the power of big business is unrestricted, and the values of individualism are paramount.

By the 1990s and early 2000s, the restructuring brought on by free trade caused nationalists to rally to a new cause — the anti-globalization movement. The critique of FDI broadened to a critique of global capital represented by transnational corporations (TNCs). Nationalists claimed globalization was leading to privatization, deregulation, and a transfer of power from the state to free markets dominated by giant TNCs. Canadians led opposition to the Multilateral Agreement on Investment (MAI), an international agreement to loosen restrictions on foreign investment.[52] The MAI was negotiated between members of the Organisation for Economic Co-operation and Development (OECD) between 1995 and 1998. It sought multilateral rules on international investment, but drew widespread criticism from non-governmental organizations (NGOs), civil society groups, and developing countries over the latitude it gave to TNCs and the possibility that the MAI would make it difficult to regulate foreign investors. Opponents argued that the MAI would threaten protection of human rights, labour, and environmental standards, adversely affect less-developed countries, and result in a "race to the bottom" among countries willing to lower their labour and environmental standards to attract foreign investment. An intense global campaign was waged against the MAI by the treaty's critics, resulting in its withdrawal.

**TABLE 6.2. SALES AND MERGERS OF CANADIAN COMPANIES TO FOREIGN OWNERSHIP**

| Company | Year of Sale | Purchaser |
|---|---|---|
| Bauer | 1994 | Nike |
| Tim Hortons | 1995 | Wendy's International |
| Canadian Pacific Railway | 1995 | Private investors |
| Cooper Canada | 1995 | Nike |
| Eaton's | 1999 | Sears |
| Seagram | 2000 | Vivendi |
| Hudson Bay Company | 2003 | B-Bay Inc. |
| Molson's | 2004 | Adolph Coors Company |
| Falconbridge | 2006 | Xstrata |
| Fairmount Hotels | 2006 | Colony Capital + Kingdom Holding Company |
| INCO | 2006 | Vale |
| Dofasco | 2006 | Arcelor SA |
| Alcan | 2007 | Rio Tinto |
| Four Season's Hotels | 2007 | Cascade Investments + Kingdom Holding Company |
| Zellers | 2011 | Target |

The FTA and NAFTA affected FDI in a particular way. In the old branch plant model, the Canadian operation of the American parent warranted, physically, a Canadian head office. With free trade, the corporate structure could be rationalized on a North American basis with a single head office in the United States. This led some critics to warn that corporate Canada was being "hollowed out." In fact, a rash of sell-offs occurred in the aftermath of the signing of NAFTA. Most were to American TNCs, as Table 6.2 reveals.

In 2007, after many of these takeovers of Canadian companies by foreign companies made headline news, the Canadian government announced a Competition Policy Review Panel of five persons, all with business interests, to review Canada's competition and investment policies. Appearing before the committee, Watkins (author of the Watkins Report referenced in this section above) said: "There is a clear implication that the issue of takeovers of Canadian companies by foreign companies is to be understood as a matter of competition, and only of competition. Why not, for example, the Sovereignty Review Panel?"[53]

Despite the overall trend toward free trade, protection, and/or foreign ownership, restrictions remained in place in some sectors, including telecommunications, cultural industries, broadcasting, transportation services, and uranium production. As well, the financial services sector remained subject to ownership restrictions of general application but not specific foreign ownership restrictions.

The case of the Saskatchewan's PotashCorp illustrated some of the inherent tensions produced by free trade combined with restrictions on foreign ownership. In the 1990s, PotashCorp expanded by buying up a number of American potash companies, and owned assets across Canada, the United States, Brazil, and the Middle East. By March 2008, due to rising potash prices, it had become one of the most valuable companies in Canada valued at almost $63 billion. In August 2010, PotashCorp became the subject of a hostile takeover bid by Anglo-Australian mining giant BHP Billiton.

Saskatchewan Premier Brad Wall launched a campaign to block the takeover, saying it was contrary to the interests of the citizens of Saskatchewan since it failed the "net benefit" test in three key areas: jobs and investment; Canadian control of an important Canadian resource; and provincial revenues. On 3 November 2010, the Government of Canada announced that it was blocking the BHP bid as it did not feel the purchase would yield a "net benefit" for Canada, and BHP withdrew its bid soon thereafter. But the case is an outlier since Investment Canada in virtually all other cases sought to welcome foreign investment rather than block it. None of the Mulroney, Chrétien, or Martin governments ever blocked a foreign investment under the *Investment Canada Act*. The first use of the Act to reject foreign investment came under the Harper government. In 2008, the sale of the space division of Canadian communications technology company MacDonald, Dettwiler & Associates (MDA), to American-based Alliant Techsystems was rejected following wide protest that the sale would transfer strategic economic and scientific assets out of Canada.

Beginning in the mid-1990s, Canada became a net exporter of capital, as the post-war trend of inward direct investment flows (mostly from American firms) was superseded by outward direct investments by Canadian corporations. By the first decade of the twenty-first century, Canada was home to more than 1,400 multinational corporations, which controlled approximately 3,700 foreign affiliates. Canada was also home to seventy-two "world class" corporations, which ranked among the top five in their line of business globally. According to Forbes, Canada ranked fifth among countries with corporations listed among the top 2,000 worldwide. Canadian firms were increasingly engaged in a wider process of internationalization, especially through foreign direct investments in Europe and Latin America.[54]

The Canadian perspective on FDI raises many important policy questions. Is FDI good for Canada, or is it a problem? If one is going to play the capitalist game, is it obvious that one ought to have one's own capitalists the better to play it? Should the state regulate FDI, or should the free market be allowed to prevail? Of course, all these questions are posed most importantly against the backdrop of the overarching Canadian-American relationship.

## 5) Shrug: The American Concern with Canadian Foreign Direct Investment

In comparison to Canada's near-obsession with the question of FDI, in the United States, FDI by Canadians generally gets little public attention or concern with various regulatory agencies involved only in examining the impact on economic competition. In 2023, the United States Surface Transportation Board approved the takeover by Canadian Pacific freight railways of Kansas City Southern in the United States. While United States Senator Elizabeth Warren urged the Board to reject the takeover for competition reasons, the Board only found positive impacts to the merger.[55] Recent takeovers by Canadian energy companies of American energy companies received little public or political attention outside of business news articles.[56] While most large Canadian banks also have retail banking operations in the United States, large American banks don't have retail operations in Canada.

Though Canadians have frequently expressed concerns over American encroachment on the Canadian economy and Canadian business, stewards of the much larger American economy have been far less concerned about Canadian investment than with the American economic and military rivalry with China. In recent years, the United States has often blocked Chinese investment in the United States, and American investment in China for national security reasons.[57] The United States has banned investment and sales by the Chinese company Huawei due to fears of its ties to the Chinese government and has urged allies to enact similar bans.[58] In 2024, the House of Representatives passed a bill to force the social media site TikTok's Chinese parent company, ByteDance, to sell TikTok or else the app would be banned on American phones.[59]

The United States has no similar restrictions on Canadian investments, but the State Department's website on the investment climate in Canada does warn Americans about some of the Canadian restrictions on FDI.[60] Perhaps the best description of what Americans think about their economic relationship with Canada was expressed in a famous recording by Canadian broadcast commentator Gordon Sinclair in 1973. His audio editorial about American technology and how Americans are always ready to bail out other country's economic problems during an emergency, while other countries never return the favour, gained widespread attention in the United States. A record of his editorial set to the music of the "Battle Hymn of the Republic" reached the Top 40 in both countries, charting higher in the United States than in Canada.[61]

## C. Taxation

### 1) The Price for Being Canadian Rather than American

Another point of comparison between Canada and the United States economic policy relates to taxation. There is a price to be paid for living in Canada rather than in the United States. The price is related to choosing a different role for government. Citizens decide what services they believe should be provided privately and which should be provided collectively (by the state). Historically, Canada has chosen a higher degree of state interventionism; consequently, taxes have tended to be higher than in the United States. The politics of taxation has been important in both countries. Decisions about what and who to tax, and how much, has been the subject of sharp debate. Recently, a deep anti-tax ethos has emerged, this despite the admonition made in 1927 by American Supreme Court Justice Oliver Wendell Holmes that "taxes are what we pay for a civilized society," a sentiment articulated much earlier by the Roman senator Cicero that "taxes are the sinews of the state."[62]

The two federal tax systems differ noticeably in their emphasis: Canada relies more on sales taxes while the United States relies more on social security taxes on wages, salaries, and payrolls. Most individuals will pay more tax in Canada than had they lived in the United States, while most businesses see little difference in the overall tax level.

In 2022, spending by all levels of government in Canada amounted to about 42 percent of GDP, while spending by all levels of government in the United States amounted to about 36 percent of GDP.[63] In comparison to other Group of Seven (G7) countries (United States, Germany, France, United Kingdom, Japan, Italy, and Canada), Canadian overall state spending is about 108.5 percent of the G7 average; spending in the United States is about 84.5 percent of the G7 average. Social spending in both countries is roughly even, at about 22 percent of GDP.[64]

According to two experts in economic policy in Canada and the United States:

> The Canadian safety net is considerably denser than that in the US, and the minimum level of support that is provided by the government is higher (and this is particularly the case for health care). The tax system is more progressive, and the federal government equalization payments to the provinces with below average taxing capacity are more extensive. The result has been a smaller increase in income inequality over the last three decades in Canada.[65]

## 2) Sources of Revenue in Canada Compared to the United States

Sources of tax revenue also vary between the two countries. Canada has a national sales tax known as the Goods and Services Tax/Harmonized Sales Tax (GST/HST), while the United States does not. The United States has a 15.3 percent national payroll tax to contribute to the Social Security and Medicare Trust Funds, while Canada imposes an 11.9 percent payroll tax on most workers to fund the Canada Pension Plan. As a result, in 2024, revenue for the United States federal government mostly comes from three sources: the individual income tax (50 percent), the Social Security and Medicare payroll tax (36 percent), and corporate income tax (9 percent).[66] In Canada the main sources of revenue are shown in Figure 6.1 for 2022–2023. The largest proportion of taxes come from personal income tax (46.4 percent), then corporate income tax (21 percent), followed by the GST/HST (10.3 percent). Other revenues (7.5 percent), Employment Insurance premiums (6 percent), other taxes and duties (4.1 percent), and proceeds from the pollution pricing framework (1.8 percent) make up the remaining sources of revenue. Tax revenues in Canada in 2022 was about 13.3 percent of GDP, whereas in the United States in 2022 it was about 11.6 percent of GDP.[67]

**FIGURE 6.1. COMPOSITION OF REVENUES FOR 2022–2023 (TOTAL: $447.8 BILLION)**

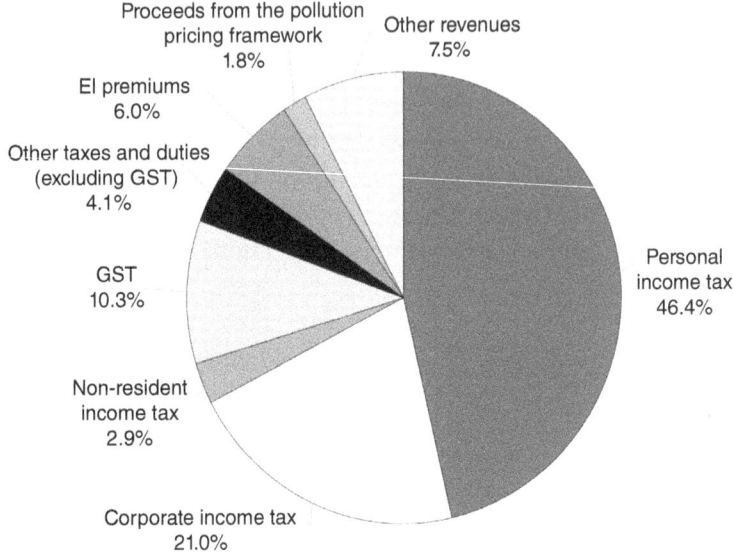

Source: Canada, Department of Finance, *Annual Financial Report of the Government of Canada Fiscal Year 2022–2023*, online: www.canada.ca/en/department-finance/services/publications/annual-financial-report/2023/report.html

## 3) Income Inequality in Canada Compared to the United States

Corporate income tax has declined as a percentage of all federal taxes in both countries in recent decades. Hence the burden of taxation has been shifting in both Canada and the United States from corporations to individuals. Moreover, the redistributive impact of taxes, once central to the idea that a progressive tax system could enhance equality, has been diminishing. This is especially the case in the United States. In the United States, income inequality has been persistently higher than in Canada for more than forty years. Comparing income inequality among the world's richest democracies in the OECD shows the United States is the most unequal in terms of income distribution, while Canada is at or below the average.[68]

The differences between shares of pre-tax income held by the richest earners of each country is striking. This is particularly the case with the share of income held by the top 10 percent (and especially the top 1 percent) of income distribution. In both countries, "the top 10% of the distribution holds a staggeringly large percentage of income — 40% in Canada and 50% in the United States in 2018."[69] The patterns in the concentration of wealth in both countries over the twentieth and into the early twenty-first centuries has followed a U-shape; in the 1920s, earnings disparities were not unlike the high concentration of wealth in very few hands today, but from the 1930s to the 1970s, disparities in income between the richest and least well off diminished.[70] In the past forty years, though, the extent of inequality has grown. For instance, since 1980, income share in Canada has increased for the highest ten percent of income earners by 11.5 percent and for the top one percent by 58.5 percent. In the United States, the figures are a 26.5 percent increase for the top ten percent and an astonishing 73.6 percent for the top one percent. Meanwhile, the bottom four-fifths of earners in Canada and the United States have seen their income share reduced.[71] In Canada, the richest 100 CEOs in 2022 made 246 times more than the average Canadian worker.[72] In the United States, also in 2022, CEOs were paid 344 times as much as a typical worker.[73]

## D. Budgeting Processes in Canada and the United States

### 1) The Complexity of Budgeting

The economic fortunes of Canada and the United States are tied very closely together. The impact of the health of the American economy is of course of more significance to Canada than vice versa. In any case, both nations pursue macroeconomic policy making through similar, yet different, budgetary processes. The similarities relate to the prominent role the budgetary process plays in each country's politics. The differences involve the ways in which revenues and expenditures are managed by each government.

The complexity of budgeting is evident in considering the tremendous number of variables that impinge on financial management in both countries. These include their own domestic economies; the global economic landscape; provincial, state, and other governments; transnational corporations; interest groups, social movements, and citizens; wars; pandemics; climate events; and recessions, among other things. Many events that originate in the United States have a profound cross-border impact, and the execution of carefully constructed financial plans can easily be sent off the rails by unforeseen crises such as the bank and real estate failures in the United States in 2008, 2022, and 2023. The collapse of the American mortgage and lending sector and bankruptcies of some of the biggest players in the American financial sector, which triggered the global recession of 2008–2009, caused economic shock waves in Canada. Decisions by the Bank of Canada and the United States Federal Reserve to raise or lower interest rates have their own effects on government budgeting.

The COVID-19 pandemic is a case in point. The Canadian federal government deficit grew from $29.3 billion in 2019–2020 to a record level of $327.7 billion, while the national debt skyrocketed to an unprecedented $1.04 trillion. All the best economic planning by the Canadian government for the 2019–2020 budget went up in smoke. No one predicted the actual impact of the rapidly developing global pandemic, and by 2020 governments in Canada had no choice but to respond to the rapidly shifting emergency with a series of astonishing budgetary measures to protect the health of Canadians and their businesses. Similar measures were needed by the American government, where the estimated cumulative financial costs of the COVID-19 pandemic related to lost output and increased rates of illness was more than $16 trillion, or roughly 90 percent of annual GDP of the United States.[74] Six COVID-19 relief laws enacted in 2020 and 2021 provided about $4.6 trillion of funding for pandemic response and recovery as of 31 January 2023, none of which were anticipated, of course, before COVID-19 struck.[75]

## 2) Budget-Making in Canada[76]

In Canada, the annual budget is the responsibility of the minister and department of finance. There is a quirky tradition surrounding the introduction of the government's annual budget that sees the minister of finance purchase new shoes to wear when the budget is delivered.[77]

> Where this curious practice began is not known, and it is not always strictly followed. But when finance ministers observe it, it usually signals something about the state of the economy and whether the budget will contain good or bad news for Canadians. Fancy new dress shoes are the usual choice. But some ministers have sported running shoes, second-hand shoes, work boots, and even mukluks. One finance minister, in trying to indicate that fiscal prudence was the order of the day, even resoled his shoes.[78]

Beyond these sartorial choices, the process for approving a federal budget in Canada is complex. It is rooted in ancient practices derived from feudal Britain where the lords and barons sought limits to the ability of the monarch to tax and spend, and ultimately to hold the monarch accountable to Parliament. "In keeping with this tradition, the Canadian federal government cannot raise taxes or spend funds without first obtaining Parliament's explicit approval through the adoption of legislation."[79] As a result, complex systems to hold the government accountable for its financial management have developed.

The finance minister and department are the key actors in the Canadian budgetary process. One prime minister allowed that his finance minister was so important that no light could be allowed to show between himself and his minister of finance.[80] Generally speaking the success or failure of policy ideas is largely dependent on the approval of the finance department, which,

> has virtually exclusive authority over the preparation of the revenue and expenditure budgets, the drafting of the budget speech, and other important economic statements.... Finance determines

taxation, trade and tariff policy, manages federal borrowing on financial markets and is the key actor overseeing and managing billions of dollars in federal transfers to provinces and territories. Regulatory policy concerning the financial sector is another of its responsibilities, and it represents Canada within international financial institutions. In addition to all of that, it is the key source for analysis and advice on the broad economic and financial affairs of the country, researching the performance of the Canadian economy from output and growth to employment and income to price stability and monetary policy to the impact of globalization, etc. In addition, this department is in constant communication with the other departments of government to coordinate initiatives that have an impact on the economy.[81]

The government of Canada follows a complex series of steps to manage the economy through its annual budget. In the spring (usually March), the finance minister presents a proposed budget for the upcoming fiscal year, and the opposition parties are given a chance to respond. The budget speech itself is a major event in the life of a government, and the media, economists, political scientists, and other academics, other governments, interest groups, think tanks, and citizens will often weigh in with their analysis of it. The budget "includes a comprehensive financial statement, including a forecast of financial requirements for government operations for the forthcoming year, and the ways and means proposed by the government to achieve its multiple objectives."[82] The budget speech has been described as "the focal point of the federal government's efforts to define and mobilize public support for its fiscal and economic agenda. As such, it is an opportunity for the federal government to define its priorities, exercise leadership, and obtain legal and political support for its policies, through both the formal processes of Parliament and direct appeals for public support."[83]

Following the reading of the budget speech, there is a debate in the House of Commons lasting several days. The House then approves the budget as an automatic vote of confidence in the government. If the majority of members of the Commons vote against the budget, that is considered a vote of no confidence, the government falls, and a new election is called. This last happened in 1979 when Prime Minister Joe Clark's Progressive Conservative minority government was defeated by a mere six votes when the opposition parties united to defeat his budget.

More recently, in 2008, the Harper Conservative government nearly lost a vote of non-confidence (as we noted in Chapter 2). It presented a budget update just six weeks after the October election, but the opposition parties threatened to defeat the government unless several measures they disliked were removed. The Conservatives had 143 seats, but the other parties together held 163 seats (the Liberals had seventy-seven seats, the NDP thirty-seven seats, and the Bloc Québécois forty-nine seats, and there were two independents). They decided to form a coalition and informed Governor General Michaëlle Jean that they demanded the right to form a new government. To avoid a sure defeat in the House of Commons, Harper advised the Governor General instead to prorogue Parliament (meaning terminate a session of Parliament). This raised a constitutional question not tested since the 1926 King-Byng affair: Was it legitimate for the Governor General to reject the advice of the prime minister, thereby giving the opposition coalition the opportunity to govern? After consulting with constitutional experts and then meeting with Harper for more than two hours on 4 December 2008, she granted his request to prorogue Parliament until 26 January 2009. The Conservatives later rewrote parts of their budget to the satisfaction of the Liberals and resumed governing.

The *British North America Act, 1867* (BNA Act, 1867), in section 102 gives Parliament the right to control public money by establishing a single consolidated revenue fund to receive all money belonging to Canada. Parliament is given authority to pay money out of the consolidated revenue fund in section 106. The importance of the principle of parliamentary approval over the raising and spending of money is explained by Donald Savoie:

Several principles underpin Parliament's role in the budget process. The first is that the government — or the executive — can have no revenue which is not sanctioned by Parliament, and the second is that the government can make no expenditures except those approved by Parliament. In addition, Parliament does not grant a permanent right to spend, so that the government must submit a new budget every year. Thus funds allocated by Parliament but not spent must lapse. Detailed spending plans are submitted annually in the form of spending "estimates." The government must also account to Parliament for its management of public moneys, both revenues and expenditures.[84]

In reality, though, the executive branch of government controls the public purse, and it is able to ensure its budget is accepted and passed in Parliament due to the practice of party discipline (see Chapter 2). The members of each party virtually always vote the way their leaders instruct them, especially with regard to signalling support for the budget. Parliament, thus, acts more as a "watchdog," conferring legitimacy on the government's financial plans, rather than determining them. As noted above, though, minority government enhances the ability of Parliament to influence the budget since the executive often must bargain with one or more of the opposition parties for their support. In return, those parties may be able to negotiate for measures they want to see included or against measures they want removed. In 2022, the NDP negotiated a deal with the minority Trudeau Liberal government to refrain from voting non-confidence for a set period of time as long as certain policies favoured by the NDP were passed by the Liberals.[85] Minority government, it has been suggested, "creates a fascinating game of cat and mouse. A government that wishes to stay in power has to try to keep the opposition divided. It typically does so by introducing measures that it hopes at least one of the major Opposition parties cannot possibly disagree with."[86]

Unlike the American Senate, the role of the Canadian Senate in the budget process is perfunctory. The Canadian Senate almost always practises deference to the House of Commons in the budget process and automatically approves the government's budget once it passes the other chamber. But there was an unusual Senate rebellion in 1990 against a proposal by Progressive Conservative Prime Minister Brian Mulroney to implement a new Goods and Services Tax (national sales tax) in Canada. Liberals still dominated the Senate at the time due to many appointments by the previous prime minister, Pierre Trudeau. It appeared that the Senate would reject the new GST, so Mulroney, for the only time in Canadian history, invoked an obscure constitutional provision that allowed him to appoint eight new senators to give him a Senate majority that approved his new tax.[87]

### 3) Budget-Making in the United States

Because budget bills are votes of no confidence in Canada, situations where the federal government shuts down due to lack of funding or when there is no planned budget for the upcoming year cannot happen in Canada. Yet situations like that happen frequently in the United States. Prior to 1921, the United States had no planned federal budget. Various spending committees in Congress would appropriate funds and then depend on the tax committees to raise enough revenue to pay for everything. The increased complexity and size of the federal government convinced Congress to create a central planning process through the *Budget and Accounting Act* of 1921, yet Congress gave that power to plan a national budget to the executive branch rather than to itself.

The law became an important component in the rise of presidential power in the United States during the twentieth century. For more than fifty years after the passage of the 1921 law, the president would send a budget proposal with taxing and spending provisions to Capitol Hill each year, Congress would argue and fight over a few parts of the president's budget and change a few things, and then pass most of the president's proposal into law. Due to perceived abuses of government budgeting during the Nixon administration, along with growing congressional and public frustration with abuses of presidential power during the Vietnam War and Watergate scandal, Congress passed the *Budget and Impoundment Control Act* in 1974. That law restored more control and power over spending and taxing decisions to Congress, as intended by the Constitution.

However, in recent decades, the increased polarization in Congress between conservative Republicans and liberal Democrats, the power of Senate filibusters, and the checks and balances system treasured as a principle of government by Americans have all led to increasing gridlock in Washington and the inability to approve any planned budget at all in most years during the twenty-first century. Instead, the United States federal government mostly operates on continuing resolutions that temporarily fund federal government operations at previous levels for three to six months at a time — without planning of priorities, few budget cuts or increases, and usually no major tax changes. Some continuing resolutions will provide emergency funding for military operations or public health or natural disaster responses.

In October 2013, congressional Republicans demanded full repeal of the *Affordable Care Act* (ACA or Obamacare — see Chapter 5) in order to pass a new continuing resolution. Democrats refused. So the federal government shut down for two weeks due to lack of funding. In December 2018, President Trump demanded funding for a border wall with Mexico in order to sign a new continuing resolution into law. Congressional Democrats refused. So on 22 December 2018, most federal agencies shut down, including financial services, transportation, housing, agriculture, the Food and Drug Administration, and national parks. That year, 800,000 federal government employees went unpaid over the Christmas holidays, though they did get back pay later on. The shutdown lasted thirty-five days until 25 January, the longest in American history, and cost $5 billion for the federal government to reopen.[88]

Congress passed several more continuing resolutions to fund the federal government temporarily in 2022 and 2023, with a constant threat of potential government shutdowns looming. With a narrow

Republican-majority House of Representatives and a Democratic-majority Senate and Democratic president in 2024, there were four more continuing resolutions approved to keep the United States government operating temporarily and few prospects for an improvement to the federal budget process in the short term.

## Conclusion

What happens when an elephant is a mouse's main relationship? The power imbalance between Canada and the United States is evident when comparing the size of their economies. Yet the two are deeply integrated, based on a long and extensive trade and economic relationship. Both exhibit a democratic political system wed to a capitalist economy. Shared outlooks foster areas of cooperation. But differing economic interests place Canada and the United States in competition with each other over many economic and trade-related issues. Consequently, management of this relationship often requires intervention at the very highest levels — prime ministers and presidents. Domestic management of the economy in each country revolves around the all-important budgetary process, deciding whom to tax and where to spend. Yet the political machinations behind this economic exercise, derived from the differing political systems in play, produce quite different approaches and means to budgeting. Yet again we see how Canada and the United States are the same, only different.

CHAPTER SEVEN

# Foreign Policy: Friends and Allies (Mostly)

### Introduction

Where foreign policy is concerned, Canada and the United States have been friends and allies — mostly. The twentieth century and early twenty-first century saw the two countries move closer and closer in a commonality of interests regarding the outside world. But irritants and disagreements arose from time to time that have tested the warmth of the relationship. This chapter explores some contemporary foreign policy relations focusing on the wars in Afghanistan and Iraq, border security, Arctic sovereignty, pipelines, and relations with Russia and China. But first, it looks at the general trends in foreign policy positions over the history of relations between the two countries to determine the extent to which their foreign policies are the same, only different.

### A. Friends and Allies (Mostly)

#### 1) The Nineteenth Century

Throughout the twentieth century, it became commonplace to refer to the forty-ninth parallel — the boundary line between Canada and the United States — as the longest undefended border in the world. This idea can be dated to the conclusion of the War of 1812 when Great Britain and the United States signed the Treaty of Ghent in 1815. Subsequently, they also signed the Rush-Bagot Treaty in 1817, which demilitarized the Great Lakes and prohibited both countries from sailing warships there. Each country was allowed to have one armed vessel with one cannon on Lake Ontario and each country to have two armed vessels with one cannon each on the other four Great Lakes. In 2006, the United States Coast Guard announced that it had armed eleven Coast Guard boats in Lakes Erie and Huron with machine guns due to smuggling and fears of terrorists, in apparent violation of the Treaty. Canada said it would view the machine guns as a law enforcement tool, not for military purposes, and so would not object.[1]

The Treaty of Ghent laid the basis for a demilitarized boundary between British North America and the United States, and marked the end of direct violent conflict between the governments of Canada and the United States. It was followed by a long period of developing deep economic and cultural relations, as well as the gradual integration of the military-industrial complex.

As we noted in Chapter 1, after the War of 1812, Americans turned to the policy of manifest destiny, which declared that it was their fate and purpose to settle the West; as such, droves of settlers moved there. This sometimes brought them into conflict with both Canada and Mexico and led to war with Mexico in the 1840s and a border dispute with Canada on the Pacific coast.

The gap between the political economies of Canada and the United States was widened by the American Civil War from 1860 to 1865, which cost some 700,000 American lives. The war helped facilitate industrial development and the emergence of the steel industry. In turn, this contributed to the building of transcontinental railways that led to the further expansion of the republic westward. The victory by the North over the South in the Civil War marked the ascendance of an economy based on industrial capitalism in the northern states over the agricultural-plantation economy of the south. America emerged as a powerfully attractive destination for growing numbers of immigrants. Many of them used Canada as a stopping-off point on their way to the United States.

A variety of political, economic, and cultural interests existed in British North America in the mid-nineteenth century. They jockeyed for position in response to the changing conditions, including through the development of a political system of dual elite accommodation in the institutions of the Province of Canada where the interests of the two cultural communities in Canada East and Canada West had to be bridged. Serious stresses and strains stretched the system to its limits as diverging economic and cultural differences emerged.

One possibility was to join the United States. But this was a minority view. After all, as noted in Chapter 1, Canadians could have opted for American republicanism several times during the American Revolution in 1776, the War of 1812, or the Rebellions in Upper and Lower Canada in 1837 and 1838. But the powerful influence of the United Empire Loyalists and the French, neither of whom were predisposed to join the United States, foreclosed that possibility.[2] Indeed, as also noted in Chapter 1, British North Americans were motivated to unite partly because of their disdain for the American model of democracy. Thus annexation to the United States was not an attractive prospect for most. Indeed, by the 1860s the American experience of civil war provided the case for enhancing the military security of British North America through the union of the colonies. In short, "a sense of military insecurity and consequent need for common defence"[3] was a contributing factor in the creation of a federal system in Canada. After all, there was a very large well-trained demobilized army in the wake of the Civil War looking for something to do. The Canadian colonies felt potential American military action was always possible.

Moreover, since slavery had been abolished in the United States as a result of the Civil War, northern expansion was a real possibility. Prior to the war, the admission of any new slave state had to be matched with the addition of a free state. This debilitated expansion and led to deadlock. Now the addition of Canada, or parts of it, could proceed without this condition. The southern plantation economy had been an important source for cotton for Britain's textile industry, and the British had been sympathetic to the South in the war. This caused friction and a deterioration in relations between the United States and Great Britain, and also contributed to the concern among Canadians that the Americans might turn their ire toward their northern neighbour. The victorious North, it was feared, might seek revenge on British North America. Another related threat existed in the form of the Fenian Brotherhood, as noted in Chapter 1. These were Irish nationalists in the United States, many of whom had fought for the North in the Civil War, and who launched armed raids into British North America to draw the attention and resources of the British army away from Ireland to make it easier to defeat the British there and achieve the goal of an independent Irish republic.[4]

This proved to be another potentially destabilizing security threat to the colonies of British North America, although admittedly it was less of a factor for those colonies that did not share a border with the United States, namely Nova Scotia and Newfoundland. Still, the military threat provided a compelling motivation for much of the leadership of British North America; it led them to look for new forms of political arrangements that might help assure some greater measure of security, and hence contributed ultimately to Confederation. On top of the military threat, the United States took economic actions that also pushed the British North American colonies into union. As noted in Chapter 6, in 1854, the American Congress had authorized a Reciprocity Treaty with the colonies — a form of free trade. But in 1866, it terminated the agreement and erected protectionist tariffs against the import of Canadian products. The pattern of protectionism versus free trade was set early on in the Canada-United States relationship.

It is against this backdrop that Canada and the United States assumed their places in relation to each other and to the broader world. The power imbalance would establish that Canada was forever the more vulnerable of the two. Retaining its ties to the British Empire was in part seen as the only viable foreign policy stance for the Canada of the late nineteenth and early twentieth centuries. Hence, Confederation was not, as noted earlier, a move to independence, as several of the most important connections to Great Britain were retained. These included the monarchy, the right of the British Parliament to amend the Canadian Constitution, and the trappings of the colonial position Canada had once held, such as the British flag and anthem. It also meant subservience in foreign policy to the British Foreign Office, which continued to set the parameters of foreign policy for Canada. Thus, when the Boer War broke out in 1899 in South Africa, Canada dutifully sent its soldiers to join the fight alongside the British. Similarly, when Britain declared war on Germany at the outset of the First World War in 1914, Canada found itself automatically at war, and again dutifully sent troops to join the fight.

The American stance on foreign affairs was strikingly different. Having violently severed its ties to the British Empire, the United States adopted a position of isolationism. It eschewed entanglements in European matters in particular, although as it grew in stature it proclaimed its sphere of influence as the western hemisphere. Diplomatic and military engagements in the Caribbean, and Central and Latin America represented the furthest reach of American imperial power at first. During the final decades of the nineteenth century, the United States expanded its territorial sovereignty across the Pacific Ocean and into the Caribbean Sea, as described in Chapter 1.

## 2) The Twentieth Century

Though the United States belatedly participated in the First World War due to threats from Germany, the United States returned to isolationist policies after that war ended. When war broke out in Europe in 1939, Canada joined quickly to support Britain, but the United States stayed out of it until December 1941, when Japan bombed the Pearl Harbor naval base in Hawaii. After the Second World War, the United States became more interventionist in world affairs, mainly at first through the policy of containment of communism. This led to American involvement in wars first in Korea in the 1950s (ostensibly as part of a United Nations-led mission), and then in Vietnam in the 1960s. The United States sent approximately 2.7 million men and women to fight in Vietnam, but Canada did not participate in the war. This led to tensions between the two countries. American policy in Vietnam was strongly criticized in much of the rest of the world, including by Canadian Prime Ministers Lester Pearson and Pierre Trudeau. After Pearson gave a speech at Temple University in Philadelphia in 1965 in which he criticized American policy in Vietnam, he was subject to a profanity-filled tirade by President Lyndon Johnson who grabbed Pearson by the lapels and snarled, "Don't you come into my living room and piss on my rug."[5]

By the end of the twentieth century, though, Canada and the United States were closely allied through several bilateral and multilateral relationships. They participated in the construction of the post-war global economic order at Breton Woods in 1944, which gave birth to the World Bank and the International Monetary Fund (IMF). They were both instrumental in the founding of the United Nations (UN) and the North Atlantic Treaty Organization (NATO). The two coordinated continental defence through the creation of the Defence Production Sharing Agreement (DPSA) in 1956 and the North American Aerospace Defence Command (NORAD) in 1958.

This is not to say that everything was rosy between the two countries. An indication of the quality of the relationship and the extent of convergence on foreign policy issues can be had by looking at relations at the top between prime ministers and presidents. Top-down relations determine much of the relationship between Canada and the United States; that is, how capably can prime ministers and presidents establish a solid working relationship and, in some cases, even a friendship? As the examples in Table 7.1 attest, the relationship is highly conditional on the informal interpersonal perceptions prime ministers and presidents develop about each other.

Foreign Policy

**TABLE 7.1. PRIME MINISTERS, PRESIDENTS, AND FOREIGN POLICY**

| Prime Minister | President | Key Issues |
| --- | --- | --- |
| King | Roosevelt | Prime Minister William Lyon Mackenzie King developed a strong professional and personal relationship with President Franklin D Roosevelt through their joint efforts as allies against Nazi Germany during the Second World War. |
| St. Laurent | Truman, Eisenhower | 1951 — While President Harry Truman supported the St. Lawrence Seaway, he was unable to get Congressional approval, and Prime Minister Louis St. Laurent prepared for Canada to build the needed infrastructure alone.<br><br>1954 — President Dwight Eisenhower signed a law passed by Congress to include the United States in the seaway's construction. |
| Diefenbaker | Kennedy | 1962 — Prime Minister John Diefenbaker on President John F Kennedy: "He's a hothead. He's a fool — too young, too brash, too inexperienced, and a boastful son of a bitch!" |
| Pearson | Johnson | 1965 — At the height of the Vietnam War, Prime Minister Lester Pearson visited President Lyndon Johnson at the White House after having given a scathing speech critical of the war. Johnson was livid, grabbed Pearson by the shirt collar, lifted the prime minister off the floor and shouted, "Don't you come into my living room and piss on my rug." |
| PE Trudeau | Nixon | 1969 — Pierre Trudeau told the National Press Club in Ottawa that living next to the United States "is in some ways like sleeping with an elephant. No matter how friendly or temperate the beast, one is affected by every twitch and grunt."<br><br>1971 — When it was revealed that President Richard Nixon called Prime Minister Pierre Trudeau "an asshole" in his private tapes, Trudeau responded with, "I've been called worse things by better people." |

*(Continued)*

**TABLE 7.1.** *(Continued)*

| Prime Minister | President | Key Issues |
|---|---|---|
| | | 1971 — After Trudeau left a session with Nixon in the Oval Office, the president said to HR Haldeman, his chief of staff: "That Trudeau, he's a clever son of a bitch." Then he said to Secretary of State Henry Kissinger: "What in the Christ is he talking about?" |
| | | Trudeau so infuriated Nixon during the visit that Nixon called him "a pompous egghead" and told Haldeman: "You've got to put it to these people for kicking the US around after what we did for that lousy son of a bitch. Give it to somebody around here." This was when Nixon ordered Haldeman to plant a negative story about Trudeau with columnist Jack Anderson. |
| | | 1972 — Nixon delivered a speech to the House of Commons: "While we do not have a wall between us, we have a great unguarded boundary. This does not mean that we are the same. This does not mean we do not have differences. But it does mean we have found a way to discuss differences in a friendly way without war." |
| Mulroney | Reagan, GHW Bush | 1985 — Prime Minister Brian Mulroney and President Ronald Reagan sing to each other when the president visits Canada: |
| | | *When Irish eyes are smiling,*<br>*Sure, 'tis like the morn in Spring.*<br>*In the lilt of Irish laughter*<br>*You can hear the angels sing.* |
| | | They then proceeded to negotiate and enact the Free Trade Agreement in 1989. |
| | | Mulroney was so close to President George HW Bush that he gave a tribute at Bush's funeral. |
| Chrétien | Clinton, GW Bush | 1999 — President Bill Clinton gave a major speech in Canada claiming the United States valued a united Canada at a time when Prime Minister Jean Chrétien was battling separatists in Quebec. |

Foreign Policy

**TABLE 7.1.** *(Continued)*

| Prime Minister | President | Key Issues |
|---|---|---|
| | | At the turn of the millennium, it was reported that White House officials privately referred to Chrétien as "Dino" (short for dinosaur). |
| | | 2001 — President George W Bush, in a speech to Congress, thanked countries all over the world for standing with the United States in its fight against terror after the attacks on the World Trade Center and the Pentagon. He did not mention Canada, where it was widely seen as an appalling snub. |
| | | 2003 — The Canadian government disagreed with Bush over the US-led war in Iraq (2003–2011). |
| Martin | GW Bush | 2005 — Prime Minister Paul Martin showed public impatience with President George W Bush over the American refusal to obey a NAFTA panel ruling over softwood lumber. |
| Harper | Obama | 2014 — Disagreements existed over confronting Syrian use of chemical weapons, negotiating trade agreements, defending Israel, and approving the Keystone oil pipeline. Prime Minister Stephen Harper was convinced President Barak Obama was captive to so many special interests that he simply would not or could not take a stand. |
| J Trudeau | Trump, Biden | 2020 — Prime Minister Trudeau was lied to by President Trump, who exaggerated and made up stories about the Canadian economy when renegotiating the North American Free Trade Agreement. In 2020, Trudeau famously paused for a full twenty-one seconds when asked a question about Trump's appalling response to anti-Black racism in America. |
| | | With Joe Biden as president, issues of free trade, American protectionism, climate change, and oil pipelines took centre stage, but a much more cordial relationship with Trudeau ensued. |

Source: Adapted from Lawrence Martin, *The Presidents and the Prime Ministers: Washington and Ottawa Face to Face: The Myth of Bilateral Bliss, 1867–1982* (Toronto: Doubleday, 1982); and Martin O'Malley & Justin Thompson, "Prime Ministers and Presidents" *CBC News* (22 November 2003), online: www.cbc.ca/canadaus/pms_presidents1.html.

As an example, after Prime Minister Brian Mulroney and President George HW Bush had both left office, Bush and his wife Barbara went to the wedding of the daughter of Brian and Mila Mulroney in September 2000. On the other hand, the difficulties in the Justin Trudeau-Donald Trump relationship were many. The unprecedented manner of Trump's approach to executive power and foreign policy — and especially his unconventional approach to traditional allies and enemies of the United States — created an unprecedented set of challenges for the Canadian-American relationship. There was much about the Trump presidency that was unprecedented:

> Indeed, in the Trump years and in their fraught two-year aftermath, the precedents tumbled like dominoes: Just as no presidents ever fomented a rebellion against the system of government they swore to preserve and protect, no presidential candidate ever sought to reverse the results of an election, no swarm of protesters ever breached the walls of the Capitol with intent to disrupt congressional proceedings, and no president ever has been impeached twice.[6]

In June 2020 in the aftermath of several highly publicized episodes of police violence against Black Americans, Trudeau was asked a question about Trump's appalling advocacy of military action against Black protestors. As noted in Chapter 6, Trudeau paused for an excruciatingly long twenty-one seconds before responding, creating a viral moment of silence that spoke legions about his views.[7]

### 3) The War in Afghanistan

The United States and Canada have very different levels of military resources. As of 2023, the United States had about 1.3 million active duty troops, and spent more than $800 billion on its military. Canada had about 70,000 active duty troops, and spent about $27 billion on the military (or about $20 billion in US dollars).

## Foreign Policy

Canada and the United States are, as noted above, members of NATO. Article 5 of the NATO treaty says that an attack on any NATO member is an attack on all NATO members; it is a mutual defence treaty. This clause has only been invoked once in its history. This was when terrorists attacked the United States on 11 September 2001 (9/11), and NATO members allied to defend the United States against Al Qaeda forces in Afghanistan. In 2001, Afghanistan had an Islamic fundamentalist government known as the Taliban, which had been in power since 1996. Its policies included requiring women to wear a burqa (full covering) in public; forbidding education for girls; and banning television, music, dancing, and kite flying. The Taliban were known to use state violence and sometimes massacred civilians in areas who resisted their religious-based edicts.

After the 9/11 attacks, the Taliban said the mastermind of the 9/11 attacks, Osama bin Laden and Al Qaeda leaders, were guests in Afghanistan. The United States responded by invading Afghanistan to overthrow the Taliban. Canada joined in and sent an infantry battle group and naval support. The ensuing war lasted twenty years until July 2021 when the last American and allied troops withdrew, and the Taliban returned to power. It was the single longest military engagement in history for both Canada and the United States.

Throughout the war, the Taliban engaged a series of suicide bombings and attacks on United States and allied country's militaries and Afghan political and military leaders, and retained control over many rural sections of the country. In total, more than 40,000 Canadian Armed Forces members served in the twelve-year campaign. The war killed 165 Canadians — 158 soldiers and seven civilians — while many Canadian veterans of the war developed post-traumatic stress disorder. More than 2,400 American troops died during the war, as did about 450 British troops. In February 2020, the United States had about 8,000 troops left in Afghanistan, Germany had 1,300, and the United Kingdom had 1,100. They were part of the Resolute Training Force whose role was to advise and train the Afghan military, which was then supposed to take the lead.

Thirty-eight countries still had armed forces totalling more than 16,000 troops in Afghanistan, including twenty-six of the twenty-nine countries in NATO at the time.[8] NATO member Iceland does not have a true military force, and Canada and France pulled out their military forces from Afghanistan in 2014.

Ironically, the first four Canadian troops to die in Afghanistan in 2002 were victims of friendly fire. The Canadian forces were running a nighttime military exercise, and Harry Schmidt, a major in the United States Illinois National Guard, flew over the Canadian military exercise and reported enemy fire to superiors on the ground. They told him to hold fire, but Schmidt dropped a laser-guided 500-pound bomb on the Canadian forces, killing four and wounding eight. A hearing held in Louisiana for Schmidt in 2004 found him guilty of dereliction of duty, docked him $5,700 in pay and gave him a reprimand.

Over time, Canada's involvement in Afghanistan became increasingly unpopular among Canadians. In 2008, Prime Minister Stephen Harper announced that all Canadian combat forces would leave Afghanistan by 2011, and they did. In March 2014, Harper withdrew several hundred Canadian military trainers from Afghanistan, making Canada the first NATO member to remove its entire military operation from the country. At the time, the United States still had 33,000 troops in Afghanistan, the United Kingdom had 5,000, and fifty other countries had small forces there.

## 4) The Iraq War

In 2003, the United States invaded Iraq and toppled the brutal regime of Saddam Hussein. But Canada did not sign on to this war. Skeptical of the George W Bush administration's claims that Hussein had "weapons of mass destruction," the Canadian government refused to declare war on Iraq. No such weapons were ever found. Prime Minister Chrétien had determined upon taking office in 1993 that he would reject the overly solicitous nature of Mulroney's attitude toward the United States. Indeed, the Liberal Party campaign platform expressly stated that the Liberals would reject a "camp-follower approach" and strike a more made-in-Canada position on foreign relations.[9] As it turned out, this was not too problematic while Bill Clinton was president. He and Chrétien got along very well on a personal level and shared many political attitudes and values.

But when George W Bush became president, relations turned frosty. Bush adopted an "us and them" attitude toward the war on terror, suggesting that any country that did not follow the American lead was with the terrorists. Not since John Diefenbaker and John Kennedy had relations between a Canadian prime minister and American president been so acrimonious. Nonetheless, a residue of good relations underpinned the tensions. The United States government publicly appreciated Canada's contribution to the war in Afghanistan and its cooperation over border security. Bush, however, interpreted some Canadian positions as anti-Americanism and suggested to Prime Minister Martin that Canadian diplomacy had sometimes taken a wrong tone in that regard.[10]

With the broadening of terrorist activity and the rise of ISIS (also known as ISIL/Islamic State/Daesh) in Syria and Iraq, the United States initiated the formation of Operation Inherent Resolve in 2014 and Canada joined under Operation Impact. Harper sent Canadian fighter jets to the region to bomb ISIL positions. After the Liberals won the October 2015 election, Trudeau announced that Canada would be withdrawing air support from the operation, which ended in February 2016, after 251 Canadian air strikes in the region, mostly in Iraq. The Trudeau government did send about 600 special forces ground troop advisers to the area. The United States and Canada continued to have military operations in the region as of 2024.

## 5) Border Security

In the early twenty-first century, most of the policy focus on the United States-Canada border focused on fear of terrorism, especially in the United States. Americans sometimes perceived Canada as underestimating the risk of terrorism, while Canadians sometimes perceived the United States as overreacting to the risk of terrorism that involved the border. Many Americans, for example, thought that some of the 9/11 hijackers arrived in the United States through Canada. This false idea extended even up to senior policy makers in some cases. In 2009, Secretary of Homeland Security Janet Napolitano had an interview with the Canadian Broadcasting Corporation (CBC), and implied that some of the 9/11 hijackers came through Canada. She quickly apologized after the interview. But Senator John McCain of Arizona, the Republican candidate for president in 2008, said on Fox News after the Napolitano interview, "Well some of the 9/11 hijackers did come through Canada, as you know." The Canadian Embassy in Washington, DC, was left to undertake heavy damage control each time.[11]

Americans made this mistake largely because they were probably thinking of Ahmed Ressam, known in the United States as the Millennium Bomber. Ressam was born in Algeria in 1967, and entered Canada with a forged French passport in 1994 and asked for asylum. Canada scheduled a refugee hearing for 1995, released Ressam into Montreal to await the hearing, and gave him $500 per month in welfare benefits. During that year, Ressam lived with Islamic fundamentalists from Algeria connected to Al Qaeda. Ressam robbed tourists some thirty to forty times and counterfeited passports, was arrested four times, and was convicted once, but did no jail time. In 1995 his refugee status was rejected in Canada when he did not show up for a hearing. A warrant for his arrest was issued, but he was not found. By then, Ressam had used a stolen baptismal form to call himself Benni Antoine Noris, and got a Canadian passport under that name. He travelled to an Al Qaeda training camp in Afghanistan, and then returned to Canada.[12]

On 14 December 1999, Ressam boarded a ferry from Victoria, British Columbia, to Port Angeles, Washington. An American Customs inspector thought Ressam was acting suspiciously, so she searched his car and found large amounts of bomb making materials. Ressam's intent was to bomb Los Angeles airport on

31 December 1999; this became known as the Millennium Plot. Ressam was convicted and sentenced to a thirty-seven-year term.

After the Millennium Plot and 9/11, the United States government responded with the Western Hemisphere Travel Initiative (WHTI), which for the first time in modern Canadian-American relations required all Canadians and Americans flying to the United States from Canada to have passports by 2007 and for those crossing land or water to have passports by 2009. While most Canadians had valid passports, as of 2023 most Americans still did not.

A deeply troubling case involving the interdependence of Canadian and American border security occurred beginning in 2002. Maher Arar was born in Syria, and emigrated to Canada in 1988. He got degrees in computer engineering from McGill University in Montreal, Quebec; lived in Ottawa with his wife and two children; became a Canadian citizen; and worked as an engineer. In September 2002, he was returning to Canada from a family vacation in Tunisia, and had to change planes at JFK Airport in New York City, where he was stopped by officials who accused him of Al Qaeda connections. As proof, the officials showed Arar an apartment rental application the American officials had gotten from the Royal Canadian Mounted Police (RCMP). It listed Abdullah Almaki as an emergency contact. Almaki was a Syrian-born Canadian citizen, and an engineer with a wife and children in Ottawa. He had gone to Syria to visit his grandmother in 2002, and was arrested by the Syrians, put in prison and tortured because the RCMP had sent Syria documents in the 1990s that showed Almaki had worked for a year in Afghanistan for a charity run by an Al Qaeda fundraiser named Ahmed Khadr.

American officials ignored Arar's Canadian passport, and sent him to Syria, where he was put in prison for a year and tortured. Syria then let him go, and he returned to Canada. Arar sued the American government, but federal judges dismissed his case, saying documents needed for a trial could not be made public due to national security concerns. The Harper government in Canada in 2007 apologized to Arar and gave him $10.5 million in compensation.[13] The United States government has never apologized to Arar.

During the early years of the 2020s, attention and controversy about the United States-Canada border turned to issues about refugees and security. The refugee issue had earlier acquired heightened attention during the Syrian civil war. While the United States admitted about 20,000 Syrian refugees during the final years of the Obama administration, Trump, while running as the 2016 Republican presidential candidate, stated that he wanted to ban all Muslims from entering the United States. (He repeated that desire in 2023 during the run-up to the presidential primary elections of 2024.) Meanwhile, Canada settled more than 44,000 Syrian refugees between 2015 and 2017, leading the United States Senate Homeland Security Committee in February 2016 to hold a hearing about potential dangers to American security of Syrian refugees in Canada.[14]

The immigration policies of the Trump administration led to Canada having its own refugee controversy at the United States border. After the 9/11 terrorist attacks, the United States and Canada signed a Safe Third Country Agreement in 2002, stating that asylum seekers must seek refugee status in the first of the two countries they enter under the assumption that both countries were safe places to live. That meant that asylum applicants seeking to enter one country from the other at a Canada-United States border crossing would be turned back to make their asylum request in the first country they entered.

However, the agreement did not cover those seeking asylum away from legal border entry points, and between 2017 and 2023, Roxham Road at the land border between Quebec and New York state became a popular point of travel for asylum seekers in the United States, who perceived their chances to be poor under the Trump administration, to make their asylum requests in Canada instead. More than 100,000 migrants crossed into Canada at Roxham Road before the United States and Canada modified their safe country agreement to include crossings between official border stations.[15]

Back in the United States, conservative supporters of Donald Trump, who had pushed for a wall at the Mexican border and who made exaggerated allegations about criminals and drugs pouring over the Mexican border into the United States, began to turn their attention to the northern border with Canada. At a 2023 debate, Republican presidential candidate Vivek Ramaswamy called for a border wall with Canada to block what he claimed, without evidence, to be large-scale fentanyl smuggling.[16] Ramaswamy was echoed by other Republican presidential candidates, including Trump, who described the border as "not so hot"; Florida Governor Ron DeSantis, who said it was the site of a worsening problem; and Nikki Haley, the former United States ambassador to the United Nations, who said she would do whatever it took to stop illegal crossings there, up to and including building a massive wall. Earlier in 2023, twenty-eight congressional Republicans formed a new Northern Border Security Caucus to bring attention to claimed threats about migrant and drug smuggling across the Canadian border.[17] Trump's 2024 campaign pledge to expel up to 11 million illegal immigrants from the United States caused tremendous trepidation in Canada, where officials feared the possibility of a tidal wave of illegal border crossings into Canada.

Canadians were not immune to making exaggerated claims of threats from the other side of the border in the early 2020s. During the COVID-19 pandemic, Canada blocked most Americans from being able to travel to Canada between March 2020 and August 2021. While the United States also blocked the entry of Canadians at land borders, Canadians were free to travel to the United States by air as much as they wanted (and then endure two-week quarantines upon their return to Canada). During the early months of the border closures, there were numerous reports of Canadians angered at the sight of United States licence plates on cars in Canada. American drivers, for example, could claim they needed to get to Alaska through Canada, and were allowed to cross with instructions to proceed as quickly as possible. Some of those drivers would then make side trips to places like Banff National Park. Some Canadians returning home with American licence plates were harassed and their cars vandalized.[18]

## 6) Arctic Sovereignty

The sector principle in international law is where international boundaries are extended over sea areas in the Arctic toward the North Pole and over land in the Antarctic to the South Pole following lines of longitude. Since 1925, under the sector principle, Canada has claimed as Canadian territory the Arctic Ocean north of Canada up to the North Pole. The United States does not recognize that claim. Under the Law of the Sea Treaty, ratified by Canada in 2003, countries had ten years after ratification to stake a territorial claim on the underwater continental shelf. In December 2013, the Harper government filed a claim with the UN that extends Canadian territory to include the North Pole and parts of the eastern hemisphere north of Russia. The Trudeau government extended the claim in 2022.[19] The United States has not ratified the Law of the Sea Treaty.

Another contentious issue related to Arctic sovereignty involves the Northwest Passage. This is the northern waterway that allows for quicker shipping trips between Europe and East Asia. Under international law, international straits between two large oceans or seas are international waters open to shipping from all nations. Canada claims that the Northwest Passage is internal Canadian waters and that other countries must get approval from Canada to send ships through the waters. The United States and many other countries disagree, arguing that the Northwest Passage is an international strait open to international shipping from all countries. To support this position, the United States has sent icebreakers and nuclear submarines through the Northwest Passage without Canadian permission, causing consternation in Canada. The significance of the passage is growing as the ice cap is melting. Climate change means that the Northwest Passage, blocked by ice through most of modern history, is opening up and will soon be a viable shipping route for longer portions of the year.

## 7) Energy Policy: Of Pipelines and Politics

The North American energy network is a constantly changing environment, subject to a variety of political, economic, social, and environmental forces. The usage of oil in North America dates to ancient times. Indigenous peoples had used petroleum seeps since the prehistoric era in, for instance, western Pennsylvania, a fact noted by settlers when they arrived in the region. The modern history of oil production dates from the early nineteenth century following the discovery of oil at Oil Creek, Pennsylvania in 1859.[20] By the middle of the nineteenth century, scientists realized kerosene could be manufactured from sufficiently large supplies of crude oil and the industry grew exponentially as the industrialization of the American economy took off. Production was at first concentrated in the western portions of New York and Pennsylvania, as well as Ohio, Kentucky, and West Virginia, and later spread to California near San Francisco and Los Angeles. In the late nineteenth century, production spread to Oklahoma, Arkansas, Kansas, Louisiana, and the Texas panhandle. For much of the nineteenth and twentieth centuries, the United States was the largest oil-producing country in the world, regaining that position in 2018.[21]

In Canada, the presence of oil in Oil Springs, Ontario was observed by early explorers and the pioneer farmers who used it for medical purposes. The first well was dug in 1858, and a refinery established in Hamilton soon thereafter. Large-scale commercial production had to wait until the discovery of significant reserves of oil in Leduc, Alberta in 1947. Imperial Oil had drilled 133 dry holes in a row, and after pouring millions of dollars into the search was about to give up on the prospect of finding commercially viable supplies. Down to their six "last chance" wells, they finally found success at Leduc No 1, about 15 kilometres west of Edmonton.[22]

Production in Canada was mainly in the hands of American-based multinational corporations, contributing to the integrated nature of the industry in North America. The Canadian sector essentially developed as an extension of the American energy economy, which supplied most of the investment capital, technology, and expertise.²³ In 1960, largely at the behest of the American oil industry and the United States State Department, the government of Prime Minister John Diefenbaker introduced the National Oil Policy. The Canadian oil market was divided into two parts: oil from western Canada was earmarked for export to the United States, while markets in central and eastern Canada were henceforth to rely on imported oil from Venezuela via American transnational oil companies. In return for a secure source of western Canadian oil, the American government exempted Canada from import quotas. In this way, Canada was able to offset the cost of importing oil for central and eastern Canada. A consequence of the National Oil Policy, though, was that it effectively blocked the possibility of construction of a pan-Canadian oil market, which would have developed had pipelines been built to supply western oil to the rest of the country. As a result, throughout the 1960s, the continental integration of the Canadian oil industry proceeded apace.²⁴

The energy crisis of the 1970s caused the American government to intensify its search for low-risk, secure, reliable, and strategically acceptable energy partners; Canada appeared to fit the bill, according to President Richard Nixon. But Canada had its own response to the energy crisis, which was to put an export tax on oil it sent abroad from western Canada to offset the rising cost of oil it imported for central and eastern Canada. World oil prices had quadrupled by 1973 due to the restrictions on the supply of oil enacted by the Organization of Petroleum Exporting Countries (OPEC), threatening the economic viability of the Canadian, American, and many other economies dependent on high levels of energy consumption. The government of Prime Minister Pierre Trudeau responded with the National Energy Program (NEP) in 1980 with the goal of stabilizing the price and supply of oil for eastern and central Canada. It also established incentives to conserve energy, increase Canadian ownership of the petroleum industry, expand exploration in Canadian frontier areas, develop alternatives to oil consumption, and ultimately establish energy self-sufficiency in Canada.

President Ronald Reagan, a staunch anti-communist and free marketer, thought he saw the rough outlines of a socialist tyranny forming north of the border exemplified by the interventionist NEP and other Trudeau government initiatives, and, along with the major players in the American transnational oil community, exerted maximum pressure on the Canadian government to rescind the NEP.[25] Meanwhile, the NEP proved domestically to be an extremely divisive policy. It did stimulate Canadian ownership in the oil industry, which jumped from 7 percent to more than 34 percent.[26] But the ideological differences between the interventionist Trudeau government and the neoconservative Albertan government proved fatal. Bumper stickers appeared in Alberta proclaiming "Let the eastern bastards freeze in the dark." The oil industry felt blindsided, having had little to no advance warning or consultation over the NEP. As political economist Stephen Clarkson concluded, "In the end, collapsing world oil prices caused the NEP to unravel and left the country's oil producers in the west securely integrated in the US market and its oil consumers in the east insecurely dependent on overseas markets."[27]

The enactment of the 1989 Canada-United States Free Trade Agreement (FTA) represents the next chapter of the continental energy saga (see Chapter 6). The FTA prohibited the application of export taxes between the two countries, reinforced free market principles for the governance of the oil relationship, and limited the possibilities of Canadian government intervention along the lines of the NEP. It expressly prohibited Canada from reducing the proportion of its oil exports to the United States unless it reduced domestic consumption by the same proportion. It also prohibited Canada from introducing a two-tiered price system as it had done with the NEP, the purpose of which had been to sell exported oil for more than the price it paid for imported oil. As a result of these constraints, Washington had succeed in preventing Canada from intervening in its domestic market in order to favour Canadian industry and consumers or restrict exports to the United States.[28]

The attitudes of American policy makers toward the continental energy sector were captured by Senator Lindsay Graham, a Republican from South Carolina, who was asked in 2010 if he thought Canadian oil was "foreign" oil. His response was "No, I consider Canadian oil part of America's energy independent strategy. I consider Canadian oil to be a reliable, safe and secure source. . . . To me, this is an extension of the United States' energy independence — by growing our ability to receive oil from Canada."[29] At the level of transnational corporations that dominate the continental energy sector, many CEOs of Canadian resource companies have often been American, thereby further blurring any distinctions that might be drawn between Canadian and American energy interests.[30] In effect, the north–south flow of Canadian oil was entrenched in the FTA, or what President Reagan had called "the economic constitution of North America."

In 2000, President George W Bush, a former oil company executive, commissioned his vice president, Dick Cheney, another former oil company executive, to provide recommendations on assuring American energy security. Cheney's report suggested expansion of the network of pipelines from Canada to the United States, in particular to further exploit the Albertan oil sands through the development of "a North American Energy Framework."[31] Along with Canada, Mexico increasingly featured prominently in America's plans for energy security. However, when the FTA was replaced with the North American Free Trade Agreement in 1994, Mexico had refused to accept the pricing and supply restrictions Canada had agreed to and that carried over from the FTA. A North American Energy Working Group was subsequently struck between the three countries whose goal was to replace the three separate energy markets with one continental market. In 2005, President George W Bush, Prime Minister Paul Martin, and Mexican President Vincente Fox announced the creation of the Security and Prosperity Partnership of North American (SPP), which included further harmonization of energy regulations, and further integration of the three energy markets. While the SPP itself was short lived and ceased to exist as of 2008 (see Chapter 6), the trend toward continentalization of the energy sector was much more entrenched.

Meanwhile, in the first two decades of the twenty-first century, the United States had become the largest oil producer in the world, largely as a result of the "shale revolution." This is the process of developing the massive reserves of unconventional oil and gas through hydraulic fracturing (or "fracking") and horizontal drilling. An important consequence for Canada of this seismic development has been to search for ways to expand its oil and gas exports to other markets beyond the United States. A series of megaprojects involving pipelines and liquefied natural gas facilities to move Canadian oil to eastern Canada and to western ports for export to Asia were initiated.

Prime Minister Stephen Harper championed Canada's oil and gas industry, especially in Alberta. He downplayed environmental concerns, including climate change, referring to the Liberal Party plan for a carbon tax as an "insane idea," comparing it to the much maligned NEP. "It is like the national energy program in the sense that the national energy program was designed to screw the West and really damage the energy sector — and this will do those things," Harper said. "This is different in that this will actually screw everybody across the country."[32] He also supported a number of major energy projects, including several pipeline projects. Growing opposition to those energy projects was met by Harper with policy measures under the umbrella of the Responsible Resource Development initiatives in 2012, "many of which intensified opposition and were roundly critiqued by opponents for placing the economy over the environment."[33]

After the 2015 election, Prime Minister Justin Trudeau's "sunny ways" was thought by many to signal an end to significant oil and gas expansion. However, various pipeline-related initiatives by the Trudeau government showed a more nuanced approach. On 29 November 2016, Trudeau approved Kinder Morgan's TMEP and Enbridge's Line 3 replacement pipelines to the United States while also rejecting Enbridge's Northern Gateway pipeline in Canada.[34] The pressing question is what explains the importance of Canada's pipelines as a part of the overall national discourse and relations with the United States?

Based on joint statements by Minister of Natural Resources Jim Carr and Minister of Transport Marc Garneau, the government made the decisions with the hope of creating more "good, middle-class jobs," protecting environmentally sensitive areas, providing access to global markets as well as North American refineries, and generating significant federal and provincial government revenues.[35] The minister of natural resources said, "It is our duty to permit infrastructure so Canada's resources get to market in a more environmentally-responsible way, creating jobs and a thriving economy."[36] Trudeau was treated to a standing ovation from oil and gas industry executives in Houston, Texas for saying, "No country would find 173 billion barrels of oil in the ground and just leave them there."[37]

Pipeline politics clearly became a prominent part of the landscape of Canadian-American relations in the early twenty-first century. The success or failure of pipelines had implications for international trade, job creation, provincial fiscal resources, and even future generations. For Albertans and many in the oil and gas industry, pipelines are a way to increase the export capacity of one of Canada's primary "staples" products and promote infrastructure development as well as jobs, development, and skills training that are promised by companies looking to expand their pipeline networks. Debt also plays a key role as the costs of constructing, maintaining, and dismantling large pipeline projects have grown over the years, largely in part due to environmental safeguards and National Energy Board (NEB) requirements. Foreign investment has a similar potential to make or break pipeline success in Canada as the primary goal of many of the pipelines is to get Canadian resources to foreign markets, either the United States, in the Asia-Pacific region, or with trading partners across the Atlantic.

Keystone XL began as a joint venture between TransCanada Corporation and ConocoPhillips to create a major extension in the network of oil sands bitumen from Hardisty, Alberta to refineries in Texas.[38] After extensive protests, legal battles, and state intervention, the United States Congress in 2015 approved a bill to bypass the usual presidential approval needed for a pipeline crossing an international border, but President Obama vetoed that bill and blocked approval of a pipeline construction permit.[39]

President Donald Trump in 2017 changed course and issued a permit to allow construction of the Keystone XL Pipeline, calling for the rest of the project to be completed with American-produced steel, but lawsuits continued to delay the process.

If the pipeline were completed, more than 20 percent of Canada's oil exports would go exclusively to the United States.[40] The reliance on the United States as a viable end-point for oil production in Canada was made clear by TransCanada's actions in the United States; through an American lobby group, the Columbia Pipeline Group, it contributed more than $925,000 over five years in the State of Nebraska alone in an attempt to exert influence on the state's majority Republican party.[41] However, in 2021, on President Biden's first day of office, he again rejected the permit to build the pipeline into the United States, after gaining support from environmentalists and Indigenous groups during his winning election campaign. Canadian attempts to get Biden to change his mind were unsuccessful.[42] Trump, in contrast, campaigned in 2024 to move the United States away from Biden's climate-centric policies to a focus on maximizing domestic oil and natural gas production.

Energy policy, broadly speaking, and oil and gas policy specifically, reveal numerous ways in which Canada and the United States are the same, only different. As Gattinger and Tohme point out:

> [B]oth countries have tremendous energy potential across multiple energy sources; both have largely market-based systems for energy development and deep bilateral energy trading relationships; both are major oil and gas producers committed to ambitious climate action; both have experienced growing division over energy and climate, with civil society playing an increasingly active role; and both are federations in which sub-national governments hold powerful policy levers.[43]

But important differences also underscore the energy policy relationship, not the least of which is the power imbalance and the differing constitutional arrangements and systems of government in both countries.

### 8) The Russian Invasion of Ukraine

In the early 2020s, Canada and the United States took similar foreign policy approaches in reaction to the Russian invasion of Ukraine and to controversial actions taken by the People's Republic of China, but the focus of the two North American countries toward these two foreign rivals differed somewhat, often for domestic political reasons.

In 2012, the Cold War legacy of Russian-American relations became a key topic during a presidential candidate debate between President Obama, a Democrat, and former Massachusetts Republican Governor Mitt Romney (who later became a US senator for Utah). At that debate, Obama criticized Romney for having labelled Russia as the number one geopolitical foe of the United States earlier in the year, at a time when the United States still had troops in Afghanistan and was between military actions in Iraq. Obama commented, "the 1980s are now calling and ask for their foreign policy back. The Cold War has been over for twenty years." Ten years later, some commentators noted that Romney may have been right.[44] When Russia invaded Ukraine in 2014, annexing the region of Crimea, and supporting allied rebel forces in the Donbas region, the Obama administration worked with European leaders, condemned the Russian occupation, and imposed economic sanctions, but took no military actions, in part because the areas Russia annexed and instigated rebellion were mainly populated by Russian speakers.[45]

During the Trump administration, Russian President Vladimir Putin had a friend in the White House. Prior to his election in 2016, Trump appealed to Russia to find and leak emails belonging to his opponent Hillary Clinton from her private server, which had become a major campaign issue. Russian agents promptly did so.

Earlier that year, Russian hackers sponsored by the government had accessed and leaked emails from the Democratic National Committee that had embarrassed the Clinton campaign.[46]

In addition, the Russian Internet Research Agency, labelled in the United States as a "troll farm," made a major effort in 2016 to spread information and misinformation on social media that assisted the Trump campaign and damaged the Clinton campaign. The American intelligence community and a bipartisan consensus of the United States Senate Intelligence Committee agreed with the conclusion that Russia tried to interfere in the 2016 presidential election to help Trump,[47] but academics dispute what impact that interference had on the election outcome.[48]

After he was elected president, Trump met Putin for a summit in Helsinki, Finland, in 2018. At a press conference following the summit, Trump was asked about the findings of his intelligence agencies that Russia had tried to interfere with the 2016 election. Trump responded that "I have President Putin, he just said it's not Russia. I will say this. I don't see any reason why it would be. So I have great confidence in my intelligence people, but I will tell you that President Putin was extremely strong and powerful in his denial today."[49]

After Russia invaded Ukraine again and more extensively in 2022, Trump in a radio interview called Putin a "genius" for his geopolitical strategy and discussed how well he and Putin got along and liked each other.[50] It was revealed during the 2024 election campaign that Trump and Putin had spoken several times after Trump had been defeated in 2020, although the Kremlin denied this was true.[51] However, President Biden and the United States Congress reacted very differently to the invasion, with leaders of both parties supporting shipments of American military weapons to support Ukraine's efforts to resist a Russian takeover. In a White House speech shortly after the 2022 invasion, President Biden referred to the Russian invasion as a flagrant violation of international law and based on false pretexts and misinformation, declared extensive economic sanctions, and called for additional defensive actions by NATO. He added that "this aggression cannot go unanswered. If it did, the consequences for America would be much worse. America stands up to bullies. We stand up for freedom. This is who we are."⁵²

But as the war continued into a second year in 2023, the usual American resistance to long-term military commitments began to appear in public opinion polls and in Congress, especially among Republican supporters of Trump primed not to think of Putin as an enemy of the United States. In late 2023, growing Republican opposition to continued military funding assistance for Ukraine prevented the United States House of Representatives for several months from approving more such funding.⁵³ In early 2024, Trump doubled down on his provocations, declaring that he would let Russia do "whatever the hell they want" to any NATO member that fails to meet spending guidelines, causing widespread consternation among the member nations.⁵⁴

Meanwhile in Canada, the early international approaches toward the Russian annexation of Crimea in 2014 followed the American pattern of condemnation and economic sanctions without any military actions. However, Prime Minister Trudeau did not join in President Trump's friendship with Putin during Trump's four years in office. The second more extensive Russian invasion of Ukraine in 2022 led to a similar but stronger reaction in Canada compared to the United States, with more universal support for the Ukrainian cause and opposition to Russian actions. The Canadian government recruited Ukrainians to settle the Prairie provinces and establish farms during the late nineteenth and early twentieth centuries and continued to welcome Ukrainian refugees from the Soviet Union for the rest of the twentieth century. This led Canada to have the second largest diaspora of Ukrainian descendants in the world by the twenty-first century (after Russia), including the Deputy Prime Minister Chrystia Freeland, who was raised by a Ukrainian mother in Alberta.⁵⁵

In 2023, the Speaker of the Canadian House of Commons, normally a non-partisan position that gets little media attention, inadvertently brought the troubled Second World War history of Ukraine into the spotlight and provided support for Russian misinformation campaigns. During the occasion when Ukrainian President Volodymyr

Zelenskyy had been invited to speak in the House of Commons, Speaker Anthony Rota invited a ninety-eight-year-old Ukrainian war veteran and constituent, Yaroslav Hunka, to attend as an "honoured guest." During the event, Speaker Rota presented Hunka, leading to two standing ovations, including from President Zelenskyy and Prime Minister Trudeau. Soon after the event, it was revealed that Hunka had served with a Ukrainian military force allied with Nazi Germany during the Second World War, and that the Ukrainian military unit had participated in war crimes. Speaker Rota soon resigned, Prime Minister Trudeau apologized to Zelenskyy, and the Russian government used the incident to bolster its claim that modern Ukraine was being run by Nazis, despite Zelenskyy being Jewish.[56]

## 9) Relations with China in the Twenty-First Century

In relations with China during the first quarter of the twenty-first century, both the United States and Canada have held to similar principles, but with a different emphasis. In the United States, controversies involving relations with China have usually focused on national security or on trade (the latter discussed in Chapter 6), while in Canada, relations with China have often focused on Chinese interference in domestic politics (as with the Russian involvement in the 2016 American election) or in the legal system.

The twenty-first century started auspiciously for Chinese relations with the United States and Canada when China joined the World Trade Organization in 2001 with American and Canadian government support. Yet relations between the two North American countries and the People's Republic of China (PRC) subsequently largely deteriorated, and not always just for international trade reasons (see Chapter 6). Both the United States and Canada expressed concerns about widespread human rights violations in China and the cancellation of civil liberties in Hong Kong.

The United States has grown increasingly concerned about the national security threats posed by growth in Chinese military technology and the country's expansionist views of territory in the

South China Sea. In 2023, there was an international incident when a Chinese balloon carrying military surveillance technology flew over several military installations in the United States before being shot down by an American military plane above the Atlantic Ocean near South Carolina. China claimed the balloon, which also flew over Western Canada, was for weather research.[57]

In 2022 and 2023, the PRC reacted to meetings by United States House Speakers Nancy Pelosi and Kevin McCarthy with the president of Taiwan by engaging in military exercises intended for intimidation and as a threat against Taiwan.[58] Government officials and agencies across the United States banned use of equipment and technology from the Chinese company Huawei due to fears of the company's ties to the PRC government.[59] As noted in Chapter 6, Congress in 2024 voted to force the Chinese owner of TikTok to sell the social media site or be banned in the United States, due to claims that the technology could be used to invade the privacy of Americans or spread Chinese government propaganda. The state of Montana passed a law to ban TikTok, though a federal judge blocked the ban in late 2023 as a potential violation of free speech.[60]

The Canadian government has similar national security concerns about China, and in 2024 it ordered TikTok Technology Canada Inc. to close its Canadian offices, although it continued to allow the TikTok app to be available to Canadians. But most news and political focus has been on attempted Chinese interference in domestic politics, in Canadian society, and in the legal system. In 2018, at the request of the United States, Meng Wanzhou, an executive with Huawei and daughter of the company's founder, was detained by the Canadian Border Services Agency at the Vancouver airport. Wanzhou was accused in the United States of violating American sanctions against Iran in Huawei business dealings. In response, China arrested two Canadian citizens working in China — Michael Spavor who ran a North Korean cultural exchange organization and Michael Kovrig, a former Canadian diplomat who worked for the International Crisis Group think tank. China accused both men of espionage and put them in prison with limited access to Canadian consular assistance. Meanwhile, Wanzhou lived under house arrest in a Vancouver mansion that she owned while fighting extradition to the United States.

China repeatedly denied that the "two Michaels" had been taken as hostages in retaliation for the detention of Wanzhou, but North Americans assumed otherwise, and the ultimate resolution of the conflict seemed to confirm the situation. In September 2021, the United States agreed to a deferred prosecution for Wanzhou, in which she admitted to lying about dealings with Iran in return for her release from house arrest and freedom to return to China on the same day as the two Michaels were released from custody in China and allowed to return home to Canada.[61] In 2023, news media in Canada reported that Michael Spavor was suing the Canadian government over his detention in China and that he had been an unwitting pawn in efforts by Michael Kovrig to provide intelligence information from China to the Canadian government.[62]

In 2023, Canada and the United States revealed the presence in both countries of Chinese "police stations" where Chinese government agents worked in large cities and attempted to intimidate or convince local members of Chinese diasporas to return to China to face criminal charges or to stop criticizing Chinese government human rights violations. The agents at the North American "police stations" would sometimes intimidate local Chinese immigrants by threatening or putting pressure on relatives still living in China.[63]

What may have been the biggest Canadian political scandal of 2023 also involved China, after it was revealed that the PRC attempted to intimidate Canadian Members of Parliament and influence outcomes in recent Canadian federal elections against candidates who spoke out on human rights violations in China. The Chinese government spread disinformation and again tried to threaten or pressure relatives or friends living in China to influence Canadian political leaders, including Conservative foreign affairs critic Michael Chong, former Conservative Party Leader Erin O'Toole, and NDP MP Jenny Kwan.[64]

When it was also revealed that some Canadian government officials were aware for several years of the attempted Chinese interference with Canadian elections and the attempted intimidation of Canadian politicians, but had not made that information public, Prime Minister Trudeau appointed a former Governor General and family friend, David Johnston, to investigate. That satisfied none of the opposition parties in Parliament, and when Johnston concluded that an official public inquiry into the issue would not be a good idea, a public and political outcry caused Johnston to resign, and Trudeau to agree to work with opposition parties to set up an official inquiry.[65] The Foreign Interference Commission was set up as a result, and heard from a variety of government officials, Canadian Security Intelligence Service (CSIS) officers, MPs, a former leader of the Official Opposition, and even the prime minister himself. Given that, according to the 2021 Census, there are more than 1.7 million Chinese Canadians residing in Canada representing 4.7 percent of the total population, the stakes surrounding Canada's relationship with China are high.

## Conclusion

This chapter has shown that even two countries as similar as Canada and the United States can have differences in their respective foreign policy positions. Shared experiences in the twentieth century like the two World Wars, the Korean War, the containment of communism during the Cold War, and the development of the modern international regime of multilateral and bilateral treaties and agreements usually brought the two countries together. But the devil is often in the details, and policy differences emerged even in areas of broad agreement. The twenty-first century brought more examples of commonality in interests as well as differences with regard to wars in Afghanistan and Iraq, border security, Arctic sovereignty, pipelines, and relations with Russia and China. Overall, the general trends in foreign policy positions over the history of relations between the two friends and allies (mostly) shows the extent to which their foreign policies are often the same, only different.

CHAPTER EIGHT

# Looking Ahead: Comparing Canada and the United States and Canadian-American Relations

There is no relationship in the world between two countries quite like that between Canada and the United States. As two historians put it:

> The Canadian-American relationship is a complex patchwork of inevitable conflict mixed with cooperation that is every bit as inevitable. The links between the two countries (and between the provinces and the United States) span every area of modern life and move across a vast array of government departments, agencies, boards, commissions, treaties, agreements, corporate and union links, and personal, professional and familial ties.[1]

The extent of the similarities in the cultures of the two countries is striking. American retail outlets like Walmart and fast food restaurants like McDonald's are ubiquitous in both countries. The term "Can-Am," short form for Canadian-American, can refer to anything from highways to sports teams to record labels to off-road vehicles to academic studies, and so on. The Royal Canadian Mounted Police once contracted with Disney Corporation to license its name and image — a name and image once thought to be one of the most distinctly unique of Canadian symbols. Culture in the form of books, magazines, newspapers, internet sites, movies, music, and fashion all tend to flow northward from the United States into Canada, with some reciprocity in that Canadian cultural producers like Justin Bieber, Drake, Joni Mitchell, Neil Young, and others seamlessly blend into the American culture machine and are frequently assumed to be American. Political ideas and trends similarly flow northward. Suggestions for fixed election dates, an elected Senate, parliamentary questioning of Supreme Court nominees, and others have seeped into the Canadian political system.

The longest undefended border in the world sees hundreds of thousands of Canadians and Americans cross it every year. More than $2 billion in goods and services cross daily. Most Canadians live within a short drive of the border. Hundreds of thousands actually live in the United States, while hundreds of thousands of Americans live in Canada. Economic integration through the Free Trade Agreement (FTA), North America Free Trade Agreement (NAFTA), and the Canada-United States-Mexico Agreement (CUSMA, also known in the United States as the United States-Mexico-Canada Agreement or USMCA and in Mexico as the Tratado entre México, Estados Unidos y Canadá or T-MEC) has proceeded with alacrity since the latter part of the twentieth century. Each country is the other's most significant foreign investor. Foreign policy initiatives have often been in sync between the two countries, which broadly share a common world view about the importance of democracy and an aversion to tyranny.

Yet the two countries are not the same. Survey research in the early twentieth century found a growing divergence in values and attitudes between Canada and the United States.[2] The Canadian perspective is often rooted in a slightly smug attitude of moral superiority. Canada has less income disparity, a miniscule gun violence problem compared to the United States, and is on the whole a much safer place to live. It is cleaner, has a more robust social safety net, and a more liberal abortion regime. Both countries are peopled by masses of immigrants, but in Canada a national pride in multiculturalism is seen as preferable to the melting pot assimilationist and jingoistic nationalism of the United States. The condition of

Indigenous peoples in both countries is roughly similar, but the policies concerning these peoples are vastly different.

The deep similarities between the two countries create a tremendous scope for cooperation. The differences create the conditions for divergent paths. Hence Ottawa can and does express and act on the national interest in situations that conflict with Washington's preferences. However, Washington can press ahead with its interests with relatively little regard for Canada if necessary. The power imbalance makes this game much more fraught for Canada.

The political story of the modern independent republic known as the United States began with revolution and continued through conquest of western parts of the North American continent, a civil war struggle to preserve or abolish slavery, further expansion into islands of the Pacific and the Caribbean, growing economic and industrial strength, a preference to avoid involvement in European wars, and eventually to international economic and military dominance.

The political story of the modern constitutional monarchy known as Canada began with support for self-government from the British Crown, in part to maintain independence from the United States; a dominion status in which the British government continued to play a major role in Canadian foreign relations and in the legal system; settlement and economic expansion into the western parts of North America; nearly automatic support for the British in two World Wars; and evolution into an increasingly independent Canada. The result is a modern polity whose politics and external relations often revolve around the United States far more than the latter country is influenced by Canadian actions.

While both countries have in recent decades usually promoted liberal democratic values at home and tried to promote them abroad, both countries have sometimes lapsed in their enthusiasm for democratic elections. After the abolition of slavery in the 1860s, most African Americans were still blocked from exercising voting rights for a hundred years by various laws and practices in Southern states. The United States in the early twenty-first century began with a questionable and still disputed result in the 2000 presidential election in which the United States Supreme Court intervened with a 5:4 vote to prevent a continued count of ballots that had gone uncounted by voting machines in Florida. After the 2020 presidential election, the losing presidential candidate continued to make false claims of rigged processes and continued to be supported by tens of millions of Americans who either believed the provably false claims or who hated the other political party so much that they did not care about democratic outcomes. In part, this helped fuel a victory by that candidate in 2024.

Most Indigenous Canadians were not allowed to vote in federal or provincial elections until the 1960s, decades after most Native Americans were granted the franchise. In 2015, the leader of the Liberal Party promised that year would be the last first-past-the-post federal election if his party won and said his party would enact a fairer system of electing candidates. His party won and soon abandoned the promise, leading to results in the federal elections of 2019 and 2021 where the Liberals won the most seats in the House of Commons, while Conservative Party candidates won more votes nationwide.

In both countries, support for democratic elections overseas has often been a lower priority than military alliances or economic trade. Both countries in the twenty-first century sometimes excoriate dictatorships for violations of human rights and lack of free elections and sometimes excuse or ignore anti-democratic practices overseas for geopolitical, military, or economic reasons.

Domestic governance in the two countries varies widely because the institutions of government are set up differently with a separately elected president and Congress in the United States and a prime minister chosen as the leader of the largest party in the Canadian House of Commons. In both countries, recent presidents and prime ministers have been accused of abusing executive branch authority by taking actions not clearly allowed by the legislative branch or under existing laws. But while this has led to fights in the United States Congress to block and limit presidential authority, the Canadian Parliament controlled by the same party as the prime minister has often limited its reaction to grumbling or to ineffective investigations by committees.

Since 1990, the United States federal government has had six shutdowns of offices and services, lasting from three days to more than a month, when the president, House of Representatives, and Senate could not agree on taxing and spending policies. Canada has had none and cannot have any, since a House of Commons vote against a budget is an automatic vote of no confidence that leads to new elections. The Canadian Senate can block a budget bill in theory, but almost never has due to its traditional deference to the elected chamber. The one near exception was in 1990 when the Senate threatened to block the new Goods and Services Tax, but the prime minister temporarily added eight new senators to approve it.

The "checks and balances" approach to politics and greater partisanship extends in the United States to the appointed judicial branch. Nominations to the Supreme Court and even for lower federal courts have become an extremely partisan affair in recent decades, with presidents choosing judges mostly due to their ideological preferences, and Senate votes based on the political views of the nominees. In Canada, while the political views of judges can play a role in who prime ministers appoint, most judicial appointments get little media attention, the political views of those selected are usually unknown to the public, there is usually no public spectacle involved with the appointments, and there is no vote of confirmation in Parliament.

The United States elects far more offices in far more elections than Canada, though the thousands of offices elected in the United States often cannot accomplish much due to the institutional checks and balances system. The diffusion of power through electing so many people who have competing goals and interests and lack of a centralizing party influence in American elections also often lead to an inability for those elected officials to accomplish what the American people claim to want out of government.

Both countries encounter abuses of their election systems by elected leaders. In the United States, gerrymandering to favour the party in power at the state level is extensive. The people who run elections are usually chosen for partisan reasons, leading to questionable fairness at times. In Canada, prime ministers call early elections whenever they think political conditions are most favourable to their parties. They can also parachute their preferred candidates into ridings over the objections of local riding associations. The United States gives voters far more chances than Canada to bypass elected leaders through the common use of voter initiatives in almost half the states.

Regionalism has played a strong role in the political development of both countries, with the United States long divided between a North and a South, and then a Midwest, a Pacific Coast, and an inland West, all with different political preferences and interests. In Canada, the dominant regional political divide between English-speaking Ontario and French-speaking Quebec has extended to separate central Canada in politics from the Atlantic provinces and the Western provinces, with British Columbia having a regional politics of its own.

The regionalism crosses the international border, with Canadian provinces and American states sharing some political similarities that make them distinct from other parts of both countries. Ideologically, the Maritime provinces of New Brunswick, Nova Scotia, and Prince Edward Island often vote similarly to the northern New England states across the border. Rural areas in those provinces and states are dominated by the fishing, logging, small farm, and tourism industries. They vote mostly for liberal candidates or moderate conservatives, and sometimes favour socialists like Bernie Sanders in Vermont or the New Democratic Party (NDP) in Canada.

Ontario has similarities to the states on the other side of the Great Lakes, such as New York, Pennsylvania, Michigan, and Illinois. Industries like car manufacturing, financial services, and mining and steel dominate. They all tend to lean liberal, but conservatives can often win.

Minnesota, Wisconsin, and North Dakota in the American Midwest have similar political histories to Manitoba and Saskatchewan across the border. They all have large agricultural sectors with some industry and, recently, oil in North Dakota and Saskatchewan. In the 1920s and 1930s, all those states and provinces were dominated by coalitions of farmers and labourers that led to the creation of strong left-wing political parties, such as the Farmer-Labor Party in Minnesota (now allied with Democrats as the DFL party in Minnesota), the Progressive Party in Wisconsin, the Non-Partisan League of North Dakota, and the Cooperative Commonwealth Federation (CCF) in Manitoba and Saskatchewan, which later became the NDP. Many of these areas are more conservative in modern politics.

Montana, Wyoming, and Idaho have strong farming and ranching interests and are rural states with some tourism, similar to Alberta in Canada, dominated by cattle ranching and resource industries (especially oil). These areas all have a populist past, with politicians who called for doing whatever sounds popular with voters and disregarding the economic consequences. Today they are mostly conservative. It is striking that the largest number of immigrants to Alberta in the late nineteenth and early twentieth centuries were Americans.

Washington state and Oregon have very similar economies and politics to British Columbia. The inland areas are agricultural and ranching and mostly conservative, and the coastal areas near Vancouver, Seattle, and Portland have economies based on shipping, fishing, logging, technology, tourism, and cultural industries (television, music), and are very liberal to socialist and strongly environmentalist.

The federal systems in both countries are designed to accommodate such regional political differences. But while the United States began as a decentralized republic, with the central government gaining in influence and power over the past century, Canada was originally intended to have a strong central government, designed to avoid American mistakes that resulted in a civil war, but has instead decentralized, often to accommodate francophones in Quebec and more recently to address Western opposition to control from Ottawa.

However, the original goals of federal government power in Canada are sometimes retained due to constitutional provisions. The federal government can use its "spending power" to intrude in areas of provincial jurisdiction. The *Criminal Code* in Canada is national, influencing how and where many policies are made, compared to the United States, where most criminal laws are determined at the state level. The United States has fifty state constitutions that organize state institutions and provide rights to residents that often go beyond those in the federal Constitution. Canadian provinces have sometimes passed laws that contain measures equivalent to those found in constitutions, but federal constitutional provisions are the most important in determining how provinces are governed.

While federal tax revenue is used in both countries to assist states and provinces with providing important government services, the United States has no current equivalent to the Canadian practice of equalization, where economically wealthy provinces share revenue with provinces that are not thriving to the same extent. While negative attitudes between voters in different states tend to focus on cultural differences (liberal views in California and New York or conservative views in Texas and Florida), in Canada, negative attitudes between voters in different provinces often focus on economic differences (between the Prairie provinces and the Maritime provinces and Quebec, for example), or on language, in the case of Quebec.

Many policy differences between the two countries relate to the existence of a federal *Criminal Code* in Canada and the existence of voter initiatives and state constitutions in the United States. Legal medical cannabis, legal recreational cannabis, and medically assisted death all existed first at the state level in the United States through passage of voter initiatives, and then later became legal nationwide in Canada under the federal *Criminal Code*. Abortion remains legal nationwide in Canada, but subject to different laws in different states in the United States, with several states moving in recent years to add reproductive freedom as a state constitutional right.

Political cultures from each country's early years of independence also continue to cause policy differences in the present day. An emphasis on liberty and freedom from government plays a strong role in American policies on guns, health care, climate change, and free speech, while the need for peace, order, and good government influence Canadian policies in those areas. The American tradition of separation of church and state has limited direct government funding of religious schools, while some provinces in Canada continue to provide direct government funding for Catholic schools.

Canada and the United States not only have the longest "undefended" border in the world, they have the longest land border, period. But the United States has almost nine times as many people as Canada, making the relationship often unequal. The United States has two major land borders — with Canada and Mexico — and domestic and international concerns over the southern border often have an impact on American policies on the northern border. Canada meanwhile only has a significant land border with one country, the United States (and a tiny land border with Greenland/Denmark on Hans Island in the Arctic).

On trade, American business interests and political leaders long perceived the Canadian economy as "hewers of wood and drawers of water" based on a resource economy. The United States in the twenty-first century still imports significant amounts of resources from Canada, such as oil, lumber, minerals, and hydroelectric power. But the Canadian economy has diversified, and manufactured items, computer services, and financial services now constitute a large share of exports across the border. While in recent decades Canada has prioritized keeping the United States economy open to Canadian exports, the United States has fluctuated between protectionism and free trade, and often put greater priority on exports to Mexico and preventing perceived unfair competition from Mexican businesses. These different priorities have become intertwined in the free trade agreements between all three countries.

On the physical border between the two countries, while it can still be called "undefended," the ease of travel and lack of supervision have been in steep decline during the twenty-first century. Following the 9/11 terrorist attacks in the United States in 2001, passport controls were implemented at the Canadian-American border for the first time. The United States also increased the use of armed ships on the Great Lakes and electronic technology at the northern border, including drones. Some American conservatives in recent decades have called for building a wall at the Canadian border, similar to demands made for the Mexican border.

From the Canadian perspective, overzealous security measures and under-zealous public health measures in the United States have led to controversies over Canadian Maher Arar being sent from John F Kennedy International Airport in New York City to torture in prison in Syria, and to Canada supporting a mostly closed border for more than a year during the COVID-19 pandemic.

Overseas, the two countries usually act with unity, fighting together in two World Wars, Korea, Afghanistan, and against the Islamic State. But Canada sometimes opposes or rebels against its militarily stronger neighbour, having declined to get involved in the Vietnam War and the 2003–2011 war in Iraq. After four Canadians were killed in friendly fire by an American in Afghanistan in 2002, Canadian public support for that mission also diminished, and Canada withdrew its armed forces seven years before most other NATO countries did.

Canadian and United States policies toward Russia and China in the twenty-first century have had similar overall approaches, but have differed on specific policies when addressing domestic political concerns or particular controversies. The main distinction came during the presidential administration of Donald Trump, who seemed to perceive Russian leader Vladimir Putin as a friend or ally.

In modern times, both countries have shared a commitment to democratic principles with regular elections and popular changes in government. But both countries have also been threatened by attacks on those democratic principles and a growing share of population that does not seem to share those commitments. In the United States, tens of millions of Americans have indicated in polls and in votes that support for democratic changes of government or respect for election results are not important in the choice of political leaders. The 6 January 2021 attack on Congress and the defeated presidential candidate's refusal to accept his defeat are only the most obvious and overt manifestations of these attitudes.

In Canada, thousands openly supported (and possibly millions latently supported) the Freedom Convoy that blocked streets in Ottawa for almost a month and several border crossings with the United States to protest COVID-19 policies in early 2022. Some uninformed protest leaders bizarrely called on the Governor General and unelected Canadian Senate to end all federal and provincial COVID-19 policies, possibly remove the Trudeau government, dismiss the House of Commons, and set up new elections. Neither has the power to do so. Many Conservative Members of Parliament, including party leader Pierre Poilievre, expressed support for the protests at times.

These challenges to democratic governance and the many other examples cited in this book demonstrate how Canada and the United States are the same, only different. Both countries share some governing principles, some elements of government institutions and election systems, significant roles for federalism and regionalism, certain types of policies, and foreign relations goals. But the differing formative historical trajectories of each nation — revolution for the United States versus evolution for Canada — may explain why approaches taken in each country often differ greatly. The degree to which Canada and the United States remain politically, economically, and culturally the same, only different in the future will largely depend on the continuing influences of their historical legacies as well as on election results and the paths that citizens and governments of both countries choose for the remainder of the twenty-first century.

# Notes

## Introduction

1 Ian L MacDonald, "JFK's Epic Speech to Parliament — An Enduring Moment in Time" *Policy Magazine* (17 May 2021), online: www.policymagazine.ca/jfks-epic-speech-to-parliament-an-enduring-moment-in-time/.
2 Margaret MacMillan, "Sleeping with a Very Cranky Elephant: The History of Canada-US Tensions" *The Sunday Magazine* (15 June 2018), online: www.cbc.ca/radio/sunday/the-sunday-edition-june-17-2018-1.4692469/sleeping-with-a-very-cranky-elephant-the-history-of-canada-u-s-tensions-1.4699017.
3 Quoted in Jane O'Grady & David Staines, eds, *Northrop Frye on Canada* (Toronto: University of Toronto Press, 2003) at 106.
4 John Bartlet Brebner, quoted in Susan Ratcliffe, ed, *Oxford Essential Quotations*, 4th ed (Oxford: Oxford University Press, 2015).
5 Innovative Research Group, "Key Value Conflicts Help Explain Differences in Canadian and American Politics" (9 October 2020), online: https://innovativeresearch.ca/canadians-and-americans-are-more-similar-than-you-might-think-but-there-are-key-differences-too/.
6 Michael Adams & Andrew Parkin, "The Differences Between Canada and the US Remain Significant" *Policy Options* (20 December 2022), online: https://policyoptions.irpp.org/magazines/december-2022/the-differences-between-canada-and-the-u-s-remain-significant/.
7 Ian Bailey, "Politics Briefing: Trade Issues High on the Agenda as Bilateral Meetings Get Under Way at Three Amigos Summit" *The Globe*

and Mail* (18 November 2021), online: www.theglobeandmail.com/politics/article-politics-briefing-trade-issues-high-on-the-agenda-as-bilateral/.

8   Susan Delacourt, "Picking a Fight with Canada Is a Bad Idea, Says Justin Trudeau, but Joe Biden Is Still 'One of the Good Guys'" *Toronto Star* (14 December 2021), online: www.thestar.com/politics/political-opinion/2021/12/14/picking-a-fight-with-canada-is-a-bad-idea-says-justin-trudeau-but-joe-biden-is-still-one-of-the-good-guys.html.

9   Andrew Coyne, "Canada Is Far from Ready for the Chaos Coming Our Way" *The Globe and Mail* (13 October 2024), online: www.theglobeandmail.com/opinion/article-canada-is-far-from-ready-for-the-chaos-coming-our-way/.

10  Andrew Phillips, "Justin Trudeau Is Already Getting It Wrong on Trump" *Toronto Star* (12 November 2024), online: www.thestar.com/opinion/star-columnists/justin-trudeau-is-already-getting-it-wrong-on-trump/article_6f2f2808-a054-11ef-88f0-fbd77dd1fa22.html.

11  Trevor Tombe, *Partners in Prosperity: Exploring the Significance of Canada-US Trade* (Toronto: Canadian Chamber of Commerce, October 2024), online: https://businessdatalab.ca/wp-content/uploads/2024/10/PartnersInProsperity_EN_Final.pdf.

12  Kelly Geraldine Malone, "Trump's Appointees Have Criticized Trudeau, Warned of Border Issues with Canada" *Toronto Star* (13 November 2024), online: www.thestar.com/news/canada/trumps-appointees-have-criticized-trudeau-warned-of-border-issues-with-canada/article_50eb116c-ba6a-591d-a59d-c4c8d52b9e7c.html.

13  *Ibid.*

14  *Ibid.*

15  Jorge Barrera, "Trump's Border Czar Says Canadian Border Is an 'Extreme' Vulnerability" *CBC News* (13 November 2024), online: www.cbc.ca/news/canada/border-czar-canada-vulnerable-1.7381797.

16  Michael Wernick, *Governing Canada: A Guide to the Tradecraft of Politics* (Vancouver: On Point Press, 2021) at 61.

17  Edward Keenan, "Remember When Canada and the US Were Friends? Joe Biden Does" *Toronto Star* (13 November 2020), online: www.thestar.com/news/world/2020/11/13/remember-when-canada-and-the-us-were-friends-joe-biden-does.html.

CHAPTER ONE | **Canadians and Americans — The Same, Only Different: Comparative History and Political Culture**

1   A note on terminology: Because "Indian" is a term used in the United States Constitution and the modern relevant agency is still called the Bureau

## Notes

of Indian Affairs, the term "Indian" is used here when discussing the United States. The term "Indian" has been largely superseded in Canada by "Aboriginal," "Indigenous," and "First Nations." In addition, in Canada there are the Metis and the Inuit. We use all these terms when discussing Canada. But Canada still uses the term "Indian" in relation to Status Indians governed under the *Indian Act* of 1876. We therefore retain use of the term "Indian" where it refers in either country to a specific title or to constitutional or legal usage, or where it is appropriate to the historical context of the issue being discussed.

2 Radha Jhappan, "The 'New World': Legacies of European Colonialism in North America," in Yasmeen Abu-Laban, Radha Jhappan & François Rocher, eds, *Politics in North America: Redefining Continental Relations* (Peterborough, ON: Broadview Press, 2008) at 27–50.

3 William M Denevan, *The Native Population of the Americas in 1942*, 2d ed (Madison, WI: University of Wisconsin Press, 1992).

4 Russell Thornton, *American Indian Holocaust and Survival: A Population History Since 1492* (Norman, OK: University of Oklahoma Press, 1990).

5 *Ibid.*

6 George R, Proclamation, 7 October 1763, reprinted in RSC 1985, App II, No. 1.

7 Edwin S Gaustad, *Roger Wiliams* (New York: Oxford University Press, 2005).

8 Margaret Newell, "Our Hidden History: Roger Williams and Slavery's Origins" *The Providence Journal* (29 August 2020), online: https://www.providencejournal.com/story/opinion/2020/08/29/our-hidden-history-roger-williams-and-slaveyrsquos-origins/42468467/.

9 Library of Congress, "Washington as Land Speculator" *George Washington Papers*, online: www.loc.gov/collections/george-washington-papers/articles-and-essays/george-washington-survey-and-mapmaker/washington-as-land-speculator/.

10 Department of State, Office of the Historian, "Proclamation Line of 173, Quebec Act of 1774 and Westward Expansion," online: https://history.state.gov/milestones/1750-1775/proclamation-line-1763.

11 Stephen Azzi, *Reconcilable Differences: A History of Canada-US Relations* (Toronto: Oxford University Press, 2014) at 2.

12 Russell J Dalton, "Political Cultures and Values," in Paul J Quirk, ed, *The United States and Canada: How Two Democracies Differ and Why It Matters* (Toronto: Oxford University Press, 2019) at 27.

13 Jonathan Gienapp, "Using Beard to Overcome Beardianism: Charles Beard's Forgotten Historicism and the Ideas-Interests Dichotomy" (2014), *Constitutional Commentary* 550, online: https://scholarship.law.umn.edu/concomm/550.

14 National Archives, Founders Online, "Thomas Jefferson to William Duane, 4 August 1812," online: https://founders.archives.gov/documents/Jefferson/03-05-02-0231.
15 John Boyko, *Blood and Daring* (Toronto: Alfred A Knopf Canada, 2013).
16 See Margaret MacMillan, *Paris 1919: Six Months That Changed the World* (New York: Random House, 2003).
17 Louis Hartz, *The Liberal Tradition in America* (New York: Harcourt Brace, 1955).
18 Seymour Martin Lipset, "Why No Socialism in the United States?" in Seweryn Bialer & Sophia Sluzar, eds, *Radicalism in the Contemporary Age*, Volume 1 (New York: Routledge, 1977).
19 Gerard W Boychuk, *National Health Insurance in the United States and Canada: Race, Territory and the Roots of Difference* (Washington, DC: Georgetown University Press, 2008).
20 30 US 1 (1831).
21 Andrew DePietro, "Counties with the Highest and Lowest Poverty Rates in the US" *Forbes* (28 February 2022), online: https://www.forbes.com/sites/andrewdepietro/2022/02/28/counties-with-the-highest-and-lowest-poverty-rates-in-the-us/.
22 David Frum, "Is America Still 'the Shining City on a Hill'?" *The Atlantic* (1 January 2021), online: https://www.theatlantic.com/ideas/archive/2021/01/is-america-still-the-shining-city-on-a-hill/617474/.
23 Richard Hofstadter, "The Paranoid Style in American Politics" *Harper's* (November 1964).
24 Pew Research Center, "Public Trust in Government 1958–2023" 19 September 2023, online: https://news.gallup.com/opinion/polling-matters/404750/public-opinion-role-government.aspx.
25 Frank Newport, "US Public Opinion and the Role of Government" Gallup Polling Matters (4 November 2022) online: https://news.gallup.com/opinion/polling-matters/404750/public-opinion-role-government.aspx.
26 See Harold Adams Innis, *The Fur Trade in Canada: An Introduction to Canadian Economic History* (Toronto: University of Toronto Press, 1970 [1930]).
27 Bayard Reesor, *The Canadian Constitution in Historical Perspective: With a Clause-by-Clause Analysis of the Constitution Acts and the Canada Act* (Scarborough: Prentice Hall, 1992) at 17.
28 *Ibid* at 18.
29 *Ibid* at 21.
30 John George Lambton, "Report on the Affairs of British North America from the Earl of Durham, Her Majesty's High Commissioner," in Robert Stanton, *Journal of the House of Assembly of Upper Canada* (Printer to the Queen's Most Excellent Majesty, 1839) at 95, online: https://books.google.ca/books?id=OZBaAAAAYAAJ&pg=PP9#v=onepage&q&f=false.

31 *Ibid* at 92.
32 *Ibid* at 9. See also David R Cameron, "Lord Durham Then and Now," in Robert C Vipond, ed, *The Daily Plebiscite: Federalism, Nationalism and Canada. Essays by David R Cameron* (Toronto: University of Toronto Press, 2021) at 65–85.
33 Gregory J Inwood, *Understanding Canadian Federalism: An Introduction to Theory and Practice* (Toronto: Pearson, 2013).
34 *Ibid* at 36.
35 Ramsay Cook, John C Ricker & John T Saywell, *Canada: A Modern Study* (Toronto: Clarke Irwin, 1963) at 83.
36 Gregory J Inwood, *Understanding Canadian Federalism: An Introduction to Theory and Practice* (Toronto: Pearson, 2013) at 36.
37 Frank Underhill, *In Search of Canadian Liberalism* (Toronto: Macmillan, 1961) at 177.
38 Richard Gwynn, *John A: The Man Who Made Us: The Life and Times of Sir John A. Macdonald*, vol 1 (Toronto: Vintage Canada, 2008) at 380.
39 Gregory J Inwood, *Understanding Canadian Federalism: An Introduction to Theory and Practice* (Toronto: Pearson, 2013) at 43.
40 Alan C Cairns, "The Living Canadian Constitution," in Peter J Meekison, ed, *Canadian Federalism: Myth or Reality?* 3d ed (Toronto: Methuen, 1971) at 143.
41 This section is based on Gregory J Inwood, *Understanding Canadian Federalism: An Introduction to Theory and Practice* (Toronto: Pearson, 2013) ch 4.
42 Hugh GJ Aitken, "Defensive Expansion: The State and Economic Growth in Canada," in Hugh GJ Aitken, ed, *The State and Economic Growth* (New York: Social Science Research Council, 1959) at 183.
43 Daniel Drache, ed, *Harold A. Innis: Staples, Markets and Cultural Change. Selected Essays* (Montreal: McGill-Queen's University Press, 1995).
44 Nelle Oosterom, "A Day for Laurier" *Canada's History* (12 September 2016), online: www.canadashistory.ca/explore/prime-ministers/a-day-for-laurier.

## CHAPTER TWO | Comparative Political Institutions: Where Does Power Lie in Each Country?

1 Stephen Brooks, Donald E Abelson & Melissa Haussman, *Understanding American Politics*, 3d ed (Toronto: University of Toronto Press, 2024) at 92.
2 Congressional Research Service, *History, Evolution, and Practices of the President's State of the Union Address: Frequently Asked Questions* (updated 5 February 2019), online: https://crsreports.congress.gov/product/pdf/R/R44770/10.
3 RW Apple Jr., "Mud on the Senate Floor: All Parties Blame One Another for Disclosures That Sting" *New York Times* (5 March 1989), online: www.nytimes.com/1989/03/05/us/mud-senate-floor-tower-debate-all-parties-blame-one-another-for-disclosures-that.html.

4   See Gregory J Inwood, *Understanding Canadian Public Administration: An Introduction to Theory and Practice*, 5th ed (Toronto: University of Toronto Press, 2025).
5   Tina Nguyen, "Trump Appointees Take Turns Praising Him in Bizarre Cabinet Meeting" *Vanity Fair* (12 June 2017), online: www.vanityfair.com/news/2017/06/donald-trump-cabinet-meeting.
6   National Constitution Center Staff, "The Man Whose Impeachment Vote Saved Andrew Johnson," National Constitution Centre (16 May 2022), online: https://constitutioncenter.org/blog/the-man-whose-impeachment-vote-saved-andrew-johnson.
7   *Myers v United States*, 272 US 52 (1926).
8   Alan Gephardt, "The Federal Civil Service and the Death of President James A Garfield" *Garfield Observer* (September 2012), online: www.nps.gov/articles/000/the-federal-civil-service-and-the-death-of-president-james-a-garfield.htm.
9   Gregory J Inwood, *Understanding Canadian Public Administration: An Introduction to Theory and Practice*, 5th ed (Toronto: University of Toronto Press, 2025).
10  Jennifer Smith, "Canadian Confederation and the Influence of American Federalism" 21 *Canadian Journal of Political Science* (1988) at 443–64, quoted in GP Browne, ed, *Documents on the Confederation of British North America* (Toronto: McClelland & Stewart, 1969) at 122.
11  See Donald J Savoie, *Governing from the Centre: The Concentration of Power in Canadian Politics* (Toronto: University of Toronto Press, 1999).
12  David Firestone with Philip Shenon, "A Hushed but Vital Issue: Thurmond's Health" *New York Times* (9 March 2001), online: www.nytimes.com/2001/03/09/us/a-hushed-but-vital-issue-thurmond-s-health.html.
13  John Locke, *Second Treatise of Government*, Salt Lake City: Project Gutenberg (22 April 2003) [1690], online: www.gutenberg.org/files/7370/7370-h/7370-h.htm.
14  Cited in FL Morton & Dave Snow, eds, *Law, Politics and the Judicial Process in Canada*, 4th ed (Calgary: University of Calgary Press, 2008) at 4.
15  *Marbury v Madison*, 5 US 137 (1803).
16  Peter H Russell, Rainer Knopff & Ted Morton, *Federalism and the Charter: Leading Constitutional Decisions. A New Edition* (Toronto: Oxford University Press, 1989) at 3.
17  See Canada, Department of Justice, "Where Our Legal System Comes From" in Canada's System of Justice, 2015, online: www.justice.gc.ca/eng/csj-sjc/just/img/courten.pdf.
18  Canada, Department of Justice, "Where Our Legal System Comes From," online: https://www.justice.gc.ca/eng/rp-pr/cp-pm/just/03.html.

19 See Kerry Wilkins, *Essentials of Canadian Aboriginal Law* (Toronto: Thomson Reuters, 2018); and Thomas Isaac, *Aboriginal Law*, 5th ed (Toronto: Thomson Reuters, 2016).
20 See Peter McCormick, *Supreme at Last: The Evolution of the Supreme Court of Canada* (Toronto: James Lormier, 2000).
21 Barry Wright, Betina Appel Kuzmarov, Rebecca Jaremko Bromwich & Vincent Kazmierski, *Looking at Law: Canada's Legal System*, 7th ed (New York: LexisNexis, 2019) at 125.
22 Canada. Office of the Commissioner for Federal Judicial Affairs, "What Is the Process for Appointing Supreme Court of Canada Judges?" online: www.fja-cmf.gc.ca/scc-csc/2023/questions-eng.html.
23 Gerard J Kennedy & Mark Mancini, "Canadian Courts Are Not Politicized in the American Way" *Policy Options* (23 January 2023), online: https://policyoptions.irpp.org/magazines/january-2023/politicized-courts-us-canada/.

## CHAPTER THREE | Comparative Elections and Voting: Do Canadians Have Too Few Electoral Choices, or Do Americans Have Too Many?

1 See PoliEngine, "How Many Politicians Are There in the United States?" (2022), online: https://poliengine.com/blog/how-many-politicians-are-there-in-the-us. See also Jennifer L Lawless, *Becoming a Candidate: Political Ambition and the Decision to Run for Office* (United Kingdom: Cambridge University Press, 2012) at 33, online: www.google.ca/books/edition/Becoming_a_Candidate/AFyNvwEACAAJ?hl=en.
2 Christine O'Donnell, "I'm Not a Witch. I'm You" *YouTube* (4 October 2010), online: www.youtube.com/watch?v=ek3OUay2uWw.
3 Warren Bowen, "Do the Math: Canadians Aren't Getting the Government They're Voting For" *CBC News* (9 June 2023), online: www.cbc.ca/news/opinion/opinion-warren-bowen-electoral-change-1.5333743.
4 Matt Kwong, "Here's How Gerrymandering Games US Elections — And Why This Pennsylvania Decision Matters" *CBC News* (24 January 2018), online: www.cbc.ca/news/world/gerrymander-explained-1.4360638.
5 Lindsay Lazarski, "Outside Expert Advises Pa. Supreme Court in Drawing Congressional District Map" *WHYY* (18 February 2018), online: https://whyy.org/articles/outside-expert-advises-pa-supreme-court-drawing-congressional-district-map/.
6 See Canada, Elections Canada, "The Role of the Electoral Boundaries Commissions in the Federal Redistribution Process," online:

www.elections.ca/content.aspx?section=res&dir=cir/red/rolecom&document=index&lang=e.

7   Katie Glueck, "Trump Throws Fit on Twitter" *POLITICO* (7 November 2012), online: www.politico.com/story/2012/11/trump-throws-fit-on-twitter-083450.

8   Robert Speel, "You'll Hear These 4 Arguments in Defense of the Electoral College. Here's Why They Are Wrong" *St. Louis Post-Dispatch* (31 March 2019), online: https://www.stltoday.com/article_079065f6-e0db-5607-acd5-8a1beaca6f9e.html.

9   CBC Archives, "The King-Byng Affair" *CBC News*, CBC/Radio Canada, 2004, online: www.cbc.ca/player/play/1776946871.

10  Canada, Elections Canada, *Limits on Contributions 2023*, online: www.elections.ca/content.aspx?section=pol&dir=lim&document=lim2023&lang=e.

11  Andre Blais, Shaun Bowler & Bernard Groffman, "Electoral and Party Systems," in Paul J Quirk, ed, *The United States and Canada: How Two Democracies Differ and Why It Matters* (Toronto: Oxford University Press, 2019) at 56.

12  *Buckley v Valeo*, 424 US 1 (1976).

13  *Citizens United v Federal Election Commission*, 558 US 310 (2010).

14  See Open Secrets: Following the Money in Politics, online: www.opensecrets.org/.

15  Frank Giustra, "America Is a Broken Nation. Here's How to Fix It in Four Easy Steps (and Why It Will Never Happen)" *Toronto Star* (7 September 2022), online: www.thestar.com/business/opinion/2022/09/07/how-to-fix-a-broken-america-in-four-easy-steps-which-will-never-happen.html.

16  Sean McMinn & Alyson Hurt, "Tracking the Money Race Behind the Presidential Primary Campaign" *NPR* (16 April 2019), online: www.npr.org/2019/04/16/711812314/tracking-the-money-race-behind-the-presidential-campaign.

17  Jordan Fabian & Skylar Woodhouse, "Biden Grows Money Edge Over Trump With $25 Million New York Haul" *Bloomberg News* (28 March 2024), online: www.bnnbloomberg.ca/biden-grows-money-edge-over-trump-with-25-million-new-york-haul-1.2052701.

18  Alison Durkee, "Trump Vs. Harris Fundraising Race: Harris Has Raised Over $1 Billion Since Becoming Nominee, Report Says" *Forbes* (9 October 2024), online: https://www.forbes.com/sites/alisondurkee/2024/10/09/trump-vs-harris-fundraising-race-harris-has-raised-over-1-billion-since-becoming-nominee-report-says/.

19  Michael Dorgan, "Harris Campaign and Allies Spent More Than $1.4B on Political Ads in Losing Race Against Trump" *Fox Business* (6 November 2024), online: https://www.foxbusiness.com/politics/harris-campaign-allies-spent-more-than-1-4b-political-ads-losing-race-against-trump.

## Notes

### CHAPTER FOUR | Federalism and Regionalism

1 See Daniel Elazar, *American Federalism: A View from the States*, 2d ed (New York: Thomas Y Crowell Company, 1972).
2 Elazar's analysis of political cultures focused on moralistic, individualistic, and traditionalistic regions. But some historians have noted a different type of social and political culture that developed in the frontier Appalachian region of British colonial America, a culture which this text will label as "Populist." See David Hackett Fischer, *Albion's Seed: Four British Folkways in America* (New York: Oxford University Press 1989) and Colin Woodard, *American Nations* (London: Penguin Books, 2011).
3 See CNN, "Exit Polls" *CNN Politics*, online: www.cnn.com/election/2020/exit-polls/president/national-results; Pew Research Centre, "Sizable Difference by Gender, Race and Ethnicity, Age and Education in Midterm Election Preferences" (23 August 2022), online: www.pewresearch.org/politics/2022/08/23/abortion-rises-in-importance-as-a-voting-issue-driven-by-democrats/pp_2022-08-23_midterms_01-01/; and Jennifer Vilcarino & Chase Harrison, "*Chart: How US Latinos Voted in the 2020 Midterm Election*" (17 November 2022), online: www.as-coa.org/articles/chart-how-us-latinos-voted-2022-midterm-election.
4 Jason Lange, Bo Erickson & Brad Heath, "Trump's Return to Power Fueled by Hispanic, Working-Class Voter Support" *Reuters* (7 November 2024), online: https://www.reuters.com/world/us/trumps-return-power-fueled-by-hispanic-working-class-voter-support-2024-11-06/.
5 Peter B Waite, ed, *The Confederation Debates in the Provinces of Canada* (Toronto: McClelland & Stewart, 1963) at 44.
6 Peter Russell, *Constitutional Odyssey: Can Canadians Become a Sovereign People?* 3d ed (Toronto: University of Toronto Press, 2004).
7 Dennis J Mahoney, "Declaration of Independence" 46 *Society* (1986) at 46–48; Philip Resnick, "Montesquieu Revisited, or the Mixed Constitution and the Separation of Powers in Canada" 20:2 *Canadian Journal of Political Science* (June 1987) at 97–115.
8 Samuel H Beer, *To Make a Nation: The Rediscovery of American Federalism* (Cambridge MA: Belknap Press, 1993). See also Barry R Weingast, "The Economic Role of Political Institutions: Market-Preserving Federalism and Economic Development" 11:1 *The Journal of Law, Economics, and Organization* (April 1995) at 1–31; and Richard Simeon & Beryl A Radin, "Reflections on Comparing Federalisms: Canada and the United States" 40:3 *Publius: The Journal of Federalism* (2010) at 357–65.
9 Simeon & Radin, above note 8 at 360.
10 KC Wheare, *Federal Government*, 4th ed (London: Oxford University Press, 1973).

11 Canada. Statistics Canada, *Foreign Direct Investment, 2022*, online: www150.statcan.gc.ca/n1/daily-quotidien/230428/dq230428b-eng.htm.
12 Quebec, Ministry of Environment, the Fight Against Climate Change, Wildlife and Parks, "The Quebec-California Carbon Market," online: www.environnement.gouv.qc.ca/changements/carbone/documents-spede/LinkingMarket.pdf; California, Air Resources Board, "At COP26: California Signs Joint Declaration with New Zealand, Québec to Cooperate in Fight Against Climate Change" Media Release (9 November 2021), online: https://ww2.arb.ca.gov/news/cop26-california-signs-joint-declaration-new-zealand-quebec-cooperate-fight-against-climate.
13 Donald Smiley, *Canada in Question. Federalism in the 1970s*, 2d ed (Toronto: McGraw-Hill Ryerson, 1976) at 54.
14 Richard Simeon, *Federal-Provincial Diplomacy: The Making of Recent Policy in Canada* (Toronto: University of Toronto Press, 2006).
15 See Gregory J Inwood, Carolyn M Johns & Patricia L O'Reilly, *Intergovernmental Policy Capacity in Canada. Inside the Worlds of Finance, Environment, Trade and Health Policy* (Montreal: McGill-Queen's University Press, 2012).
16 *The Attorney General of Ontario v The Attorney General of Canada*, [1897] AC 199, [1896] UKPC 20.
17 *Canada (AG) v Alberta (AG) and others*, [1921] UKPC 107, [1922] 1 AC 191.
18 *Fort Frances Pulp and Paper Company Ltd v Manitoba Free Press Co Ltd and others (Ontario)*, [1923] UKPC 64, [1923] AC 695.
19 [1925] UKPC 2, [1925] AC 396.
20 *Canada (AG) v Ontario (AG) and others*, [1937] UKPC 6.
21 *Reference Re Anti-Inflation Act*, [1976] 2 SCR 373.
22 *Reference re Greenhouse Gas Pollution Pricing Act*, 2021 SCC 11.
23 [1881] UKPC 50.
24 *Reference re Pan-Canadian Securities Regulation*, 2018 SCC 48.
25 *Canada (AG) v Ontario (AG) and others*, [1937] UKPC 7.
26 [1978] 2 SCR 191.
27 [1978] 2 SCR 545 [*CIGOL*].
28 *Reference Re Resolution to Amend the Constitution*, [1981] 1 SCR 753.
29 *United States v Lanza*, 260 US 377 (1922).
30 *United States v Alfonso D Lopez, Jr*, 514 US 549 (1995).
31 *Printz v United States*, 521 US 898 (1997).
32 *Pruneyard Shopping Center v Robins*, 447 US 74 (1980).
33 *Robinson Twp v Pa Pub Util Comm'n*, 83 A3d 901 (Pa 2013).
34 David Gelles & Mike Baker, "Judge Rules in Favor of Montana Youths in a Landmark Climate Case" *New York Times* (14 August 2023), online: www.nytimes.com/2023/08/14/us/montana-youth-climate-ruling.html.

35 See Gregory J Inwood, *Understanding Canadian Federalism: An Introduction to Theory and Practice* (Toronto: Pearson, 2013) at 113–15.
36 National Popular Vote, online: www.nationalpopularvote.com/.
37 *Constitution Act, 1982*, s 91, being Schedule B to the *Canada Act 1982* (UK), 1982, c II.
38 *Heart of Atlanta Motel, Inc v United States*, 379 US 241 (1964).
39 *Wickard v Filburn*, 317 US 111 (1942).
40 *Gonzales v Raich*, 545 US 1 (2005).
41 Canada, Department of Finance, *Federal Transfers to Provinces and Territories*, online: www.canada.ca/en/department-finance/programs/federal-transfers.html#Major.
42 *Constitution Act, 1982*, being Schedule B to the *Canada Act 1982* (UK), c II, s 36(2).
43 Canada, Government of Canada, "Equalization Program" (18 May 2023), online: www.canada.ca/en/department-finance/programs/federal-transfers/equalization.html.
44 *South Dakota v Dole*, 483 US 203 (1987).
45 US Const art 1 § 8.
46 17 US 316.

## CHAPTER FIVE | Comparative Public Policy: Similar Countries, Dissimilar Policies

1 *R v Parker*, 2000 CanLII 5762 (Ont CA).
2 Alex Malyshev & Sarah Ganley, "What Rescheduling to Schedule III Would Mean for the Cannabis Industry" *Reuters* (12 September 2023), online: www.reuters.com/legal/litigation/what-rescheduling-schedule-iii-would-mean-cannabis-industry-2023-09-12/.
3 *R v Morgentaler*, [1988] 1 SCR 30.
4 *Roe v Wade*, 410 US 113 (1973).
5 Meredith Blake, "The Woman Behind 'Roe vs. Wade' Didn't Change Her Mind on Abortion. She Was Paid" *Los Angeles Times* (19 May 2020), online: www.latimes.com/entertainment-arts/tv/story/2020-05-19/roe-v-wade-jane-roe-norma-mccorvey-hulu-doc-abortion.
6 *Planned Parenthood of Southeast Pennsylvania v Casey*, 505 US 833 (1992).
7 *Dobbs v Jackson Women's Health Organization*, 597 US 215 (2022).
8 Allison McCann & Amy Schoenfeld Walker, "Tracking Abortion Bans Across the Country" *New York Times* (8 January 2024), online: www.nytimes.com/interactive/2022/us/abortion-laws-roe-v-wade.html.
9 *Carter v Canada*, 2015 SCC 5.
10 Canada, Department of Justice, *Canada's Medical Assistance in Dying (MAID) Law*, online: www.justice.gc.ca/eng/cj-jp/ad-am/bk-di.html.

11  Canada, Parliament of Canada, *Medical Assistance in Dying in Canada: Choices for Canadians. Report of the Special Joint Committee on Medical Assistance in Dying*. February 2023, 44th Parliament, 1st Session.

12  Masih Khalatbari & Robert Cribb, "Surge in Medically Assisted Deaths Under Canada's MAID Program Outpaces Every Other Country" *Toronto Star* (27 January 2024), online: www.thestar.com/news/investigations/surge-in-medically-assisted-deaths-under-canada-s-maid-program-outpaces-every-other-country/article_29028f96-bc6b-11ee-8f67-03bf29ac7d34.html.

13  Oregon Health Authority, *Oregon Death with Dignity Act 2022 Data Summary* (8 March 2023), online: www.oregon.gov/oha/PH/PROVIDERPARTNERRESOURCES/EVALUATIONRESEARCH/DEATHWITHDIGNITYACT/Documents/year25.pdf.

14  James Farney & Clark Banack, *Faith, Rights, and Choice: The Politics of Religious Schools in Canada* (Toronto: University of Toronto Press, 2023).

15  *Adler v Ontario*, [1996] 3 SCR 609.

16  *Lemon v Kurtzman*, 403 US 602 (1971).

17  *Zelman-Simmons v Harris*, 536 US 639 (2002).

18  Mike McShane, "Oh What a Year (For School Choice)" *Forbes* (19 December 2023), online: www.forbes.com/sites/mikemcshane/2023/12/19/oh-what-a-year-for-school-choice/.

19  COVID-19 Tracker, online: https://covid19tracker.ca/.

20  Centers for Disease Control and Prevention, *COVID Data Tracker*, online: https://covid.cdc.gov/covid-data-tracker/#datatracker-home.

21  Canada, Health Canada, *Government of Canada Announces Deductions and Next Steps to Curb Private Health Care Paid Out-of-Pocket* (10 March 2023), online: www.canada.ca/en/health-canada/news/2023/03/government-of-canada-announces-deductions-and-next-steps-to-curb-private-health-care-paid-out-of-pocket.html.

22  Antonia Maioni & Pierre Martin, "Health Care in Canada and the United States," in David M Thomas & Christopher Sands, eds, *Canada and the United States: Differences That Count*, 5th ed (Toronto: University of Toronto Press, 2023) at 252.

23  *Ibid*.

24  PBS News, "How Canada Got Universal Health Care and What the US Could Learn," *PBS News Hour* (31 August 2020), online: www.pbs.org/newshour/health/how-canada-got-universal-health-care-and-what-the-u-s-could-learn.

25  Ross University School of Medicine, "US vs. Canadian Healthcare: What Is the Difference?" (11 May 2021), online: https://medical.rossu.edu/about/blog/us-vs-canadian-healthcare.

26 Eric C Schneider, Arnav Shah, Michelle M Doty, Roosa Tikkanen, Katharine Fields & Reginald D Williams II, "Mirror, Mirror 2021: Reflecting Poorly: Health Care in the US Compared to Other High-Income Countries" *The Commonwealth Fund* (4 August 2021), online: www.commonwealthfund.org/publications/fund-reports/2021/aug/mirror-mirror-2021-reflecting-poorly.
27 Maioni & Martin, above note 22 at 263–64.
28 *Chaoulli v Quebec*, 2005 SCC 35.
29 Stephen Brooks, *Canadian Democracy*, 8th ed (Toronto: Oxford University Press, 2015) at 345.
30 Commonwealth of Massachusetts, "Health Care Reform for Individuals" (13 November 2023), online: https://www.mass.gov/info-details/health-care-reform-for-individuals.
31 State of Hawaii, "About Prepaid Health Care," online: https://labor.hawaii.gov/dcd/home/about-phc/.
32 Peter Hirschfeld, "Eight Years After Shumlin's 'Crushing' Reversal, Single-Payer Health Care Movement Presses On" *Vermont Public* (1 March 2022), online: www.vermontpublic.org/vpr-news/2022-03-01/eight-years-after-shumlins-crushing-reversal-single-payer-health-care-movement-presses-on.
33 Ashley Kirzinger, Alex Montero, Liz Hamel & Mollyann Brodie, "5 Charts About Public Opinion on the Affordable Care Act" *KFF* (14 April 2022), online: www.kff.org/health-reform/poll-finding/5-charts-about-public-opinion-on-the-affordable-care-act-and-the-supreme-court/.
34 See Bernd Debusmann Jr, "Why Is Canada's COVID Death Rate So Much Lower than US?" *BBC News* (14 February 2022), online: www.bbc.com/news/world-us-canada-60380317.
35 Jennifer Mascia & Chip Brownlee, "A Decade of Mass Shootings, By the Numbers" *The Trace* (5 October 2023), online: www.thetrace.org/2023/10/mass-shootings-gun-violence-how-many/.
36 Centers for Disease Control and Prevention, "Assault or Homicide" *National Center for Disease Statistics* (29 December, 2023), online: www.cdc.gov/nchs/fastats/homicide.htm.
37 *Ibid*.
38 [1987] 2 SCR 636.
39 Rick Ungar, "Here Are the 23 Executive Orders on Gun Safety Signed Today by the President" *Forbes* (16 January 2013), online: www.forbes.com/sites/rickungar/2013/01/16/here-are-the-23-executive-orders-on-gun-safety-signed-today-by-the-president/.
40 Paul LeBlanc, "Video Surfaces of Marjorie Taylor Greene Confronting Parkland Shooting Survivor with Baseless Claims" *CNN* (28 January 2021), online: www.cnn.com/2021/01/27/politics/marjorie-taylor-greene-david-hogg-video/index.html.

41 Giffords Law Center to Prevent Gun Violence, "Gun Laws," online: https://giffords.org/lawcenter/gun-laws/.

42 See Kathryn Harrison, "Environmental Policy: Climate Change," in Paul J Quirk, ed, *The United States and Canada: How Two Democracies Differ and Why It Matters* (Toronto: Oxford University Press, 2019) at 196–218.

43 British Columbia, *British Columbia's Carbon Tax*, online: https://www2.gov.bc.ca/gov/content/environment/climate-change/clean-economy/carbon-tax.

44 Canada, Environment and Natural Resources, "How Carbon Pricing Works," online: www.canada.ca/en/environment-climate-change/services/climate-change/pricing-pollution-how-it-will-work/putting-price-on-carbon-pollution.html.

45 *Reference re Greenhouse Gas Pollution Pricing Act*, 2021 SCC 11.

46 Rachel Aiello, "Poilievre Pans Trudeau's Carbon Pricing Pivot, Liberals Pitch Pause as 'Great News'" *CTV News* (27 October 2023), online: www.ctvnews.ca/politics/poilievre-pans-trudeau-s-carbon-pricing-pivot-liberals-pitch-pause-as-great-news-1.6620250.

47 Gayathri Vaidyanathan, "Biden Signs Historic Climate Bill as Scientists Applaud" *Nature* (16 August 2022), online: www.scientificamerican.com/article/biden-signs-historic-climate-bill-as-scientists-applaud/.

48 *R v Keegstra*, [1990] 3 SCR 697.

49 CBC News, "NS Man Guilty of Hate Crime in Cross-Burning" (9 November 2010), online: www.cbc.ca/news/canada/nova-scotia/n-s-man-guilty-of-hate-crime-in-cross-burning-1.925313.

50 Shanifa Nasser, "Kevin Johnston Ordered to Pay $2.5M for 'Hateful, Islamophobic' Remarks Against Restaurant Chain Owner" *CBC News* (13 May 2019), online: www.cbc.ca/news/canada/toronto/kevin-johnston-paramount-2-5-million-mohamad-fakih-1.5134227.

51 *Smith v Collin*, 439 US 916 (1978).

52 *RAV v City of St Paul*, 505 US 377 (1992).

53 *Snyder v Phelps*, 562 US 443 (2011).

54 *Ford v Quebec (AG)*, [1988] 2 SCR 712.

55 Don Terry, "Arizona Court Strikes Down Law Requiring English Use" *New York Times* (29 April 1998), online: www.nytimes.com/1998/04/29/us/arizona-court-strikes-down-law-requiring-english-use.html.

56 *English Language Unity Act* of 2023, HR 997, s 1109.

## CHAPTER SIX | Trade and Economic Policy: The Long and Winding Road

1 Goldwin Smith, *Canada and the Canadian Question* (Toronto: University of Toronto Press, 1971 [1891]) at 5.

## Notes

2  Cited in Geoffrey Hale, *So Near, Yet So Far: The Public and Hidden Worlds of Canada-US Relations* (Vancouver: UBC Press, 2012) at 13.
3  Edelgard Mahant & Graham Mount, *Invisible and Inaudible in Washington: American Policies Toward Canada* (Vancouver: UBC Press, 1999).
4  See Livingston T Merchant, *Neighbours Taken for Granted: Canada and the United States* (New York: Frederick A Praeger, 1965) and Charles F Doran, *Forgotten Partnership: US-Canada Relations Today* (Baltimore: Johns Hopkins University Press, 1984).
5  United States Department of State, "US Relations With Canada," online: www.state.gov/r/pa/ei/bgn/2089.htm#travel.
6  Canada, Government of Canada, "Canada-United States Relations," online: www.international.gc.ca/country-pays/us-eu/relations.aspx?lang=eng.
7  See particularly Alan Gotlieb, *I'll Be with You in a Minute, Mr. Ambassador: The Education of a Canadian Diplomat in Washington* (Toronto: University of Toronto Press, 1991).
8  New Republic Staff, "Boring Headline Contest" *New Republic* (14 February 2011), online: https://newrepublic.com/article/83443/boring-headline-contest.
9  See Stephen Azzi, *Reconcilable Differences: A History of Canada-US Relations* (Toronto: Oxford University Press, 2014).
10  See Cy Gonick, *Canada Since 1960: A People's History* (Toronto: James Lorimer & Company, 2016).
11  Kari Levitt, *Silent Surrender* (Toronto: Gage, 1970).
12  Cited in Ramsay Cook, *The Maple Leaf Forever: Essays on Nationalism and Politics in Canada* (Toronto: Macmillan, 1971) at 46.
13  See Paul Kellogg, *Escape from the Staple Trap: Canadian Political Economy After Left Nationalism* (Toronto: University of Toronto Press, 2016).
14  Cited in Greg Albo & Chris Bailey, "Beyond Economic Nationalism: Clashes with Canadian Capitalism," in Cy Gonick, ed, *Canada Since 1960: A People's History* (Toronto: James Lorimer & Company, 2016) at 364.
15  *Hansard*, 14 April 1972 at 1328. Cited in Gregory J Inwood, *Continentalizing Canada: The Politics and Legacy of the Macdonald Royal Commission* (Toronto: University of Toronto Press, 2005) at 29-30.
16  Cited in Graham Fraser, *Playing for Keeps: The Making of the Prime Minister, 1988* (Toronto: McClelland & Stewart, 1989) at 344.
17  Jeffrey M Ayres, *Defying Conventional Wisdom: Political Movements and Popular Contention against North American Free Trade* (Toronto: University of Toronto Press, 1998) at 25.
18  James Thomson, *Making North America: Trade, Security and Integration.* Toronto: University of Toronto Press, 2014) at 59.
19  Inwood, *Continentalizing Canada*, above note 15.

20 Stephen Clarkson, *Uncle Sam and Us* (Toronto: University of Toronto Press, 2002) at 30.
21 Bruce G Doern & Brian Tomlin, *Faith and Fear: The Free Trade Story* (Toronto: Stoddart, 1992) at 26.
22 See Derek Burney, *Getting It Done: A Memoir* (Montreal: McGill-Queen's University Press, 2005).
23 Clarkson, *Uncle Sam and Us*, above note 20 at 32.
24 See Helen Dewar, "NAFTA Wins Final Congressional Test" *Washington Post* (November 21, 1993), online: www.washingtonpost.com/archive/politics/1993/11/21/nafta-wins-final-congressional-test/4b98cac1-c6cc-4128-b65e-a92b05565b92/; Public Citizen, "Final House Vote on NAFTA" (17 November 1993), online: www.citizen.org/article/final-house-vote-on-nafta/; and Tod Robberson, "Mexico's NAFTA Vote: Rancor, no Suspense" *Washington Post* (24 November 1993), online: www.washingtonpost.com/archive/politics/1993/11/24/mexicos-nafta-vote-rancor-no-suspense/ddd6c560-ab22-4a91-a340-df5bca4d6ba4/.
25 M Angeles Villarreal & Ian F Fergusson, *The North American Free Trade Agreement*, Congressional Research Service (16 April 2016), online: www.fas.org/sgp/crs/row/R42965.pdf; Canada, Government of Canada, "North American Free Trade Agreement (NAFTA) — Fast Facts," online: www.international.gc.ca/trade-commerce/trade-agreements-accords-commerciaux/agr-acc/nafta-alena/fta-ale/facts.aspx?lang=eng.
26 US Bureau of Labor Statistics, Current Employment Statistics survey, series ID CES3000000001, manufacturing industry, US Department of Labor (6 February 2018), online: www.bls.gov/ces/.
27 Public Citizen, "Trade Adjustment Assistance Database," online: www.citizen.org/tradeadjustment-assistance-database. See also United States General Accounting Office, "Trade Adjustment Assistance: Improvements Necessary, but Programs Cannot Solve Communities' Long Term Problems," online: www.gao.gov/assets/gao-01-988t.pdf and Robert E Scott, "NAFTA-Related Job Losses Have Piled Up Since 1993" *Economic Policy Institute* (16 December, 2003), online: https://www.epi.org/publication/webfeatures_snapshots_archive_12102003/.
28 Patrick Gillespie, "Trump Hammers America's 'Worst Trade Deal'" *CNN Business* (27 September 2016), online: https://money.cnn.com/2016/09/27/news/economy/donald-trump-nafta-hillary-clinton-debate/.
29 Eric Miller, "Remaking NAFTA: Its Origin, Impact and Future" *Canadian Global Affairs Institute Policy Paper* (August 2017) at 10.
30 Adrian Morrow, Barrie McKenna & Stephanie Nolen, "From NAFTA to USMCA: Inside the Tense Negotiations That Saved North American Trade" *The Globe and Mail* (5 October 2018), online: https://www.theglobeandmail.

## Notes

com/business/article-from-nafta-to-usmca-inside-the-tense-negotiations-that-saved-north/.

31  Stephen Azzi, *Reconcilable Differences: A History of Canada-US Relations* (Toronto: Oxford University Press, 2014).

32  GlobalTV News, "Trump Slams Canada on NAFTA" (26 September 2018), online: https://globalnews.ca/video/4490794/trump-slams-canada-on-nafta. See also Catherine Porter, "Before the Smiles, Mounting Tensions Between Trudeau and Trump" *New York Times* (8 June 2018), online: www.nytimes.com/2018/06/08/world/canada/canada-trudeau-trump-us-group-of-7.html.

33  CBC News, "Trudeau Pauses for 21 Seconds Before Answering Question About Trump's Response to US Protests" (2 June 2020), online: www.youtube.com/watch?v=SeaDi-0Nz8w.

34  Katie Simpson, "From Clashes to Candy, the Evolution of Chrystia Freeland's Relationship with Her US Trade Counterpart" *CBC News* (10 October 2018), online: www.cbc.ca/news/politics/freeland-lighthizer-evolution-of-a-trade-relationship-1.4856319.

35  Jeff Cox, "Trump Signs Steel and Aluminum Tariffs That Exempt Canada and Mexico and Leave Door Open to Other Countries" *CNBC* (8 March 2018), online: www.cnbc.com/2018/03/08/trump-signs-tariffs-that-exempt-canada-and-mexico-open-door-to-others.html.

36  Government of British Columbia, "Stumpage and Export Fees" (1 November 2023), online: https://www2.gov.bc.ca/gov/content/taxes/natural-resource-taxes/forestry/stumpage.

37  Canada, Global Affairs Canada, *Softwood Lumber*, online: www.international.gc.ca/controls-controles/softwood-bois_oeuvre/index.aspx?lang=eng.

38  Office of the United States Trade Representative, "Statement by Neena Moorjani, Spokeswoman for US Trade Representative Rob Portman, Office of the United States Trade Representative" (8 December 2005), online: https://ustr.gov/archive/Document_Library/Spokesperson_Statements/Statement_of_Neena_Moorjani,_Spokesperson,_Regarding_the_Softwood_Lumber_Issue.html.

39  Jeff Yoders, "US Doubles Tariffs on Canadian Softwood Lumber and Contractors Expect Higher Prices" *Engineering News-Record* (30 November 2021), online: www.enr.com/articles/53119-us-doubles-tariffs-on-canadian-softwood-lumber-contractors-expect-higher-prices.

40  Canada, Global Affairs Canada, *Softwood Lumber: Recent Developments*, online: www.international.gc.ca/controls-controles/softwood-bois_oeuvre/recent.aspx?lang=eng.

41  Canada, Global Affairs Canada, *Minister Ng Welcomes NAFTA Dispute Panel Ruling on US Duties on Canadian Softwood Lumber* (5 October 2023), online: https://www.canada.ca/en/global-affairs/news/2023/10/

minister-ng-welcomes-nafta-dispute-panel-ruling-on-us-duties-on-canadian-softwood-lumber.html.

42 Gregory J Inwood, *Continentalizing Canada: The Politics and Legacy of the Macdonald Royal Commission* (Toronto: University of Toronto Press, 2005).

43 See Stephen Clarkson, *Does North America Exist? Governing the Continent After NAFTA and 9/11* (Toronto: University of Toronto Press, 2008) at 42–43.

44 For the official announcement, see Office of the Press Secretary, The White House (4 February 2011), online: https://obamawhitehouse.archives.gov/the-press-office/2011/02/04/joint-statement-president-obama-and-prime-minister-harper-canada-regul-0. For a critique by the Council of Canadians, see Stewart Trew, "Say No to New Regulations" *Council of Canadians* (1 September 2011), online: https://canadians.org/analysis/say-no-new-regulations-canadian-us-manufacturers-brief-ambassadors-their-common-cause/.

45 Canada, Public Safety Canada, *Beyond the Border Action Plan* (4 February 2011), online: www.publicsafety.gc.ca/cnt/brdr-strtgs/bynd-th-brdr/ctn-pln-en.aspx.

46 Josh Dawsey, Damien Paletta & Erica Werner, "In Fundraising Speech, Trump Says He Made Up Trade Claim in Meeting with Justin Trudeau" *Washington Post* (14 March 2018), online: www.washingtonpost.com/news/post-politics/wp/2018/03/14/in-fundraising-speech-trump-says-he-made-up-facts-in-meeting-with-justin-trudeau/.

47 Christopher Sands, "Was President Biden's Ottawa Visit Good for US-Canada Relations?" *Policy Options* (29 March 2023), online: https://policyoptions.irpp.org/magazines/march-2023/biden-visit-us-canada-relations/.

48 Canada, Statistics Canada, *Foreign Direct Investment, 2022* (18 April 2023), www150.statcan.gc.ca/n1/daily-quotidien/230428/dq230428b-eng.htm.

49 See Michiel Horn, *The League for Social Reconstruction: Intellectual Origins of the Democratic Left in Canada, 1930–1942* (Toronto: University of Toronto Press, 1980).

50 See Neil Bradford, "Structuring Canada's National Policy Debate: The Royal Commission on Canada's Economic Prospects," in Gregory J Inwood & Carolyn M Johns, eds, *Commissions of Inquiry and Policy Change: A Comparative Analysis* (Toronto: University of Toronto Press, 2014) at 49–69.

51 Canada, Privy Council Office, *Foreign Ownership and the Structure of Canadian Industry: Report of the Task Force on the Structure of Canadian Industry* (Ottawa: Queen's Printer, 1968).

52 See Maude Barlow, Lori Wallach, & Tony Clarke, *MAI: The Multilateral Agreement on Investment and the Threat to American Freedom* (Toronto: Stoddart, 1998).

53 Mel Watkins, "Why Foreign Ownership Still Matters in 2008: Submission to Competition Policy Review Panel" *Briefing Paper: Trade and Investment Series* (Canadian Centre for Policy Alternatives, 2008), 9, 1, 1.

54 Jerome Klassen & William Carroll, "Transnational Class Formation? Globalization and the Canadian Corporate Network" 17:2 *Journal of World-Systems Research* (2011) at 379.
55 Niraj Chockshi & Mark Walker, "US Approves $31 Billion Merger of Two Big Railroads" *New York Times* (15 March 2023), online: www.nytimes.com/2023/03/15/business/canadian-pacific-kansas-city-southern-merger.html.
56 "AltaGas Launches $8.4-Billion Takeover of US Power Company WGL Holdings" *CBC News* (25 January 2017), online: www.cbc.ca/news/canada/calgary/altagas-takeover-wgl-holdings-1.3952336.
57 Noah Berman, "President Biden Has Banned Some US Investment in China. Here's What to Know," *Council on Foreign Relations* (29 August 2023), online: www.cfr.org/in-brief/president-biden-has-banned-some-us-investment-china-heres-what-know.
58 Noah Berman, Lindsay Maizland & Andrew Chatzky, "Is China's Huawei a Threat to US National Security?" *Council on Foreign Relations* (8 February 2023), online: www.cfr.org/backgrounder/chinas-huawei-threat-us-national-security.
59 Scott Nover, "The Grim Reality of Banning Tik Tok" *Time Magazine* (15 March 2024), online: https://time.com/6952889/tiktok-ban-freedom-of-speech-essay/.
60 United States, Department of State, *2023 Investment Climate Statements: Canada*, online: www.state.gov/reports/2023-investment-climate-statements/canada/.
61 William Borders, "Canadian Record Hailing US a Hit" *New York Times* (13 June 1974), online: www.nytimes.com/1974/01/13/archives/canadian-record-hailing-us-a-hit-journalist-tired-of-hearing.html.
62 Cited in Trevor Hancock, "Taxes Are the Price We Pay for Civilization" *Victoria Times Colonist* (3 June 2015), online: www.timescolonist.com/opinion/trevor-hancock-taxes-are-the-price-we-pay-for-civilization-4623145.
63 International Monetary Fund, "Government Expenditure, Percent of GDP 2022," online: www.imf.org/external/datamapper/exp@FPP/FRA/JPN/GBR/SWE/ESP/ITA/ZAF/IND/CAN/USA.
64 OECD Date, *Social Spending*, online: https://data.oecd.org/socialexp/social-spending.htm.
65 William Keech & William Scarth, "Economic Policy," in Paul J Quirk, ed, *The United States and Canada: How Two Democracies Differ and Why It Matters* (Toronto: Oxford University Press, 2019) at 185.
66 United States Treasury, "How Much Revenue Has the US Government Collected This Year?" *Fiscal Data*, online: https://fiscaldata.treasury.gov/americas-finance-guide/government-revenue/.
67 World Bank, "Tax Revenue (% of GDP) — Canada, United States" *Data*, https://data.worldbank.org/indicator/GC.TAX.TOTL.GD.ZS?end=2022&locations=CA-US&start=1972&view=chart.

68   Organisation for Economic Cooperation and Development, "Income Inequality" *Data*, online: https://data.oecd.org/inequality/income-inequality.htm.
69   Sarah Burkinshaw, Yaz Terajima & Carolyn A Wilkins, "Income Inequality in Canada" *Bank of Canada Staff Discussion Paper* (26 July 2022), online: www.bankofcanada.ca/wp-content/uploads/2022/07/sdp2022-16.pdf.
70   John Harles, "Choose Your Parents Wisely: Economic Inequality and Mobility in Canada and the United States," in David M Thomas & Christopher Sands, eds, *Canada and the United States: Differences That Count*, 5th ed (Toronto: University of Toronto Press, 2023) at 273.
71   *Ibid*.
72   David Macdonald, "Canada's New Gilded Age: CEO Pay in Canada in 2022" (Ottawa: Canadian Centre for Policy Alternatives, January 2024), online: https://policyalternatives.ca/sites/default/files/uploads/publications/National%20Office/2024/01/canadas-new-gilded-age.pdf.
73   Josh Bivens & Jori Kandra, "CEO Pay Slightly Declined in 2022 but It Has soared 1,209.2% Since 1978 Compared with a 15.3% Rise in Typical Workers' Pay" Economic Policy Institute (21 September 2023), online: www.epi.org/publication/ceo-pay-in-2022/#:~:text=In%202022%2C%20CEOs%20were%20paid,wage%20earners%20in%20the%20U.S.
74   David M Cutler & Lawrence H Summers, "The COVID-19 Pandemic and the $16 Trillion Virus" National Library of Medicine (2 November 2020), online: www.ncbi.nlm.nih.gov/pmc/articles/PMC7604733/#:~:text=The%20estimated%20cumulative%20financial%20costs,GDP%20of%20the%20United%20States.
75   US Government Accountability Office, "COVID-19 Relief: Funding and Spending as of Jan. 31, 2023" (28 February 2023), online: www.gao.gov/products/gao-23-106647.
76   Parts of this section are based on Gregory J Inwood, *Understanding Canadian Public Administration: An Introduction to Theory and Practice*, 5th ed (Toronto: University of Toronto Press, 2025).
77   Amy Minsky, "The Finance Minister's New Shoes: A Purely Canadian, Though Mysterious, Tradition" *Global News* (20 April 2015).
78   Gregory J Inwood, *Understanding Canadian Public Administration: An Introduction to Theory and Practice*, 5th ed (Toronto: University of Toronto Press, 2025) at 344.
79   Canada, Library of Parliament, *The Parliamentary Financial Cycle* (Ottawa: Library of Parliament, 2021) at 2.
80   Donald J Savoie, *Governing From the Centre: The Concentration of Power in Canadian Politics* (Toronto: University of Toronto Press, 1999) at 156.
81   Gregory J Inwood, *Understanding Canadian Public Administration: An Introduction to Theory and Practice*, 5th ed (Toronto: University of Toronto Press, 2025) at 349.

82 Peter Harder & Evert Lindquist, "Expenditure Management and Reporting in the Government of Canada: Recent Developments and Backgrounds," in Jacques Bourgault, Maurice Demers & Cynthia Williams, eds, *Public Administration and Public Management: Experiences in Canada* (Sainte-Foy, QC: Les Publications du Quebec, 1997) at 73.
83 Geoffrey Hale, *The Politics of Taxation in Canada* (Peterborough: Broadview, 2002) at 120.
84 Donald J Savoie, *The Politics of Public Spending in Canada* (Toronto: University of Toronto Press, 1990) at 26.
85 Canada, Prime Minister of Canada, *Delivering for Canadians Now: A Supply and Confidence Agreement from March 22, 2022 until when Parliament rises in June of 2025*, online: https://pm.gc.ca/en/news/news-releases/2022/03/22/delivering-canadians-now.
86 Patrick Malcolmson & Richard Myers, *The Canadian Regime: An Introduction to Parliamentary Government in Canada*, 4th ed (Toronto: University of Toronto Press, 2009) at 48.
87 CBC News, "When Brian Mulroney Upsized the Senate to Pass the GST" *CBC News Archives* (27 September 2018), online: www.cbc.ca/archives/when-brian-mulroney-upsized-the-senate-to-pass-the-gst-1.4839649.
88 Andrew Restuccia, Burgess Everett & Heather Caygle, "Longest Shutdown in History Ends After Trump Relents on Wall" *Politico* (25 January 2019), online: www.politico.com/story/2019/01/25/trump-shutdown-announcement-1125529.

## CHAPTER SEVEN | Foreign Policy: Friends and Allies (Mostly)

1 CBC News, "US Puts Machine-Guns on Great Lakes Coast Guard Vessels" (15 March 2006), online: www.cbc.ca/news/canada/u-s-puts-machine-guns-on-great-lakes-coast-guard-vessels-1.622621.
2 Gregory J Inwood, *Understanding Canadian Federalism: An Introduction to Theory and Practice* (Toronto: Pearson, 2012) at 43.
3 KC Wheare, *Federal Government*, 4th ed (London: Oxford University Press, 1973) at 37.
4 See Sharon Adams, "The Battle of Ridgeway" *Legion: Canada's Military History Magazine* (1 June 2021), online: https://legionmagazine.com/en/the-battle-of-ridgeway/.
5 JDM Stewart, "Prime Ministers and Presidents: What Defines a 'Good Relationship'?" *Policy: Canadian Politics and Public Policy*, online: www.policymagazine.ca/prime-ministers-and-presidents-what-defines-a-good-relationship/.
6 David Shribman, "Jan. 6 Panel's Likely Recommendation of Criminal Charges for Trump Would Smash Another Precedent" *The Globe and Mail*

(16 December 2022), online: www.theglobeandmail.com/world/us-politics/article-jan-6-committee-trump-prosecution/.

7   Catherine Porter, "Trudeau's 21-Second Pause Becomes the Story in Canada" *New York Times* (22 January 2021), online: www.nytimes.com/2020/06/03/world/canada/trudeau-canada-george-floyd-protests.html.

8   North Atlantic Treaty Organization, "Resolute Support Mission (RSM): Key Facts and Figures" (February 2020), online: www.nato.int/nato_static_fl2014/assets/pdf/2020/2/pdf/2020-02-RSM-Placemat.pdf.

9   Liberal Party of Canada, *Creating Opportunity: The Liberal Plan for Canada* (Ottawa: Liberal Party of Canada, 1993) at 106, online: www.poltext.org/sites/poltext.org/files/plateformesV2/Canada/CAN_PL_1993_LIB_en.pdf.

10  Denis Stairs, "Challenges and Opportunities for Canadian Foreign Policy in the Paul Martin Era" 58:4 *International Journal* (Autumn 2003) at 481–506.

11  CBC News, "McCain Defends Napolitano, Insists 9/11 Perpetrators Came from Canada" (24 April 2009), online: www.cbc.ca/news/world/mccain-defends-napolitano-insists-9-11-perpetrators-came-from-canada-1.830149.

12  PBS Frontline, "Ahmed Ressam's Millennium Plot," online: www.pbs.org/wgbh/pages/frontline/shows/trail/inside/cron.html.

13  Ian Austen, "Canada Reaches Settlement With Torture Victim" *New York Times* (26 January 2007), online: www.nytimes.com/2007/01/26/world/americas/26cnd-canada.html.

14  Susana Mas, "Canada's Syrian Refugee Plan Raises Concerns of 'Shortcuts,' Homeland Security Committee Hears" *CBC News* (3 February 2016), online: www.cbc.ca/news/politics/canada-syrian-refugee-plan-us-senate-committee-shortcuts-1.3431698.

15  Morgan Lowrie, "RCMP Demolish Last Structure at Quebec's Roxham Road Migrant Crossing" *CTV News* (26 September 2023), online: https://montreal.ctvnews.ca/rcmp-demolish-last-structure-at-quebec-s-roxham-road-migrant-crossing-1.6575998.

16  Alexander Panetta & Katie Simpson, "Republican Presidential Candidate Proposes Border Wall with Canada" *CBC News* (9 November 2023), online: www.cbc.ca/news/world/vivek-ramaswamy-canada-border-wall-1.7023226.

17  Alan Smith, "Republicans Zero in on a New Border — The One with Canada" *NBC News* (23 January 2024), online: www.nbcnews.com/politics/2024-election/republicans-northern-border-canada-rcna135169.

18  Sophia Harris, "Canadian Drivers with US Licence Plates Harassed by Fellow Canadians" *CBC News* (3 July 2020), online: www.cbc.ca/news/business/canada-u-s-border-harassment-u-s-license-plates-banff-1.5634534.

19  Eilís Quinn, "Canada Extends Continental Shelf Claim, Increasing Overlaps with Russia in Arctic" *Eye on the Arctic Radio Canada International* (22 December 2022), online: www.rcinet.ca/eye-on-the-arctic/2022/12/22/

canada-extends-continental-shelf-claim-increasing-overlaps-with-russia-in-arctic/.

20 Rob Wile, "153 Years Ago Today, An Unemployed Sick Man Drilled The First Modern Oil Well" *Business Insider* (27 August 2012), online: www.businessinsider.com/edwin-drake-first-modern-oil-well-153-years-ago-2012-8.

21 Cutler Cleveland, "The History of Oil Production in the United States" Boston University: Institute for Global Sustainability (11 September 2023), online: https://visualizingenergy.org/the-history-of-oil-production-in-the-united-states/.

22 Wallis Snowdon, "Leduc No. 1: Seven Decades Ago, a Single Oil Well Changed Alberta History" *CBC News* (13 February 2017), online: www.cbc.ca/news/canada/edmonton/leduc-oil-discovery-anniversary-oil-boom-history-1.3980331.

23 Larry Pratt & John Richards, *Prairie Capitalism: Power and Influence in the New West* (Toronto: McLelland & Stewart, 1979).

24 Stephen Clarkson, *Does North America Exist? Governing the Continent after NAFTA and 9/11* (Toronto: University of Toronto Press, 2008) at 184.

25 Gregory J Inwood, *Continentalizing Canada: The Politics and Legacy of the Macdonald Royal Commission* (Toronto: University of Toronto Press, 2005) at 38.

26 *Ibid* at 185.

27 *Ibid*.

28 Stephen Clarkson & Matto Mildenberger, *Dependent America? How Canada and Mexico Construct US Power* (Toronto: University of Toronto Press, 2011) at 76.

29 "US Senator Sold on the Oil Sands" *Globe and Mail* (17 September 2020), cited in Stephen Clarkson & Matto Mildenberger, *Dependent America? How Canada and Mexico Construct US Power* (Toronto: University of Toronto Press, 2011) at 57.

30 Clarkson and Mildenberger, above note 29 at 70.

31 United States, National Energy Policy Development Group, *Reliable, Affordable, and Environmentally Sound Energy for America's Future: Report of the National Energy Policy Development Group [Cheney Report]* (Washington, DC: May 2001) at xv.

32 CBC News, "PM: Dion's Carbon Tax Would 'Screw Everybody'" (20 June 2008), online: www.cbc.ca/news/canada/pm-dion-s-carbon-tax-would-screw-everybody-1.696762.

33 Monica Gattinger & Julien Tohme, "Canada-US Energy Futures in an Age of Climate Change: Balancing Market, Environment, and Security Imperatives in Uncertain, Disruptive Times," in David M Thomas & Christopher Sands, eds, *Canada and the United States: Differences That Count*, 5th ed (Toronto: University of Toronto Press, 2023) at 356.

34 Alex Boutilier & Bruce Campion-Smith, "Liberals Approve Trans Mountain Pipeline, Reject Northern Gateway Plan" *Toronto Star* (29 November 2016),

online: www.thestar.com/news/canada/2016/11/29/liberals-approve-trans-mountain-line-3-pipeline-projects.html.

35 Canada, Natural Resources Canada, "Government of Canada Announces Pipeline Plan That Will Protect the Environment and Grow the Economy" (29 November 2016), online: www.canada.ca/en/natural-resources-canada/news/2016/11/government-canada-announces-pipeline-plan-that-will-protect-environment-grow-economy.html.

36 *Ibid*.

37 Jeremy Berke, "'No Country Would Find 173 Billion Barrels of Oil in the Ground and Just Leave Them': Justin Trudeau Gets a Standing Ovation at an Energy Conference in Texas" *Business Insider* (10 March 2017), online: www.businessinsider.com/trudeau-gets-a-standing-ovation-at-energy-industry-conference-oil-gas-2017-3.

38 Evan Vucci, "A Chronological History of Controversial Keystone XL Pipeline Project" *CBC News* (1 January 2017), online: www.cbc.ca/news/politics/keystone-xlpipeline-timeline-1.3950156.

39 Gregory Korte & David Jackson, "Obama Administration Rejects Keystone Pipeline" *USA Today* (6 November 2015), online: www.usatoday.com/story/news/politics/2015/11/06/obama-reject-keystone-pipeline/75293270/.

40 Rahul Kalvapalle, "Will Keystone XL Be Good for Canada? Depends Who You Ask" *Global News* (25 January 2027), online: http://globalnews.ca/news/3203600/willkeystone-xl-be-good-for-canada-depends-who-you-ask/.

41 Kate Aronhoff, "Meet the Nebraskans Who Could Stop Keystone XL (Again)" *In These Times* (6 April 2017), online: https://inthesetimes.com/article/meet-the-nebraskans-who-could-stop-keystone-xl-again.

42 Matthew Brown, "Keystone XL Pipeline Nixed After Biden Stands Firm on Permit" *AP News* (9 June 2021), online: https://apnews.com/article/donald-trump-joe-biden-keystone-pipeline-canada-environment-and-nature-141eabd7cca6449dfbd2dab8165812f2.

43 Gattinger & Tohme, above note 33 at 347–38.

44 Chris Cillizza, "It's Time to Admit It: Mitt Romney Was Right About Russia" *CNN: The Point* (27 February 2022), online: www.cnn.com/2022/02/22/politics/mitt-romney-russia-ukraine/index.html.

45 Nick Robertson, "Obama Defends 2014 Crimea Response: 'We Challenged Putin with the Tools We Had at the Time'" *The Hill* (22 June 2023), online: https://thehill.com/blogs/blog-briefing-room/4063939-obama-defends-2014-crimea-response-in-cnn-interview/.

46 Dylan Scott, "July 27, 2016: Trump Publicly Asked Russia to Find Hillary's Emails. They Acted Within Hours" *Vox* (13 July 2018), online: www.vox.com/policy-and-politics/2018/7/13/17569264/mueller-indictment-trump-russia-email-hack.

## Notes

47 Andrew Desiderio & Martin Matishak, "Senate Intel Russia Probe Enters Homestretch with Key Unanimous Approval" *Politico* (6 April 2020), online: www.politico.com/news/2020/04/06/senate-intel-report-russia-169194.

48 Gregory Eady et al, "Exposure to the Russian Internet Research Agency Foreign influence Campaign on Twitter in the 2016 US Election and its Relationship to Attitudes and Voting Behavior" 14 *Nature Communications* (2023) at 62.

49 Jordyn Phelps & Meridith McGraw, "Trump Casts Doubt on US Intelligence, Calls Putin's Meddling Denial 'Strong and Powerful'" *ABC News* (16 July 2018), online: https://abcnews.go.com/Politics/stakes-high-expectations-low-trump-putin-meet-helsinki/story?id=56603366.

50 Joseph Gedeon, "Trump Calls Putin 'Genius' and 'Savvy' for Ukraine Invasion" *Politico* (23 February 2022), online: www.politico.com/news/2022/02/23/trump-putin-ukraine-invasion-00010923.

51 Katherine Doyle, "Trump and Putin Have Talked as Many as 7 Times Since 2021, New Book Claims" *NBC News* (8 October 2024), online: https://www.nbcnews.com/politics/donald-trump/trump-putin-talked-many-7-2021-new-book-claims-rcna174528.

52 United States, The White House, "Remarks by President Biden on Russia's Unprovoked and Unjustified Attack on Ukraine" (24 February 2022), online: www.whitehouse.gov/briefing-room/speeches-remarks/2022/02/24/remarks-by-president-biden-on-russias-unprovoked-and-unjustified-attack-on-ukraine/.

53 Joan E Greve, "US 'Out of Money' for Ukraine: Six Things to Know About the Aid Standoff" *The Guardian* (4 December 2023), online: www.theguardian.com/us-news/2023/dec/04/republicans-oppose-ukraine-funding-white-house.

54 Nick Patton Walsh, "Trump's Incendiary NATO Remarks Send Very Real Shudders Through Europe" *CNN* (12 February 2024), online: www.cnn.com/2024/02/12/europe/trump-nato-putin-europe-analysis-intl/index.html.

55 Leyland Cecco, "In Canada, World's Second Largest Ukrainian Diaspora Grieves Invasion" *The Guardian* (3 March 2022), online: www.theguardian.com/world/2022/mar/03/canada-ukraine-diaspora-relief-efforts-russia-attack.

56 John Paul Tasker, "Anthony Rota Resigns as Speaker after Honouring Ukrainian Veteran Who Fought with Nazi Unit" *CBC News* (28 September 2023), online: www.cbc.ca/news/politics/speaker-anthony-rota-resignation-1.6978422.

57 Cloe Kim, "Chinese Spy Balloon Did Not Collect Information, Says Pentagon" *BBC* News (29 June 2023), online: www.bbc.com/news/world-us-canada-66062562.

58 John Ruwitch & Emily Feng, "Taiwan's President Tsai Meets Kevin McCarthy Despite China's Warnings" *NPR* (5 April 2023), online: www.npr.org/2023/04/05/1167872114/kevin-mccarthy-taiwan-president-tsai-meeting-california-china.

59 Noah Berman, Lindsay Maizland & Andrew Chatzky, "Is China's Huawei a Threat to US National Security?" *Council on Foreign Relations* (8 February 2023), online: www.cfr.org/backgrounder/chinas-huawei-threat-us-national-security.

60 Sapna Maheshwari & Amanda Holpuch, "Why Countries Are Trying to Ban TikTok" *New York Times* (12 December 2023), online: www.nytimes.com/article/tiktok-ban.html.

61 CBC News, "The Meng Wanzhou Huawei Saga: A Timeline" *CBC News* (24 September 2021), online: www.cbc.ca/news/meng-wanzhou-huawei-kovrig-spavor-1.6188472.

62 Adam Zivo, "It Turns Out It Was One Michael and Another Michael" *National Post* (18 November 2023), online: https://nationalpost.com/opinion/adam-zivo-it-turns-out-it-was-one-michael-and-another-michael.

63 CBC News, "Alleged Chinese Police Stations Still Open in Quebec, Despite Minister's Claims" (1 May 2023), online: www.cbc.ca/news/politics/alleged-chinese-police-stations-still-open-1.6828345.

64 Paula Newton & Caitlin Hu, "Canada's Ex-conservative Party Leader Says Chinese Misinformation Campaign Targeted Him in Last Election" *CNN* (21 May 2023), online: www.cnn.com/2023/05/30/americas/canada-china-otoole-intl/index.html.

65 Darren Major, "What We Know So Far About the Public Inquiry into Foreign Interference" *CBC News* (7 September 2023), online: www.cbc.ca/news/politics/how-will-foreign-interference-inquiry-work-1.6959808.

## CHAPTER EIGHT | Looking Ahead: Comparing Canada and the United States and Canadian-American Relations

1 Norman Hillmer & JL Granatstein, *For Better or Worse: Canada and the United States into the Twenty-First Century* (Toronto: Thomson Nelson, 2007) at 321.

2 See Michael Adams, "American Backlash, Canadian Compromise: 30 Years of Divergence," in David M Thomas & Christopher Sands, eds, *Canada and the United States: Differences That Count* (Toronto: University of Toronto Press, 2023) at 56–72 and Michael Adams, *Fire and Ice: The United States, Canada and The Myth of Converging Values* (Toronto: Penguin, 2009).

# Bibliography

## Canadian Court Cases

*Adler v Ontario*, [1996] 3 SCR 609

*The Attorney General of Ontario v The Attorney General of Canada*, [1897] AC 199, [1896] UKPC 20

*Canada (AG) v Alberta (AG) and others*, [1921] UKPC 107, [1922] 1 AC 191

*Canada (AG) v Ontario (AG) and others*, [1937] UKPC 6

*Canadian Industrial Gas & Oil Ltd v Government of Saskatchewan et al*, [1978] 2 SCR 545

*Carter v Canada*, 2015 SCC 5

*Chaoulli v Quebec*, 2005 SCC 35

*Citizens Insurance Co of Canada and Queen Insurance Co v Parsons (Canada)*, [1881] UKPC 50

*Ford v Quebec (AG)*, [1988] 2 SCR 712

*Fort Frances Pulp and Paper Company Ltd v Manitoba Free Press Co Ltd and others (Ontario)*, [1923] UKPC 64, [1923] AC 695

*R v Keegstra*, [1990] 3 SCR 697

*R v Morgentaler*, [1988] 1 SCR 30

*R v Parker*, 2000 CanLII 5762 (Ont CA)

*R v Vaillancourt*, [1987] 2 SCR 636

*Reference re Anti-Inflation Act*, [1976] 2 SCR 373

*Reference re Pan-Canadian Securities Regulation*, 2018 SCC 48

*Reference re Resolution to Amend the Constitution*, [1981] 1 SCR 753

*Reference re Greenhouse Gas Pollution Pricing Act*, 2021 SCC 11

*Toronto Electric Commissioners v Colin G Snider and others (Ontario)*, [1925] UKPC 2, [1925] AC 396

## United States Court Cases

*Buckley v Valeo*, 424 US 1 (1976)

*Cherokee Nation v Georgia*, 30 US 1 (1831)

*Citizens United v FEC*, 558 US 310 (2010)

*Dobbs v Jackson Women's Health Organization*, 597 US 215 (2022)

*Gonzales v Raich*, 545 US 1 (2005)

*Heart of Atlanta Motel, Inc v United States*, 379 US 241 (1964)

*Lemon v Kurtzman*, 403 US 602 (1971)

*McCulloch v Maryland*, 17 US 316 (1819)

*Myers v United States*, 272 US 52 (1926)

*Planned Parenthood v Casey*, 505 US 833 (1992)

*Printz v United States*, 521 US 898 (1997)

*Pruneyard Shopping Center v Robins*, 447 US 74 (1980)

*RAV v City of St Paul*, 505 US 377 (1992)

*Robinson Twp v Pa Pub Util Comm'n*, 83 A3d 901 (Pa 2013).

*Roe v Wade*, 410 US 113 (1973)

*Smith v Collin*, 439 US 916 (1978)

*Snyder v Phelps*, 562 US 443 (2011)

*South Dakota v Dole*, 483 US 203 (1987)

*United States v Alfonso D Lopez, Jr*, 514 US 549 (1995)

*United States v Lanza*, 260 US 377 (1922)

*Wickard v Filburn*, 317 US 111 (1942)

*Zelman-Simmons v Harris*, 536 US 639 (2002)

## Secondary Sources, Government Publications, and Journal Articles

ADAMS, MICHAEL. "American Backlash, Canadian Compromise: 30 Years of Divergence," in David M Thomas & Christopher Sands, eds, *Canada and the United States: Differences That Count*, 5th ed (Toronto: University of Toronto Press, 2023).

———. *Fire and Ice: The United States, Canada and The Myth of Converging Values* (Toronto: Penguin, 2009).

ADAMS, MICHAEL & ANDREW PARKIN. "The Differences between Canada and the US Remain Significant." *Policy Options*, 20 December 2022, online: https://policyoptions.irpp.org/magazines/december-2022/the-differences-between-canada-and-the-u-s-remain-significant/.

ADAMS, SHARON. "The Battle of Ridgeway." *Legion: Canada's Military History Magazine*, 1 June 2021, online: https://legionmagazine.com/en/the-battle-of-ridgeway/.

AIELLO, RACHEL. "Poilievre Pans Trudeau's Carbon Pricing Pivot, Liberals Pitch Pause as 'Great News.'" *CTV News*, 27 October 2023, online: www.ctvnews.ca/politics/poilievre-pans-trudeau-s-carbon-pricing-pivot-liberals-pitch-pause-as-great-news-1.6620250.

AITKEN, HUGH GJ. "Defensive Expansion: The State and Economic Growth in Canada," in Hugh GJ Aitken, ed, *The State and*

*Economic Growth,* New York: Social Science Research Council, 1959 at 183–221.

ALBO, GREG & CHRIS BAILEY. "Beyond Economic Nationalism: Clashes with Canadian Capitalism," in Cy Gonick, ed, *Canada Since 1960: A People's History* (Toronto: James Lorimer and Company, 2016) at 358–97.

APPLE JR., RW. "Mud on the Senate Floor: All Parties Blame One Another for Disclosures That Sting." *New York Times*, 5 March 1989, online: www.nytimes.com/1989/03/05/us/mud-senate-floor-tower-debate-all-parties-blame-one-another-for-disclosures-that.html.

ARONHOFF, KATE. "Meet the Nebraskans Who Could Stop Keystone XL (Again)," in *These Times*, 6 April 2017, online: https://inthesetimes.com/article/meet-the-nebraskans-who-could-stop-keystone-xl-again.

AUSTEN, IAN. "Canada Reaches Settlement with Torture Victim." *New York Times*, 26 January 2007, online: www.nytimes.com/2007/01/26/world/americas/26cnd-canada.html.

AYRES, JEFFREY M. *Defying Conventional Wisdom: Political Movements and Popular Contention against North American Free Trade* (Toronto: University of Toronto Press, 1998).

AZZI, STEPHEN. *Reconcilable Differences: A History of Canada-US Relations* (Toronto: Oxford University Press, 2014).

BAILEY, IAN. "Politics Briefing: Trade Issues High on the Agenda as Bilateral Meetings Get Under Way at Three Amigos Summit." *The Globe and Mail*, 18 November 2021, online: www.theglobeandmail.com/politics/article-politics-briefing-trade-issues-high-on-the-agenda-as-bilateral/.

BARRERA, JORGE. "Trump's Border Czar Says Canadian Border Is an 'Extreme' Vulnerability." *CBC News*, 13 November 2024, online: www.cbc.ca/news/canada/border-czar-canada-vulnerable-1.7381797.

## Bibliography

BEER, SAMUEL H. *To Make a Nation: The Rediscovery of American Federalism* (Cambridge, MA: Belknap Press, 1993).

BERKE, JEREMY. "'No Country Would Find 173 Billion Barrels of Oil in the Ground and Just Leave Them': Justin Trudeau Gets a Standing Ovation at an Energy Conference in Texas." *Business Insider*, 10 March 2017, online: http://www.businessinsider.com/trudeau-gets-a-standing-ovation-at-energy-industry-conference-oil-gas-2017-3.

BERMAN, NOAH. "President Biden Has Banned Some US Investment in China. Here's What to Know." *Council on Foreign Relations*, 29 August 2023, online: www.cfr.org/in-brief/president-biden-has-banned-some-us-investment-china-heres-what-know.

BERMAN, NOAH, LINDSAY MAIZLAND & ANDREW CHATZKY. "Is China's Huawei a Threat to US National Security?" *Council on Foreign Relations*, 8 February 2023, online: www.cfr.org/backgrounder/chinas-huawei-threat-us-national-security.

BIVENS, JOSH & JORI KANDRA. "CEO Pay Slightly Declined in 2022 but It Has Soared 1,209.2% Since 1978 Compared with a 15.3% Rise in Typical Workers' Pay." *Economic Policy Institute*, 21 September 2023, online: www.epi.org/publication/ceo-pay-in-2022/#:~:text=In%202022%2C%20CEOs%20were%20paid,wage%20earners%20in%20the%20U.S.

BLAIS RE, SHAUN BOWLER & BERNARD GROFFMAN. "Electoral and Party Systems," in Paul J Quirk, ed, *The United States and Canada: How Two Democracies Differ and Why It Matters* (Toronto: Oxford University Press, 2019) at 48–78.

BLAKE, MEREDITH, "The Woman Behind 'Roe vs. Wade' Didn't Change Her Mind on Abortion. She Was Paid." *Los Angeles Times*, 19 May 2020, online: www.latimes.com/entertainment-arts/tv/story/2020-05-19/roe-v-wade-jane-roe-norma-mccorvey-hulu-doc-abortion.

BORDERS, WILLIAM. "Canadian Record Hailing US a Hit." *New York Times*, 13 June 1974, online: www.nytimes.com/1974/

01/13/archives/canadian-record-hailing-us-a-hit-journalist-tired-of-hearing.html.

BOUTILIER, ALEX & BRUCE CAMPION-SMITH. "Liberals Approve Trans Mountain Pipeline, Reject Northern Gateway Plan." *Toronto Star*, 29 November 2016, online: www.thestar.com/news/canada/2016/11/29/liberals-approve-trans-mountain-line-3-pipeline-projects.html.

BOWEN, WARREN. "Do the Math: Canadians Aren't Getting the Government They're Voting For." *CBC News*, 9 June 2023, online: www.cbc.ca/news/opinion/opinion-warren-bowen-electoral-change-1.5333743.

BOYCHUK, GERARD W. *National Health Insurance in the United States and Canada: Race, Territory and the Roots of Difference* (Washington, DC: Georgetown University Press, 2008).

BOYKO, JOHN. *Blood and Daring* (Toronto: Alfred A Knopf Canada, 2013).

BRADFORD, NEIL. "Structuring Canada's National Policy Debate: The Royal Commission on Canada's Economic Prospects," in Gregory J Inwood & Carolyn M Johns, eds, *Commissions of Inquiry and Policy Change: A Comparative Analysis* (Toronto: University of Toronto Press, 2014) at 49–69.

BRITISH COLUMBIA. *British Columbia's Carbon Tax*, online: https://www2.gov.bc.ca/gov/content/environment/climate-change/clean-economy/carbon-tax.

BROOKS, STEPHEN. *Canadian Democracy*, 8th ed (Toronto: Oxford University Press, 2015).

BROOKS, STEPHEN, DONALD E ABELSON & MELISSA HAUSSMAN. *Understanding American Politics*, 3rd ed (Toronto: University of Toronto Press, 2024).

BROWN, MATTHEW. "Keystone XL Pipeline Nixed After Biden Stands Firm on Permit." *AP News*. 9 June 2021, online: https://apnews.com/article/donald-trump-joe-biden-keystone-pipeline-canada-environment-and-nature-141eabd7cca6449dfbd2dab8165812f2.

BURKINSHAW, SARAH, YAZ TERAJIMA & CAROLYN A WILKINS. "Income Inequality in Canada." *Bank of Canada Staff Discussion Paper.* 26 July 2022, online: www.bankofcanada.ca/wp-content/uploads/2022/07/sdp2022-16.pdf.

BURNEY, DEREK H. *Getting It Done: A Memoir* (Montreal: McGill-Queen's University Press, 2005).

CAIRNS, ALAN C. "The Living Canadian Constitution," in Peter J Meekison, ed, *Canadian Federalism: Myth or Reality?* 3d ed (Toronto: Methuen, 1971) at 86–99.

CALIFORNIA, AIR RESOURCES BOARD. "At COP26: California Signs Joint Declaration with New Zealand, Québec to Cooperate in Fight Against Climate Change," online: https://ww2.arb.ca.gov/news/cop26-california-signs-joint-declaration-new-zealand-quebec-cooperate-fight-against-climate.

CAMERON, DAVID R. "Lord Durham Then and Now," in Robert C Vipond, ed, *The Daily Plebiscite: Federalism, Nationalism and Canada* (Toronto: University of Toronto Press, 2021) at 65–85.

CANADA, DEPARTMENT OF FINANCE. *Annual Financial Report of the Government of Canada Fiscal Year 2022–2023*, online: www.canada.ca/en/department-finance/services/publications/annual-financial-report/2023/report.html.

———. *Canada's Medical Assistance in Dying (MAID) Law*, online: www.justice.gc.ca/eng/cj-jp/ad-am/bk-di.html.

———. *Federal Transfers to Provinces and Territories,* online: www.canada.ca/en/department-finance/programs/federal-transfers.html#Major.

———. "Where Our Legal System Comes From," in *Canada's System of Justice*, 2015, online: www.justice.gc.ca/eng/csj-sjc/just/img/courten.pdf.

CANADA, ELECTIONS CANADA. *Limits on Contributions 2023*, online: www.elections.ca/content.aspx?section=pol&dir= lim&document=lim2023&lang=e.

———. "The Role of the Electoral Boundaries Commissions in the Federal Redistribution Process," online: www.elections.ca/content.aspx?section=res&dir=cir/red/rolecom&document=index&lang=e.

CANADA, ENVIRONMENT AND NATURAL RESOURCES. "How Carbon Pricing Works," online: www.canada.ca/en/environment-climate-change/services/climate-change/pricing-pollution-how-it-will-work/putting-price-on-carbon-pollution.html.

CANADA, GLOBAL AFFAIRS CANADA. *Softwood Lumber*, online: www.international.gc.ca/controls-controles/softwood-bois_oeuvre/index.aspx?lang=eng.

———. *Softwood Lumber: Recent Developments*, online: www.international.gc.ca/controls-controles/softwood-bois_oeuvre/recent.aspx?lang=eng.

———. *Minister Ng Welcomes NAFTA Dispute Panel Ruling on US Duties on Canadian Softwood Lumber*, online: www.canada.ca/en/global-affairs/news/2023/10/minister-ng-welcomes-nafta-dispute-panel-ruling-on-us-duties-on-canadian-softwood-lumber.html.

CANADA, GOVERNMENT OF CANADA. "Canada-United States Relations," online: www.international.gc.ca/country-pays/us-eu/relations.aspx?lang=eng.

———. "North American Free Trade Agreement (NAFTA) — Fast Facts," online: www.international.gc.ca/trade-commerce/trade-agreements-accords-commerciaux/agr-acc/nafta-alena/fta-ale/facts.aspx?lang=eng.

———. "Equalization Program," 18 May 2023, online: www.canada.ca/en/department-finance/programs/federal-transfers/equalization.html.

CANADA, HEALTH CANADA. *Government of Canada Announces Deductions and Next Steps to Curb Private Health Care Paid Out-of-Pocket*, 10 March 2023, online: www.canada.ca/en/health-canada/news/2023/03/government-of-canada-announces-deductions-and-next-steps-to-curb-private-health-care-paid-out-of-pocket.html.

CANADA, LIBRARY OF PARLIAMENT. *The Parliamentary Financial Cycle* (Ottawa: Library of Parliament, 2021).

CANADA, NATURAL RESOURCES CANADA. "Government of Canada Announces Pipeline Plan That Will Protect the Environment and Grow the Economy," 29 November 2016, online: www.canada.ca/en/natural-resources-canada/news/2016/11/government-canada-announces-pipeline-plan-that-will-protect-environment-grow-economy.html.

CANADA, OFFICE OF THE COMMISSIONER FOR FEDERAL JUDICIAL AFFAIRS. "What Is the Process for Appointing Supreme Court of Canada Judges?" online: www.fja-cmf.gc.ca/scc-csc/2023/questions-eng.html.

CANADA, PARLIAMENT OF CANADA. *Medical Assistance in Dying in Canada: Choices for Canadians. Report of the Special Joint Committee on Medical Assistance in Dying*, February 2023, 44th Parliament, 1st Session.

CANADA, PRIME MINISTER OF CANADA. *Delivering for Canadians Now: A Supply and Confidence Agreement from March 22, 2022 Until When Parliament Rises in June of 2025*, online: https://pm.gc.ca/en/news/news-releases/2022/03/22/delivering-canadians-now.

CANADA, PRIVY COUNCIL OFFICE. *Foreign Ownership and the Structure of Canadian Industry: Report of the Task Force on the Structure of Canadian Industry* (Ottawa: Queen's Printer, 1968).

CANADA, PUBLIC SAFETY CANADA. *Beyond the Border Action Plan*, 4 February 2011, online: www.publicsafety.gc.ca/cnt/brdr-strtgs/bynd-th-brdr/ctn-pln-en.aspx.

CANADA, STATISTICS CANADA. *Foreign Direct Investment, 2022*, 18 April 2023, online: www150.statcan.gc.ca/n1/daily-quotidien/230428/dq230428b-eng.htm.

CBC ARCHIVES. "The King-Byng Affair." *CBC News*. CBC/Radio Canada, 2004, online: www.cbc.ca/player/play/1776946871.

CBC NEWS. "Alleged Chinese Police Stations Still Open in Quebec, Despite Minister's Claims." 1 May 2023, online: www.cbc.ca/news/politics/alleged-chinese-police-stations-still-open-1.6828345.

——. "AltaGas Launches $8.4-Billion Takeover of US Power Company WGL Holdings." 25 January 2017, online: www.cbc.ca/news/canada/calgary/altagas-takeover-wgl-holdings-1.3952336.

——. "McCain Defends Napolitano, Insists 9/11 Perpetrators Came from Canada." 24 April 2009, online: www.cbc.ca/news/world/mccain-defends-napolitano-insists-9-11-perpetrators-came-from-canada-1.830149.

——. "The Meng Wanzhou Huawei Saga: A Timeline." 24 September 2021, online: www.cbc.ca/news/meng-wanzhou-huawei-kovrig-spavor-1.6188472.

——. "NS Man Guilty of Hate Crime in Cross-Burning." 9 November 2010, online: www.cbc.ca/news/canada/nova-scotia/n-s-man-guilty-of-hate-crime-in-cross-burning-1.925313.

——. "PM: Dion's Carbon Tax Would 'Screw Everybody.'" 20 June 2008, online: www.cbc.ca/news/canada/pm-dion-s-carbon-tax-would-screw-everybody-1.696762.

——. "Trudeau Pauses for 21 Seconds Before Answering Question About Trump's Response to US Protests." 21 June 2020, online: www.youtube.com/watch?v=SeaDi-0Nz8w.

——. "US Puts Machine-Guns on Great Lakes Coast Guard Vessels." 15 March 2006, online: www.cbc.ca/news/canada/u-s-puts-machine-guns-on-great-lakes-coast-guard-vessels-1.622621.

———. "When Brian Mulroney Upsized the Senate to Pass the GST." *CBC News Archives*, 27 September 2018, online: www.cbc.ca/archives/when-brian-mulroney-upsized-the-senate-to-pass-the-gst-1.4839649.

CECCO, LEYLAND. "In Canada, World's Second Largest Ukrainian Diaspora Grieves Invasion." *The Guardian*, 3 March 2022, online: www.theguardian.com/world/2022/mar/03/canada-ukraine-diaspora-relief-efforts-russia-attack.

CENTERS FOR DISEASE CONTROL AND PREVENTION. *COVID Data Tracker*, online: covid.cdc.gov/covid-data-tracker/#datatracker-home.

———. "Assault or Homicide." *National Center for Disease Statistics*. 29 December 2023, online: www.cdc.gov/nchs/fastats/homicide.htm#print.

CHOCKSHI, NIRAI & MARK WALKER. "US Approves $31 Billion Merger of Two Big Railroads." *New York Times*, 15 March 2023, online: www.nytimes.com/2023/03/15/business/canadian-pacific-kansas-city-southern-merger.html.

CILLIZZA, CHRIS. "It's Time to Admit It: Mitt Romney Was Right About Russia." *CNN: The Point*, 27 February 2022, online: www.cnn.com/2022/02/22/politics/mitt-romney-russia-ukraine/index.html.

CLARKSON, STEPHEN. *Does North America Exist? Governing the Continent after NAFTA and 9/11* (Toronto: University of Toronto Press, 2008).

———. *Uncle Sam and US: Globalization, Neoconservatism, and the Canadian State* (Toronto: University of Toronto Press, 2002).

CLARKSON, STEPHEN & MATTO MILDENBERGER. *Dependent America? How Canada and Mexico Construct US Power* (Toronto: University of Toronto Press, 2011).

CLEVELAND, CUTLER. "The History of Oil Production in the United States." Boston University: Institute for Global

Sustainability, 11 September 2023, online: https://visualizingenergy.org/the-history-of-oil-production-in-the-united-states/.

COMMONWEALTH OF MASSACHUSETTS. "Health Care Reform for Individuals, 13 November 2023, online: www.mass.gov/info-details/health-care-reform-for-individuals.

CONGRESSIONAL RESEARCH SERVICE. *History, Evolution, and Practices of the President's State of the Union Address: Frequently Asked Questions*. Updated 5 February 2019, online: https://crsreports.congress.gov/product/pdf/R/R44770/10.

*Constitution Act, 1982,* being Schedule B to the *Canada Act 1982* (UK), 1982, c II, ss 36(2) and 91.

COOK, RAMSAY. *The Maple Leaf Forever: Essays on Nationalism and Politics in Canada* (Toronto: Macmillan, 1971).

COOK, RAMSAY, JOHN C RICKER & JOHN T SAYWELL. *Canada: A Modern Study* (Toronto: Clarke Irwin, 1963).

COVID-19 TRACKER. Online: https://covid19tracker.ca/.

COX, JEFF. "Trump Signs Steel and Aluminum Tariffs That Exempt Canada and Mexico and Leave Door Open to Other Countries." *CNBC*, 8 March 2018, online: www.cnbc.com/2018/03/08/trump-signs-tariffs-that-exempt-canada-and-mexico-open-door-to-others.html.

COYNE, ANDREW. "Canada Is Far from Ready for the Chaos Coming Our Way." *The Globe and Mail*, 13 October 2024, online: www.theglobeandmail.com/opinion/article-canada-is-far-from-ready-for-the-chaos-coming-our-way/.

CNN. "Exit Polls." *CNN Politics*, online: www.cnn.com/election/2020/exit-polls/president/national-results

CUTLER, DAVID M & LAWRENCE H SUMMERS. "The COVID-19 Pandemic and the $16 Trillion Virus." *National Library of Medicine*, 2 November 2020, online: www.ncbi.nlm.nih.gov/pmc/articles/PMC7604733/#:~:text=The%20estimated%20

cumulative%20financial%20costs,GDP%20of%20the%20United%20States.

DALTON, RUSSELL J. "Political Cultures and Values," in Paul J Quirk, ed, *The United States and Canada: How Two Democracies Differ and Why It Matters* (Toronto: Oxford University Press, 2019) at 27–47.

DAWSEY, JOSH, DAMIEN PALETTA & ERICA WERNER. "In Fundraising Speech, Trump Says He Made Up Trade Claim in Meeting with Justin Trudeau." *Washington Post*, 14 March 2018, online: www.washingtonpost.com/news/post-politics/wp/2018/03/14/in-fundraising-speech-trump-says-he-made-up-facts-in-meeting-with-justin-trudeau/.

DEBUSMANN JR., BERND. "Why Is Canada's COVID Death Rate So Much Lower than US?" *BBC News*, 14 February 2022, online: www.bbc.com/news/world-us-canada-60380317.

DELACOURT, SUSAN. "Picking a Fight with Canada Is a Bad Idea, Says Justin Trudeau, but Joe Biden Is Still 'One of the Good Guys.'" *Toronto Star*, 14 December 2021, online: www.thestar.com/politics/political-opinion/2021/12/14/picking-a-fight-with-canada-is-a-bad-idea-says-justin-trudeau-but-joe-biden-is-still-one-of-the-good-guys.html.

DENEVAN, WILLIAM M. *The Native Population of the Americas in 1942*, 2d ed (University of Wisconsin Press, 1992).

DEPARTMENT OF STATE, OFFICE OF THE HISTORIAN. "Proclamation Line of 173, Quebec Act of 1774 and Westward Expansion," online: https://history.state.gov/milestones/1750-1775/proclamation-line-1763.

DEPIETRO, ANDREW. "Counties with the Highest and Lowest Poverty Rates in the US." *Forbes*, online: www.forbes.com/sites/andrewdepietro/2022/02/28/counties-with-the-highest-and-lowest-poverty-rates-in-the-us/?sh=7805b7c965ec.

DESIDERIO, ANDREW & MARTIN MATISHAK. "Senate Intel Russia Probe Enters Homestretch with Key Unanimous

Approval." *Politico*, 6 April 2020, online: www.politico.com/news/2020/04/06/senate-intel-report-russia-169194.

DEWAR, HELEN. "NAFTA Wins Final Congressional Test." *Washington Post*, 21 November 1993, online: www.washingtonpost.com/archive/politics/1993/11/21/nafta-wins-final-congressional-test/4b98cac1-c6cc-4128-b65e-a92b05565b92/.

DOERN, G BRUCE & BRIAN TOMLIN. *Faith and Fear: The Free Trade Story* (Toronto: Stoddart, 1992).

DORAN, CHARLES F. *Forgotten Partnership: US-Canada Relations Today* (Baltimore: Johns Hopkins University Press, 1984).

DORGAN, MICHAEL. "Harris Campaign and Allies Spent More Than $1.4B on Political Ads in Losing Race Against Trump." *Fox Business*, 6 November 2024, online: https://www.foxbusiness.com/politics/harris-campaign-allies-spent-more-than-1-4b-political-ads-losing-race-against-trump.

DOYLE, KATHERINE. "Trump and Putin Have Talked as Many as 7 Times since 2021, New Book Claims." *NBC News*, 8 October 2024, online: https://www.nbcnews.com/politics/donald-trump/trump-putin-talked-many-7-2021-new-book-claims-rcna174528.

DRACHE, DANIEL, ed. *Harold A. Innis: Staples, Markets and Cultural Change. Selected Essays* (Montreal: McGill-Queen's University Press, 1995).

DURKEE, ALISON. "Trump Vs. Harris Fundraising Race: Harris Has Raised Over $1 Billion Since Becoming Nominee, Report Says." *Forbes*, 9 October 2024, online: https://www.forbes.com/sites/alisondurkee/2024/10/09/trump-vs-harris-fundraising-race-harris-has-raised-over-1-billion-since-becoming-nominee-report-says/.

EADY, GREGORY ET AL. "Exposure to the Russian Internet Research Agency Foreign Influence Campaign on Twitter in the 2016 US Election and its Relationship to Attitudes and Voting Behavior." 14:62 *Nature Communications* (2023).

ELAZAR, DANIEL. *American Federalism: A View from the States*, 2d ed (New York: Thomas Y Crowell Company, 1972).

*English Language Unity Act of 2023*, HR 997, S 1109.

FABIAN, JORDAN & SKYLAR WOODHOUSE. "Biden Grows Money Edge Over Trump With $25 Million New York Haul." *Bloomberg News*, 28 March 2024, online: www.bnnbloomberg.ca/biden-grows-money-edge-over-trump-with-25-million-new-york-haul-1.2052701.

FARNEY, JAMES & CLARK BANACK. *Faith, Rights, and Choice: The Politics of Religious Schools in Canada* (Toronto: University of Toronto Press, 2023).

FIRESTONE, DAVID with PHILIP SHENON. "A Hushed but Vital Issue: Thurmond's Health." *New York Times*, 9 March 2001, online: www.nytimes.com/2001/03/09/us/a-hushed-but-vital-issue-thurmond-s-health.html.

FISCHER, DAVID HACKETT. *Albion's Seed: Four British Folkways in America* (New York: Oxford University Press, 1989).

FRASER, GRAHAM. *Playing for Keeps: The Making of the Prime Minister, 1988* (Toronto: McClelland & Stewart, 1989).

FRUM, DAVID. "Is America Still 'the Shining City on a Hill'?" *The Atlantic*, 1 January 2021.

GATTINGER, MONICA & JULIEN TOHME. "Canada-US Energy Futures in an Age of Climate Change: Balancing Market, Environment, and Security Imperatives in Uncertain, Disruptive Times," in David M Thomas & Christopher Sands, eds, *Canada and the United States: Differences That Count*, 5th ed (Toronto: University of Toronto Press, 2023) at 347–68.

GAUSTAD, EDWIN S. *Roger Williams* (New York: Oxford University Press, 2005).

GEDEON, JOSEPH. "Trump Calls Putin 'Genius' and 'Savvy' for Ukraine Invasion." *Politico*, 23 February 2022, online: www.politico.com/news/2022/02/23/trump-putin-ukraine-invasion-00010923.

GELLES, DAVID & MIKE BAKER. "Judge Rules in Favor of Montana Youths in a Landmark Climate Case." *New York Times*, 14 August 2023, online: www.nytimes.com/2023/08/14/us/montana-youth-climate-ruling.html.

GEORGE, R. Proclamation, 7 October 1763, reprinted in RSC 1985, App II, No. 1.

GEPHARDT, ALAN. "The Federal Civil Service and the Death of President James A. Garfield." *Garfield Observer*, September 2012, online: www.nps.gov/articles/000/the-federal-civil-service-and-the-death-of-president-james-a-garfield.htm.

GHITZA, YAIR & JONATHON ROBINSON. "What Happened in 2020 National Analysis." *Catalist*, 8 July 2022, online: https://catalist.us/wh-national/.

GIENAPP, JONATHAN. "Using Beard to Overcome Beardianism: Charles Beard's Forgotten Historicism and the Ideas-Interests Dichotomy" (2014). *Constitutional Commentary*, 550, online: https://scholarship.law.umn.edu/concomm/550.

GIFFORDS LAW CENTER TO PREVENT GUN VIOLENCE. "Gun Laws," online: https://giffords.org/lawcenter/gun-laws/.

GILLESPIE, PATRICK. "Trump Hammers America's 'Worst Trade Deal.'" *CNN Business*, 27 September 2016, online: https://money.cnn.com/2016/09/27/news/economy/donald-trump-nafta-hillary-clinton-debate/.

GIUSTRA, FRANK. "America Is a Broken Nation. Here's How to Fix It in Four Easy Steps (And Why It Will Never Happen)." *Toronto Star*, 7 September 2022, online: www.thestar.com/business/opinion/2022/09/07/how-to-fix-a-broken-america-in-four-easy-steps-which-will-never-happen.html.

GLOBALTV NEWS. "Trump Slams Canada on NAFTA," 26 September 2018, online: https://globalnews.ca/video/4490794/trump-slams-canada-on-nafta.

GLUECK, KATIE. "Trump Throws Fit on Twitter." *POLITICO*, 7 November 2012, online: www.politico.com/story/2012/11/trump-throws-fit-on-twitter-083450.

GONICK, CY, ed. *Canada Since 1960: A People's History* (Toronto: James Lorimer & Company, 2016).

GOTLIEB, ALLAN. *I'll Be with You in a Minute, Mr. Ambassador: The Education of a Canadian Diplomat in Washington* (Toronto: University of Toronto Press, 1991).

GOVERNMENT OF BRITISH COLUMBIA. "Stumpage and Export Fees," 1 November 2023, online: https://www2.gov.bc.ca/gov/content/taxes/natural-resource-taxes/forestry/stumpage.

GRANT, GEORGE. *Lament for a Nation: The Defeat of Canadian Nationalism* (Ottawa: Macmillan of Canada, 1965).

GREVE, JOAN E. "US 'Out of Money' for Ukraine: Six Things to Know about the Aid Standoff." *The Guardian*, 4 December 2023, online: www.theguardian.com/us-news/2023/dec/04/republicans-oppose-ukraine-funding-white-house.

GWYNN, RICHARD. *John A: The Man Who Made Us: The Life and Times of Sir John A. Macdonald*, vol 1 (Toronto: Vintage Canada, 2008).

HALE, GEOFFREY. *So Near, Yet So Far: The Public and Hidden Worlds of Canada-US Relations* (Vancouver: UBC Press, 2012).

———. *The Politics of Taxation in Canada* (Peterborough, ON: Broadview, 2002).

HANCOCK, TREVOR. "Taxes Are the Price We Pay for Civilization." *Victoria Times Colonist*, 3 June 2015, online: www.timescolonist.com/opinion/trevor-hancock-taxes-are-the-price-we-pay-for-civilization-4623145#:~:text=More%20than%20a%20hundred%20years,the%20sinews%20of%20the%20state.%E2%80%9D

HARDER, PATER & EVERT LINDQUIST. "Expenditure Management and Reporting in the Government of Canada: Recent Developments and Backgrounds," in Jacques Bourgault, Maurice Demers & Cynthia Williams, eds., *Public Administration and Public Management: Experiences in Canada* (Sainte-Foy, QC: Les Publications du Quebec, 1997).

HARLES, JOHN. "Choose Your Parents Wisely: Economic Inequality and Mobility in Canada and the United States," in David M Thomas & Christopher Sands, eds, *Canada and the United States: Differences That Count*, 5th ed (Toronto: University of Toronto Press, 2023) at 272–93.

HARTZ, LOUIS. *The Liberal Tradition in America* (New York: Harcourt Brace, 1955).

HARRIS, SOPHIA. "Canadian Drivers with US Licence Plates Harassed by Fellow Canadians." *CBC News*, 3 July 2020, online: www.cbc.ca/news/business/canada-u-s-border-harassment-u-s-license-plates-banff-1.5634534.

HARRISON, KATHRYN. "Environmental Policy: Climate Change," in Paul J Quirk, ed, *The United States and Canada: How Two Democracies Differ and Why It Matters* (Toronto: Oxford University Press, 2019) at 196.

HILLMER, NORMAN & JL GRANATSTEIN. *For Better or Worse: Canada and the United States into the Twenty-First Century* (Toronto: Thomson Nelson, 2007).

HIRSCHFELD, PETER. "Eight Years After Shumlin's 'Crushing' Reversal, Single-Payer Health Care Movement Presses On." *Vermont Public*, 1 March 2022, online: www.vermontpublic.org/vpr-news/2022-03-01/eight-years-after-shumlins-crushing-reversal-single-payer-health-care-movement-presses-on.

HOFSTADTER, RICHARD. "The Paranoid Style in American Politics." *Harper's*, November 1964.

HORN, MICHIEL. *The League for Social Reconstruction: Intellectual Origins of the Democratic Left in Canada, 1930-1942* (Toronto: University of Toronto Press, 1980).

INNIS, HAROLD ADAMS. *The Fur Trade in Canada: An Introduction to Canadian Economic History* (Toronto: University of Toronto Press, 1970 [1930]).

INNOVATIVE RESEARCH GROUP. "Key Value Conflicts Help Explain Differences in Canadian and American Politics," 9 October 2020, online: https://innovativeresearch.ca/canadians-and-americans-are-more-similar-than-you-might-think-but-there-are-key-differences-too/.

INTERNATIONAL MONETARY FUND. "Government Expenditure, Percent of GDP 2022," online: www.imf.org/external/datamapper/exp@FPP/FRA/JPN/GBR/SWE/ESP/ITA/ZAF/IND/CAN/USA.

INWOOD, GREGORY J. *Continentalizing Canada: The Politics and Legacy of the Macdonald Royal Commission* (Toronto: University of Toronto Press, 2005).

———. *Understanding Canadian Federalism: An Introduction to Theory and Practice* (Toronto: Pearson, 2013).

———. *Understanding Canadian Public Administration: An Introduction to Theory and Practice*, 5th ed (Toronto: University of Toronto Press, 2025).

INWOOD, GREGORY J, CAROLYN M JOHNS & PATRICIA L O'REILLY. *Intergovernmental Policy Capacity in Canada. Inside the Worlds of Finance, Environment, Trade and Health Policy* (Montreal: McGill-Queen's University Press, 2012).

ISAAC, THOMAS. *Aboriginal Law*, 5th ed (Toronto: Thomson Reuters, 2016).

JHAPPAN, RADHA. "The 'New World': Legacies of European Colonialism in North America," in Yasmeen Abu-Laban, Radha Jhappan & François Rocher, eds, *Politics in North*

America: Redefining Continental Relations* (Peterborough, ON: Broadview Press, 2008) at 27–50.

KALVAPALLE, RAHUL. "Will Keystone XL Be Good for Canada? Depends Who You Ask." *Global News*, 25 January 2027, online: http://globalnews.ca/news/3203600/will-keystone-xl-be-good-for-canada-depends-who-you-ask/.

KEECH, WILLIAM & WILLIAM SCARTH. "Economic Policy," in Paul J Quirk, ed, *The United States and Canada: How Two Democracies Differ and Why It Matters* (Toronto: Oxford University Press, 2019) at 173–95.

KEENAN, EDWARD. "Remember When Canada and the US Were Friends? Joe Biden Does." *Toronto Star*, 13 November 2020, online: www.thestar.com/news/world/2020/11/13/remember-when-canada-and-the-us-were-friends-joe-biden-does.html.

KELLOGG, PAUL. *Escape from the Staple Trap: Canadian Political Economy after Left Nationalism* (Toronto: University of Toronto Press, 2016).

KENNEDY, GERARD J & MARK MANCINI. "Canadian Courts Are Not Politicized in the American Way." *Policy Options*, 23 January 2023, online: https://policyoptions.irpp.org/magazines/january-2023/politicized-courts-us-canada/.

KHALATBARI, MASIH & ROBERT CRIBB. "Surge in Medically Assisted Deaths Under Canada's MAID Program Outpaces Every Other Country." *Toronto Star*, 27 January 2024, online: www.thestar.com/news/investigations/surge-in-medically-assisted-deaths-under-canada-s-maid-program-outpaces-every-other-country/article_29028f96-bc6b-11ee-8f67-03bf29ac7d34.html.

KIM, CLOE. "Chinese Spy Balloon Did Not Collect Information, Says Pentagon." *BBC* News, 29 June 2023, online: www.bbc.com/news/world-us-canada-66062562.

KIRZINGER, ASHLEY, ALEX MONTERO, LIZ HAMEL & MOLLYANN BRODIE. "5 Charts About Public Opinion on the Affordable Care Act." *KFF*, 14 April 2022, online: www.kff.org/health-reform/poll-finding/5-charts-about-public-opinion-on-the-affordable-care-act-and-the-supreme-court/.

KLASSEN, JEROME & WILLIAM CARROLL. "Transnational Class Formation? Globalization and the Canadian Corporate Network." 17.2 *Journal of World-Systems Research* (2011) at 379–402.

KORTE, GREGORY & DAVID JACKSON. "Obama Administration Rejects Keystone Pipeline." *USA Today*, 6 November 2015, online: www.usatoday.com/story/news/politics/2015/11/06/obama-reject-keystone-pipeline/75293270/.

KWONG, MATT. "Here's How Gerrymandering Games US Elections — And Why This Pennsylvania Decision Matters." *CBC News*, 24 January 2018, online: www.cbc.ca/news/world/gerrymander-explained-1.4360638.

LAMBTON, JOHN GEORGE. "Report on the Affairs of British North America from the Earl of Durham, Her Majesty's High Commissioner," in Robert Stanton, *Journal of the House of Assembly of Upper Canada* (Printer to the Queen's Most Excellent Majesty, 1839), online: https://books.google.ca/books?id=OZBaAAAAYAAJ&pg=PP9#v=onepage&q&f=false.

LANGE, JASON, BO ERICKSON & BRAD HEATH. "Trump's Return to Power Fueled by Hispanic, Working-Class Voter Support." *Reuters*, 7 November 2024, online: https://www.reuters.com/world/us/trumps-return-power-fueled-by-hispanic-working-class-voter-support-2024-11-06/.

LAWLESS, JENNIFER L. *Becoming a Candidate: Political Ambition and the Decision to Run for Office* (Cambridge: Cambridge University Press, 2012), online: www.google.ca/books/edition/Becoming_a_Candidate/AFyNvwEACAAJ?hl=en.

LAZARSKI, LINDSAY. "Outside Expert Advises Pa. Supreme Court in Drawing Congressional District Map." *WHYY*, 18 February 2018, online: https://whyy.org/articles/outside-expert-advises-pa-supreme-court-drawing-congressional-district-map/.

LEBLANC, PAUL. "Video Surfaces of Marjorie Taylor Greene Confronting Parkland Shooting Survivor with Baseless Claims." *CNN*, 28 January 2021, online: www.cnn.com/2021/01/27/politics/marjorie-taylor-greene-david-hogg-video/index.html.

LEVITT, KARI. *Silent Surrender: The Multinational Corporation in Canada* (Toronto: Gage, 1970).

LIBERAL PARTY OF CANADA. *Creating Opportunity: The Liberal Plan for Canada* (Ottawa: Liberal Party of Canada, 1993), online: www.poltext.org/sites/poltext.org/files/plateformesV2/Canada/CAN_PL_1993_LIB_en.pdf.

LIBRARY OF CONGRESS, "Washington as Land Speculator." *George Washington Papers*, online: www.loc.gov/collections/george-washington-papers/articles-and-essays/george-washington-survey-and-mapmaker/washington-as-land-speculator/.

LIPSET, SEYMOUR MARTIN. "Why No Socialism in the United States?" in Seweryn Bialer & Sophia Sluzar, eds, *Radicalism in the Contemporary Age*, vol 1 (New York: Routledge, 1977).

LOCKE, JOHN. *Second Treatise of Government*. Salt Lake City: Project Gutenberg, 22 April 2003 [1690], online: www.gutenberg.org/files/7370/7370-h/7370-h.htm.

LOWRIE, MORGAN. "RCMP Demolish Last Structure at Quebec's Roxham Road Migrant Crossing." *CTV* News, 26 September 2023, online: https://montreal.ctvnews.ca/rcmp-demolish-last-structure-at-quebec-s-roxham-road-migrant-crossing-1.6575998.

MACDONALD, DAVID. "Canada's New Gilded Age: CEO Pay in Canada in 2022" (Ottawa: Canadian Centre for Policy Alternatives, January 2024), online: https://policyalternatives.ca/sites/default/files/uploads/publications/National%20Office/2024/01/canadas-new-gilded-age.pdf.

MACDONALD, IAN L. "JFK's Epic Speech to Parliament — An Enduring Moment in Time." *Policy Magazine*, 17 May 2021, online: www.policymagazine.ca/jfks-epic-speech-to-parliament-an-enduring-moment-in-time/.

MACMILLAN, MARGARET. *Paris 1919: Six Months That Changed the World* (New York: Random House, 2003).

———. "Sleeping with a Very Cranky Elephant: The History of Canada-US Tensions." *The Sunday Magazine*, 15 June 2018, online: www.cbc.ca/radio/sunday/the-sunday-edition-june-17-2018-1.4692469/sleeping-with-a-very-cranky-elephant-the-history-of-canada-u-s-tensions-1.4699017.

MAHANT, EDELGARD & GRAEME S MOUNT. *Invisible and Inaudible in Washington: American Policies Toward Canada* (Vancouver: UBC Press, 1999).

MAHESHWARI, SAPNA & AMANDA HOLPUCH. "Why Countries Are Trying to Ban TikTok." *New York Times*, 12 December 2023, online: www.nytimes.com/article/tiktok-ban.html.

MAHONEY, DENNIS J. "Declaration of Independence." *Society* 46 (1986) at 46–48.

MAIONI, ANTONIA & PIERRE MARTIN, "Health Care in Canada and the United States," in David M Thomas & Christopher Sands, eds, *Canada and the United States: Differences That Count*, 5th ed (Toronto: University of Toronto Press, 2023) at 251–71.

MAIONI, ANTONIA & THEODORE R MARMOR. "Healthcare," in James Quirk ed, *The United States and Canada: How Two*

*Democracies Differ and Why It Matters* (Toronto: Oxford University Press, 2019) at 242–65.

MAJOR, DARREN. "What We Know So Far About the Public Inquiry into Foreign Interference." *CBC News*, 7 September 2023, online: www.cbc.ca/news/politics/how-will-foreign-interference-inquiry-work-1.6959808.

MALCOLMSON, PATRICK & RICHARD MYERS. *The Canadian Regime: An Introduction to Parliamentary Government in Canada*, 4th ed (Toronto: University of Toronto Press, 2009).

MALONE, KELLY GERALDINE. "Trump's Appointees Have Criticized Trudeau, Warned of Border Issues with Canada." *Toronto Star*, 13 November 2024, online: www.thestar.com/news/canada/trumps-appointees-have-criticized-trudeau-warned-of-border-issues-with-canada/article_50eb116c-ba6a-591d-a59d-c4c8d52b9e7c.html.

MALYSHEV, ALEX & SARAH GANLEY. "What Rescheduling to Schedule III Would Mean for the Cannabis Industry." *Reuters*, online: www.reuters.com/legal/litigation/what-rescheduling-schedule-iii-would-mean-cannabis-industry-2023-09-12/.

MARTIN, LAWRENCE. *The Presidents and the Prime Ministers: Washington and Ottawa Face to Face: The Myth of Bilateral Bliss 1867–1982* (Toronto: Doubleday, 1982).

MAS, SUSANA. "Canada's Syrian Refugee Plan Raises Concerns of 'Shortcuts,' Homeland Security Committee Hears." *CBC News*, 3 February 2016, online: www.cbc.ca/news/politics/canada-syrian-refugee-plan-us-senate-committee-shortcuts-1.3431698.

MASCIA, JENNIFER & CHIP BROWNLEE. "A Decade of Mass Shootings, By the Numbers." *The Trace*, 5 October 2023, online: www.thetrace.org/2023/10/mass-shootings-gun-violence-how-many/.

MCCORMICK, PETER. *Supreme at Last: The Evolution of the Supreme Court of Canada* (Toronto: James Lorimer, 2000).

MCMINN, SEAN & ALYSON HURT. "Tracking the Money Race Behind the Presidential Primary Campaign." *NPR*, 16 April 2019, online: www.npr.org/2019/04/16/711812314/tracking-the-money-race-behind-the-presidential-campaign.

MCSHANE, MIKE. "Oh What a Year (For School Choice)." *Forbes*, 19 December 2023, online: www.forbes.com/sites/mikemcshane/2023/12/19/oh-what-a-year-for-school-choice/?sh=2e25d2344f9c.

MERCHANT, LIVINGSTON T. *Neighbours Taken for Granted: Canada and the United States* (New York: Frederick A Praeger, 1965).

MILLER, ERIC. "Remaking NAFTA: Its Origin, Impact and Future." *Canadian Global Affairs Institute Policy Paper*, August 2017.

MINSKY, AMY. "The Finance Minister's New Shoes: A Purely Canadian, Though Mysterious, Tradition." *Global News*, 20 April 2015.

MORROW, ADRIAN, BARRIE MCKENNA & STEPHANIE NOLEN. "From NAFTA to USMCA: Inside the Tense Negotiations That Saved North American Trade." *The Globe and Mail*, 5 October 2018.

MORTON, FL & DAVE SNOW, eds. *Law, Politics and the Judicial Process in Canada*, 4th ed (Calgary: University of Calgary Press, 2008).

NASSER, SHANIFA. "Kevin Johnston Ordered to Pay $2.5M for 'Hateful, Islamophobic' Remarks Against Restaurant Chain Owner." *CBC News*, 13 May 2019, online: www.cbc.ca/news/canada/toronto/kevin-johnston-paramount-2-5-million-mohamad-fakih-1.5134227.

NATIONAL ARCHIVES, FOUNDERS ONLINE. "Thomas Jefferson to William Duane, 4 August 1812," online: https://founders.archives.gov/documents/Jefferson/03-05-02-0231.

NATIONAL CONSTITUTION CENTER STAFF. "The Man Whose Impeachment Vote Saved Andrew Johnson." National Constitution Centre, 16 May 2022, online: https://constitutioncenter.org/blog/the-man-whose-impeachment-vote-saved-andrew-johnson.

NATIONAL POPULAR VOTE. Online: www.nationalpopularvote.com/.

NEW REPUBLIC STAFF. "Boring Headline Contest." *New Republic*, 14 February 2011, online: https://newrepublic.com/article/83443/boring-headline-contest.

NEWELL, MARGARET. "Our Hidden History: Roger Williams and Slavery's Origins." *The Providence Journal*, 29 August 2020.

NEWPORT, FRANK. "US Public Opinion and the Role of Government." *Gallup Polling Matters*, 4 November 2022, online: https://news.gallup.com/opinion/polling-matters/404750/public-opinion-role-government.aspx.

NEWTON, PAULA & CAITLIN HU. "Canada's Ex-conservative Party Leader Says Chinese Misinformation Campaign Targeted Him in Last Election." *CNN*, 21 May 2023, online: www.cnn.com/2023/05/30/americas/canada-china-otoole-intl/index.html.

NEW YORK TIMES. "Tracking Abortion Bans Across the Country," 8 January 2024, online: www.nytimes.com/interactive/2022/us/abortion-laws-roe-v-wade.html.

NGUYEN, TINA. "Trump Appointees Take Turns Praising Him in Bizarre Cabinet Meeting." *Vanity Fair*, 12 June 2017, online: www.vanityfair.com/news/2017/06/donald-trump-cabinet-meeting.

NORTH ATLANTIC TREATY ORGANIZATION. "Resolute Support Mission (RSM): Key Facts and Figures," February 2020, online: www.nato.int/nato_static_fl2014/assets/pdf/2020/2/pdf/2020-02-RSM-Placemat.pdf.

NOVER, SCOTT. "The Grim Reality of Banning Tik Tok." *Time Magazine*, 15 March 2024, online: https://time.com/6952889/tiktok-ban-freedom-of-speech-essay/.

O'DONNELL, CHRISTINE. "I'm Not a Witch. I'm You," online: www.youtube.com/watch?v=ek3OUay2uWw.

OECD DATE. *Social Spending*, online: https://data.oecd.org/socialexp/social-spending.htm.

## Bibliography

OFFICE OF THE PRESS SECRETARY. The White House, 4 February 2011, online: https://obamawhitehouse.archives.gov/the-press-office/2011/02/04/joint-statement-president-obama-and-prime-minister-harper-canada-regul-0.

OFFICE OF THE UNITED STATES TRADE REPRESENTATIVE. "Statement by Neena Moorjani, Spokeswoman for US Trade Representative Rob Portman, Office of the United States Trade Representative," 8 December 2005, online: https://ustr.gov/archive/Document_Library/Spokesperson_Statements/Statement_of_Neena_Moorjani,_Spokesperson,_Regarding_the_Softwood_Lumber_Issue.html.

O'GRADY, JANE & DAVID STAINES, eds. *Northrop Frye on Canada* (Toronto: University of Toronto Press 2003).

O'MALLEY, MARTIN & JUSTIN THOMPSON. "*Prime Ministers and Presidents*." *CBC News*, 22 November 2003, online: www.cbc.ca/canadaus/pms_presidents1.html.

OOSTEROM, NELLE. "A Day for Laurier." *Canada's History*, 12 September 2016, online: www.canadashistory.ca/explore/prime-ministers/a-day-for-laurier.

OPEN SECRETS: FOLLOWING THE MONEY IN POLITICS. Online: www.opensecrets.org/.

OREGON HEALTH AUTHORITY. Oregon Death with Dignity Act 2022 Data Summary, online: www.oregon.gov/oha/PH/PROVIDERPARTNERRESOURCES/EVALUATIONRESEARCH/DEATHWITHDIGNITYACT/Documents/year25.pdf.

ORGANISATION FOR ECONOMIC COOPERATION AND DEVELOPMENT. "Income Inequality." *Data*, online: https://data.oecd.org/inequality/income-inequality.htm.

PANETTA, ALEXANDER & KATIE SIMPSON. "Republican Presidential Candidate Proposes Border Wall with Canada." *CBC News*, 9 November 2023, online: www.cbc.ca/news/world/vivek-ramaswamy-canada-border-wall-1.7023226.

PATTON WALSH, NICK. "Trump's Incendiary NATO Remarks Send Very Real Shudders Through Europe." *CNN*, 12 February 2024, online: www.cnn.com/2024/02/12/europe/trump-nato-putin-europe-analysis-intl/index.html.

PBS FRONTLINE. "Ahmed Ressam's Millennium Plot," online: www.pbs.org/wgbh/pages/frontline/shows/trail/inside/cron.html.

PBS NEWS. "How Canada Got Universal Health Care and What the US Could Learn." *PBS News Hour*, 31 August 2020, online: www.pbs.org/newshour/health/how-canada-got-universal-health-care-and-what-the-u-s-could-learn.

PEW RESEARCH CENTER. "Public Trust in Government 1958–2023," 19 September 2023, online: https://news.gallup.com/opinion/polling-matters/404750/public-opinion-role-government.aspx.

———. "Sizable Difference by Gender, Race and Ethnicity, Age and Education in Midterm Election Preferences," 23 August 2022, online: www.pewresearch.org/politics/2022/08/23/abortion-rises-in-importance-as-a-voting-issue-driven-by-democrats/pp_2022-08-23_midterms_01-01/.

PHELPS, JORDYN & MERIDITH MCGRAW. "Trump Casts Doubt on US intelligence, Calls Putin's Meddling Denial 'Strong and Powerful.'" *ABC News*, 16 July 2018, online: https://abcnews.go.com/Politics/stakes-high-expectations-low-trump-putin-meet-helsinki/story?id=56603366.

PHILLIPS, ANDREW. "Justin Trudeau Is Already Getting It Wrong on Trump." *Toronto Star*, 12 November 2024, online: www.thestar.com/opinion/star-columnists/justin-trudeau-is-already-getting-it-wrong-on-trump/article_6f2f2808-a054-11ef-88f0-fbd77dd1fa22.html.

POLIENGINE. "How Many Politicians Are There in the United States? (2022), online: https://poliengine.com/blog/how-many-politicians-are-there-in-the-us.

PORTER, CATHERINE. "Before the Smiles, Mounting Tensions Between Trudeau and Trump." *New York Times*, 8 June 2018, online: www.nytimes.com/2018/06/08/world/canada/canada-trudeau-trump-us-group-of-7.html.

PRATT, LARRY & JOHN RICHARDS. *Prairie Capitalism: Power and Influence in the New West* (Toronto: McLelland & Stewart, 1979).

PUBLIC CITIZEN. "Final House Vote on NAFTA," 17 November 1993, online: www.citizen.org/article/final-house-vote-on-nafta/.

———. "Trade Adjustment Assistance Database," online: www.citizen.org/tradeadjustment-assistance-database.

QUEBEC, MINISTRY OF ENVIRONMENT. The Fight Against Climate Change, Wildlife and Parks, "The Quebec-California Carbon Market," online: www.environnement.gouv.qc.ca/changements/carbone/documents-spede/LinkingMarket.pdf.

QUINN, EILÍS. "Canada Extends Continental Shelf Claim, Increasing Overlaps with Russia in Arctic." *Eye on the Arctic Radio Canada International*, 22 December 2022, online: www.rcinet.ca/eye-on-the-arctic/2022/12/22/canada-extends-continental-shelf-claim-increasing-overlaps-with-russia-in-arctic/.

QUIRK, PAUL J, ed. *The United States and Canada: How Two Democracies Differ and Why It Matters* (Toronto: Oxford University Press, 2019).

RATCLIFFE, SUSAN, ed. *Oxford Essential Quotations*, 4th ed (Oxford: Oxford University Press, 2015).

REESOR, BAYARD. *The Canadian Constitution in Historical Perspective: With a Clause-by-Clause Analysis of the Constitution Acts and the Canada Act* (Scarborough, ON: Prentice Hall, 1992).

RESNICK, PHILIP. "Montesquieu Revisited, or the Mixed Constitution and the Separation of Powers in Canada." 20 *Canadian Journal of Political Science* (June 1987) at 97–115.

RESTUCCIA, ANDREW, BURGESS EVERETT & HEATHER CAYGLE. "Longest Shutdown in History Ends After Trump Relents on Wall." *Politico*, 25 January 2019, online: www.politico.com/story/2019/01/25/trump-shutdown-announcement-1125529.

ROBBERSON, TOD. "Mexico's NAFTA Vote: Rancor, no Suspense." *Washington Post*, 24 November 1993, online: www.washingtonpost.com/archive/politics/1993/11/24/mexicos-nafta-vote-rancor-no-suspense/ddd6c560-ab22-4a91-a340-df5bca4d6ba4/.

ROBERTSON, NICK. "Obama Defends 2014 Crimea Response: 'We Challenged Putin with the Tools We Had at the Time'." *The Hill*, 22 June 2023, online: https://thehill.com/blogs/blog-briefing-room/4063939-obama-defends-2014-crimea-response-in-cnn-interview/.

ROSS UNIVERSITY SCHOOL OF MEDICINE. "US vs. Canadian Healthcare: What Is the Difference?" 11 May 2021, online: https://medical.rossu.edu/about/blog/us-vs-canadian-healthcare.

RUSSELL, PETER. *Constitutional Odyssey: Can Canadians Become a Sovereign People?* 3d ed (Toronto: University of Toronto Press, 2004).

RUSSELL, PETER H, RAINER KNOPFF & TED MORTON. *Federalism and the Charter: Leading Constitutional Decisions. A New Edition* (Toronto: Oxford University Press, 1989).

RUWITCH, JOHN & EMILY FENG. "Taiwan's President Tsai Meets Kevin McCarthy Despite China's Warnings." *NPR*, 5 April 2023, online: www.npr.org/2023/04/05/1167872114/kevin-mccarthy-taiwan-president-tsai-meeting-california-china.

SANDS, CHRISTOPHER. "Was President Biden's Ottawa Visit Good for US-Canada Relations?" *Policy Options*, 29 March 2023, online: https://policyoptions.irpp.org/magazines/march-2023/biden-visit-us-canada-relations/.

SAVOIE, DONALD J. *Governing from the Centre: The Concentration of Power in Canadian Politics* (Toronto: University of Toronto Press, 1999).

———. *The Politics of Public Spending in Canada* (Toronto: University of Toronto Press, 1990).

SCHNEIDER, ERIC C, ARNAV SHAH, MICHELLE M DOTY, ROOSA TIKKANEN, KATHARINE FIELDS & REGINALD D WILLIAMS II. "Mirror, Mirror 2021: Reflecting Poorly: Health Care in the US Compared to Other High-Income Countries." *The Commonwealth Fund*, 4 August 2021, online: www.commonwealthfund.org/publications/fund-reports/2021/aug/mirror-mirror-2021-reflecting-poorly.

SCOTT, DYLAN. "July 27, 2016: Trump Publicly Asked Russia to Find Hillary's Emails. They Acted Within Hours." *Vox*, 13 July 2018, online: www.vox.com/policy-and-politics/2018/7/13/17569264/mueller-indictment-trump-russia-email-hack.

SCOTT, ROBERT E. "NAFTA-Related Job Losses Have Piled up Since 1993." *Economic Policy Institute*, 16 December 2003.

SHRIBMAN, DAVID. "Jan. 6 Panel's Likely Recommendation of Criminal Charges for Trump Would Smash Another Precedent." *The Globe and Mail*, 16 December 2022, online: www.theglobeandmail.com/world/us-politics/article-jan-6-committee-trump-prosecution/.

SIMEON, RICHARD. *Federal-Provincial Diplomacy: The Making of Recent Policy in Canada. With a New Preface and Postscript* (Toronto: University of Toronto Press, 2006).

SIMEON, RICHARD & BERYL A RADIN. "Reflections on Comparing Federalisms: Canada and the United States." 40:3 *Publius: The Journal of Federalism* (2010) at 357–65.

SIMPSON, KATIE. "From Clashes to Candy, the Evolution of Chrystia Freeland's Relationship with her US Trade Counterpart." *CBC News*, 10 October 2018, online: www.cbc.ca/news/politics/freeland-lighthizer-evolution-of-a-trade-relationship-1.4856319.

SMILEY, DONALD. *Canada in Question. Federalism in the 1970s*, 2d ed (Toronto: McGraw-Hill Ryerson, 1976).

SMITH, ALAN. "Republicans Zero in on a New Border — The One with Canada." *NBC News*, 23 January 2024, online: www.nbcnews.com/politics/2024-election/republicans-northern-border-canada-rcna135169.

SMITH, GOLDWYN. *Canada and the Canadian Question* (Toronto: University of Toronto Press, 1971 [1891]).

SMITH, JENNIFER. "Canadian Confederation and the Influence of American Federalism." 21:3 *Canadian Journal of Political Science* (1988) at 443–64. Quoted in GP Browne, *Documents on the Confederation of British North America* (Toronto: McClelland & Stewart, 1969).

SNOWDON, WALLIS. "Leduc No. 1: Seven Decades Ago, a Single Oil Well Changed Alberta History." *CBC News*, 13 February 2017, online: www.cbc.ca/news/canada/edmonton/leduc-oil-discovery-anniversary-oil-boom-history-1.3980331.

SOSSIN, LORNE & PETER H RUSSELL. *Parliamentary Democracy in Crisis* (Toronto: University of Toronto Press, 2009), online: www.google.ca/books/edition/Parliamentary_Democracy_in_Crisis/f9uIZ12yh-UC?hl=en&gbpv=0.

SPEEL, ROBERT. "You'll Hear These 4 Arguments in Defense of the Electoral College. Here's Why They Are Wrong." *St. Louis Post-Dispatch*, 31 March 2019.

STAIRS, DENIS. "Challenges and Opportunities for Canadian Foreign Policy in the Paul Martin Era." 58:4 *International Journal* (Autumn 2003) at 481–506.

STATE OF HAWAII. "About Prepaid Health Care," online: https://labor.hawaii.gov/dcd/home/about-phc/.

STEWART, JDM. "Prime Ministers and Presidents: What Defines a 'Good Relationship'?" *Policy: Canadian Politics and Public*

*Policy*, online: www.policymagazine.ca/prime-ministers-and-presidents-what-defines-a-good-relationship/.

TASKER, JOHN PAUL. "Anthony Rota Resigns as Speaker After Honouring Ukrainian Veteran Who Fought with Nazi Unit." *CBC News*, 28 September 2023, online: www.cbc.ca/news/politics/speaker-anthony-rota-resignation-1.6978422.

TERRY, DON. "Arizona Court Strikes Down Law Requiring English Use." *New York Times*, 29 April 1998, online: www.nytimes.com/1998/04/29/us/arizona-court-strikes-down-law-requiring-english-use.html.

THOMAS, DAVID M & DAVID N BIETTE, eds. *Canada and the United States: Differences That Count*, 4th ed (Toronto: University of Toronto Press, 2014).

THOMPSON, JAMES. *Making North America: Trade, Security and Integration* (Toronto: University of Toronto Press, 2014).

THORNTON, RUSSELL. *American Indian Holocaust and Survival: A Population History Since 1492* (Norman, OK: University of Oklahoma Press, 1990).

TOMBE, TREVOR. *Partners in Prosperity: Exploring the Significance of Canada-US Trade* (Toronto: Canadian Chamber of Commerce, October 2024), online: https://businessdatalab.ca/wp-content/uploads/2024/10/PartnersInProsperity_EN_Final.pdf.

TREW, STEWART. "Say No to New Regulations." *Council of Canadians*, 1 September 2011, online: https://canadians.org/analysis/say-no-new-regulations-canadian-us-manufacturers-brief-ambassadors-their-common-cause/.

UNDERHILL, FRANK. *In Search of Canadian Liberalism* (Toronto: Macmillan, 1961).

UNGAR, RICK. "Here Are the 23 Executive Orders on Gun Safety Signed Today by The President." *Forbes*, 16 January 2013, online: www.forbes.com/sites/rickungar/2013/01/16/

here-are-the-23-executive-orders-on-gun-safety-signed-today-by-the-president/.

UNITED STATES, DEPARTMENT OF STATE. *2023 Investment Climate Statements: Canada*, online: www.state.gov/reports/2023-investment-climate-statements/canada/.

———. "US Relations With Canada," online: http://www.state.gov/r/pa/ei/bgn/2089.htm#travel.

UNITED STATES GENERAL ACCOUNTING OFFICE. "Trade Adjustment Assistance: Improvements Necessary, but Programs Cannot Solve Communities' Long Term Problems," online: www.gao.gov/assets/gao-01-988t.pdf.

UNITED STATES, NATIONAL ENERGY POLICY DEVELOPMENT GROUP. *Reliable, Affordable & Environmentally Sound Energy for America's Future: Report of the National Energy Policy Development Group [Cheney Report]* (Washington, DC, May 2001).

UNITED STATES, THE WHITE HOUSE. "Remarks by President Biden on Russia's Unprovoked and Unjustified Attack on Ukraine," 24 February 2022, online: www.whitehouse.gov/briefing-room/speeches-remarks/2022/02/24/remarks-by-president-biden-on-russias-unprovoked-and-unjustified-attack-on-ukraine/.

UNITED STATES, TREASURY. "How Much Revenue Has the US Government Collected This Year?" *Fiscal Data*, online: https://fiscaldata.treasury.gov/americas-finance-guide/government-revenue/.

US BUREAU OF LABOR STATISTICS. Current Employment Statistics survey, series ID CES3000000001, manufacturing industry, US Department of Labor, 6 February 2018, online: http://www.bls.gov/ces/.

US Const. art. 1 § 8.

US GOVERNMENT ACCOUNTABILITY OFFICE. "COVID-19 Relief: Funding and Spending as of Jan. 31, 2023," 28 February 2023, online: www.gao.gov/products/gao-23-106647.

VAIDYANATHAN, GAYATHRI. "Biden Signs Historic Climate Bill as Scientists Applaud." *Nature*, 16 August 2022, online: www.scientificamerican.com/article/biden-signs-historic-climate-bill-as-scientists-applaud/.

VILCARINO, JENNIFER & CHASE HARRISON. "*Chart: How US Latinos Voted in the 2020 Midterm Election*," 17 November 2022, online: www.as-coa.org/articles/chart-how-us-latinos-voted-2022-midterm-election.

VILLARREAL, M ANGELES & IAN F FERGUSSON. *The North American Free Trade Agreement*. Congressional Research Service, 16 April 2016, online: www.fas.org/sgp/crs/row/R42965.pdf.

VUCCI, EVAN. "A Chronological History of Controversial Keystone XL pipeline Project." *CBC News*, 1 January 2017, online: http://www.cbc.ca/news/politics/keystone-xlpipeline-timeline-1.3950156.

WAITE, PB, ed. *The Confederation Debates in the Provinces of Canada*, Carleton Library Edition (Toronto, McClelland & Stewart, 1963).

WASHINGTON POST. "How Much Money Is Behind Each Campaign?" *The Washington Post* (WP Company, 2016), online: www.washingtonpost.com/graphics/politics/2016-election/campaign-finance/.

WATKINS, MEL. "Why Foreign Ownership Still Matters in 2008: Submission to Competition Policy Review Panel." *Briefing Paper: Trade and Investment Series* [Canadian Center for Policy Alternatives, 2008]. 9, 1, 1.

WEINGAST, BARRY R. "The Economic Role of Political Institutions: Market-Preserving Federalism and Economic Development." 11:1 *The Journal of Law, Economics, and Organization* (April 1995) at 1–31.

WERNICK, MICHAEL. *Governing Canada: A Guide to the Tradecraft of Politics* (Vancouver: One Print UBC Press, 2021).

WHEARE, KC. *Federal Government*, 4th ed (London: Oxford University Press, 1973).

WILE, ROB. "153 Years Ago Today, an Unemployed Sick Man Drilled the First Modern Oil Well." *Business Insider*, 27 August 2012, online: www.businessinsider.com/edwin-drake-first-modern-oil-well-153-years-ago-2012-8.

WILKINS, KERRY. *Essentials of Canadian Aboriginal Law* (Toronto: Thomson Reuters, 2018).

WOODARD, COLIN. *American Nations* (London: Penguin Books, 2011).

WORLD BANK. "Tax Revenue (% of GDP) — Canada, United States." *Data*, online: https://data.worldbank.org/indicator/GC.TAX.TOTL.GD.ZS?end=2022&locations=CA-US&start=1972&view=chart.

WRIGHT, BARRY, BETINA APPEL KUZMAROV, REBECCA JAREMKO BROMWICH & VINCENT KAZMIERSKI. *Looking at Law: Canada's Legal System*, 7th ed (New York: LexisNexis, 2019).

YODERS, JEFF. "US Doubles Tariffs on Canadian Softwood Lumber and Contractors Expect Higher Prices." *Engineering News-Record*, 30 November 2021, online: www.enr.com/articles/53119-us-doubles-tariffs-on-canadian-softwood-lumber-contractors-expect-higher-prices.

ZIVO, ADAM. "It Turns Out It Was One Michael and Another Michael." *National Post*, 18 November 2023, online: https://nationalpost.com/opinion/adam-zivo-it-turns-out-it-was-one-michael-and-another-michael.

# Index

Abortion rights, 183–186
Abrams, Stacey, 128
*Act of Union, 1840,* 45
Adams, John, 76
Adams, Michael, 3
*Adler v Ontario,* 189
Administration of elections, 127–128
Alliant Techsystems, 248
Al Qaeda, 276
American Civil War, 50, 80, 264
American exceptionalism, 31
American FDI in Canada, 239–250.
  *See also* trade and economic
  relations, Canada–United States
  FTA, impact on, 246
  importance of, 244
  in mining and smelting
    industry, 241
  NAFTA, impact on, 246
  nationalist critiques of, 241–245
  1956 Pipeline Debate, 241–242
  in petroleum and natural gas
    industry, 241
  Watkins Report recommendations,
    242, 247
American federalism, 148–149, 169
  centralized model, 149
  criminal laws, 166
  federal spending power, 177
  gun laws, 166
  intellectual discourses on, 149–150
  intergovernmental accords and
    agreements, 169
  intragovernmental relations,
    156–157
  judicial federalism, 168
  judicial interpretation in, 165–169
  National Popular Vote Interstate
    Compact, 169
  raising and spending money under,
    175–176
  rationale for, 153
  Regional Greenhouse Gas
    Initiative, 169
American imperialism, 29–30
American military weapons, 289
American oil industry, 282
American party system. *See* Democratic
  and Republican parties
American policy, 268
American regionalism, 138–141
  political cultures, 138–140
  voting and policy demands, impact
    on, 140–141

American Revolution, 18–38, 42, 143
   American elections of 1844, 28
   Boston Tea Party, 19
   British *vs* local militias, 20
   Declaration of Independence of 1776, 40
   distinct political cultures, development of, 21–22
   1821 revolution, 27
   *Gaspee* episode, 19
   Great Lakes region as part of United States, 20
   Intolerable Acts (Coercive Acts), 19
   manifest destiny, 25, 27
   Mexican-American War, 27–28
   peace treaty, 20
   taxation policies of British, 18–21
   United States Constitution, formation of, 22–25
   War of 1812, 25–27
American society, political cultures of, 138–139
   Blue States and Red States, 140–142
   political movements and, 140
   voting and policy demands, 140
American Thirteen Colonies, 40, 143
American transnational oil companies/community, 282–283
Anti-abortion movement, 184
Anti-involvement America First campaign, 32
Anti-Muslim views, 209–210
Arctic Sovereignty, 280
Articles of Confederation, 22–25
   Article XI, 22
   governance, conflicts about ideas of, 22–24
   government powers, 22
Assisted death policy, 186–189
   medical assistance in dying, 187–188
Aztecs, 12
Azzi, Stephen, 21, 234

Balfour Declaration of 1926, 60
Ballot initiatives, 133–135
Banff National Park, 279
Battle of Plains of Abraham, 17
Bennett, RB, 59
Biden, Joe, 4–6, 8, 74, 111, 120, 125, 130, 133, 183, 204, 208, 238–239
Bilingualism, 212
Black, William Anderson, 88
Bloc Québécois, 114
*Board of Commerce* case, 160
Boer War, 267
Boone, Daniel, 15
Borden, Robert, 58, 81
Border Security, 275–280
Boston Tea Party, 19
Boychuk, Gerard, 31
British army, 266
British Cabinet-parliamentary system, 127
British Columbia massacre, 1996, 199
British Commonwealth of Nations, 60
British East India Company, 19
British Empire, 267
British Foreign Office, 267
Brock, Isaac, 41
Brown, George, 47–48
Brown, John, 19
Brown, Russell, 105
*Buckley v Valeo*, 130
Budgetary processes
   in Canada, 255–259
   complexity of, 253–254
   in United States, 259–261
Bureaucracy, 82, 138–139, 155
Bureau of Indian Affairs (BIA), 35
Bush, George W, 37, 77, 123, 274, 275
Business Council on National Issues (BCNI), 229
Butler, Carrie, 89
ByteDance, 249

# Index

Cahokia, 12
Campbell, Kim, 146
Canada Development Corporation (CDC), 226, 244–245
Canada-United States border, 278
Canada-United States-Mexico Agreement (CUSMA), 232, 234
Canada *vs* United States, similarities and differences, 1–8, 21
abortion, women's right to, 3
Biden and Trump, Trudeau's relationship with, 5–7
carbon emissions, cap-and-trade regulations of, 154
citizens, perceptions of, 4
concentration of wealth, patterns of, 253
cross-border relations and politics, 4–8, 27–29, 153–154
cultural issues, 3
economic opportunities, attitudes toward, 2–3
economy and trade, government involvement in, 2
foreign policy, 6–8
forty-ninth parallel, 28
government, responsibility and accountability of, 78
gun culture, 3, 199–200
history of slavery, 28–29
income inequality, 252–253
political cultures, 2–3
populations, 25, 29, 41, 47, 55–56, 65–66, 86–87, 119, 121, 142, 151, 211–212
slavery, 28–29
social services, access to, 3
social spending, 250–251
spread of democratic institutions, 50
stereotypes, 3
television shows, 3–4
Canadian air strikes, 275

Canadian-American relations, 4–8, 27–29, 153–154, 206–207, 272, 286, 295
budgetary processes, 253–261
foreign direct investment, 153, 221–226, 239–250
taxation, 250–253
trade and economic relations, 154, 207, 218–239
Canadian Border Services Agency, 292
Canadian Broadcasting Corporation (CBC), 62, 276
Canadian Constitution, 94, 267. *See also* policy making
*Anti-Inflation Act, 1975*, 161
Bill of Rights, 95
British model, 93–94
*British North America Act, 1867* (BNA Act, 1867), 48–51, 57–58, 83, 103, 158, 164, 171, 179–180, 189, 257
*Canada Elections Act*, 125–126, 128
*Canada Health Act*, 192, 196, 198
Canadian Charter of Rights and Freedoms, 95, 99, 105, 125, 130, 164, 180, 183–184, 186, 201–202, 208, 211, 213
*Constitution Act*, 1867, 159
*Constitution Act*, 1982, 164, 179–180
*Consumer Packaging and Labelling Act*, 212
*Criminal Code*, 89, 97, 105, 165–166, 186, 200–201, 204, 208, 209
*Electoral Boundaries Readjustment Act*, 118
*Emergencies Act*, 198
*Greenhouse Gas Pollution Pricing Act, 2021*, 207
*Income Tax Act*, 128
*Official Languages Act*, 212
official national languages, 211–214
*Pan-Canadian Securities Regulation*, 163
*Parliament of Canada Act*, 125

371

provincial government powers, 97
*Reference re Greenhouse Gas Pollution Pricing Act*, 162, 207
Canadian FDI in United States, 239, 248–249
  restrictions, 249
  takeovers, 248–249
Canadian federalism, 149–150, 169
  courts on, impact of, 165
  decentralized model, 149, 170–171
  executive, 155–156
  federal spending power, 177
  intellectual discourses on, 149–150
  intergovernmental accords and agreements, 169
  intergovernmental relations, conduct of, 155
  judicial interpretation in, 157–165
  provincial/regional interests, representation of, 170–171
  raising and spending money under, 173–175
  rationale for, 152–153
Canadian House of Commons, 290
Canadian identity, 244
*Canadian Industrial Gas & Oil Ltd v Government of Saskatchewan*, 164
Canadian Manufacturers Association, 229
Canadian oil market, 282
Canadian parliament. *See also* Canadian Senate; House of Commons, Canada
  laws, proposal and passage of, 89
  United States Congress, comparison with, 90–91
Canadian party system
  Bloc Québécois, 114, 146–147, 187, 257
  Coalition Avenir Québec, 115
  Green Party, 114, 187
  national Conservative Party, 114, 193, 221

national Liberal Party, 114, 193, 221
New Democratic Party, 88, 114–115, 147–148, 187, 193, 229, 230, 243, 257, 258
Progressive Conservative Party, 64, 115, 144–145, 184, 189, 196, 226–227, 229, 242, 257, 259
provincial party systems, 115
Reform Party, 146–147
Saskatchewan Party, 115
United Conservatives, 115, 195
Canadian Radio Broadcasting Corporation (CRBC), 222
Canadian regionalism, 141–148
  Atlantic provinces, 143
  central Canadian settlement, 143
  English and French, division between, 142–143
  Indigenous peoples and settler, relationship between, 141–142
  Macdonald's policy, 144–145
  Ontario political culture, 144
  regional voting patterns, 145–148
  Western provinces, 144–145
Canadian resource companies, 284
Canadian Senate, 51, 83, 87–88
  appointments, duration of, 87
  on budget process, 258–259
  power of, 83–84
  senators, distribution of, 87–88
Canadian symbols, 295
Canadian territory, 280
Candidate selection in elections, 111–113. *See also* elections and voting, Canada and United States
Carbon tax, 207
*Carter v Canada*, 186
Cartier, Jacques, 39
Castle, Mike, 111
Catholic taxpayer-funded Catholic school systems, 189–190
Champlain, Samuel de, 39
*Chaoulli v Quebec*, 196

# Index

Charles II, King, 23
Charlottetown Accord of 1992, 134, 146
Château Clique of Lower Canada, 41–43, 46, 143–144
Cheney, Dick, 77, 284
*Cherokee Nation v Georgia*, 33
Chrétien, Jean, 73, 146–147, 230
*Citizens Insurance of Canada and Queen Insurance v Parsons (Canada)*, 162
*Citizens United v Federal Election Commission*, 131
Civil service system, in Canada and United States, 81–82
Civil War 1861–1865, 28–29
Clark, Joe, 257
Clarkson, Stephen, 229
Climate change policy, 206–208
  in Canada, 207
  North American climate change action, 206
  taxes on fossil fuels, 207
  in United States, 207–208
Clinton, Bill, 74, 133, 214, 232, 275
Clinton, Hillary, 122, 140, 288
Coalition Avenir Québec, 115
Coast Guard boats, 264
Cold War, 32–33, 36, 194
Cold War legacy of Russian-American relations, 288
Coles, Sidney, 113
Collin, Frank, 210
Colonial settlement in Canada and the United States, 141–143
  American Settlement, 16–17, 27
  conservative and church-dominated (Catholic) society, 16–17
  modern American society, basis for, 138–139
  in Quebec, Canada, 39–40
  Royal Proclamation, impact of, 13–15, 17–18

Seven Years' War, effect of, 17
Spanish, 16
Treaty of Paris, effect of, 17–18
Columbia Pipeline Group, 287
Communism, 32
Concordia University massacre, 1992, 199
Conference of New England Governors and Eastern Canadian Premiers, 154
Constitutional Convention of 1787, 23–24
Continentalism, 153
Cooperative Commonwealth Federation (CCF), 114, 300
Council of Federation, 156
Council of Great Lakes Governors, 154
Courts, in Canada and United States. *See* legal system in Canada; legal system in United States
COVID-19
  deaths, related, 191–192
  pandemic, 279, 304
  policies, 305
*Criminal Code of Canada*, 89, 97, 105, 165–166, 186, 200–201, 204, 208–209, 302
Crosbie, John, 226–227

*Dawes Act* of 1887, 35
Defence Production Sharing Agreement (DPSA), 268
Democratic and Republican parties, 114–115, 120–121, 123–125, 128, 136, 140
  on budget proposal, 259–261
Democratic National Committee, 289
Diefenbaker, John, 95, 223, 234, 242
Disney Corporation, 295
District of Columbia statehood movement, 86
Division of powers, 154–173
  judicial interpretations, 157–169
  legislative powers, distribution of, 158–159

provincial power, 97, 152, 157–160, 162, 164–165, 171
residual power, 97, 152, 159, 171–173, 175
*Dobbs v Jackson Women's Health Organization*, 185
Douglas, Tommy, 193
Duck, Donald, 118
Duke, David, 111
Durham, Lord, 42, 143

Eagle, Faith Spotted, 123
École Polytechnique massacre, 1989, 198–199, 201
Education system, Canada, 189–190
Elazar, Daniel, 138
Elections and voting, Canada and United States
  ballot initiatives, 133–135
  by-elections, 126–127
  candidate selection, 111–113
  for county coroner, 110
  demographic changes and voting patterns, 140–141, 145
  election dates, 72–74, 124–126
  elections, administration of, 127–128
  electoral systems, 115–117
  federal election, opportunity to vote in, 110
  financial provisions, 128–133
  frequency of voting, 109–110
  influence of lobbyists, 132
  for judges, 110
  legislative districts, creation of, 117–119
  non-confidence motion, effect of, 127
  party leaders and presidential candidates, selection of, 119–121
  party system, 113–115
  presidential and prime ministerial candidacy, 121–124
  presidential elections, 119–121, 136
  special elections, 126
  timing and style of, 124–127
  voters' rights and secrecy of vote, 127
  voter turnout, 120
Electoral College system, 121–124
Electoral systems, 115–117
  Canadian federal general elections, 116
  first-past-the-post system, 115–116
  ranked choice voting, 117
*Employment and Social Service Act Reference*, 164
Energy policy, 287
Executive federalism, 155–156
Executive institution, Canada. *See also* legislative institution, Canada
  accountability, 68
  bill in parliament, passing of, 69
  Cabinet, size and composition of, 76
  election, timing of, 72
  executive branch leadership, selection of, 71–72
  executive branch members, choosing of, 68
  fusion of power, 68
  Governor General, appointment of, 71–72
  House of Commons, 72
  ministerial responsibilities, 78–79
  office and removal before term, terms of, 72–73
  party discipline, 69
  prime minister, powers of, 69
  Throne Speech, 75–76
Executive institution, United States, 67–92. *See also* legislative institution, United States
  bill in parliament, passing of, 69
  Cabinet, size and composition of, 77–78
  Cabinet members, presidential firings of, 79–80

# Index

Cabinet's political role, 79-81
checks and balances, system of, 68-69, 151
Congress, presidential address to, 75-76
division of power, 68
election, timing of, 73-74
impeachment, 74
office and removal before term, terms of, 74-75
party discipline, 69
president, powers of, 69-71
prohibitions, 69
United States Congress, freedoms of, 69

Faithless electors, 123
Family Compact of Upper Canada, 41-44, 46, 143-144
Fathers of Confederation, 29, 49-50, 52, 94, 149, 152, 157, 159, 162, 165, 171-172
Federalism, federal systems, 137, 148-154. *See also* division of powers
accords and agreements, 169
British authority on, 150
centralized *vs* decentralized, 149, 152, 170-171
citizens in a federal state, 150
division of powers, 151, 154-173
executive, 155-156
intergovernmental relations, 151
national harmony, role in, 151
quasi-federalism, 171
raising and spending money, 173-177
rationale for, 152-153
rights and freedoms, 167-169
two-level system, 149
Federal-provincial diplomacy, 156
Federal spending power, 176, 177
Federal states, 151
Feinstein, Dianne, 88
Fenian Brotherhood, 50
Fenian raids, Canada, 50

"54-40 or fight" campaign, 28
Financial provisions of elections, 128-133
candidates, expenses limits for, 129-130
contribution limits, 129
spending limits, 129-131
Super PACs creation of, 131
third party spending, 130
Firearms deaths, Canada and United States, 199
First Nations, 146
First World War, 30, 267
Ford, Christine Blasey, 106
*Ford v Quebec*, 213
Foreign direct investments (FDI). *See* American FDI in Canada; Canadian FDI in United States
Foreign Investment Review Agency (FIRA), 244-245
*Fort Frances Pulp and Paper Company v Manitoba Free Press and others*, 161
Fossil fuels, 206-207
Freeland, Chrystia, 6
Free speech and hate speech, 208-211
Free Trade Agreement (FTA), 296
between Canada and other countries, 236-237
between Canada and United States, 226-230, 246
French forts, 16
Front de libération du Québec (FLQ), 62-63
Fur trade, 15-17, 141-142
Fusion of powers, 46, 68-69

Garfield, James, 81
Gaspee Days, 19
George III, King, 16
Gerrymandering, 117-119
Ghent Treaty, 27
Goods and Services Tax, 299
Gordon, Walter, 241-242

Gosar, Paul, 92
Grant, George, 224
Gray, Herb, 244
Great Depression era
   in Canada, 58–60
   in United States, 30–31
Great Lakes, 304
Greene, Marjorie Taylor, 204
Greenhouse gases emissions, 206
Green Party, 114
Guistra, Frank, 132
Guiteau, Charles, 81
Gun control law, 198–206
   in Canada, 199–202
   firearms acquisition certificates, 201
   restrictions and established
      controls, 201
   in United States, 202–206
*Gun-Free School Zones Act,* 166

Haldane, Lords Richard, 160
Hamilton, Alexander, 48
Harper, Elijah, 146
Harper, Stephen, 72, 77, 86, 104–105,
   115, 222, 257
Harris, Kamala, 4, 8, 74, 121, 133
Harrison, Kathryn, 206
Hartz, Louis, 30, 31
Head, Sir Francis Bond, 43
Health care policy, 191–198
Health system, Canada, 192
   COVID-19 related policies and
      outcomes, 197–198
   health care
      access to, 197
      cost of, 195
      spending, 195
   health insurance, 193
   pharmacare program, 193
   private for-profit health care
      facilities, use of, 196
   private health insurance, 195–196
   private sector, role of, 195
Health system, United States, 192–193

   affordability, 198
   COVID-19 related policies and
      outcomes, 197–198
   health care
      cost of, 195
      spending, 194
      health insurance, 196–197
      health outcomes, 195, 198
   Medicare and Medicaid, 193
Hobbs, Katie, 128
Hofstadter, Richard, 36
Hogg, David, 204
Holmes, Oliver Wendell, 250
Homan, Tom, 7–8
Homicide rate, Canada and United
   States, 200
House of Commons, Canada, 51, 66,
   68–69, 72, 75, 78, 83–84, 87–91,
   104, 107, 115–116, 119, 121, 125–127,
   145–146, 172, 181, 225, 229, 231
   budget speech, debate on, 256–259
   election of, 88
   Government and Opposition sides, 87
   leader of party, 119
   legislative districts, creation of, 119
   marijuana legalization, 181
   ministerial responsibility
      towards, 78
   number of ridings, 87
   passing of bills, 83, 172, 181, 184
Howe, CD, 241, 241
Hudson's Bay Company, 28
Huron Lakes, 264
Hydro Quebec, 63

*Indian Removal Act*, 1830, 34
*Indian Reorganization Act*, 35
Indigenous peoples, 11–16
   between British Crown and,
      constitutional relationship, 14
   Canada' relationship with, 56–57,
      141–142
   economic relations, 13, 15
   estimated population, 12, 16–17

## Index

European settlers and, violence between, 14
French and British, relations between, 13
fur trade, 15–17
history of, 11–12
as military allies, 13
rights of, 13–14
slavery of, 15, 24–25, 29
United States' relationship with, 33–36
Individualists, 138–139
*Inflation Reduction Act, 2022*, 5
Intergovernmental agreements, 169
International Crisis Group, 292
International Monetary Fund (IMF), 268
Intolerable Acts (Coercive Acts), 19
Investment Canada, 245
Iraq War, 274

Jamestown, 16
Jean, Michaëlle, 85
Jefferson, Thomas, 26–27, 76
Johnson, Andrew, 80
Johnson, Lyndon, 222
Judiciary
  administration of justice, 97
  Court Systems, 98–102
  judges and courts, powers of, 92–95
  judicial decisions, reversing of, 95–96
  judicial review, 94, 157–158
  notwithstanding clause, Canada, 96
  partisan appointments of judges, 106
  partisan considerations, 103, 105
  Supreme Courts, 102–106

Kasich, John, 123
Kavanaugh case, 106
*Keegstra* case, 209
Kemp, Brian, 128

Kennedy, John, 37, 234
Kennedy, Robert, 203
Key, Francis Scott, 26
Keynes, John Maynard, 31
King, Dr. Martin Luther, 203
King, William Lyon Mackenzie, 59, 61, 221
Ku Klux Klan (KKK), 111

*Labour Conventions* case, 161
Laurier, Wilfrid, 55–56, 221
Law of the Sea Treaty, 280
Laws, proposal and passage of
  *Aretha Franklin Congressional Gold Medal Act*, United States, 92
  Canadian parliament, 89
  *Granite Mountain Hotshots Commemorative Coin Act*, United States, 92
  *Prince Congressional Gold Medal Act*, United States, 92
  United States Congress, 89, 91–92
League of Nations, 30
Legal system in Canada
  Aboriginal rights, 98–99
  Civil Code, 98
  civil law, 98
  common law, basis of, 98
  *Criminal Code*, 165–166
  English common law and French civil law traditions, 98
  federal and provincial courts, 99–100
  federalism, influence of, 99
  judges, appointment of, 99–104
  Judicial Committee of the Privy Council, 95, 103, 159–162, 164–165
  Supreme Court and, 99–100, 158, 168
Legal system in United States. *See also* Court Systems, United States
  appellate courts, 101
  bankruptcy courts, 101

federal and state laws, relationship between, 100–101
federal courts
  of appeal, 100–101
  levels of, 101
  power of, 102
federal judicial power, 101–102
judges, impeachment of, 102
judicial independence, 102
reference cases, 102–103
Supreme Courts, 100–101, 118, 168
tax court, 101
trial courts, 100–101
Legislative districts, creation of, 117–119
Legislative institution, Canada, 83–84. *See also* executive institution, Canada
  Canadian Senate, power of, 83–84
  House of Commons, approval of, 83
  Independent Advisory Board for Senate Appointments, 84
  parliament, proroguing, 85–86
  partisanship, 84
  regional interests, 83
Legislative institution, United States, 84–85. *See also* executive institution, United States; United States Congress
  *Affordable Care Act* (Obamacare), repeal of, 85
  minority interests, representation of, 84
  Senate, powers of, 85
*Lemon v Kurtzman*, 190
Les Patriotes, 43
Lévesque, René, 63
Levitt, Kari, 223
Liberal and Conservative parties, Canada, 113–114
Liberal individualism, 31
Liberal Party campaign, 274
Lighthizer, Robert, 8

Lincoln, Abraham, 29, 80
Lindbergh, Charles, 32
Lipset, Seymour Martin, 21, 31
Lobbyists, 132
*Local Prohibition* case, 160

MacDonald, Dettwiler & Associates (MDA), 248
Macdonald, Sir John A, 48, 53, 144, 152, 221, 240
Mack, Richard, 167
Mackenzie, William Lyon, 43–44
Madison, James, 68
Maher, Bill, 111
Manifest destiny, 25, 27, 29–31
*Marbury v Madison*, 94
Marijuana legalization, 166–167, 173, 181–183, 185
  grow plants, permission to, 181
  medical use, 181–182
  recreational use, 181–182
Marjory Stoneman Douglas school shooting, 2018, 204
Martin, Paul, 73, 77
Massey Royal Commission on Arts and Letters, 223
*McCulloch v Maryland*, 177
Meech Lake Accord, 145–146
Mega-constitutional politics, 150
Mercer, Rick, 4
Mexican-American War, 27–28
Mexico, 5, 8, 30
  American settlers with slaves in, 27
  border with United States, 279
  Canada and United States, trilateral relationship between, 230–234
  population, 25, 41
  United States, free trade agreements with, 64
Millennium Plot, 277
Ministry of Federal-Provincial Affairs, 1961, 156

Montesquieu, Baron de, 150
Moore, Roy, 112
Moralists, 138-140
*Morgentaler* case, 183, 186
Mulroney, Brian, 83-84, 145-147, 184, 226-229, 234, 244-245, 247, 259
Multilateral Agreement on Investment (MAI), 245
Myer, Dillon, 35
Myers, Frank, 80-81
*Myers v United States*, 80

Nadon affair, 104
*Napoleonic Code*, 98
Narragansett Bay, 19
National Energy Board (NEB), 286
National Energy Program (NEP), 245, 282
National Instacheck System (NICS), 203-204
National Oil Policy, 282
National Rifle Association (NRA), 203
Navigation Acts, 19
New Amsterdam (New York), 16-17
New Democratic Party (NDP), 300
New England, 14, 16, 138, 154
New France (Quebec), 16-17
New Spain (West Indies), 16
9/11 attacks, 273
Nixon, Richard, 33, 219, 225, 234
Non-confidence motion, 127
North American Aerospace Defence Command (NORAD), 268
North American energy network, 281
North American Energy Working Group, 284
North American Free Trade Agreement (NAFTA), 7-8, 230-231, 246, 284
  sunset clause, 233
  Trump administration's contentious demands, 233-234

North Atlantic Treaty Organization (NATO), 268, 273-274, 289-290
Northwest Passage, 280
Norton, Eleanor Holmes, 86-87
Nova Scotia shootings, 2020, 199

Obama, Barack, 31, 37, 112, 133, 182-183, 194, 197, 204, 237
October Crisis of 1970, 63
O'Donnell, Christine, 111-112
Official national languages, 211-215
Oil Creek, 281
Operation Inherent Resolve, 275
Organization of Petroleum Exporting Countries (OPEC), 282
Osborne, Dan, 113

Pacific Northwest Economic Region, 154
Paley Report, 1952, 221
Papineau, Joseph, 43
Paris Treaty, 1763, 16, 40
*Parker* case, 181
Parkin, Andrew, 3
Parti Québécois, 63
Partisan gerrymandering, 117
Party systems, in Canada and United States, 113-115. *See also* Canadian party system; Democratic and Republican parties
*Patriation Reference*, 164
Paul, Ron, 123
"Peace, order and good government" (POGG) of Canada, 159-162
Pearl Harbor naval base, 267
Pearson, Lester, 32, 193, 222, 242
Pennamite-Yankee wars, 23
Petro Canada, 244, 245
Phelps, Fred, 211
Pike, Zebulon, 26
*Planned Parenthood of Southeast Pennsylvania v Casey*, 185
Plymouth (Massachusetts), 16
Poilievre, Pierre, 7, 120

Policy making
  abortion rights, 183–186
  assisted death, 186–189
  in Canada, 179–180
  climate change, 206–208
  Constitutions and, 179–181
  free speech and hate speech,
    208–211
  gun control, 198–206
  health care, 191–198
  marijuana legalization, 181–183
  official national languages, 211–215
  parameters, 180
  religious schools, government
    funding for, 189–191
  in United States, 180–181
Political culture, Canada, 22, 25–26.
  *See also* Canadian party system;
    Quebec
  *Act of Union, 1840*, 46–48
  American draft dodgers in, 33
  Asian immigration in, 65–66
  Atlantic Canadian political
    culture, 143
  Balfour Declaration, 1926, 60
  Bennett's reforms, 59
  bicameral national Parliament, 51
  British colony, features of, 52–53
  *British North America Act, 1867*,
    48–51, 57–58, 83, 103
  Canadian identity and nationalism,
    41–42, 55, 60, 65
  *Charter of Rights and Freedoms*, 64
  *Civil Service Act, 1918*, 81–82
  concentration of power, 46
  Confederacy, trade and recognition
    of, 29
  Confederation of Canada, 48–52
  *Constitutional Act, 1791*, 40
  cultural dualism, 46–47
  cultural individualism, 143
  education system, 62
  *Emergencies Act*, 63
  English population in, 21, 45
  Fenian raids, 50
  French-English relations in, 40, 55,
    65, 142–143
  French settlers, influx of, 39
  *Gradual Civilization Act* of 1857, 57
  *Gradual Enfranchisement Act* of
    1869, 57
  Great Depression, effect of, 58–60
  immigration policies, 65
  *Indian Act, 1876*, 57
  Indigenous population,
    marginalization of, 56–57
  industrialization and urbanization
    in, 63
  King's reforms, 59–60
  Lord Durham's Report, 1839, 44–46
  Macdonald's policy and its impact,
    144–145
  *Manitoba Schools Act, 1890*,
    55–56
  Massey Commission, 1951, 65
  *Military Service Act*, 1917, 58
  National Policy of 1879, 53–55
  "New Deal" for, 59
  October Crisis of 1970, 63
  Ontario political culture, 144
  Ontario's Regulation 17/1913, 56
  path to nationhood, 38
  political economy, 53–56
  population diversity, 65–66
  population growth, 41
  post-Second World War, 61–62
  Quebec colony, creation of, 19,
    39–40, 62–64
  Quiet Revolution, 62
  regionalism in, 31–32
  Seven Years' War (1756–1763), 39–40
  staples-based economy, 53, 55, 62
  Statute of Westminster, 1931, 60
  Upper and Lower Canada
    rebellions in, 42–46, 50
    tension between, 40
  veterans, "affirmative action"
    program for, 62

war efforts, 30, 32
*War Measures Act*, 63
*Wartime Elections Act*, 58
Western provinces, 144-145
women's voting rights, 58
world wars, contribution to, 30, 32, 57-58, 60-61
Political culture, United States, 192. *See also* American Revolution; Democratic and Republican parties
American policy in Vietnam, 32
anti-communist policy, 32
economic policies following economic disruption, 30-31
*Hatch Act* of 1939, 82
immigration numbers to, 38
as imperial power, 33
isolationist attitudes among Americans, 32
liberal individualism, 31
manifest destiny, ideology of, 25, 27, 29-31
military intervention overseas, 33
modern political culture of, 36-38
Native Americans and government entities, relationship between, 33-36
Operation Relocation, 1952, 35
*Pendleton Civil Service Reform Act* of 1883, 81-82
presidential vetoes, 71
racial equality, 31, 37-38
Spain over colonial control of Cuba, war on, 30
*Tenure of Office Act*, 80
world wars, contributions in, 30, 32, 35
Populists, 139, 140
PotashCorp, 247
Powell, Colin, 123
Power in executive branch
of Canadian prime minister, 69

of queen/king and Governor General, 70
symbolic, 70
of United States president, 70-71
Proroguing parliament, 85-86
President, United States
choosing of, 72
as Commander-in-Chief of Armed Forces, 71
powers of, 69-71
selecting Supreme Court justices, role in, 71
veto power, 71
Presidential candidacy, 121-124
Presidential elections, 119-121, 136
Prime ministerial candidacy, 121-124
Prince Edward Island, ridings of, 87
Printz, Jay, 167
Psilocybin, legalization of, 135
Public service
in Canada, 81-82
in United States, 82
*Public Service Board v Dionne*, 164
Puritans, 16

Quebec, 149, 152, 154, 156, 207, 211-212, 218
Bloc Québécois party, 114, 146-147
Charter of Human Rights and Freedoms, 196
City mosque shooting, 2017, 199
Civil Code, 98
Coalition Avenir Québec, 115
*Constitutional Act, 1791* and, 40-41
creation of, 39-40, 62-64
as distinct society, 145-146
economic nationalism, 63
new parties and movements, 62-63
official national languages, 213-214
political culture of, 143, 145
private health care, 195
*Quebec Act, 1774*, 19, 40, 98
Quiet Revolution, 171

referendums and its consequences, 63–64
social/cultural aspects, 63
Question Period, 75
Quiet Revolution, 62

*RAV v City of St Paul*, 210
Reagan, Ronald, 36, 219, 227–228, 234
Reciprocity Treaty, with colonies, 266
Recreational marijuana, legalization of, 134–135
*Reference re Pan Canadian Securities Regulation*, 163
*References re Greenhous Gas Pollution Pricing Act*, 162
Regional Greenhouse Gas Initiative, 208
Regionalism, 154
  in Canada, 141–148
  in United States, 138–141
Residual power, 152, 159, 171–173
Resolute Training Force, 273
Responsibility and accountability of government, 78–81
Revere, Paul, 20
Robinson, Lisa, 113
*Roe v Wade*, 95, 105, 184–185
Romney, Mitt, 74, 196–197
Roosevelt, Franklin, 26
Royal Canadian Mounted Police (RCMP), 277
Royal Commission on Aboriginal Peoples (RCAP), 99
Royal Commission on Canada's Economic Prospects, 241
Royal Proclamation of 1763, 13–15, 17–18, 20, 40
Rubio, Marco, 7
Rush-Bagot Treaty, 264
Russell, Peter, 150
Russian Internet Research Agency, 289
*R v Keegstra*, 209
*R v Morgentaler*, 183, 186

*R v Ndhlovu*, 105
*R v Parker*, 181
*R v Vaillancourt*, 201

Safe Third Country Agreement, 278
Same-sex marriage, 112
Sanders, Bernie, 114–115, 123, 140–141
Sandy Hook massacre, 2012, 204
Saskatchewan Party, 115
School voucher programs, United States, 190–191
Second World War, 267
  Canada's contribution, 32, 60–61
  United States's contribution, 32
Secord, Laura, 41
Security and Prosperity Partnership (SPP), 237–238
  of North American, 284
Separation of powers, 46, 150, 153
Sessions, Jeff, 111, 182–183
Seven Years' War (1756–1763), 17, 39–40, 139
Seward, William, 29
Sifton, Sir Clifford, 144
Silent Surrender study, 223
Simeon, Richard, 156
*The Simpsons* television show, 3
Singh, Jagmeet, 120
Slavery, 28–29
  abolition of, 24–25, 29
  of Indigenous peoples, 15
Smiley, Donald, 155
Smith, Albert, 210
*Smith v Collin*, 210
Snyder, Albert, 211
*Snyder v Phelps*, 211
Sons of Liberty, 19
Soros, George, 131, 204
*South Park* television show, 3–4
*The Spirit of Laws*, 150
*Stamp Act* of 1765, 18–19
Stanton, Edwin, 80
"The Star-Spangled Banner," 27
Stefanik, Elise, 7

# Index

Stock market crash
   1929, 30–31
   2008, 31
Strange, Luther, 111–112
Super PACs, 131
Supremacy clause, 97, 152–153, 177
Supreme Courts, 102–106
   of Canada, 99–100, 158
   political scandal and controversy over appointments, 103–106
   reference cases, 102–103
   of United States, 100–101, 118, 168, 168
Symbolic power, 70
Syrian-born Canadian citizen, 277
Syrian refugees, 278

Taxation, Canada *vs* United States, 250–253
   pre-tax income, 253
   tax revenue, sources of, 251–252
   without representation, 18, 22, 34, 86
Taxpayer-funded school systems, 189
Taylor, Charles, 225
*Tea Act, 1773*, 19
Tea Party movement, 2009, 19, 140
Tecumseh, Shawnee Chief, 26, 41
*Termination Act, 1953*, 35–36
*This Hour Has 22 Minutes*, 4
Throne Speech, 75–76
Thurmond, Strom, 88
Toltecs, 12
*Toronto Electric Commissioners v Snider and others (Ontario)*, 131
Tory, John, 22, 189
Tower, John, 77
Townshend Acts of 1767, 18–19
Township, Robinson, 168
Trade and economic relations, Canada–United States, 154, 218–239
   American protectionism and, 4, 144–145, 225, 227–228, 232–233, 235–236, 238–239

Automotive Agreement (Auto Pact), 222
   background, 220–221
   in cultural industries, 222–223
   Defence Production Sharing Agreement, 222
   free trade agreement, 226–230, 234
   Mexico, trilateral relationship with, 230–234
   patterns, 218
   policies, American influence in, 223–226
   pre-free trade and free trade eras, 219–220
   quiet diplomacy, 220, 232
   Security and Prosperity Partnership, 237–238
   Softwood Lumber Agreement, 234–235
   special relationship, 224, 232
Traditionalists, 139, 140
Trail of Tears, 34
TransCanada Corporation, 286
Trans-Pacific Partnership, 232
Tratado entre México, Estados Unidos y Canadá (T-MEC), 232, 234
Treaty of Ghent, 264
Trudeau, Justin, 4, 5, 72–73, 77, 84, 86, 105, 116, 120, 186, 193, 202, 207, 209, 234, 238
Trudeau, Pierre, 32–33, 145, 225, 234, 244
Trump, Donald, 4, 6–8, 37, 74, 112, 120, 122, 124, 128, 130–131, 133, 140, 194, 232–233, 234, 260, 287
   impeachment of, 74–75

Uihlein, Richard, 131
Uncle Sam, 216
Underhill, Frank, 49
United Empire Loyalists, 21, 143, 265
United Nations, 32
United Nations-led mission, 268

United States Coast Guard, 264
United States Congress, 86–89
   Congress members, number of, 86
   divisions in, 140–141
   House of Representatives, 86–87
   non-voting delegates, 86
   proposal and passage of laws, 89, 91–92
   "taxation without representation," 86
United States Constitution, 68, 112, 165. *See also* policy making
   Arizona amendment, 214–215
   Articles of Confederation, 22–24
   Bill of Rights, 180, 203
   *Brady Handgun Violence Protection Act,* 167
   *Budget and Accounting Act* of 1921, 259
   *Civil Rights Act*, 173
   Constitutional Convention of 1787, 23–24
   *Death with Dignity Act*, 187–188
   electoral votes (Twenty-third Amendment), 122
   environmental rights, 168–169
   free speech
      clauses, 208
      protection, 215
   *Gun Control Act*, 1968, 203
   *Gun-Free School Zones Act* of 1990, 166
   gun law, 202
   individual rights, 167–168
   *Inflation Reduction Act*, 208, 239
   *Investment Canada Act*, 247
   legality of marijuana, 166–167, 173
   national government, powers of, 152
   Native American reservations and status, 33–36
   necessary and proper clause, 177
   official national languages, 214–215
   *Patient Protection and Affordable Care Act*, 192, 194, 196–197, 260
   Pledge of Allegiance, 170
   referendums, 133–134
   residual powers clause, 172–173
   shared power, 177
   slavery, abolition of, 24–25, 29
   State of Union address, 75–76
   state to administer elections, role of, 128
   supremacy clause, 97, 152–153, 177
   Thirteenth Amendment, 24–25, 29
   *Trading with the Enemy Act*, 242
United States International Trade Commission (USITC), 235
United States-Mexico-Canada Agreement (USMCA), 232, 234
United States Senate Homeland Security Committee, 278
United States Senate Intelligence Committee, 289
*United States v Alfonso D Lopez, Jr*, 166
US Postal Service, 37

*Vaillancourt* case, 201
Versailles Treaty, 30
Vikings, 12
Viktora, Robert, 210
Voter initiatives, 134–135
Voting practice. *See* elections and voting, Canada and United States
Vuong, Kevin, 113

Wall, Brad, 247
Waltz, Mike, 7
War in Afghanistan, 272
War of 1812, 25–27, 41–42, 264–265
   Fort McHenry, British bombardment of, 26–27
   Indigenous tribes, role of, 26
   key goal, 26
   York, American attack on, 26
Warren, Elizabeth, 248–249
Washington, George, 15–16, 75–76
Washington-Williams, Essie Mae, 89

Watergate scandal, 37
Watkins, Mel, 242
Watson, William, 160
Western Governors' Association, 154
Western Hemisphere Travel Initiative (WHTI), 277
Western Premiers' Conference, 154
*Wickard v Filburn*, 173

Williams, Roger, 14–15
Wilson, Woodrow, 30, 76
Winthrop, John, 36
World Bank, 268
World Trade Organization (WTO), 232

*Zelman-Simmons v Harris*, 190

# About the Authors

**Dr. Greg Inwood** is a professor in the Department of Politics and Public Administration at Toronto Metropolitan University (formerly Ryerson University). He completed a PhD in political science at the University of Toronto, and he holds an MA in political science and an Honours BA in history, both from the University of Western Ontario. His teaching and research interests include the political economy of Canadian-American relations, Canadian federalism and intergovernmental relations, and public administration. He is a past winner of the Canadian Political Science Association Donald Smiley Prize for *Continentalizing Canada: The Politics and Legacy of the Macdonald Royal Commission* (University of Toronto Press, 2005), for "the best book published in English or in French in a field relating to the study of government and politics in Canada." He has published books and articles on commission of inquiry, Canadian federalism, and Canadian public administration. He is also the author of one of the leading textbooks in the field of Canadian public administration, *Understanding Canadian Public Administration: An Introduction to Theory and Practice*, 5th ed (University of Toronto Press, 2025).

**Dr. Robert Speel** is an associate professor of political science at Penn State Erie, The Behrend College, and has been an adjunct professor of politics and public administration at Toronto Metropolitan University (formerly Ryerson University). He received a PhD in government from Cornell University and undergraduate degrees in political science and sociology from the University of Pennsylvania. His teaching and research interests include United States elections and government institutions, public policy, state and local politics, ethnic and racial politics, and comparative Canadian politics. He is the author of *Changing Patterns of Voting in the Northern United States* (Penn State University Press, 1998) and a large number of articles that have appeared in academic journals and popular news media.

# About the Editor

**Gregory Tardi**, BCL, LLB, DJur, is the general editor of the Understanding Canada Collection. He is a member of the Barreau du Québec and serves both as president of the Institute of Parliamentary and Political Law and as editor of the *Journal of Parliamentary and Political Law*. He has served as legal counsel with Elections Canada and at the House of Commons. He has taught at McGill, York, and Queen's universities and at the University of Ottawa, and he is the author of several books, including *The Theory and Practice of Political Law*, *Anatomy of an Election*, and, in the Understanding Canada collection, *Political Law in Canada*.